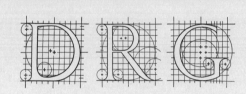

DAVID R. GODINE
1970
* Fifty Years *
2020
PUBLISHER

Godine at Fifty

GODINE AT FIFTY

A Retrospective of Five Decades in the Life of
an Independent Publisher

DAVID R. GODINE

DAVID R. GODINE · *Publisher* · BOSTON

A GUIDE TO IMPRINT MARKS
see page 261 for a longer description of each

 NONPAREIL

 VERBA MUNDI

 IMAGO MUNDI

 POCKET PARAGON

Published in 2021 by
David R. Godine, Publisher, Inc.
www.godine.com

Book designed and typeset by Sara Eisenman

FIRST PRINTING, 2021
Printed in the Czech Republic

Library of Congress Cataloging-in-Publication Data

Names: Godine, David R., author.
Title: Godine at fifty : a retrospective of five decades in the life of an
independent publisher / David R. Godine.
Description: Boston : David R. Godine, Publisher, 2021. | Includes
bibliographical references and index. | Summary: "David R. Godine,
Publisher's founder and namesake gives a personal tour of the most
memorable books he published during his 50 year career. From his
earliest days as a letter press printer to the present digital era,
Godine maintained a tradition of an independent publishing, surviving
against all odds: these books are the reason why"— Provided by publisher.
Identifiers: LCCN 2021004503 | ISBN 9781567926767 (hardcover)
Subjects: LCSH: David R. Godine, Publisher—Catalogs. | Publishers'
catalogs—United States. | United States—Imprints—Catalogs.
Classification: LCC Z1217.D38 G63 2021 | DDC 015.73—dc23
LC record available at https://lccn.loc.gov/2021004503

Contents

Introduction & Brief History of the Press [vii]

1. *Early Letterpress & Fine Printing* [1]

2. *Woodcut & Wood Engraving* [10]

3. *Fiction* [17]

4. *Short Stories* [29]

5. *Literature in Translation* [36]

6. *Poetry* [43]

7. *Essays & Criticism* [58]

8. *Words, Language & Usage* [69]

9. *Biography & Autobiography* [73]

10. *History* [90]

11. *Photography* [105]

12. *Art* [124]

13. *Architecture* [135]

14. *Children's Books* [147]

15. *Nautical & Maritime* [173]

16. *Music* [185]

17. *Gardening* [197]

18. *Cooking & Cuisine* [207]

19. *Typography* [213]

20. *Calligraphy* [231]

21. *Natural History* [239]

22. *Humor* [249]

23. *The Sporting Life* [253]

24. *Outliers & Other Works of Unclassifiable but Undeniable Genius* [257]

Posters [262]

Ephemera [264]

Bindings [265]

Typographers, Calligraphers, & Designers [266]

Index [267]

This book is dedicated to Morton R. Godine & Paul Siskind,
anchors and compass who,
despite all evidence to the contrary,
kept the faith and the ship afloat.

No matter how they are framed, histories of publishing companies always read like self-serving promotions. I suppose this one is no different, and I can't pretend the author isn't biased in its favor. But among the lasting pleasures of publishing, what Frank Swinnerton once referred to as "the last refuge of the grasshopper mind," is that each book presents different challenges and demands different solutions. Most people think it is writers who create books. This is nonsense. Writers create *texts* for books, often accompanied by illustrative material, revealing captions, and helpful back matter. But it is publishers who convert this material into something that is readable, useful and hopefully attractive and affordable.

I have always construed the verb "publish" as a synonym for "making books public." That is the primary responsibility of any publisher. No matter how carefully edited, how elegantly designed, how beautifully produced and how aggressively sold, unless and until a book reaches the market for which it was intended, the publisher has not fulfilled his primary mission. No publisher succeeds every time or with every book. And certain genres, like poetry, which every self-respecting publisher has a moral obligation to support, present marketing and sales challenges that are Dantesque in the purity of their hopelessness.

The effort of this publishing company has been, for better and often for worse, to publish books in a wide variety of fields – most of which interest me personally. Since we started as printers and had ink under our fingernails for the first decade, the long and broad history of printing, printers, and the graphic arts have held particular interest. I sail wooden boats, fish with flies, and weed gardens, so these activities are represented. The issue of properly reproducing a full-tone image, a photograph, with tiny halftone dots has always fascinated me, so the list has always been receptive to photography and its history. Growing up in a close suburb of Boston played a large part in the company's aesthetic and editorial orientation. Boston, which used to fancy itself "the Athens of America," takes history, and especially *its* history, seriously and has more than enough of it to infiltrate even the most indifferent psyche. My grandmother would take me to the Boston Garden to feed the ducks and we would wander through the diverse neighborhoods of the old West End, subsequently leveled in the name of urban development. I attended private schools from the second grade, from grade six to grade twelve at the Roxbury Latin School, founded in 1640 and the oldest secondary school in continuous operation in

the country. American history physically stood at the front door in the form of Joseph Warren, the first real hero of the Revolution slain at Bunker Hill. Early on I would ride the MBTA into Park Street to buy stamps and most of old Boston still survived – the Haymarket, Cornhill, Jacob Wirth's, even the Old Howard. For a nickel, I would ride to Cambridge to listen to Joan Baez, Rolf Cahn and Eric von Schmidt and Maria Muldaur sing at Club 47.

History was everywhere and it was tangible. I was surrounded by figures like Walter Muir Whitehill at the Boston Athenaeum, Bill Bond, Phil Hofer, Eleanor Garvey and Roger Stoddard at Harvard's Houghton Library, Steve Riley at the Massachusetts Historical Society, Harold Hugo at The Meriden Gravure Company, and Rocky Stinehour and Freeman Keith at The Stinehour Press. Each was deeply involved in the city, its institutions and its past.

My life as a publisher really began at Dartmouth College, the smallest, the most distanced, rural and probably most conservative of the Ivy League schools. When I attended, it was an all-male institution and there was little in the way of night life or distractions. The Hopkins Center had just opened and in the basement was a small workshop full of interesting equipment: an etching press and lithography press, cases of type and an ancient Washington hand press (soon to be replaced by a more functional and precise Vandercook 15). In the front office sat a smallish man with graying hair, a moustache, and a twinkle in his eye. This was Professor Ray Nash, the head of Dartmouth Publications, a scholar of the history of graphic art, a fine teacher and a devoted mentor. For three years I haunted this workshop, learning the physical techniques of cutting a woodblock with a knife, engraving on endgrain block with a burin, biting an etching plate, printing a lithograph and setting and printing type. Having attended and survived Roxbury Latin, I had acquired enough book learning to bluff my way through any course. I was in every way a mediocre student, but I had a genuine passion for making books and for printing, and my senior year I was awarded one of the College's twelve Senior Fellowships that allowed me to skip all formal classes and travel. I spent a term at Oxford with Nash, mostly holed up in the Bodleian reading room, looking at incunables and sixteenth-century French printing, another two weeks in France at the Bibliothèque nationale, a week in Greece at the Gunneidus. I came home to mud season in New Hampshire to finish my senior project: a collection of lyric verse I had set by hand in different typefaces, each poem with a note on the type.

This was printed four-up on a Vandercook proof press in the insane edition of 500 copies. At 112 pages, this entailed 14,000 passes through a handfed cylinder press. To compound the insanity, no one had ever informed me of the necessity of including copyright. I still possess a letter from Mr. Alfred Knopf, to whom I had proudly sent a copy, reading, "Dear Mr. Godine, thank you so much for your gift of *Lyric Verse: A Printer's Choice*; a fine piece of printing. However, before you proceed too much further in this, your chosen profession, I strongly urge you to observe one of the more important conventions of our trade known as copyright. I've enclosed a small booklet for your edification." Mr. Hegel of Macmillan was not so forgiving. I had included three poems of Yeats, who at that time was going for $35/line. So began my illustrious career in publishing.

In many ways, it was Harold McGrath at Leonard Baskin's Gehenna Press in Northampton who was our godfather. After graduating Dartmouth, serving in the Army, and earning a one-year "advanced" degree in education at Harvard, I decided to follow my first love, printing. And the best printing within driving distance, or perhaps anywhere in the country, was in Baskin's little shop with its oriental rugs in Northampton, Massachusetts. For reasons I still cannot explain, Baskin took a liking to me and hired me as an "apprentice" for four days a week at the rate of $125/week (which he couldn't afford, then or ever). It was an act of unspeakable generosity, for he needed an "apprentice" as much as a Buick needed a fifth hole. This was Harold's domain and he was probably not consulted, but took the appointment of someone who knew next to nothing about serious printing gracefully and spent the next months showing me the ropes – how to insert paper into the jaws of the Thomson Laureate without losing a finger, how to create the make readies for Leonard's detailed and exquisite engravings that required endless fussing with thin strips of India paper (at which Harold was a genius), and how to run the big Kelly Two 38″ cylinder press which was pretty much held together with baling wire and gum, and which Harold would periodically kick and swear at. Into this mix came Lance Hidy, who had begun printing at Jonathan Edwards College at Yale where he had, from what I can tell *ex nihilo*, produced some superb work. Baskin must have recognized Lance's talents immediately, for he took him on as a "student" at once. Lance moved to Northampton that year and began showing up at the press. Martha Rockwell was the third member of the founding team. A student at Bennington College, I had known her from her days at the Putney School. She was an excellent "comp," devoted and careful, but was hampered by being selected for the 1970 Olympic Team in cross-country skiing. She took this very seriously.

I think we all learned more than we ever realized from Harold, who, with relentless good humor, would watch us make a mess of jobs, pick up the pieces, inform us (again and again) that the secret of good printing was "maximum pressure and minimum ink," and reveal the mysteries of double rolling, make readies, and printing handmade paper dry. He was infinitely patient, and I will always remember how he would fondly tease Martha, who was shy, modest and reticent and whom he adored, by breaking out into an extravagant rendition of "My Wild Irish Rose" every time she pulled up to the curb in her battered Saab. So, the earliest "imprints" were really printed at Gehenna: James Agee's *Letter to Father Flye*, Marvell's *To His Coy Mistress*, and our most ambitious project, Thoreau's *Civil Disobedience* (remember, this was 1969, not exactly America's most pacific year). The shop contained mostly Monotype, most of it cast by MacKenzie and Harris in San Francisco and shipped cross-country in long galleys packed in wooden crates. Today, this sounds insane, but back then it worked just fine, as did printing on all rag handmade paper, which was going at about $60-80/ream. We soon figured out that the English handmades, Hammer & Anvil, Tovil, Crown & Sceptre, were lovely to contemplate in the abstract but were so heavily sized that they handled like sheet metal. There was simply no way to print them from soft Monotype metal without dampening and expect more than a few hundred impressions. The Italian papers, especially the Amalfis and Fabrianos, were softer, far easier to handle and held the ink well, as did a number of German sheets like Nideggen and Frankfurt.

Two years earlier, I had found an abandoned cow barn on the property of James Lawrence in Brookline, Massachusetts. This was the last "working farm" left in the town. James, a very formal but very liberal Democrat, gave me permission to use it for ten years at the rent of one book a year. It needed everything – new windows, a furnace, floors, electricity, a cesspool and plumbing. But my family had recently sold the old family business to Beatrice Foods and I was left with a small legacy or, to be precise, a trust fund. I went through this very quickly over time, but both my father and the family's trustee, Paul Siskind, were enormously indulgent, perhaps far too indulgent, as we slowly worked our way through the challenges of bringing in enough electricity to run a press, a furnace big enough to heat an uninsulated barn, wooden floors, doors, and finally, a working bathroom. We were plowing through capital pretty quickly, but since we did most of this work ourselves and my father had plenty of "friends in the trade" willing to help us out, we were more or less ready to print by 1970. We were fortunate to be surrounded by institutions that understood the value of good letterpress work, and found ourselves engaged in all kinds of work, from diplomas for Harvard to promotional material for Wellesley College to entire books for the Imprint Society. These and wedding, birth and event announcements were our bread and butter, but even as early as 1970 we had in mind the hope of doing our own publishing and creating our own list. I think our attitudes toward publishing were fairly well summarized in our very first prospectus. To a large degree they still hold, for I have never seen Godine as a "private" press, or a hobby, although I'd be the first to admit that any number of our books were "privished" rather than published.

But the basic guidelines were in place from the beginning and still bear repeating, for they express the central ideals that have governed us ever since:

1) To offer a wide selection of books of permanent editorial and textual importance.
2) To provide these books in quantities and at prices that are attractive to all lovers of good books.
3) To maintain in all books the highest production standards; to produce books of typographic distinction that delight the mind while not distracting the eye.

Although a bit over the top, at least this didn't suggest a private press. The aim was always to keep prices low, quality high and print runs as large as possible. If there were a model, it was far closer to Francis Meynell's Nonesuch Press than William Morris's Kelmscott.

In the *Times Literary Supplement* of September 1954, Alfred and Blanche Knopf placed an ad reading:

"A curious thing about book publishing is that it displays small monopolies within the widest possible range of free and unrestricted competition. The publisher secures by contract with its author the sole and exclusive right to publish a given book, but he competes with that author and that book with virtually all his colleagues."

There were a few more curious anomalies of the profession he could have added

1) Publishing is among the very few businesses that sell its products on a fully returnable basis. We don't really "sell" books; we more or less loan them out to customers in the hope they might sell and we might someday be paid.
2) Almost alone among manufacturers, publishers print the retail price of their products right there on the flap or in the bar code. We set the price, not the retailer, who is thereby given very little latitude to price according to need.
3) Since the turn of the last century, it is a profession that sells goods over whose production it has little control. No publisher today maintains its own presses; it may dictate the specifications, but the actual printing is done elsewhere – often overseas. In this sense books (hardware) have much in common with their software counterparts.

By 1973 it was clear that surviving as printers would require us to switch from a letterpress to an offset shop. This would mean starting over with a technique unfamiliar to all of us. The prospect wasn't appealing. It would also require a capital investment in equipment that I knew

would put us in debt for years and there was plenty of competition from larger and far better funded companies. Publishing seemed a less dangerous route. You didn't need a degree to do it. And it had three huge advantages that no one should take for granted. First, I was lucky enough to have been born into an English-speaking family and English was fast becoming the *lingua franca* of the world (and here I mean the world of scientific, cultural and political discourse). Second, the work your authors wrote and you published were by and large protected by copyright. Third, starting a publishing company required little capital nor an extensive "product line." No exams were required and the first amendment protected almost anything you chose to produce. We had wet our feet already with a number of books, but we were babes in the woods when it came to sales, marketing and distribution. But we had both youth and energy going for us, and the timing was perfect. Terrified of being left behind by the Soviet Union, federal money was pouring into libraries, and libraries were given broad latitude as to how it was spent. A review in *Publishers Weekly* or *Library Journal*, even a bad review, would guarantee a minimum sale of a thousand copies. The last quarter of the last century saw only about 40-50,000 new titles per year being published in this country; it was possible, even as a small publisher, to make a mark, to get a book reviewed, to come to know the people who made the industry tick. But, as we discovered, starting a publishing house and keeping it alive were two different skills. As Sir Stanley Unwin observed in the first page of his fine "Publisher's Bible," *The Truth About Publishing*, "It is easy to become a publisher, but difficult to remain one; the mortality in infancy is higher than in any other profession."

I was always lucky in the people who decided to associate with the press: Lance Hidy, Michael Bixler, Peggy Duhamel, Nancy McJennett, Katy Homans, Michael Pietsch, George Gibson, David Allender, Andre Bernard, Susan Barba, Winnie Danenberger, Nat Herold, Nan Sorensen… Still others, like Bill Goodman, Mark Polizzotti and Sue Berger Ramin in editorial and Steve Dyer, Bill Luckey and Heather Tamarkin in production, cut their teeth elsewhere but decided to join this little ship of fools. Many are still active. Publishing is, and has to be, more or less a team sport; employees have brought their own interests to the table, often with spectacular results. The life of a publisher is often challenging, sometimes daunting, occasionally rewarding, but never dull. Every book has its own idiosyncrasies and demands, each author comes with their own peculiar strengths and weaknesses. Because we were small, there was a very fluid understanding of "job description"; we all did a little bit of everything, including suggesting appropriate titles for the list, attending to the needs of authors, selling books out of our trunks, sorting the mail and emptying the trash.

No one should read any of the above and infer, for even a nanosecond, that Godine operated like a well-oiled machine. The challenges, and the failures, were frequent and persistent. The company was consistently undercapitalized, always starved for cash. The unsung heroes were certainly the string of business managers, from Bill Wiseman, Ellen Faran, and Tom Novak to Christine Sargent, among many others who had to put off and humor creditors with one side of their mouth while trying to collect money with the other. There was never any reserve for paying royalties, and when those days of reckoning came twice a year, it often took a full two months of dedicated work to manually tabulate sales, apply them to the terms of each contract, and find the cash to pay them, or at least some of them. Budgets never existed; bills were paid as and when enough cash was available and vendors soon learned that we were probably not a "credit problem" (all the invoices were eventually paid) but certainly a "collection challenge." The company was saved again and again by cash infusions, first from my fast-diminishing trust and later from generous investors who almost certainly knew they were putting their money in a company more on grounds of compassion than projected returns. To all of them, but especially to Robert Richardson, the first and most sympathetic, and later to Alan Ecker, who became deeply involved with the company's finances, go my eternal thanks. I think it was my father who was the first to be horrified when I told him we had never filed a tax return. He sent his personal accountant, Lester Kahn, to the barn to see what he could do. Lester, mild-mannered and earnest, arrived and asked "to see my books." I was thrilled. I began with the sixteenth century and was working my way into the seventeenth when Lester interrupted to say these were not exactly "the books" he had in mind. All we had to offer were a series of small checkbooks that hadn't been balanced in years.

In retrospect, my father's suggestion that I might take a little time off to either attend business school or work for another publisher to see how the business actually functioned, was probably sound. But as any parent knows, even the best advice is often ignored and the optimism of youth generally prevails. So we carried on.

Over the years we have had multiple homes. The first was the barn on the Lawrence estate in Brookline. Then we moved to the Ames-Webster Back Bay mansion on the corner of Dartmouth Street and Commonwealth Avenue. The wrought iron gates, ornate interior and La Farge stained glass were misleading; the rent was a very reasonable $3/square foot and we had a parking space to boot. We spent a happy decade there before moving to considerably grander space on the third floor of Horticultural Hall. After seven years of steadily increasing rent, we realized this was untenable and retreated to a small, modest cape in Lincoln, just off the railroad tracks. But we always considered ourselves a "Boston" publisher and after two years moved back into the city to 9 Hamilton Place, just a few blocks from the former offices of Ticknor & Fields. The last move, in 2010, was to 15 Court Square, a totally bland, undistinguished office building, close to where Dwiggins practiced on Cornhill and within spitting distance of the Old State House and the former City Hall.

The list of editors, sales managers, designers, production supervisors, business managers, assistants and interns would fill a small phone book. It is impossible in this space to list or thank them all, but I am fully aware that our survival and occasional triumphs owe much, and probably more, to them as they do to me. There were times of real disagreements over projects, strategies and the use of funds. That we managed to survive for as long as we did is as much a testament to their patience and forbearance as to any talents on my part. These comrades in arms, and the book buyers and sellers I visited on my sales rounds through New England, Colorado and the Far West, were probably the best part of my publishing experience.

I have accumulated a substantial library devoted to the history of publishing. These always make for interesting, and often useful, reading. I have a few perennial favorites, including Herbert Bailey's *The Art and Science of Book Publishing*, Fredric Warburg's *An Occupation for Gentlemen*, Michael Howard's equivalent fifty-year history *Jonathan Cape, Publisher,* and Bennett Cerf's *At Random.* But among the more amusing quips comes from the writer James Thurber who, having been on the lists of four different publishers, was asked by Cass Canfield, the legendary editor and publisher of Harper & Row, whether he would consider making Harper his permanent home. Thurber replied (in part), "Planned publisherhood is not the easiest thing in the world, as you know. It's like planned parenthood—you can never tell what's going to happen between the covers." I think this nails why it is not only "an occupation for gentlemen" but also one that offers the prospects of surprise, even excitement. You never *do* know who you are going to meet, what you are going to learn, or how one book will present yet another set of entirely new and perplexing challenges. I once was walking the shores of a pond with a distinguished printer, one of the best, and asked him why he had pursued *his* career, easily as difficult as publishing, for so many years. He replied that he didn't much believe in the Afterlife and that making books, good books, books that would endure, was his own small way of "leaving his footprints in the sands of time." I think, looking over the books I've selected for this retrospective, that few publishers of ours or any size have ever tackled such a broad variety of titles, in such a broad range of subjects, and consistently brought them to life at such a high level of execution. It's my hope that at least one in each of the twenty-four categories will leave its footsteps in the sands of time. And maybe a few more, if I'm lucky.

Lance Hidy, Harold McGrath and David Godine at Harold's 75th birthday party in 1996

Early Letterpress & Fine Printing

....I had found an abandoned cow barn (above) on the property of James Lawrence in Brookline, Massachusetts, and as we slowly worked our way through the challenges of bringing in enough electricity to run a press, a furnace big enough to heat an uninsulated barn, wooden floors, doors, and finally, a working bathroom. We were plowing through capital pretty quickly too, but since we did most of this work ourselves and my father had plenty of "friends in the trade" willing to help us out, we were more or less ready to print by 1970. Peggy Duhamel (left) bends over the Vandercook to adjust type wearing her favorite deerskin vest with fringe.

Andrew Marvell: *To His Coy Mistress*
1969. 8 pp, 4 × 5½″ $2.50 sc

This brief poem, set by hand with the label and title page in Jan van Krimpen's Cancelleresca Bastarda and the brief text in Arrighi, was printed at Leonard Baskin's Gehenna Press in Northampton, Massachusetts. It has the modest distinction of being the earliest publication bearing a Godine imprint. And it's certainly a modest beginning—just six pages of Marvell's little triumph of "time's wingèd chariot hurrying near," and his excuses for seduction admirably expressed and equally convincing. We sewed it in a French marbled paper and cast it on the waters for $2.50. In the following years we issued a number of these small pamphlets and booklets, some more ambitious than others, and all priced at or under $5.00. Among my favorites are Beatrice Warde's *The Rescuing Mouse* (1969), James Agee's *Last Letter to Father Flye* (1969), Joel Barlow's *The Hasty Pudding* (1969), Robert Browning's *The Pied Piper of Hamelin* (1970), *An Unpublished Letter of Junipero Serra* (1970), and Pierre Gassendi's *Peiresc & His Books* (1970). All were printed on fine, acid-free paper, handsewn, and, with the exception of *The Vulture* (page 4), issued in editions of fewer than 500. Though no effort was made for consistency in size, price, paper, or typeface, all were printed on imported handmade sheets and hand sewn.

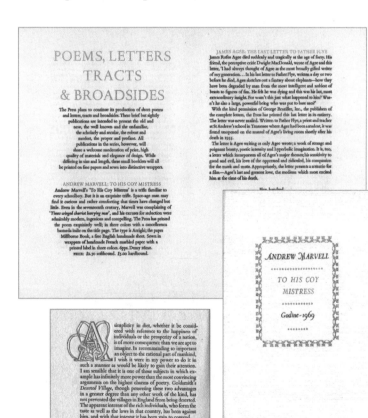

ABOVE TOP: Spread from the first 1970 prospectus, Andrew Marvell's *To His Coy Mistress*, the first Godine title printed at the Gehenna Press
LEFT: Lance Hidy's drop cap A for our edition of Joel Barlow's *The Hasty Pudding*

Henry David Thoreau, *Civil Disobedience*
1969. 44 pp, 5⅜ × 8⅝″ $10.00 hc

A Plea for Captain John Brown
1969. 44 pp, 5⅜ × 8⅝″ $10.00 hc

Both titles were set in Monotype Bell and printed letterpress on an impossibly hard English handmade sheet. As the type quickly wore down after a few hundred impressions, we learned our lesson; heavily sized English mould-made paper from the Hayle Mill in Kent needed to be printed damp, which was time consuming and, given the deckled edges and their irregularities, tricky. We quickly abandoned the English handmades in favor of softer and less heavily sized Italian and French sheets, and especially the laid cream sheet we bought in quantity from England's Hale Paper Company. This laid ivory paper was so forgiving we labeled it "Hale Miracle Laid."

Given the anxieties, unrest and political upheaval of the late sixties and early seventies, it is perhaps not surprising that these were the first two titles we decided to issue as books, both by that essential New England contrarian, Henry David Thoreau. *Civil Disobedience* is well known, but having attended Dartmouth College, which had a tortured relationship with slavery during the Civil War, I felt his *A Plea for Captain John Brown* had in many ways more resonance and political punch. Although I think Thoreau greatly oversimplified the man and his political position, he had understandably harsh words for the role Massachusetts played in quelling the insurrection at Harper's Ferry and engineering his capture: "She sent the marines there, and she will have to pay the penalty for her sins." My opinion of both Brown and Thoreau changed as I have aged. Brown was a thoroughgoing fanatic who had failed at almost every initiative he had undertaken. His only point of consistency was his insistent antagonism to the institution of slavery, a fact made clear in 1837 when, sitting in the back of a congregation in Hudson, Ohio, he rose his right hand and swore, "Here, before God, in the presence of these witnesses, from this time I consecrate my life to the destruction of slavery." Twenty-two years later, this businessman who had failed twenty times in six states, beaten his children, defaulted on debts, he assembled a group of antislavery men in Kansas in 1856 and dragged five proslavery settlers from their cabins in the middle of the night and hacked them to death. In 1859, he marched to Harper's Ferry, took a stand in an engine house and was quickly surrounded by Federal forces led by Robert E. Lee. Determined to die a martyr, he wrote his wife that he would be able to "recover all the lost capital by only hanging a few moments by the neck." He was right on at least two counts: slavery was the issue, often unacknowledged and unspoken, but increasingly visible and urgent as the war proceeded. It was the South's adherence to that insidious and embedded policy that was at the core of its decision to secede, and they saw Brown's death as a clear signal that the die was cast, that the North was intractable, and their existence threatened. The North, especially the rabid and uncompromising abolitionists from Massachusetts, would seize on his martyrdom as evidence of how deeply felt and embedded was the antipathy towards slavery. Thoreau conveniently fails to mention that Brown (whom he refers to as "an angel of light") and his gang were ruthless killers. Like other intellectuals from the North – Melville, Longfellow, Emerson, Greeley – he felt free to condemn the institutions of the South but somehow, when time came to enlist, failed to volunteer. Only Whitman, among the great mid-nineteenth-century writers, saw real action and put his life on the line. As Frederick Douglass would write of Brown's action, "it was as the burning sun to my taper light – mine was bounded by time, his stretched away to the boundless shores of eternity. I could live for the slave, but he could die for him."

Civil Disobedience, printed in 1969 at the Gehenna Press, included one of only two wood engravings I ever created for publication, which incorporates the initials of myself, Martha Rockwell, and Lance Hidy, who provided an engraved portrait of Brown. We were the original trio who really founded the press. *A Plea* was printed on the Kelly #3 in the barn in Brookline. For both, a small, limited edition was handsomely bound in quarter leather by Arno Werner.

Stephen Spender: *The Generous Days*
1969 (1970). 32 PP, 5⅜ × 8⅜″ $10.00 HC, $25.00 DELUXE

I cannot remember how we came to publish this slight work by Spender. But he was the first living author to visit us in person, and we printed his book at the Barn on a soft off-white Rives paper. I remember his day at the press in 1969, wandering absent-mindedly around the premises with his shock of ash white hair and bright blue eyes and with very little attention paid to the exposed and dangerous moving parts of the presses. Susan Rae, our extremely competent Kelly #3 press operator, observed he was "an accident waiting to happen." Although dated 1969, the book was actually issued in 1970 in an edition of 150 copies, of which fifty copies with marbled sides were bound in quarter leather by Gray Parrot. The image displays the two best poems in the book, the title poem and Spender's homage to Auden, "the young bow-tied near-albino undergraduate with rooms on Peck Quad," at Oxford University, which both attended and where Spender would often boast that he never passed an examination. Ever. He might well have been attracted to us because of his past experience with type and printing. In 1930, he helped Auden with the hand setting and printing of Auden's first book, *Poems* of 1930. He was also closely allied with America, its artists and its writers. In 1965 he was appointed our US Consultant of Poetry by the Library of Congress. In 1971, Random House issued our book in a trade edition, shooting directly from our type, never asking permission or providing any credit.

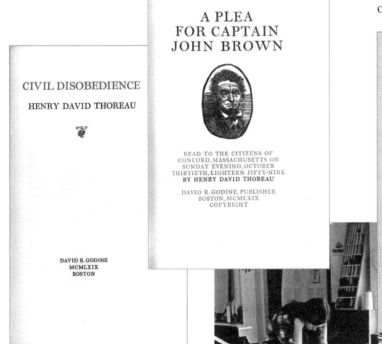

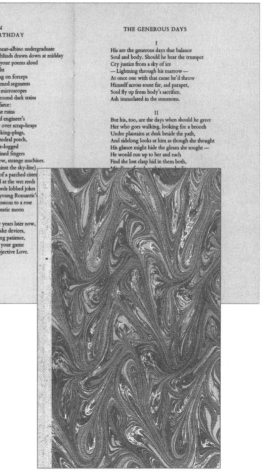

ABOVE: Title pages for both Thoreau titles set in Monotype Bell, and displaying Lance Hidy's talents as both a typographer and wood engraver in *A Plea for Captain John Brown*
RIGHT: Susan Rae checking proof sheets on the stone with the Heidelberg in the foreground
FAR RIGHT: Trade binding & title page of Stephen Spender's *The Generous Days*

Samuel Johnson: *The Vulture*

1970. 8 PP, 4½ × 5½″ $2.50 SC

The small, eight-page pamphlet, printed in Van Dijck and containing a single wood engraving by Lance Hidy, is probably as subversive as anything we issued. In 1970, we were all keenly aware of the Vietnam War, and this brief, acidic parable by Johnson, appearing in *The Idler* on September 9, 1758, seemed to speak to that sorry conflict more forcefully than any anti-war polemic appearing in the contemporary press. In it, an old matriarch of a vulture is overheard explaining to a confused youngster why mankind makes it so easy for vultures to survive. "'Man,' said the mother, 'is the only beast who kills that which he doesn't devour.'" Moreover, she goes on to explain "that men had only the appearance of animal life, being really only vegetables with a power of motion, and that as the boughs of an oak are dashed together by a storm, that swine may fatten upon the falling acorns, so men are by some unaccountable power driven against another, till they lose their motion, that vultures may be fed." And thus it is that man "shews by his eagerness and diligence that he is, more than any of the others, a friend to vultures."

Andrew Marvell: *The Garden*

1970. 20 PP, 6¼ × 9″ $100.00 HC

By 1970, we were firmly ensconced in the barn in Brookline, and we were working one very large flatbed letterpress, a Kelly #3 with a 40″ bed, and a smaller, hand-cranked Vandercook 219. On the latter we printed a hundred copies of Marvell's quiet, charming celebration of a garden on an unsized Amatruda Amalfi paper, set in Jan van Krimpen's elegant chancery italic, Cancelleresca Bastarda. We only had enough type to set two pages at a time, distribute the type and start again. Many consider it the most elegant and precious of the titles we issued in these "letterpress" years. In 2004, it was cited in the Kelly/Hutner *A Century for the Century* that selects and describes one hundred outstanding books from the twentieth century. Along with the Thomas Boreman, opposite, it is certainly the most elusive and expensive of our limited editions. The sheets were sent abroad to England, bound in linen over boards. Arno Werner provided quarter leather drop cases.

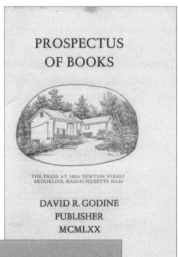

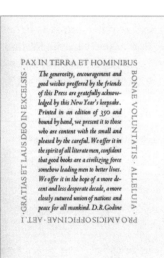

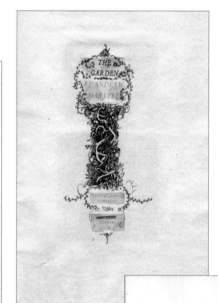

LEFT: A preliminary sketch, later discarded by Lance Hidy of the title page of *The Garden*
BELOW: A page from *The Garden* showing the handset Cancelleresca Bastarda and an etching from Marvell's *The Garden*

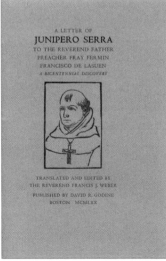

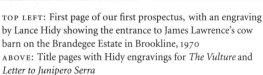

TOP LEFT: First page of our first prospectus, with an engraving by Lance Hidy showing the entrance to James Lawrence's cow barn on the Brandegee Estate in Brookline, 1970
ABOVE: Title pages with Hidy engravings for *The Vulture* and *Letter to Junipero Serra*

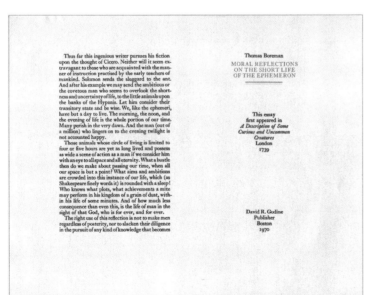

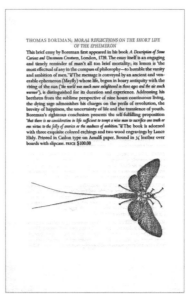

Thomas Boreman: *The Short Life of the Ephemeron*

1970. 26 PP, 5½ × 8¼″ $100.00 HC

Lance Hidy had printed an almost identical edition of this while he was a student at Jonathan Edwards College at Yale, where he had been a Scholar of the House. Dale Roylance, a longtime friend of the press, urged us to reissue it with new etchings, and 125 copies were printed, this time on the lovely gray Amalfi paper we had first encountered at The Gehenna Press. The wings of the insects were painted by hand with tiny brushes. Typographically, I suppose *The Garden* is the superior book, but I love this edition, for it demonstrates what can be accomplished with only one size of type (12-point Caslon Old Face). With its elegant binding of very thin boards covered with linen, its three-color paper label and title page, and the very even inking we were able to accomplish on the Vandercook, it shines for me as the real "bijou" of our early titles.

FAR LEFT: Label for the Boreman, and page from our second 1970 *Prospectus of New Books*
LEFT: From our 1971 prospectus announcing *Moral Reflections*
BELOW: Lance Hidy's etched roundel of the ephemeron hatch with the tiny bodies and wings painted in by hand

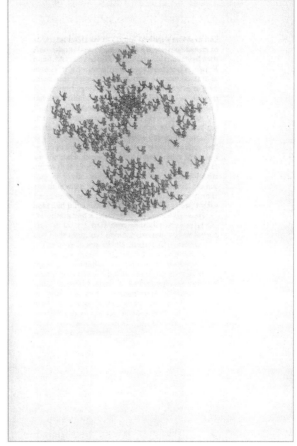

LEFT: Title and sample page of the Boreman, the entire book handset in one size of Caslon Old Face
BELOW: Greg Schelkun checking proof on the feeding table of the big Kelly #3

Charles Wadsworth: *Views from the Island*
1970. 86 PP, 10 × 12⅝″ $175.00 HC, $300.00 DELUXE

Charles Wadsworth walked in one afternoon in the pouring rain bearing examples of his complex and beautiful collograph-intaglio prints and his poetry. Lance and I were immediately struck by both, and we decided to take on his book as a project, which it certainly was. As with most of our early books, the type was set in Monotype Centaur by MacKenzie & Harris of San Francisco and shipped to us in long wooden boxes. We broke these down into pages, printing them two-up on Nideggen, a sheet we came to love as much for its color, imperfections and wavy laid lines as its print quality. The plates were printed separately on an etching press by Waddy, as we came to call him, who inked each one of them separately and who observed that "like all intaglio mediums, it is less easily controlled than relief mediums such as wood engraving and wood-cut. In compensation, it has an enormous range and seems peculiarly suited to a person whose bent and training is that of a painter." The book was assembled, and the prints guarded in separately, by Ivan Ruzicka, who also made the individual paste papers for the sides. The vellum spine was lettered by John Benson.

This was, to be sure, an 'artist's book' (although we didn't promote it as such), but both the poetry and Waddy's Afterword seemed to me then, and seem to me now, particularly intelligent and evocative. Collectors (and especially poetry collectors) seldom actually read their books; this one is well worth the effort.

BELOW: A spread from Wadsworth's *Views from the Island* showing a full-page impression of a Wadsworth intaglio collograph

Gerard Manley Hopkins: *The Wreck of the Deutschland*
Introduction by James Dickey
1971. 32 PP, 6½ × 10¼″ $6.00 HC, $4.00 SC

James Dickey had come to Dartmouth for a talk and brief seminar in 1966 while I was an undergraduate. He had yet to publish his novel *Deliverance*, which was on the bestseller list for months, but he still managed to attract a large, enthusiastic audience. Afterwards, I participated in an impromptu guitar jam session (he was a pretty good guitarist) and got to know him better. When we began issuing our own titles, I wrote to ask if there was anything he might suggest for us to print. He suggested Hopkins's *The Wreck of the Deutschland*, about which he had written a longish essay, calling it "probably the most important poem of the nineteenth century" and one that, in style, construction, and innovation, came together in a way in which "the whole concept of what can be done with the English verse line, the English language, was changed." It is not a happy poem, for it concerns death at sea, the tragic drowning of five nuns aboard the foundering "Deutschland." Its thirty-five stanzas in their eight-line, "sprung rhythm" configurations provided the talented Dutch designer Bram de Does plenty of room, and the result, set in Jan van Krimpen's elegant Lutetia italic and bound in patterned paper boards, is a small triumph of bookmaking.

LEFT & BELOW: Patterned paper cover, paper label and sample of a page of Hopkins's *The Wreck of Deutschland*, set in van Krimpen's elegant Lutetia italic and printed at Joh. Enschedé en Zonen in Holland

Sir Thomas Browne: *A Letter to a Friend, Upon the Occasion of the Death of His Intimate Friend*
Edited with a Postscript by Sir Geoffrey Keynes
1971. 52 PP, 7½ × 11″ $50.00 HC

Sir Geoffrey Keynes, scholar, bibliographer, surgeon, and collector, was an early friend of the press, doubtless viewing in us a late twentieth-century reincarnation of Francis Meynell's Nonesuch Press, with some of the capital and energy and none of the brains. In Keynes's opinion, this eloquent letter by the erudite Norwich doctor on the death of his friend demanded a separate and finely printed third appearance. It displayed all the writing skills that Keynes, a fellow doctor and equally prolific writer, admired. Like all of Browne's work, it was, in Keynes's words, "subtly illuminated with literary reference and moral reflection," and provided a text whose density elicited his comment "As in all Browne's work the extremity of his own erudition provides endless material for more and more editorial annotation." Keynes rises to the occasion with a long Postscript explaining both the purpose of the letter and its unusual relationship to the author's medical practice. Equally interesting was the Fell type cast from the original matrices and used for its setting. Brought to Oxford University by Bishop Fell in the seventeenth century, the copy was handset and displayed in three sizes, including erudite shoulder notes to the main text. The book was entirely composed by a single Scots apprentice, whom I met in person during a visit to Sir Geoffrey in 1972. Printed on a specially made and watermarked English rag paper, it was issued in an edition of 750 copies, in a slipcase with a binding in quarter leather by Robert Burlen of Boston.

Richard Wilbur: *Seed Leaves*
1973. 24 PP, 6½ × 10″ $60.00 *sewn softcover inserted in marbled boards*

Richard Wilbur's terse, radiant poem is subtitled "Homage to R.F." and it is clear that New England's greatest contemporary poet in the formal, pastoral tradition was paying homage to the great, gray (but not, by any means, virtuous) eminence, Robert Frost. We had earlier set and printed Wilbur's memorable poem "The Writer" for a reception held for friends at New York's Grolier Club in 1972, and that poem, like so much of Wilbur's work, more or less presents a universe in a few short stanzas.

The poem arose, in Wilbur's words, "from vegetable gardening, from many years' kneeling in contemplation of cotyledons." But as in so much of Frost, the apparently simple rhyming quatrains mask a deeper, darker meaning: his disappointment in the sixties, a time of "what seemed a mood of abdication, and by misunderstandings about how we may connect with the whole of things." Brief (in all, twenty-four pages), but powerful, it included Charles Wadsworth's three collograph-intaglio prints, perhaps just a touch *too* pretty for the message. Still, it is as fine a poetry title as we have issued. Set in Palatino italic and printed at Will and Sebastian Carter's Rampant Lions Press just outside of Cambridge, England, it is, like Christopher Fry's *Root and Sky*, also printed there and containing Wadsworth collographs, a splendid example of the printer's art.

BELOW: Spreads from Richard Wilbur's *Seed Leaves,* one of 160 copies printed at the Rampant Lions Press by Will and Sebastian Carter shows Hermann Zapf's elegant Palatino italic and Wadsworth's separately printed collographs.

LEFT *&* BELOW: Title page and chapter opening of Browne's *A Letter to a Friend,* all handset in the Fell types cast from the original matrices at Oxford's Clarendon Press

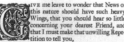

John Donne: *Deaths Duell*

Edited with a Postscript by Sir Geoffrey Keynes
1973. 64 PP, 7½ × 10¾″ $12.00 TRADE HC, $40.00
DELUXE

Sir Geoffrey Keynes suggested a reprint of John Donne's final sermon before King Charles I, delivered on 25 February 1631, just five weeks before his death. Although not first printed until 1632, plans for it were very much on Donne's mind during his final days. The title page recalls the first edition of 1632 and the facing verso reproduces the engraved portrait of Donne in a winding sheet by Martin Droeshout. When Donne, then Dean of St Paul's Cathedral, delivered the sermon, he was probably fully aware he was dying–most likely, according to Keynes, of gastric cancer. His audience was equally aware, for by then he was reduced to flesh and bones. Izaak Walton, in his 1640 biography of Donne, observed "Many that then saw his tears and heard his faint and hollow voice, professing they thought the Text prophetically chosen, and that Dr. Donne had preach't his own Funeral Sermon."

The book was designed by John Dreyfus, set in Erhardt, and printed at the Cambridge University Press under the supervision of the University Printer, Brooke Crutchley, on a special Hale Paper Company mold-made sheet containing a watermark designed by Bram de Does. It remains among our great scholarly editions, and I am forever indebted to Sir Geoffrey for the care and attention he lavished on every aspect of its production.

Hans Holbein: *The Dance of Death*

Introductory Essay by Amy T. Montague
1974. 160 PP, 5 × 7″ $11.50 HC

Philip Hofer owned an almost complete proof set of the woodcuts designed by Hans Holbein and cut by Hans Lützelburger for that sixteenth-century favorite, *The Dance of Death*. He had taken a particular fancy to Katy Homans, a Radcliffe undergraduate, and Amy Montague from Wellesley, both then working in our barn in Brookline. Amy did a fine job of writing an exhaustive history of editions of *The Dance of Death*, and Philip provided the background for the Holbein cuts and explained his acquisition of an incomplete second "von Lanna" series in 1936 from which the reproductions for the process letterpress blocks were made. Although small in size, they are uniformly, in Amy's words, "monumental in concept." Katy printed the book four-up on our 32″ Heidelberg press, inking and printing the blocks perfectly. The original French quatrains and Latin biblical quotations were set and printed as they appeared in the original editions on the facing versos. We printed a thousand copies, 100 for Philip's Cygnet Press and the rest for "the trade" at $11.50, one of the greatest bargains in our distinguished history of underpricing. For the text, scholarship, design and presswork, credit here goes entirely to Amy, Katy, and Philip, with an appreciative nod to the ever-generous scholar/bibliographer Eleanor Garvey, Hofer's right hand in the Department of Printing and Graphic Arts at Harvard's Houghton Library. We merely added our name and got out of the way.

RIGHT & BELOW: Title-page spread showing the poet/preacher in his winding sheet in an engraving by Martin Droeshout from John Donne's *Deaths Duell*

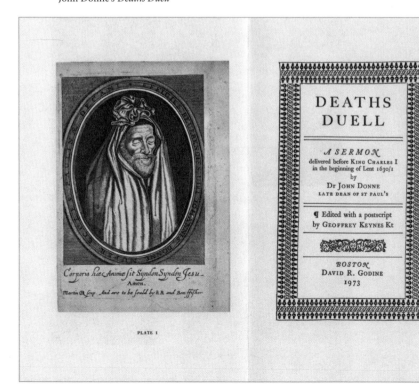

Anthony Hecht: *The Venetian Vespers*

1979. 28 PP, 5½ × 9⅜" $75.00 HC

Dimitri Hadzi was teaching sculpture at Harvard when I first met him. A talented artist and skilled printmaker, he teamed up with his friend Tony Hecht to illustrate this lovely poem told in the voice of a shy, studious, asthmatic with "an eye for ciphers and riddling things" who loses his parents, is raised by his uncle, and finds himself marooned in Venice after WWI. The blank verse is as dense and weighty as Piranesi's *Carceri*, here echoed in the rich intaglio blacks of Hadzi's strong, dramatic drypoints printed directly from the plates. The text, set in Dante by Michael and Winnifred Bixler, was printed on a soft Italian laid sheet with the letterpress by Carol Blinn. The combination makes for a very satisfactory book, substantially enhanced by the unique paste-paper cover sides evoking Venice that Carol created especially for each book.

RIGHT *&* BELOW: Binding for Hecht's *Venetian Vespers* showing the paste-paper covers Carol Blinn fashioned for the sides of each copy and the richly inked intaglios of Dimitri Hadzi

OPPOSITE *&* ABOVE: Cover and a spread from our edition of Holbein's *The Dance of Death* and with the Lützelburger/Holbein blocks printed directly from linecuts made from Philip Hofer's unique set of proofs

THE VENETIAN VESPERS

BY ANTHONY HECHT

ETCHINGS BY
DIMITRI HADZI

DAVID R. GODINE · PUBLISHER
BOSTON

Jacques Hnizdovsky and Gordon DeWolf:
Flora Exotica
1972. 96 PP, 9 × 12" $12.50 HC

I first encountered the work of Hnizdovsky at an exhibition arranged by Dale Roylance at Yale's Sterling Library. It was not difficult to spot a master at work, and, as it turned out, Jacques was a man of many talents: woodcuts, painting, ceramics, and sculpture among them. He was almost pathologically modest, and possessed self-doubts about his achievement that accompanied him his entire life. In his Afterview, he was transparent about this, "The idea of plants executed as woodcuts is not new to me. While still in school in 1944 I conceived the idea of creating a series of trees in woodcuts… without adequate experience I accumulated so many self-doubts that I have given up on the project but also all woodcuts and print-making for many years." The doubts accompanied him when he emigrated to America in 1948 and were still bubbling when we commissioned him to produce a suite of fifteen plants on wood, as his genius for reducing the complex to the essential, whether it was a plant, a sheep or snarled hair, was compelling. He had an ability to make order out of chaos, to reduce a pot of zebrina or a vase of roses to clear and recognizable patterns of symmetry and geometry. He could take the complexity of a sunflower seed head and make it comprehensible. We engaged Gordon DeWolf, then the horticultural taxonomist of the Arnold Arboretum, to write what turned out to be equally austere and revealing prose descriptions and printed the book from line blocks as the wood was too fragile to stand up to the Kelly #3. The book was beautifully printed, and the hand-colored woodcuts of the deluxe edition were especially lovely, but the type, Centaur in the 14-point size, was far too light. Hnizdovsky died too young, in 1985, and I doubt he ever recognized in himself the genius he surely was. An artist, I often thought, who would have been totally at home working as a monk in a Medieval scriptorium.

A Medieval Bestiary
Translated and introduced by T.J. Elliott
1971. 64 PP, 8¾ × 11¼" $12.50 HC, $25.00 DELUXE

A student of English literature, T.J. Elliott had located and translated a hitherto unknown medieval English bestiary, written in an East Midland hand of the thirteenth century. We liked it and commissioned Gillian Tyler, who had studied with Max Beckmann at the Brooklyn Museum School and was then living in Thetford, VT, to engrave fifteen charming and fanciful engravings. The book was printed (absurdly) in three colors on a nice Mohawk sheet. In Elliott's translation the text is accessible and of some interest; every animal has, of course, its own attributes and, through the accompanying allegory, is somehow connected to the Christian world, which put man first and foremost, with nature, especially animals, many leagues behind. But the religious context has trouble subduing the secular voice that surfaces again and again. And it is difficult not to look at Tyler's wily fox, ferocious panther and serene doves without admiring the coupling of ancient natural history text with a thoroughly modern aesthetic interpretation.

OPPOSITE & BELOW: Handcolored woodcuts from Hnizdovsky & DeWolf, *Flora Exotica*
RIGHT: Three-color title page from Elliott & Tyler's *A Medieval Bestiary*

Medieval Latin Lyrics
Translated & introduced by Brian Stock
Original woodcuts by Fritz Kredel
1972. 76 PP, 7¼ × 11″ $10.00 HC, $40.00 DELUXE

I don't recall what impelled us to do this anthology of medieval love poems that were published "for both the serious scholar and the interested layman." I don't think there was anything especially scholarly about the edition, although it did have the advantage of the Latin original being published opposite the Stock translation. The catalogue copy (which sounds like me) reads "Translations, like attractive women, tend to be either beautiful or faithful. These fall into the latter category, a judgment that should require no apology." I'm not sure I'd have the courage to repeat that statement today. The real justification for the book was the inclusion of five woodcuts by Fritz Kredel, among the very last he designed and cut, and that the book was nicely designed and very well printed in Bruce Rogers's Centaur and Warde's Arrighi type. The so-called "deluxe" edition, printed on a special handmade paper with its patterned paper binding, repurposed from commercial wallpaper, was especially attractive. I still have, and still use, the original Kredel applewood blocks, and they continue to hold up well after decades of use.

Tom Killion: *The Coast of California*
1988. 80 PP, 12 × 11¼″ $40.00 HC

William Everson was for years both printer and poet in residence at the Santa Cruz campus of the University of California. He wrote his own books, designed and set the type, and printed them on a handpress. It seems every master has at least one pupil who takes his genius to heart and passes it on to the next generation. Killion was that talent, as both poet and printer (as with Everson), but also as an artist. In his 1979 limited edition survey of the California coast appeared a portrayal of the shore in wood and linoleum cuts accompanied by his own poetry that gave his readers a tour both inspiring and sufficiently detailed to convey real and useful information.

This massive limited edition was not only a *tour de force* of printing and design, but a literal tour of the majestic strand of bays, lagoons, mountains, and beaches known as the California coast. I not only admired the artwork, so reminiscent of Hokusai, but also the writing. Still, there seemed to be no way to issue a book that size in the trade and make it affordable. With the help of Tom, who rewrote some of the text and reworked the design, and the printing skills of Martino Mardersteig at the Stamperia Valdonega, we were able to issue a revised and expanded version in 1988 at what was a very reasonable price, while still coming fairly close to both the spirit and the content of the original edition. This was one of only two titles we issued set in the elegant typeface Lutetia of Jan van Krimpen.

LEFT & BELOW: Title and interior page showing the Kredel woodcuts printed in red, and the "wallpaper" binding for the special copies

BELOW & OPPOSITE: The jacket and an interior full-page linoleum cut from Killion's *The Coast of California* showing Point Reyes from Double Point

William Smith: *Birds and Beasts*
Illustrated with woodcuts by Jacques Hnizdovsky
1990. 40 PP, 7 × 10″ $10.00 HC

This was an effort, really an excuse, to gather between covers the delightful poems of William Jay Smith and marry them with the woodcuts of Jacques Hnizdovsky. The two had collaborated for some time on the book, gathering the best of Hnizdovsky's vigorous cuts and linking them to existing poems. The trick was a) to make the book affordable while b) designing it in a way that displayed the humor and whimsy of the verse and images and c) printing his woodcuts, reduced in size and printed from linecuts by letterpress on an uncoated paper, so they preserved at least a semblance of relief. This was admirably accomplished by printer/bookdealer/publisher W. Thomas Taylor of Austin, Texas who both designed and printed the book on Mohawk Superfine with the titles in red set in Cochin and the text in Garamond Bold, types that held up nicely against the strong line of the cuts.

Ian Niall: *English Country Traditions*
Wood engravings of Christopher Wormell
1990. 72 PP, 7 × 9″ $30.00 HC *for members of Hoc Volo*

A confection of a book, this contains the detailed, exquisite wood engravings of Christopher Wormell and the delightful text of Ian Niall bringing the (barely) surviving traditions of English country life to the printed page. It is Bewick two hundred years later: beekeeping, fishing, wildfowling, and blacksmithing, as well as lesser-known trades like hop-picking, hurdle-making, and Morris dancing. Cut with a burin on the endgrain of boxwood, this was a particularly English tradition that was rediscovered and redefined by Bewick in the late eighteenth century and kept alive in the twentieth by practitioners like Eric Gill, Reynolds Stone, and Leo Wyatt. Wormwell had only been at it a few years when this was published, but he was already a master, and his delicately shaded and exquisitely cut blocks, about the size of a medium oyster shell, show off nicely against the very white paper and the equally delicate Monotype Van Dijck.

Beehives

ABOVE: Poetry of William Jay Smith and greatly reduced woodcuts of Jacques Hnizdovsky printed letterpress in two colors
RIGHT: The quite amazingly detailed and fine-cut wood engravings by Christopher Wormell to accompany Ian Niall's descriptions of English country traditions

Eric Gill: *The Engravings*
Edited with extensive notes by Christopher Skelton
1990. 480 PP, 9 × 11⅞" $75.00 HC

This was a major effort. A large folio of some 480 pages, it reproduces some 680 wood engravings that Gill produced over his long and prolific career. He was 24 when he began, entering into his diary in 1905, "Tried wood engraving a little in the evening." Like sculpture, type design, stone cutting, and inscriptional lettering, it didn't take him long to master the craft. His work, like his typefaces and his lettering, is instantly recognizable, and his range of subject and engraving skills are breathtaking. The book was originally organized and published by his nephew, Christopher Skelton, who issued it as a limited edition in 1983. Our edition contains Gill's complete oeuvre in the medium – from the religious subjects to the erotic fantasies, from his designs for *The Canterbury Tales* and *The Four Gospels*, to the revealing portraits and tiny pressmarks. All were reproduced full size, often in color, with a complete checklist of books containing his work and a ten-page index to the engravings. Moreover, it was issued at a list price an ordinary mortal could afford. We went on to issue an illustrated catalogue of his sculpture as well as his highly influential *Essay on Typography*, which appears in the Typography section.

Welford Dunaway Taylor: *The Woodcut Art of J.J. Lankes*
1999. 128 PP, 9½ × 8⅞" $40.00 HC

The name of the woodcut artist Julius John Lankes (1884–1960) is regrettably almost forgotten today. This is unfortunate as he was, in addition to being a genuine American original, a talented artist (arguably the first real woodcut *artist* this country produced) and the author of the first reliable and comprehensive text on woodcutting published in North America. Self-educated, stubborn, irritable and crotchety, he made friends with artists, authors and printers, and often unmade them with equal facility. He worked exclusively in the East, and his woodcuts, mostly of scenery and structures, range from northern Vermont to his adopted Commonwealth, Virginia. He was regularly commissioned to illustrate, or provide frontispieces for, trade books, the most famous certainly being those he created for Robert Frost's poetry. But his range of interests were considerable – portraits, landscapes, bookplates and ephemera of all kinds, an artist for hire for every subject and need. In addition to Frost's, Taylor's illustrations appear in work all over the literary map, from Robert Tristram Coffin to Glenway Wescott. His *A Woodcut Manual*, issued by Henry Holt in 1932 and containing many of his designs, is still rewarding and necessary reading on the history and technique of woodcutting. In this retrospective tribute Taylor covers his entire career: his masterful views of Virginia, his amusing Christmas cards, his illustrations of weather sayings and Bucks County stone barns. And for the truly devoted, there is an extensive list of the books he illustrated, publications on and by him, and a collation of his prints. All you need to know about a talented, neglected American artist who was probably his own worst enemy.

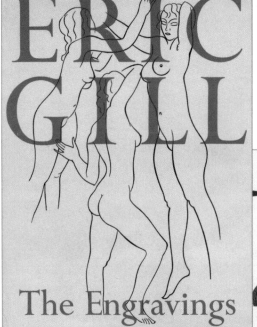

ABOVE *&* RIGHT: Jacket and a full-page plate of a Gill engraving for the Golden Cockerel edition of *The Four Gospels* from Skelton's *The Engravings*

ABOVE: Lankes woodcut of a Pennsylvania barn from Taylor's *The Woodcut Art of J.J.Lankes*

Mary Azarian: *The Four Seasons*
2000. 112 PP, 12 × 9″ $40.00 HC

Mary had been a friend to the press since we first published *A Farmer's Alphabet* in 1981. Since then she had been cutting and coloring her own woodcuts for any number of clients and by 2000, it seemed high time that a collection be put together that featured and reproduced these efforts in full color. Designed by Dean Bornstein, arranged by the seasons, and set in a light version of ITC Golden Cockerel type that Eric Gill designed for *The Four Gospels*, it is a fine tribute to a splendid artist who had for forty years been gracing books with strong and striking woodcuts that bear her very personal stamp of originality. Her special affection for plants and gardening is reflected in many of the spreads, and these colored woodcuts are, I believe, as beautiful and as personal as any work created in the medium. In my Preface about her and the woodcut tradition in which she worked, I wrote, "I recall visiting Mary at her first farm. Her studio stood away from the house and there she was furiously at work cutting basswood. This was no delicate, fussy operation. She knew exactly what she wanted and the chips flew. Looking back over the years I have known her and her work, I am surprised how little she and it have changed. She is still the same person I met twenty-five years ago – hardworking, self-deprecating, passionate about her work in a quiet way (and about bridge in a not so quiet way)." Twenty years, and many books later, this still obtains.

David R. Godine: *Five Decades of the Burin: The Wood Engravings of John DePol*
Foreword by Timothy D. Murray
2004. 96 PP, 5¼ × 8″ $30.00 HC

For fifty years John DePol, almost entirely self-taught, was providing engravings for publishers, advertisers, and the United States Banknote Corporation. His work was everywhere. He must have slept very little. When I was asked by the organizers of the APHA conference and Susan Brynteson, the Director of Libraries at the University of Delaware, to deliver a talk on his work, I suggested we create a book that would highlight his achievements decade by decade and provide a brief outline of his life. They agreed and the book, designed by Jerry Kelly, was printed in time for the conference and I suspect to John's great relief, as he passed away shortly thereafter. In the tall, narrow format, we were able to stack a number of his better images and even print many of them in two colors as he intended. Unlike Leo Wyatt or Reynolds Stone, who were essentially lettering artists (although Stone was very skilled as a draughtsman), DePol was essentially an artist who found in wood engraving the perfect medium to express himself – and you can't look at a DePol engraving without recognizing the artist behind the image. His work for The Stone House Press, the Typophiles, John Anderson's Pickering Press and the exquisite cuts he produced for John Fass's Hammer Creek Press are among the best the last century had to offer in this medium. In terms of sheer productivity, probably no one since Gustave Doré outstripped him, but Doré didn't execute the actual engravings, and John did.

LEFT & LEFT BELOW: A Mary Azarian specialty: a hand-colored nocturnal snow scene for the cover and a self-portrait of her reading in bed with the quote by Rose Macaulay.

Barry Moser: *Wood Engraving*
2006. 112 PP, 7½ × 10″ $25.00 SC

Many books have been written about the art and craft of engraving on the end grain with a burin, but few are as lucid, as passionate, or as practical as Barry's exegesis, not only on how to make a wood engraving but, in a greater sphere, how to think about life and transfer it to a medium of black and white. What is most helpful about the book is the series of excellent photographs showing how to hold and sharpen the tools and how to incise the smooth surface of a boxwood block. After all the work Barry had done with and for us, it seemed a natural tribute and was probably the easiest "manual" of its kind we ever attempted. It is a relief to everyone involved that the book has been reissued by the Brandeis University Press.

Barry Moser: *One Hundred Portraits*
2010. 144 PP, 7½ × 10″ $35.00 HC

For as long as we have been in business, Barry Moser has been creating books, drawings, illustrations, and watercolors. An indefatigable artist, still creating and still teaching at the age of 80, he has provided material for over 200 books, not a few of them ours and dating all the way back to the seventies. This brings together his black-and-white engraved portraits, a staple of his career that began with his first book, *The Red Flag*, published in 1970 and included Whistler's portrait. Nearly thirty years later, he published his edition of the King James Bible, in which over half of the images are portraits.

For this edition, he gathered an even 100 of his favorites plus fifty new portraits, ranging from musicians (Chopin, "Blind" Willie Johnson, Wagner, Sibelius) to poets (Blake, Frost, Hall, Kumin, Wilbur) to an extended selection of his favorite writers (Welty, Melville, Poe, Twain, Hawthorne, Austen, O'Connor). Looking at their faces, we can see the insight of an artist who knows the person through their work and makes *us*, looking at these faces staring back at us with mixtures of fear, confidence, grim determination and confusion, want to know *them*—to go back to the work that inspired them with the same intensity and insight of an artist at his best, one who never puts himself between the subject and the viewer.

It is fair to say that, along with Leonard Baskin, Moser has exploited black-and-white engraving more extensively and sensitively than any contemporary artist. His illustrations have informed and adorned countless titles. For this, his friend Ann Patchett wrote an elegant appreciation while Barry contributed an afterword addressing the challenges of portraiture.

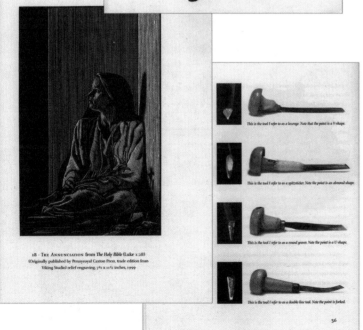

18 · THE ANNUNCIATION from *The Holy Bible* (Luke 1:28)
(Originally published by Pennyroyal Caxton Press, trade edition from Viking Studio) relief engraving, 7¾ x 11½ inches, 1999

36

JAMES ABBOTT MCNEILL WHISTLER · *American painter and etcher, 1834–1903* (2001)   WINSLOW HOMER · *American painter, 1836–1910* (2002)

ABOVE: Portraits of James McNeil Whistler & Winslow Homer from Moser's *One Hundred Portraits*

Fiction

Edmund Wilson: *Memoirs of Hecate County*
Afterword by John Updike
1980. 472 PP, 5 × 7½″ $8.00 SC

"An obscene book in violation of subdivision 1 of section 1141 of the Penal Law…would tend to deprave or corrupt those whose minds were open to such immoral influences." New York Court of Appeals. November 13, 1947

We now know, from his journals as well as his correspondence, that Wilson's sexual appetite was at least as prodigious as his literary output. Here, in his only sustained work of fiction, published by Doubleday in 1946, is the book that ignited a firestorm and whose few, occasional, and relatively mild passages would hardly shock, much less deprave and corrupt, the sensibilities of a modern twelve-year-old. The book was soon withdrawn from circulation and by some unremembered fortune, we were able to obtain reprint rights to it and include John Updike's incisive commentary as an Afterword. Our edition followed the text of his revised edition of 1959, but it still remained Wilson's "favorite among my books" one to which he could not understand "why the people who interest themselves in my work never pay any attention." One reason, as Updike points out, is that Wilson was a compulsive and consistently serious moralizer, and he was always in deadly earnest. For most of America, sex was something to be "tolerated as joke, as a night's prank," an act that "Wilson, with the dogged selfless honesty of a bookworm presses his nose, and ours, into with such solemn satisfaction." The fact that Anna, his uninhibited working-class lover, fell prey in print to a Waspy (and always earnest) patrician probably didn't help his case. If there had only been the slightest tone of levity, of self-deprecation, some sense that sex might just possibly provide a little amusement or diversion, the court might well have let him off. Still, it deserves to hold its place in our literature. As Updike concludes, "No longer shocking, and never meant to be, this 'memoir' remains, I think, a work of exemplary merit, still the most intelligent attempt by an American male to dramatize sexual behavior as a function of, rather than a suspension of, personality."

Paula Fox: *Desperate Characters*
1980. 176 PP, 5¼ × 8″ $7.00 SC

Both Bill Goodman, our editorial director at the time, and Irving Howe loved this book. Howe, in his Afterword, submits two forms of the American novel: "those sprawling 'open forms' like *Moby Dick* and *Leaves of Grass*" and the other "tradition, at least as distinguished, in which everything – diction, form, language – is fiercely compressed, and often enough, dark-grained as well." He offers this classic by Paula Fox as a prime example of the latter. The Bentwoods, the novel's central characters, live a life of determined organization and cultivated neatness. Everything is, or must seem to be, perfect. Even the New York street on which they live assumes "at night… a quiet earnest look, as though it were continuing to try to improve itself in the dark." Their forced serenity is shattered by the bite of an allegedly rabid cat, strangely the only character in the novel that displays any emotion or elicits any real sympathy. The two characters, Otto and Sophie, move in separate spheres; Sophie engages us immediately with her inherently ordered and well-intentioned (if always fastidious) liberal leanings, but Otto grows on you. He's the more interesting, the more unpredictable character. But neither of them really connect, either in a marriage of fifteen years or in Fox's minutely observed narrative of their lives together. At the end Fox says what the reader already knows, "They had been married for fifteen years. What did she know about what he thought? She knew him in the density of their lives together, not outside of it." I found this book perversely encouraging; even compulsively neat people can lead inwardly messy lives.

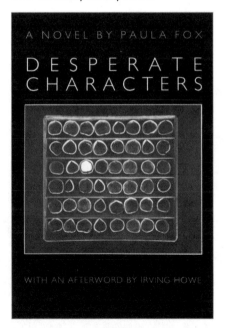

ABOVE: Olivia Parker's somewhat mysterious photograph provides a suitably restrained image for this quietly devastating novel, *Desperate Characters*.
OPPOSITE: Covers for our paperback editions of K.C. Constantine featuring his Balzic thrillers

K.C. Constantine :
The Man Who Liked Slow Tomatoes
1982. 256 PP, 5⅞ × 8¼″ $13.95 HC

Always a Body to Trade
1983. 256 PP, 5⅞ × 8¼″ $12.95 HC

Upon Some Midnights Clear
1985. 240 PP, 5½ × 8¼″ $15.95 HC

The Rocksburg Railroad Murders &
The Blank Page
1981. 356 PP, 5½ × 8″ $7.95 SC *Double Detective #1*

The Judge and His Hangman & The Quarry
1983. 256 PP, 5½ × 8″ $7.95 SC *Double Detective #2*

The Man Who Liked to Look at Himself &
A Fix Like This
1983. 352 PP, 5½ × 8″ $8.95 SC *Double Detective #3*

During Bill Goodman's reign as editor, he quite sensibly suggested that we include a few crime novels and writers in our repertoire. Aiding us was Robin Winks, Bill's good friend from Yale, but it was certainly Bill who discovered and nurtured K.C. Constantine, who was as mysterious to us as a human being as he was talented as an author. In all we published nine of his titles, first in hardcover, then in trade paperback, later as one of our "Double Detectives" and finally in mass market. All crime writers need a single figure, a central character, to set the tone and define the action. Constantine's was Mario Balzic, the chief of police of Rocksburg, PA, a small coal mining town in western Pennsylvania where Balzic was so close to his people that nothing ever moved, or even sat still, without his knowing how and why. With Balzic, you encounter tavern owner Dom Muscotti, Rocksburg's "official bookmaker" who serves as his charismatic drinking companion; Father Marrazo, a man more or less of the cloth; and the wily Mo Valcanas who, even slightly sober, is the best lawyer around. The crimes are generally blue collar; no embezzlement or Ponzi schemes here. Mostly murder, and occasionally grisly crime. But for gutsy, unfiltered language, and a detective you have to love, you really can't do much better than these nine by Constantine.

Liam O'Flaherty: *Famine*
Afterword by Thomas Flanagan
1982. 462 PP, 5½ × 8¼″ $19.00 HC, $10.00 SC

This early Nonpareil, initially issued in hardcover, presents a moving and somber account of Ireland's Great Potato Famine of 1845–49. But it is far more than a fine historical novel. Composed by one of Ireland's more erratic and problematic writers, whom Thomas Flanagan in his Afterword calls "the odd man out of modern Irish literature," it takes on not only the large theme of a mass struggle for food, bread, freedom, and representation, but the even larger issue of a people being crushed by callous misgovernment and treated as if in a state of martial insurrection instead of being destroyed by famine. It looks upon the Irish people with love while providing an appallingly realistic portrait of what life was actually like during those five years of extreme and extended poverty. O'Flaherty's career peaked with this book; it was widely read and celebrated in the US only to disappear from view, much as he did as a writer, after its original publication in 1937. In Flanagan's words "those gifts that have allowed him to move among the elementals of human experience," resulted in his masterpiece, certainly among the great historical narratives of our time.

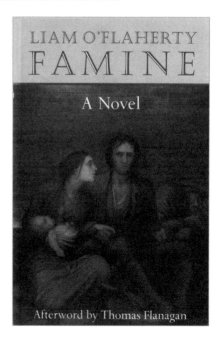

Joy Kogawa: *Obasan*
1982. 256 PP, 5½ × 8½" $13.00 HC

The United States was not alone in its disgraceful treatment of native Japanese following the bombing of Pearl Harbor. The attack spread fear and terror along the entire Western Coast, which braced itself for an invasion that was expected at any moment. That fear and anger soon turned against the Nisei and their families in Canada, viewing many of them as disloyal, possible fifth columnists and probably spies. The narrator of the book is five in 1941 when her mother leaves her to visit her relatives in Japan, to perish (as she learns later) in the bombing of Nagasaki. In the meantime, her family is shorn of its rights and possessions, the men press-ganged, and the women and children herded into concentration camps dispersed across the country.

Naomi is sent to live with her aunt Obasan, the novel's poignant center, whose silent response to insult and injury becomes the barrier through which Naomi must push to find her history – and her life. This was Kogawa's first novel, written as fiction but based on facts. When it was first published in Canada in 1981, it was awarded the Books in Canada First Novel Award and named the Canadian Authors' Association 1982 Book of the Year. It is memorable not only as an emotionally wrenching piece of fiction, but because the anger and bitterness is balanced by integrity, wit and ultimately something close to forgiveness.

ABOVE: Woodcut created by Rita Grasso for the jacket of Kogawa's *Obasan*
RIGHT: Jeanne Titherington's delicate pencil portrait of an aging Charles Dickens for Busch's *The Mutual Friend*

Frederick Busch: *The Mutual Friend*
1983. 240 PP, 5½ × 8¼" $6.00 SC   ◆ɕ

We had issued a number of original novels from the prolific Fred Busch (before his death in 2006 he would write a total of sixteen novels and six collections of short stories), but this Nonpareil reissue of the original Harper *&* Row edition, is my favorite. Dickens's last work, *Our Mutual Friend*, is certainly his darkest, his most acerbic (it's about money, money and money) and most savagely satirical. It is not a novel from a happy writer. Busch takes on Dickens in his later years, beginning with his American tour of 1867–1868, as seen through the lens of his "mutual friend" and general factotum George Dolby. Through his eyes we see Dickens, his world and his contemporaries. More has probably been written about Dickens than any novelist of the nineteenth century, and he was clearly a hero of, and model for, Fred Busch, who here attempts to show him in all his monomaniacal and slightly paranoid humanity. Through various voices, we see his life as it was ending, and to an extent, as it was lived. We meet Barbara, the learned Jewish prostitute, and Kate, his abandoned and estranged wife. We see him through the lens of his peers and witness his struggles to maintain his reputation and project charisma at all costs. It is yet another take on Dickens by a writer who knew his work thoroughly and made every attempt to present this most gifted, conflicted and empathetic of writers with all his faults and gifts. It tries to get to the heart of his actions, his motives and his human character. Angus Wilson got it right when he wrote "Mr. Busch gives us Dickens in all his genius and makes us understand how that genius worked. It is the performance only possible to a man steeped in Dickens's life and writings, but the learning is presented to us, as Dickens would have wished, in joyous and horrific entertainment." And it affirms as Oscar Wilde's observation, which Dickens would have endorsed, that "there is only one thing in the world worse than being talked about, and that is not being talked about."

John Banville: *Kepler*
1983. 196 pp, 5½ × 8¼" $14.00 HC

Mefisto
1986. 240 pp, 5½ × 8¼" $18.00 HC

We had the good fortune to publish the first four books of John Banville in this country, of which *Mefisto* and *Kepler* were the most substantial. *Kepler* won the 1981 Guardian Prize for Fiction and was hailed in the TLS as "a first rate historical novel which manages to cram in more detail, verve and insight than many a novel three times its length." Seamus Heaney would endorse this: "From the start John Banville had tremendous linguistic resource, an appetite for ideas, a relish of people and periods. *Kepler* is a novel of great scope, written with deepened authority, a jubilant achievement that further secures the writer's reputation as the most exciting and ambitious young novelist in Ireland today." I am sure Bill Goodman spotted Banville on the advice of Benedict Kiely, for, being Irish, they both shared a love of the language and diction that often approached poetry. *Kepler* concerns itself with the German astronomer and mathematician who was instrumental in the inevitable change from the geocentric vision of the Catholic Middle Ages to the modern era. Out of the ignorance, hypocrisy, superstition, and misery of his time, Kepler managed to dig out the truth, and in Banville's hands, he becomes a surprisingly modern and sympathetic figure. He laid the groundwork for Newton and formulated an astronomical model of our solar system that held until Einstein. In *Mefisto*, a work of fiction and sustained imagination and invention, the hero is again a man whose life is based in facts, and it takes as its theme the price any true scientist, or artist, must pay to pursue their calling. For both titles, James Marsh produced the extraordinary cover illustrations while Julian Waters contributed the calligraphy.

Howard Frank Mosher: *Disappearances*
1984. 272 pp, 6 × 9" $9.00 SC

The year is 1932, the heart of the Depression, just before the repeal of Prohibition, and Wild Bill, who is temperamentally precisely the opposite of what his name suggests, is celebrating his fourteenth birthday. The place is Vermont, just south of the Canadian border, the proverbial "Northeast Kingdom." Bill's Dad, Quebec Bill, desperate to preserve his threatened herd of cattle through the long winter, resorts to the family trade, something considerably more dangerous than milking cows but reliably profitable: whiskey smuggling. He takes his son on a voyage into the reaches of Canada where the lines between fantasy and reality become blurred and the suspense never quits. This was Mosher's first novel, a startling, exuberant and totally original debut that not only told a story that no one who reads it will ever forget, but also speaks to the peculiarities and idiosyncrasies of people and place, filling it with details of farming, timbering, and surviving in the most challenging topography in New England. Part gothic thriller, part fantasy, part family saga, and pure rollicking adventure, it remained on our list for decades before joining Mosher's other titles at Houghton Mifflin. Everyone who read it loved it. The stuff of legends.

ABOVE: Quebec Bill rides the rapids in a birchbark canoe, smuggling a load of whiskey across the US/Canadian border in *Disappearances,* Mosher's picaresque and rollicking first novel.
LEFT: James Marsh provided the artwork and Julian Waters the calligraphy for these striking jackets for two of the four early Banville novels published by Godine: *Mefisto* and *Kepler*.

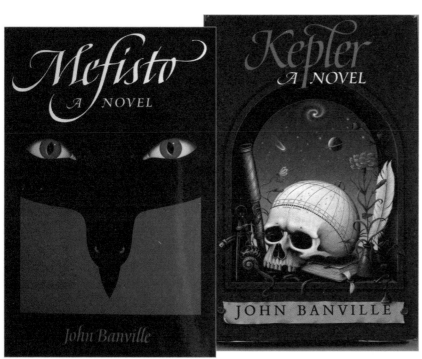

Jeannette Haien: *The All of It*

1986. 158 PP, 5 × 7" $15.00 HC

Jeannette Haien taught music in New York and summered in Ireland. This was not only her first novel but one written well into her middle age. If you fly fish, you have only to read the first few chapters to be seduced, not only by the description of Father Declan's miserable day of salmon fishing a beat in western Ireland, but the slowly emerging story of Enda and Kevin Denehy, who have sweetly been living a lie, a revelation with which the Father, when Enda finally manages to divulge, to "tell the all of it," must then deal. As only the Irish and the Catholic clergy can.

William Maxwell: *So Long, See You Tomorrow*

1989. 142 PP, 5½ × 8¼" $10.00 SC

Hilton Kramer, art critic, essayist, and founder of *The New Criterion*, was an early and strong supporter of our efforts, and we used to have periodic lunches at the Yale Club to discuss what he saw as the sorry state of American letters. After a prolonged dismissal of American writers, I asked him what he did like and might fit into our Nonpareil list. Without hesitation he brought up the name of William Maxwell, longtime right hand to William Shawn at *The New Yorker* and a writer, as I soon discovered, of considerable range and talent. His books had all been published, appropriately, by Knopf, but had never appeared in paperback. Over a period of years,

we managed to put seven of them back in print: *Ancestors; Chateau; Old Man at the Railroad Crossing; Over by the River; So, Long, See You Tomorrow; They Came Like Swallows;* and *Time Will Darken It.* We used his daughter Brooke's artwork for most of the covers. Everyone seemed happy with this arrangement, and it was surely a major investment for a small press, until Andrew Wylie took him on as a client and that was the end of it. He was a close friend of Sylvia Townsend Warner and edited a volume of her letters. When I worked for the Book-of-the-Month Club, I was astonished to learn that their first main selection, in 1929, was her strange and memorable *Lolly Willowes.* A brave choice indeed. Under the editorship of Chris Carduff, most of Maxwell's work is now available in a handsome two-volume edition from the Library of America, a well-deserved and long overdue recognition of a genuine American master.

Paul Horgan: *A Distant Trumpet*

Preface by Paul Horgan and an Introduction by C.P. Snow

1991. 656 PP, 5½ × 8½" $17.00 SC

We issued this classic of the American West to celebrate the 30th anniversary of its publication. Set in the 1880s, called by the *New York Times* "the finest novel yet on the Southwest," this was the Southwest of Arizona and New Mexico, still basically Native American territory, hosting the last gasp of resistance by a variety of tribes, here uniformly categorized as Apache. The fulcrum of the book is

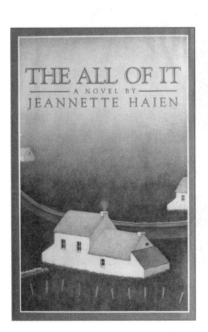

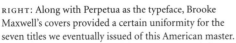

RIGHT: Along with Perpetua as the typeface, Brooke Maxwell's covers provided a certain uniformity for the seven titles we eventually issued of this American master.

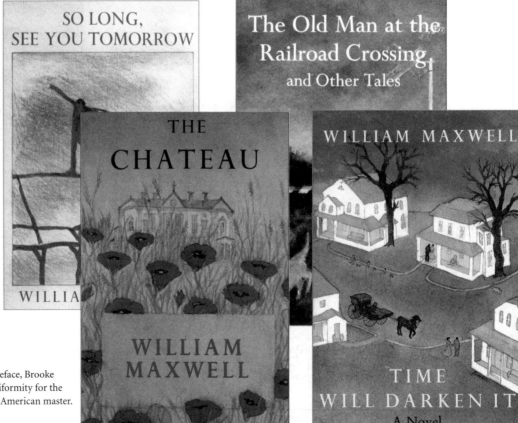

the question of whether they will be exterminated or, with putative solicitude, exported to Florida to join other tribes. The book is long on facts and incidents; it took Horgan ten years to write and the effort is reflected in its historical detail and his palpable love for the land and its people. It was a dangerous life; the climate was brutal (these were the years before air conditioning and the opera). Between the two antagonists, the concepts of "organization," "responsibility," "ownership," and "political hierarchy" were almost diametrically opposed. The characters are memorable: Matthew Hazard, just out of West Point, young, stalwart, intelligent and competent; his immediate superior, Major Prescott, a foreshadowing of what Matthew may become in the years ahead; the idiosyncratic and scholarly Major Quait, who genuinely wants to understand the Indians but is bound by his orders; and finally the Apache scout, White Horn, in service and fiercely loyal to the US Army and especially the officers he serves.

The terrain, the tenacity, the centuries of adaptation to a hostile environment are all on the side of the Native Americans, but the US Army has modern munitions, an endless supply of both personnel and weaponry, and, above all, it has time. The capitulation is almost a foregone conclusion. While not many are comfortable with it or the terms, at least it promised to preserve the tribes, and there is hope held out that someday in the future, they might be allowed to return. That hope is soon dashed. In an act of overt betrayal, the government reverses its decision and

its promise; they will stay forever in Florida. Even White Horn, who has served the government faithfully, and dangerously, for decades, is interned along with the enemies he helped subdue. Horgan's military background, and his familiarity with a part of the country he clearly loves and the scholarship he brought to its writing (there are over fifty first-hand sources listed in his Postscript), are on full display. But so, more subtly, is his Catholicism, his sense of morality, his fascination with ethical choices. Honor and trust play their respective roles in our history. In few instances have those virtues been more sorely tested or abused than in our relationships with Native Americans.

Sarah Orne Jewett: *The Country of the Pointed Firs*
Pencil drawings by Douglas Alvord
1991. 220 PP, 7¼ × 10″ $25.00 HC

Is this a novel? A classic text, first published in 1896 by Houghton Mifflin, it is set on the remote and depopulated post–Civil War Maine Coast, one of three American novels that Willa Cather (who, when she wrote her in Preface to the 1925 edition, was far better known than Jewett) predicted "which have the possibility of a long life. . ." She hoped "the student of American literature in far distant years to come will take up this book and say, 'A masterpiece.'" A collection of interrelated short stories and characters, without sex, without intrigue, without the so-called "narrative arc," and, quite remarkably almost entirely without men, it has increasingly captured an appreciative and deeply loyal audience. Really a series of short beautifully rendered and interconnected sketches, it evokes the loneliness and inexorable decline of coastal New England after the Civil War. But it is far more than just a period piece. Her "Dunnet Landing" may not have been a real place, but it is populated with real people and her prose brings them all to life: sea captains remembered from her childhood; widows living alone but self-sufficient and sympathetic; Mrs. Todd, the book's central character, who may well have been modeled on a real herbalist from Tennant's Harbor. They are all present, castaways, survivors, recluses, "Antigones on the Theban plain," a rich assembly of characters she remembered and recreated from the rounds she made with her father, Dr. Theodore Jewett of South Berwick, ME. As F.O. Matthiessen points out, "in these loosely connected sketches, [Jewett] has acquired a structure, independent of place. Her scaffolding is simply the unity of her vision." Some of the stories, and certainly most of the characters, could have been found a good century later when we published our illustrated edition with black-and-white pencil drawings by Douglas Alvord. Closely observed, carefully rendered, and modeled on "real Mainers," they capture that rock-bound coast in all its austere and self-reliant glory and reflect all the haunting reality of Jewett's prose.

Sena Jeter Naslund: *Sherlock in Love*
1993. 240 PP, 5½ × 8¼″ $22.00 HC

This book belongs to Mark Polizzotti, our invaluable editor who joined the company after his stint at Random House in New York and worked as editor, designer, copywriter, translator, and general keeper of the peace for years before leaving us for Boston's Museum of Fine Arts and thence to running the publishing program at New York's Metropolitan Museum of Art. The author was directed our way by Roger Weingarten, the director of the MFA writing program at Vermont College who had boundless faith in Naslund as both a writer and a future literary star (he was right on both counts). The book itself takes the familiar domain of Sherlock Holmes as its basis and creates a pastiche that not only honors his memory but introduces even more mysteries to those he left behind. What unutterable secrets went to the grave with him? Why is the now-venerable Doctor Watson suddenly deciding to write his old friend's biography and why is he receiving death threats as a result? What do Holmes's celebrated Stradivarius and a long unpublished adventure have in common? And, above and more mysterious than all else, who was his one true love? These are the worlds Naslund seeks to unlock, cleverly recreating the world of Holmes and Watson, and expanding on this long-familiar trope to create an engaging and powerful narrative of her own. Naslund would go on to a distinguished career, but we managed to publish another fine book of hers, a collection of her novellas and short stories, *The Disobedience of Water* in 1999, the same year as her breakthrough novel, *Ahab's Wife* turned *Moby-Dick* on its ear.

John Buchan: *The Four Adventures of Richard Hannay: The Thirty-Nine Steps, Greenmantle, Mr. Standfast, and The Three Hostages*
Introduction by Robin Winks
2001. 688 PP, 6 × 9″ $21.00 HC

John Buchan, brilliant scholar, refined diplomat, the epitome of an Edwardian gentleman (with all the prejudices that accompanied his generation), was born in Perth and remained his entire life as Scots as the thistle, grouse, and gorse to which his stories invariably return. Raised to the peerage as Lord Tweedsmur in 1935 (one of only three writers, along with C.P. Snow and Jeffrey Archer, so honored in the twentieth century). He died the popular Governor General of Canada in 1940. Although he clearly hoped to be remembered as a scholar and diplomat, his fame has rested primarily on the fiction he wrote, primarily as a pastime, throughout his career. He survives most vividly as the creator of some of the more memorable characters in fiction. And of the many he created, none was more memorable than Richard Hannay – clearly his alter ego – an unsuspecting London visitor drawn, almost against his will, into the underworld of political intrigue, a man of sure instincts, sound judgment, and almost preternatural physical and mental skills. In other words, the idealized English man of action, a certified avatar of 007. This volume includes four adventures in a single volume. Robin Winks writes in his excellent Introduction, "The basic formula for spy fiction was laid down by John Buchan, master of the Scottish landscape. . . One takes an attractive hero, slightly introspective though not debilitatingly so… endows this hero with some special expertise acquired in some remote place. . . one places this hero in some environment in which he is less comfortable… then

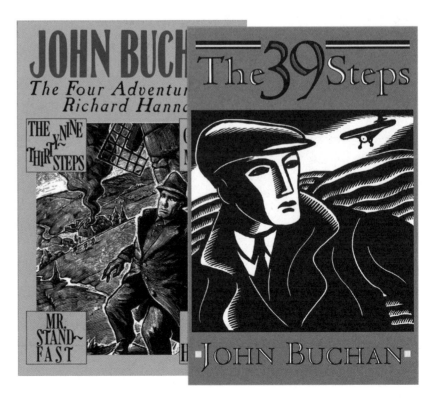

one plunges him by accident (as in *The Thirty-Nine Steps*) or design (as in *Greenmantle*) into a perilous situation. Let him be drawn, against his best judgement, into a mystery he only vaguely comprehends. Set him a task to perform, place obstacles in his path, then set the clock ticking …" This framework provided the model for masters as diverse as Forsyth, Fleming, Le Carré and Grisham. And in this grand 700-page compendium of nonstop entertainment, Buchan demonstrates why he will always be considered among the masters of the form.

Marian Engel: *Bear*

2003. 126 PP, 5 × 8″ $10.00 SC

I was working as the editor of Quality Paperback Book Club in New York when I was first introduced to this little gem of a feminist novel. It had just been awarded Canada's highest literary honor, the Governor General's Award in 1976. Margaret Atwood considered it among the best novels she'd ever read. I was dubious—a mousy librarian sent to a remote Ontario island to inventory the archives of the departed Colonel Jocelyn Cary. Cary, it turns out, has a number of secrets, but the most enduring and surprising is a pet bear he keeps chained behind his castle. Our heroine soon meets this gentle, unassuming creature and "wonders whether it would be good company." It proves to be good company indeed. Shocking and intimate company. She falls in with, well, she actually falls *in love* with the bear – with predictable results. But when I finished it, in one sitting, I recognized it as a real masterpiece. No one has ever told the story of a lonely, insecure but highly intelligent woman better than Marian Engel. And if it takes sex with a bear to bring the central character out of her shell and into the world of the living, so be it. Engel died in 1985, after a tragic fight with cancer.

Kit Bakke: *Miss Alcott's E-mail: Yours for Reforms of All Kinds*

2006. 274 PP, 5½ × 8½″ $25.00 HC

If you can make the leap of faith and buy into the proposition that a modern-day Bryn Mawr activist could communicate by email with Louisa May Alcott, this is a book to consider. Long before Greta Gerwig's film adaptation of *Little Women*, Kit Bakke realized Louisa May Alcott was a woman far ahead of her time. She is, and should be recognized as, far more than the author of *Little Women*. "Her abolitionist zeal, her women's rights advocacy, her hospital work, her crazy commune days, her heartfelt desire to leave her world a better place, her humor and energy all materialized in front of me," Bakke writes, "Louisa was serious when she signed her letters, 'Yours for reforms of all kinds.'" Serious biographies of Alcott are everywhere, but what if a confirmed radical, a member of the Weathermen while a student at Bryn Mawr for God's sake, were able to reach out and converse with Alcott on the problems and issues facing the twentieth-first century. The miracle of the book is that you soon believe in a correspondence that Alcott writes with a quill pen and that is received in Times New Roman. Bakke is nearly the same age as Alcott when she died of mercury poisoning in 1888. The scholarship and research are impressive; the issues Bakke raises and to which Alcott responds are as timely and intractable today as they were 150 years ago. Bakke moves back in time just as Alcott moves forward, meeting somewhere in the middle, the letters passing back and forth as the two minds tangle. Bakke's interwoven essays, revealing her own past, setting out the highlights of Alcott's life and work, while putting both lives in context, are triumphs of dual biography. Two engaging and thoroughly modern women make for a fascinating book.

LEFT: A fine woodcut by Wesley Bates with its almost invisible hand moving affectionately across a recumbent bear, anticipates the contents of this short but compelling novel.
RIGHT: Both the title and the peace symbol on Ms. Alcott's left cheek suggest Ms. Bakke's approach to her life and work may not be entirely conventional.

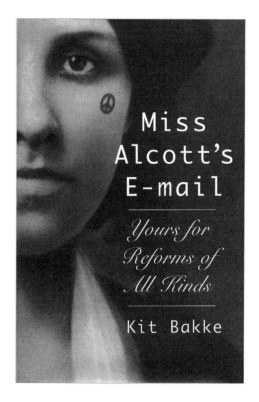

Flora Thompson: *Lark Rise to Candleford*
Introduction by H.J. Massingham
2008. 576 PP, 5½ × 8½" $19.00 SC

Flora Thompson was born in 1876 in a small hamlet in Oxfordshire and died in Devon. She doesn't stray very far from home in this classic, probably the finest distillation of English country life at the turn of the last century between covers. In 1945, the three books forming the trilogy were combined as one and that is what forms the platform for this Nonpareil reissue, along with the introduction by the historian H.J. Massingham and the charming wood engravings by Julie Neild. Massingham correctly calls the books "a triune achievement: a triumph of evocation in the resurrecting of an age that, being transitional, was the most difficult to catch as it flew; another in diversity of rural portraiture engagingly blended with autobiography, and the last in the overtones and implications of a set of values which is the author's 'Message.'" There is no question that the books were largely autobiographical; Thompson could write convincingly about the English poor because she was born among them. She could describe the routines that Laura, her alter ego, engaged as an assistant postmistress in a town four miles from her birth because she lived that job. The story follows her path, now told in the third person by the author who serves here as both a participant in the drama and an outside observer of and commentator on the events. In small but telling details, she captures the slow demise of a bucolic rural England as it slowly adjusts to the modern age. Telegraph wires and radios appear, foretelling the gradual decay of the rituals and

rites of passage that had kept agrarian England close to the land and the landscape. The story grows with the population, as does Laura from her work in a small hamlet, to a village and finally to a town. And there's little question that the cast of characters is based on the memorable characters she encountered. It is somewhat ironic that a series of books, authored by a young woman whose education was insufficient to qualify her to stand for a Civil Service examination, should have been published by the Oxford University Press, inspired two plays that ran in London for years, and a ten-part, often repeated BBC television series.

N. John Hall: *Correspondence: An Adventure in Letters*
2010. 248 PP, 6 × 9" $25.00 HC

I suspect that writing this book was Jack Hall's clever device to display his knowledge of, and affection for, Victorian literature and the colorful personalities who produced it. An acknowledged expert on Trollope and Beerbohm, he devises for the novel a clever ruse: suppose a retired bank clerk from New Jersey named Larry Dickerson inherits a mass of valuable letters from his great-great-grandfather who happened to be bookseller in Victorian London who had corresponded at length with the leading literary lights of his generation. To Dickens and Thackeray, Eliot and Trollope, Butler and Hardy, he would pose the simple series of questions: Why do you write? How do you write? From what sources do you find your characters and your ideas? What do you imagine will be the purpose, usefulness and fate of your novels? And what do you think of your peers and competitors? *Mirabile dictu*, most of them replied with predictably interesting answers. And the batch of letters have come down to Larry intact. Hall had clearly thought long and hard about these issues, but how to put them all together as a novel? The clever expedient was to publish an epistolary journey between Larry, intent on extracting as much money as possible from this windfall, and Stephen Nicholls, the patient and helpful head of Christie's manuscript department in London, who leads him through the intricacies of the auction process and introduces him to the wonders of the Victorian mind, a domain Larry eventually embraces with enthusiasm. It is part suspense novel (will he sell or not?), part Vic Lit 101, and part *tour de force*, because Hall, using the letters as his entrées into the Victorian era, does indeed introduce us to the minds and aesthetics of the foremost novelists of the period. We watch as bluff, blunt, unschooled Larry emerges as an educated, determined Victorianist, and somehow, for those of us who might have found Dickens too melodramatic, Trollope too prolix, Thackeray too allusive and Hardy too pessimistic, we go along with him for the ride.

William Kotzwinkle: *Swimmer in the Secret Sea*

2010. 96 PP, 4⅝ × 6½" $10.00 SC

I cannot remember when I first read this book. I was certainly unmarried, had never had children, and had no concept of what losing a child must be like. But I remember that even then it brought tears to my eyes. It is a short book with the largest of themes: life, death, and renewal. It first appeared in *Redbook*, was reissued in a number of editions, and came to rest as Nonpareil #104 on our list, the shortest adult book we ever published, and surely among the most powerful. Kotzwinkle, without subtracting from its mystery, manages to destroy any sentimental illusions we might harbor about childbirth, reminding us how very close is the distance between life and death, hope and disillusionment. I have never asked, but it is hard to believe that writing of such power and precision could have been anything but autobiographical.

Erskine Childers: *The Riddle of the Sands*
Preface by Brigadier E.F. Parker

2019. 248 PP, 7 × 10" $17.00 SC

This is not only one of the greatest spy stories ever written, it was actually a book that initiated the genre, a book Ken Follett described as "the first modern thriller." First published in 1903, it set the tone and rhythms for the modern spy thriller, but its two heroes, old Oxford pals, are far from typical. Charles Carruthers, the narrator, a minor official in the British Foreign Office, is asked by Arthur Davies, an expert yachtsman who seems somewhat adrift, to accompany him for a bit of duck hunting and sailing on the Frisian Coast of the North Sea. But Davies has other plans; he explains that a man has made a covert attempt on his life and he requires Carruthers's knowledge of the German language and his sharp wit to determine why. We soon learn, through a series of increasingly revealing encounters, the reason: The Germans are planning the intense development of the hazardous shoal coastline for their Navy and as a means to control the approaches to the North Sea. The plot may have been fiction, but it was prophetic in its exposure of German strategy and British naval weaknesses. Churchill used it to determine the placement of multiple naval bases. And Childers knows ropes from lines – he presents a nautical picture that is precisely drawn, geographically accurate, and with all the details of sailing, navigation, and seamanship entirely true to life.

Howard Moss & Edward Gorey: *Instant Lives*
2019. 96 PP, 4¼ × 6¾″ $20.00 HC

First published fifty years ago, this delicious combination of totally fabricated and consistently inventive short biographies by *New Yorker* editor Howard Moss and the bleakly hilarious pen-and-ink drawings by Edward Gorey combine for a droll and delightful anthology of imaginary lives. They're all here: the Alcott sisters sculpting fudge, the rise of Emily Dickinson's ruthless witch hazel business, the Brontë sisters trapped at Haworth in a downpour waiting for a drunken and menacing Branwell to fix the drains, the oversized Gertrude Stein throwing a "typical salon-type affair for which the house had become notorious" and duking it out with Picasso for a painting. The advance reviews on the back ad are hilarious. Virginia Woolf: "Leonard and I stayed up half the night. It took us hours to burn it." George Eliot: "A houseboat of conjecture that slowly sinks in a river of contrivance." Flaubert: "A major work on a minor scale, and just possibly the other way around." We reset it nicely to a pocket-size format in a two-color design by Sara Eisenman.

Instant Lives & MORE

WRITTEN BY

Howard Moss

DRAWINGS BY

Edward Gorey

DAVID R. GODINE
PUBLISHER, BOSTON

LEFT, ABOVE: The title page and jacket of *Instant Lives* is set in a suitably gothic, vaguely threatening typeface.

OPPOSITE: The covers initiated, designed and art-directed by Josh Bodwell for the three-volume 2019 reissue of Dubus's *The Cross Country Runner*, *The Winter Father*, and *We Don't Live Here Anymore*

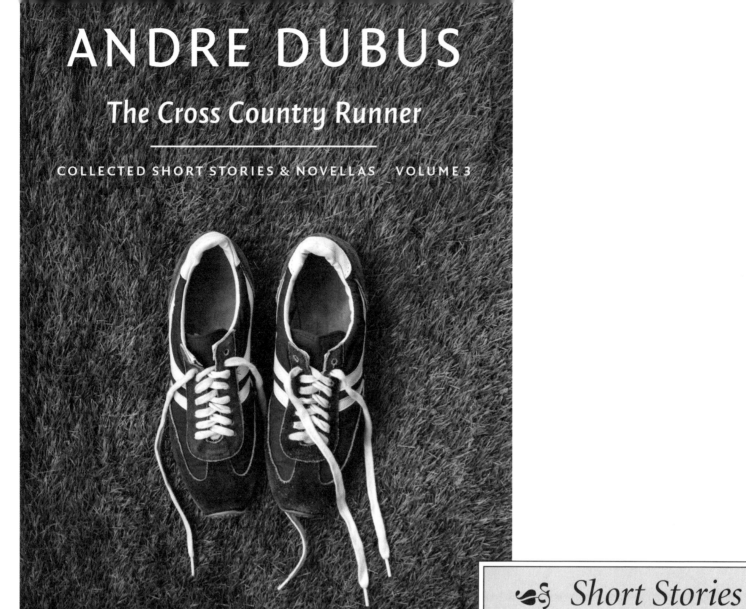

ANDRE DUBUS

The Cross Country Runner

COLLECTED SHORT STORIES & NOVELLAS   VOLUME 3

Introduction by **TOBIAS WOLFF**

ANDRE DUBUS

We Don't Live Here Anymore

COLLECTED SHORT STORIES & NOVELLAS   VOLUME 1

Introduction by ANN BEATTIE

Short Stories

ANDRE DUBUS

The Winter Father

OLLECTED SHORT STORIES & NOVELLAS   VOLUME 2

Introduction by RICHARD RUSSO

Howard Nemerov: *Stories, Fables & Other Diversions*
1971. 124 PP, 6 × 9½″ $7.50 HC

Howard Nemerov was, and with good reason will probably remain, far better known as a poet than an essayist
or short story writer. That said, I found his stories enchanting, and we issued *Stories, Fables & Other Diversions*
in 1971, our first foray into the thicket of contemporary
fiction. Nemerov had a sly sense of humor, and he always
wandered around Middlebury's Breadloaf campus with
his green bookbag looking slightly bemused by everything
he saw. That humor, his slightly out of kilter take on the
world, comes through nicely in these stories. As usual, it
was hopelessly overproduced. Set in Monotype Bembo,
printed at the Stinehour Press in an edition of 2,000 copies, with title page and jacket calligraphy by John Benson,
it received a number of favorable reviews, one of which,
in the *Washington Post*, referred to us as "a small press,"
a designation to which I ungraciously and indignantly
objected. The innocent reviewer, quite rightfully, wrote
me back informing me what a fool I was, observing I was
lucky to have the book noticed at all and someday I would
accept, even welcome, the attention. He was, of course,
absolutely right.

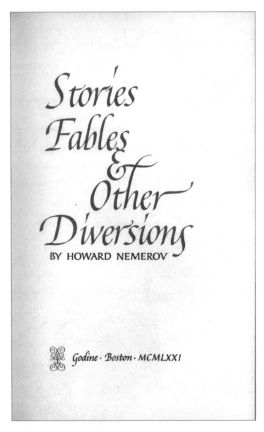

ABOVE: John Benson provided the lovely calligraphy for
Nemerov's *Stories, Fables & Other Diversions*.

Andre Dubus: *Separate Flights*
1975. 240 PP, 6 × 9″ $9.00 HC

Way back in the seventies, there was a long article in
Publishers Weekly about young and prescient New York
agents. The one I liked the sound of was Philip Spitzer.
So I called him up, and we set a date to meet in New
York for hamburgers at some cheap and accessible joint.
When I asked whom he represented who he especially
liked, without hesitation he came up with Andre Dubus,
his favorite writer but one he couldn't possibly sell; all
he wanted to write were short stories. "He'll never write
a novel. Don't even ask him the question." I paid for the
burgers, took back the manuscript in a paper bag, and read
it that evening. I was bowled over. This was the real thing. I
called Phil the next morning and said I couldn't pay much
but whatever he wanted, I'd come up with. We settled on
some derisory figure, and the first book of the seven we
ultimately published was *Separate Flights*, a title which, to
my shame, occupied only a half-page and fifteen lines in
our 1975 Spring catalogue. Andre, it turned out, had many
friends – from Richard Yates to John Yount to Toby Wolff –
and the book was widely and favorably reviewed. That year
he also won the *Boston Globe*'s first Laurence L. & Thomas
Winship Award for the outstanding book of New England
origin. It is still, in my opinion, his best collection. And,
alone among the books announced that season, still in
print. In retrospect, the jacket design, which made it look
like a textbook on bipolar disease, was probably a big mistake, and the book went through countless design permutations in subsequent softcover editions. Andre remained
loyal to us for years (he was both a faithful Catholic and an
exemplary Marine whose motto "Semper Fidelis" was one
he both took seriously and could be applied with particular precision to his character). Only after a tragic automobile accident in which he lost one leg and the use of the
other trying to rescue a motorist from harm, did he leave
us to publish with Knopf. He needed the money for his
treatments, and there was no blame or bitterness on either
side. He even called me himself to break the news.

Of all the fiction authors we have published over the
years, Andre will always remain my favorite. Short stories
were what he wanted to write and he knew he could do
them well, specializing in what George Core perceived as
"adroitly revealing the process by which a person gradually and almost unconsciously wakes up to himself and
the people close to him, and the theme of recognition is
beautifully counterpointed by the protagonist's yearning for communion." In Dubus's stories, the protagonists
were often women, and few male writers of his, or any,
generation were able to render their nuanced and complex
character as he did. He stuck to short stories. Money
held no interest for him, and he and our longtime editor
Bill Goodman remained on the closest terms. Our 1975

catalogue copy of this first collection read "Dubus is a piti-less observer of marriage and adultery, guilt and remorse, the anxieties of children and the terror of adults. These stories are not elaborate fictions, but startlingly realistic evocations of the disruptions that beset daily life." I think that description still holds. Andre's life was bedrocked on the Catholic belief in the redemptive power of grace and pity. In 1988, we issued a selection of his best stories. In 2018, spearheaded by Josh Bodwell, we issued a handsome and complete three-volume collection of his entire work, including previously unpublished material, and new fore-words by Ann Beattie, Richard Russo and Tobias Wolff.

FROM TOP DOWN: Early paperback iterations of Dubus and Elkin paperback covers with a later, slightly more contemporary, attempt of Elkin's *Searches and Seizures*

Stanley Elkin: *Searches and Seizures*
1978. 320 PP, 5½ × 9¼″ $6.00 SC

The Franchiser
Foreword by William Gass
1978. 356 PP, 5½ × 8½″ $10.00 SC

On our very first Nonpareil list, issued in 1978, we had two masters from Washington University, William Gass and Stanley Elkin. Gass received the recognition he deserved, but Stanley, despite ten novels and four collections of short stories and novellas, was never really able to break through. Maybe this was because he was billed and perceived as a "comic writer," a sure kiss of death (although most of his humor was plenty dark), and partly, in my opinion, because humor, especially when forced and laid on thick, is better applied in small doses. Elkin's shtick (to use good Yiddish slang) was best enjoyed in the shorter forms, especially the novellas. This collection of three novellas is vintage Elkin. Wry, mildly wicked, slightly mad, and very Jewish (though he would never admit it), it consists of three stories: *The Making of Ashenden, The Condominium* ("At first one thought it was a new metal alloy, or perhaps a new element. There were those who thought it had to do with big business, industrial stuff—combines, cartels. Others thought it was a sort of prophylactic."), and the best, *The Bailbondsman*, which features the Phoenician, among the oiliest characters in American fiction, who "loves a contract like the devil" and leaves a palpable slick on the printed page.

In his novel, *The Franchiser*, which we reissued in 1988, you get a sense of why Elkin had problems gaining an au-dience: the plots were never straightforward, the language baroque, and the sentences lasted forever. The wit was serial, sharp and funny but often mitigated by its density. You moved from comedy to tragedy without skipping a beat. Its "hero," Ben Flesh, an orphaned bachelor, lives to build a fast food empire and he does so by cloning a web of franchised industries, an activity that Elkin uses to sati-rize American consumerism and capitalism. But at some point the reader wants to settle down, push the humor aside, get serious, and get on with the *story*.

Both Elkin and John Irving taught at Breadloaf, Middle-bury's summer writing school, and gave the required read-ings of a work in progress. I heard them both. Irving read the first chapter of *The World According to Garp*, and the audience was on the edge of their chairs, begging for more. It had "bestseller" written all over it. Stanley read *The Bail-bondsman*, among his best. The student audience laughed and hooted, left admiring the skill, style and humor, and realized they could never come close to cloning it.

Benedict Kiely: *The State of Ireland*
Introduction by Thomas Flanagan
1980. 400 PP, 5½ × 8⅛″ $15.00 HC

I give Bill Goodman full credit for finding Benedict Kiely, one of Ireland's most important storytellers in its long, discursive narrative tradition. This was his first collection to be published in the US and one of six subsequent books we issued by this still-underrated Irish master. Kiely was perhaps best in these short stories, for in his longer novels, he could be a little *too* Irish for American tastes – often oblique, at times long-winded. But in the short form, he was an Irish master and in his front-page *New York Times* review, Guy Davenport wrote that "this choice collection of stories is welcome both as a development of the genre and an introduction to Benedict Kiely as master of it."

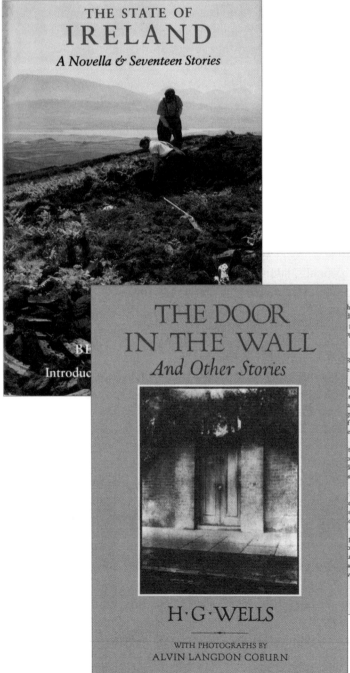

H.G. Wells: *The Door in the Wall*
Photographs by Alvin Langdon Coburn
1980. 162 PP, 5⅝ × 8″ $11.00 HC ℘

"Our business," author Wells wrote to photographer Coburn, "is to see what we can and render it." He underscored himself this by sketching with a pen, while his American collaborator Coburn rendered with a camera. Seldom have writing and image converged more powerfully than in this collection of eight stories and ten photographs, faithfully reproduced in duotone from the stunning 1911 edition published by Mitchell Kennerley and designed and typeset by Fred and Bertha Goudy. These are tales that both echo and reconfirm his great contributions to science fiction with *War of the Worlds*, *The Invisible Man*, *The Time Machine*, and *The Island of Doctor Moreau*, all published around two decades earlier. The stories, as all his writing, reflect his background in science (his first published book was a *Text-Book of Biology*) and his fascination with the future. They were stories that invariably took the reader beyond everyday reality – poignant accounts of missed chances, suggestions of what might have been, bleak premonitions of a possibly blessed future whose promise is destroyed by new forms of warfare, introductions of diseases, efforts to perfect the human race through genetic engineering and vivisection. Every story demonstrates his capacity for myth-making in which an active and dynamic deity, in the form of a man or an alien species or a mechanical device would try to determine the future. He would be nominated for the Nobel Prize four times, but was never awarded it.

THE EDGE OF THE BLACK COUNTRY

LEFT & ABOVE: The jacket photographs of Alvin Langdon Coburn grace the jacket and illustrate the short story "The Cove" accompanied by his title, "The Edge of the Black Country" in *The Door in the Wall*.

Coburn's photographs are no less haunting than the texts – otherworldly, loosely based on the stories but not tied to them, never "illustrative" in the usual sense. The book is among the few collaborations between modern author and artist, word and image, working in harmony but coming at the subjects from two separate directions.

William Gass: *In the Heart of the Heart of the Country and Other Stories*
New and Expanded Preface by William Gass
1981. 254 PP, 5½ × 8¼″ $16.00 HC

The prose of Gass, in fact anything written by Gass, is as immediately identifiable as a fugue by Bach. The language is lush, the connections not immediately apparent. The stories try hard to come from the heart, "because the heart really confesses to intelligence its deeper needs, and few of the stories one has at the top of one's head to tell get told, because the mind does not always possess the voice for them." This collection, originally published by Knopf in 1968, went through seven or eight printings, and what I found the most moving, in addition to the stories themselves that contained his most unforgettable work of fiction, "The Petersen Kid," was his "Revised and Expanded Preface." It is about literature, the role literature plays in our lives, as part of their very fabric. And its sad and slow disappearance from the landscape. You can't read a paragraph like this without detecting real rage:

No court commands our entertainments, requires our flattery, needs our loyal enlargements or memorializing lies. Fame is not a whore we can ring up. The public spends its money at the movies. It fills stadia with cheers; dances to organized noise; while books die quietly, and more rapidly than their authors. Mammon has no interest in our service.

This is the voice of an angry author. Angry in 1981, before the digital revolution had even cut its eye teeth, and dead at 93 in 2017, when it was in full swing. I sometimes wonder what Gass would have written today were he asked to revise his revisions.

Short Shorts: An Anthology of the Shortest Stories
Edited by Irving Howe and Ilana Wiener Howe
Introduction by Irving Howe
1982. 288 PP, 5 × 7½″ $13.00 HC

This anthology of very short confections, none of them more than 2,500 words and most of them closer to only 1,500. In other words, not just short stories but *really* short stories, ones that, in Irving Howe's words, "need to be especially bold. They stake everything on a stroke of inventiveness … The voice of the writer brushes, so to say, against his flash of invention. And then, almost before it begins, the fiction is brought to a stark conclusion – abrupt, bleeding, exhausting." It was a powerful collection, including writers as diverse as Tolstoy and de Maupassant, Lawrence and Kafka, Babel and Paley. The stories were so powerful you really *had* to read them in short spurts. Designed by Carol Goldenberg at the beginning of her distinguished career and set in Trump Medieval, it was an eclectic collection that only a writer of Howe's breadth of reading and interest could have assembled.

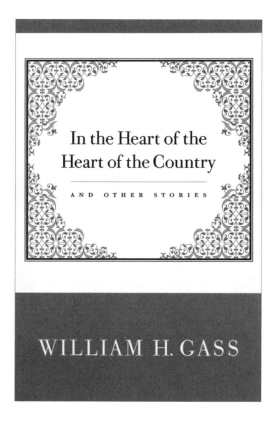

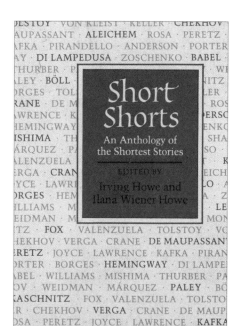

FAR LEFT: Our third iteration of a paperback cover for Bill Gass's short story collection
LEFT: Jacqueline Sakwa provided the calligraphy and Carol Goldenberg the design for this fine and appropriately small format volume of very short stories assembled by Irving and Ilana Wiener Howe.

W.P. Kinsella: *The Moccasin Telegraph and Other Tales*

1984. 192 PP, 5½ × 8¼″ $13.00 SC

Dance Me Outside: More Tales from the Ermineskin Reserve

1994. 192 PP, 5½ × 8¼″ $13.00 SC

W.P. Kinsella is today best remembered for *Shoeless Joe* and *The Iowa Baseball Confederacy*, which became the bases for the timeless movie *Field of Dreams*. Born in 1935, and living most of his life in Western Canada, he was equally gifted as a short story writer, and you come away from these two books, both set on the Ermineskin Indian Reserve and starring the irrepressible Silas Ermineskin, its resident eighteen-year-old scribe, quickly realizing that his heart was very much with its residents. The short story, really a connected sequence of vignettes, provides the perfect vehicle to introduce a wider, and whiter, audience to what he perceived life was really like for Native Americans living on a reservation. The colorful cast of characters includes Silas's girlfriend, Sadie One-wound; his best buddy, the incorrigible and sometimes malign Frank Fencepost; and Mad Etta, the 400-pound, take-no-prisoners medicine woman who dispenses advice, and occasionally wisdom, from a tree trunk chair. And if Silas can't create enough havoc for himself, he sure knows how to find it. Poignant but unsentimental, often laugh-out-loud funny, these down to earth stories reflect the best of lyric storytelling.

Wright Morris: *Collected Stories: 1948-1986*

1989. 288 PP, 5½ × 8¼″ $11.00 SC

I think Wright Morris was among the most important, and overlooked, writers of the last century. He authored nearly twenty novels, two collections of short stories, three memoirs, four books of essays and five splendid volumes of his own photography. Everyone was ready to talk about him and praise him – he was even awarded the 1981 National Book Award for *Plains Song* which we reissued in 1991. It seems few were willing to keep his work in print. A second opportunity came when Harper *&* Row was willing to sell the rights to his *Collected Stories, 1948-1986*, in George Garrett's words "bringing together old favorites and new friends in harmonious celebration." Containing twenty-five of his best, it shows his steady and subtle development as a writer, understated, almost casual, but willing to tackle a variety of themes, characters, and topographies. There is nothing flashy about his writing; most sentences begin with a "The" and follow the standard subject, verb and object prescription – perhaps none of them shout "Maestro at work," but for a career of solid storytelling, here compressed to a mere 288 pages, he is, along with William Maxwell, among the great tale-spinners of his generation.

ABOVE: Although Tim Girvin's exuberant calligraphy might have been appropriate for many covers, I am not sure it is appropriate for Wright Morris's traditional writing style.
LEFT: The idiosyncratic cover design and lettering of Steven Guarnaccia instantly catches the reader's eye and interest for this collection of reservation tales by W.P. Kinsella.

Jorge Luis Borges: *The Library of Babel*
Etchings by Erik Dezmazières
2000. 48 PP, 6 × 9" $20.00 HC

Of all Borges's stories, this one, his vision for and of the ideal library, his tribute to "The Universe, which others call the library … the feverish library, whose random volumes constantly threaten to transmogrify into others, so that they affirm all things, deny all things, and confound and confuse all things" is Borges at his most transcendentally fustian, baroque, and brilliant. It is, deservedly, considered among his most famous and eloquent meditations,

the one that remains foremost in most people's minds. When I was in Andrew Fitch's New York gallery and saw what the French etcher and engraver Erik Dezmazières had conceived as his interpretations of the story, I knew it would make a glorious package, the perfect visual counterpoint to Borges's visionary prose, right down to his interpretation of the famous "Imaginary Alphabet." Obtaining the rights to the story was another matter, but persistence prevailed and in 2000 we issued a lovely, small octavo containing the newly set story with Erik's etchings in a beautiful cloth binding. Designed by Carl W. Scarbrough, set in Mardersteig's Dante, and printed duotone by the Stinehour Press, bound in full linen with a paper label, it is, in every way, a delightful combination of art and literature – an "artist's book" that, at $20, was a gift the average consumer could also afford.

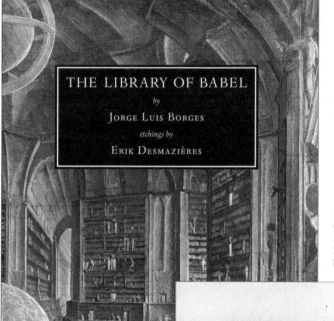

LEFT & BELOW: The hand-colored jacket image and an interior spread showing an etching of Dezmazières and the Dante typeface of Giovanni Mardersteig in our elegant presentation of Borges's best-loved short story, *The Library of Babel*

– Plate III –
Alphabet imaginaire

THE UNIVERSE (which others call the Library) is composed of an indefinite, perhaps infinite number of hexagonal galleries. In the center of each gallery is a ventilation shaft, bounded by a low railing. From any hexagon one can see the floors above and below — one after another, endlessly. The arrangement of the galleries is always the same: Twenty bookshelves, five to each side, line four of the hexagon's six sides; the height of the bookshelves, floor to ceiling, is hardly greater than the height of a normal librarian. One of the hexagon's free sides opens onto a narrow sort of vestibule, which in turn opens onto another gallery, identical to the first — identical in fact to all. To the left and right of the vestibule are two tiny compartments. One is for sleeping, upright; the other, for satisfying one's physical necessities. Through this space, too, there passes a spiral staircase, which winds upward and downward into the remotest distance. In the vestibule there is a mirror, which faithfully duplicates appearances. Men often infer from this mirror that the Library is not infinite — if it were, what need would there be for that illusory replication? I prefer to dream that burnished surfaces are a figuration and promise of the infinite.... Light is provided by certain spherical fruits that bear the name "bulbs." There are two of these bulbs in each hexagon, set crosswise. The light they give is insufficient, and unceasing.

Like all the men of the Library, in my younger days I traveled; I have journeyed in quest of a book, perhaps the catalog of catalogs. Now that my eyes can hardly make out what I myself have written, I am preparing to die, a few leagues from the hexagon where I was born. When I am dead, compassionate hands will throw me over the railing; my tomb will be the unfathomable air, my body will sink for ages, and will decay and dissolve in the wind engendered by my fall, which shall be infinite. I declare that the Library is endless. Idealists argue that the hexagonal

– 19 –

THE
OBSCENE BIRD
OF NIGHT
JOSÉ DONOSO

José Donoso: *The Obscene Bird of Night*
Translated by Hardie St. Martin *&* Leonard Mades
1979. 442 PP, 5½ × 8⅛″ $7.00 HC

A fustian, haunting jungle of a novel, this, the most
famous and widely read of Donoso's works, was hailed
as "a masterpiece" by Luis Buñuel and "one of the great
novels not only of Spanish America, but of our time" by
Carlos Fuentes. It was among the first of a stream of surreal, fantastic, and totally original fiction exploding out
of South America in the early seventies, a movement for
which Donoso himself coined the term "The Boom" in a
1977 essay, and which came to be known in this country as
"magical realism." This story centers on the last member
of the aristocratic Azcoitia family, a monstrous mutation
whose identity and appearance are kept from view (and
himself) through the expedient of a collection of freaks
chosen as his companions. It was recognized as a triumph
of imaginative, visionary writing, and an avatar of many
of the themes that would mark the movement: confusion
of identity, the meaning and use of illusion and deception,
the darker side of what might otherwise be called humor.
Born in Chile, self-exiled against the dictatorship of Pino-
chet, Donoso wrote in many forms. We had previously had
the pleasure of publishing a hardcover collection of his
short stories, *Charleston & Other Stories*, in 1977.

Aharon Appelfeld: *Badenheim 1939*
Translated by Dalya Bilu
1980. 160 PP, 5 × 7½″ $10.00 HC

The Age of Wonders
Translated by Dalya Bilu
1981. 278 PP, 5 × 7½″ $13.00 HC

It is Austria in the summer of 1939 and the usual retinue
of Jewish vacationers are heading for their favorite spa
outside of Vienna. The atmosphere seems calm to them,
but for the reader, ominous signs begin to appear gradually, and slowly but surely you can foresee the lineaments
of disaster unfolding. Even in the last few pages, when they
are all led to the boxcars and to a fate that we are all too
aware was awaiting them, they remain oblivious and trust-
ing, lambs to the slaughter. The prose is dry and matter of
fact, which makes the story all the more memorable and
devastating. Appelfeld was unknown in this country when
we published this, the result of Irving Howe's bringing it to
Bill Goodman's attention and then to a front-page review
by Howe in the *New York Times*. Like its successor, *The Age
of Wonders*, which we published in 1981 and which also
received a front-page *New York Times* review, it remains in
print to this day, a tribute to Goodman's good taste and
our willingness to take a small chance on a great author.

OPPOSITE: A striking cover for Donoso's hallucinatory tale of deformity in the jungle, and the third iteration in our attempt to capture it, by Lorraine Louie
RIGHT: We issued these first books of Appelfeld in small for-mats with delicate and restrained pencil drawings by Nancy Lawton that gave no hint of the annihilation of Austrian Jewry.

Robert Musil: *Five Women*

Translated by Eithne Wilkins *&* Ernst Kaiser
Preface by Frank Kermode
1986. 224 PP, 5⅜ × 8″ $9.00 SC   ⬤

Musil, as more and more of his work appears in modern translation, has gradually taken his place as a major writer, the Austrian equivalent of his contemporaries Rilke, Mann, and Kafka, and a central figure in the modernist movement. He is best known for his magnum opus, *The Man Without Qualities,* but here, in these five short stories, you can perceive them as being as crucial to understanding that masterpiece as Joyce's *Dubliners* is to understanding *Ulysses.* It is another face, but the same face, one that is in turn sensual, extravagant, mystical, and autobiographical. As Frank Kermode notes in his Preface, these are "elaborate attempts to use fiction for its true purposes, the discovery and registration of the human world." And it is anything but bloodless. There is always present the animality of sex. As V.S. Pritchett perceived, "In his descriptions of love affairs and especially the portraits of women in love, Musil is truly original; in managing scenes of physical love, he has not been approached by any writer in the last fifty years." It is little wonder that Musil came from a society, and a country, that also gave us Klimt and Schiele, whose women exude the same sexuality.

Georges Perec: *Life A User's Manual*

Translated by David Bellos
1987. 608 PP, 6⅛ × 9¼″ $25.00 HC   ⬤

My surprising and usually effective approach when asking about new books from a foreign publisher is to simply inquire what is the most important book on their back or frontlist that has yet to be published in the U.S. In the case of François Samuelson, who was then heading up the French Publishers Association in New York, the answer came without hesitation, "No question; it is Perec's *La Vie mode d'emploi.* The problem is that no one will be able to translate it." As it turned out, someone was indeed hard at work translating it – David Bellos, who was then a professor at the University of Manchester and is now a Professor Emeritus at Princeton. Of course, I knew nothing of Perec or the Oulipo group with which he was so closely involved, but Bellos was a patient teacher and in 1987, we published *Life A User's Manual,* a triumph of both design and typesetting, and arguably the most important novel the house has issued. This was followed by seven other books by Perec, including *A Void,* an entire novel without the letter e, and one which in my wildest dreams I was convinced no one could translate. But Gilbert Adair managed it, and rather convincingly. Thanks to David Bellos, we now have all of Perec's major, and most of his minor, works in print – and the cult seems to grow every year.

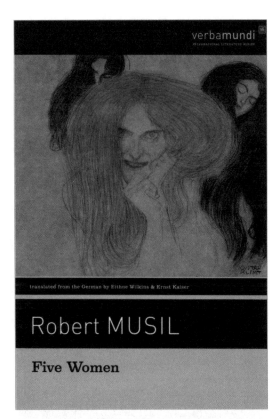

ABOVE: Gustav Klimt's drawing of the Gorgon's head provides the perfect counterpoint to the fin de siècle's steamy eroticism contained in the stories of Musil's *Five Women.*
RIGHT: The artist Jane Goldman played on a familiar Balthus painting to suggest the jigsaw universe contained and described in Perec's doorstop masterpiece of a novel *Life A User's Manual.*

Goran Tunstrom: *The Christmas Oratorio*
Translated by Paul Hoover
1995. 348 PP, 5½ × 8¼″ $24.00 HC ●

A grand fresco of a novel by Sweden's foremost contemporary writer, *The Christmas Oratorio* is Tunstrom's great tableau of family dynamics, ambition, and desire. The story begins in the 1930s, when the family matriarch, Solveig Nordensson, is accidentally killed. The family, hoping to start afresh, moves to another town, but the emotional burden created by her death follows them – geographically, emotionally, and viscerally – through three generations of family life. The saga ends only when the grandson, Victor, the heir to the family's tortured legacy, finds redemption for himself, and a modicum of release for the reader, by staging Bach's *Christmas Oratorio*, a performance that had been planned by Solveig herself a half a century earlier. If

the term "magical realist" can be applied with any accuracy to a Swede – one with a predilection for death and sorrow, capable of creating a novel whose plot unwinds with the surreal emotional complexity of a Bergman film – Tunstrom would be first in line.

Patrick Modiano: *Missing Person*
Translated by Daniel Weissbort
2005. 192 PP, 5½ × 8¼″ $17.00 HC ●

Honeymoon
Translated by Barbara Wright
1995. 128 PP, 5½ × 8¼″ $20.00 HC ●

Early in October of 2014, I received a call from the *Washington Post* informing me that Patrick Modiano had just been awarded the Nobel Prize for Literature. I was stunned. We had three Modiano titles in print at that time, two of his best novels as well as the quite wonderful children's book, *Catherine Certitude*, on which he had collaborated with Sempé. Up till that point, none of them had sold very well, and we still had copies packed away in dusty cartons from the first printings. That day, the phones at the warehouse began ringing at 8am, and by 9:30, we had sold every copy. By 5pm, the back orders were in the thousands.

I looked at our records, and the previous year we had sold a grand total of seventeen copies of his masterpiece, *Missing Person*, the book awarded the Prix Goncourt in 1978. We rushed a paperback of both his novels into print and sold over 40,000 of them combined in the next year. It just goes to show, if you're lucky enough to win an award, the Nobel is the one to choose. Modiano's books are like a giant jigsaw puzzle; you probably have to read all of them to put the pieces together, but there are common themes: the murky, dark days of the Nazi occupation of France and Paris, that black hole of the French collective memory; the crossover between film and literature, and between predictable detective thrillers and film noir, all smoky cafes and insubstantial figures crossing bridges in the fog. Curiously, his children's book, *Catherine Certitude,* a full-size picture book illustrated by the inimitable Sempé, is the most revealing, providing glimpses into the shady career of his father, the anxiety of both being half-Jewish and dealing with what is clearly smuggled merchandise, the undercover louche figures who clearly passed in and out of his early life rendered in his descriptions and Sempé's watercolors. All the books are filled with mystery, ambiguity, and lost leads. The title *Missing Person* is especially apt; people, objects, thoughts, and connective tissue are *missing*. But in all of these works, Modiano comes across as a superb storyteller, an author who grabs and holds your attention, a genuine wizard with words – and the three translations, by Daniel Weissbort, Barbara Wright, and William Rodarmor, really do his prose justice.

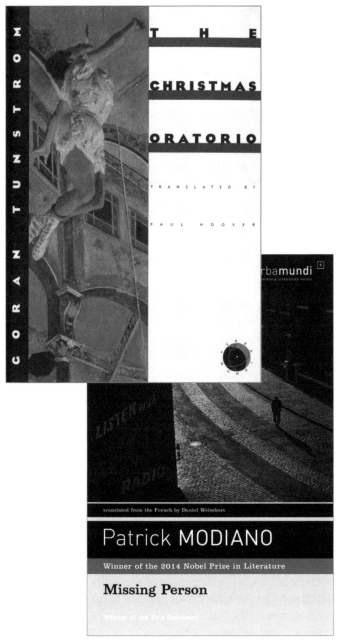

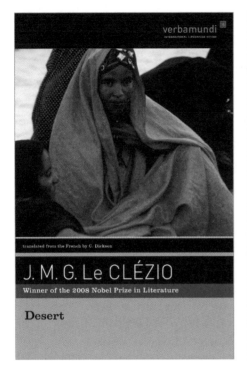
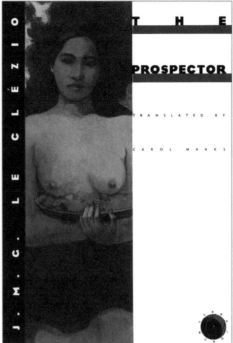
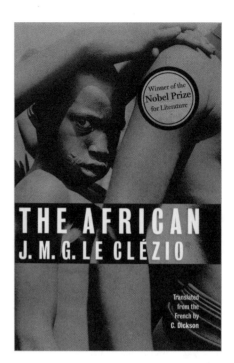

J.M.G. Le Clézio: *Desert*
Translated by C. Dickson
2009. 254 PP, 5½ × 8½″ $26.00 HC ◉

The Prospector
Translated by Carol Marks
1993. 352 PP, 5½ × 8¼″ $22.95 HC ◉

The African
Translated by C. Dickson
2013. 116 PP, 5 × 7½″ $23.00 HC ◉

In the seventies and eighties I used to make regular trips to the Frankfurt Book Fair, the largest and most inclusive gathering of its kind. The alleged aim was selling rights, but the real fun was sniffing around. The booths were arranged by country, the catalogues freely available, the rights people and often the editors (more to be trusted) were there to spread their particular gospel. Only a handful of American publishers were seriously interested in translating and publishing foreign literature, and we were among the few. On the way back from one of these trips, I visited the venerable house of Gallimard in Paris, certainly the most important literary publisher in the country and one that had steadfastly represented world literature for the entire century. I asked the head of the house, and the family, Mr. Antoine Gallimard, whom he considered their most important French authors who had never been adequately represented in the US. Without thinking too hard, he rattled off three names: J.M.G. Le Clézio, Patrick

Modiano, and Sylvie Germain. I had never heard of any of them but took his word for it and bought the rights.

To my considerable astonishment, on Yom Kippur morning of 2008, I received a call informing me that Le Clézio had just been awarded the 2008 Nobel Prize for Literature. The prize goes to an author for a body of work, not a particular title. We and one other publisher, the Curbstone Press, were the only houses in the US to have *any* of his books in print, in our case two. Having a Nobel Prize winner was, for a small publisher like Godine, not only totally unexpected but an exercise in endurance. The warehouse was swamped. We received orders from bookstores we never knew existed. Both books were completely sold out by 10 AM, and we had to scramble for a reprint.

The Swedish Academy, in awarding Le Clézio the Nobel Prize for Literature, praised *Desert* as the author's "definitive breakthrough as a novelist." The moving, multigenerational saga begins with images of a lost tribe in the African desert and ends in the *haut monde* salons of Paris. In two parallel narratives, it has all the hallmarks of Le Clézio's fiction and his primary obsessions: the disappearance and fragility of culture (highlighted here by the nomads and their revolt against colonial rule), the geography and persistence of poverty, the sense of lost identity that comes with colonization and displacement, the increasing threat to indigenous people everywhere. The book's second narrative features Lalla, born in Morocco, who encounters European culture as an immigrant to Marseilles, where she is unwanted, uninvited, and ignored. Although he wasn't born in Mauritius and never lived there, his second book, *The Prospector*, reflects his love for his Mauritian heritage. A tiny speck in the Indian Ocean, home to a flux of cultures, a racial, ethnic, and linguistic mix of British, French,

Indian and native ancestries, he refers to it as his "little fatherland." It clearly represents for the author something of a paradise and something of a paradigm, and its presence is infused, in one way or another, in all his writing. As a novel, it contains a roll call of all the great myths rooted in the colonial experience. Another influence, I think, was his father who served as a doctor in Nigeria in the British Army after 1948 and whom Le Clézio was sent to live with as a small boy. The father routinely ignores him; there is no emotional bond to be found, but the boy is free to roam the countryside and begins to understand and absorb the myriad native cultures of the continent. This is touchingly recounted in his memoir we published as *The African*. Le Clézio winters in Albuquerque with his wife, speaks fluent English, and resembles a matinee idol. But his genius lies in finding and articulating a legend and a language for the uprooted and dispossessed; for cultures, languages and ethnicities at risk and in peril; for, as the Academy put it, exploring "humanity beyond and below reigning civilization."

Dino Buzzati: *The Tartar Steppe*
Translated by Stuart C. Hood
1995. 208 pp, 5½ × 8½" $13.95 SC

Dino Buzzati, among Italy's greatest storytellers, spent his working life as a reporter for *Corriere della Sera*, a newspaper based in Milan. That quality of an outsider looking in, of telling a story from a distance with all the attendant details, infuses this 1940 novel, his best-known book, with the quality of a closely observed, and matter-of-factly reported, fantasy or fable. Drogo, the hero, is sent to a

remote fortress in the midst of an unnamed desert. There he lives out his obsession of an imminent attack by the Tartars. Through decades, he lives this dream, and, as his friends leave to marry and raise children, Drogo remains, observing the endless and useless protocols of military life and scanning the horizon for an enemy that will never appear, will never provide him with his moment of military glory. Part of the excitement, or rather message, of the book is that the reader knows exactly what is happening, while Drogo is oblivious, determined to live out his vision, certain his dream will any day turn into reality.

Franz Werfel: *The Forty Days of Musa Dagh*
Originally translated by Geoffrey Dunlop
Revised & expanded by James Reidel
Preface by Vartan Gregorian
2012. 936 pp, 5½ × 8½" $23.00 SC

This massive historical novel, first published to international acclaim in 1933 and Werfel's acknowledged masterpiece, was the book that brought the world's attention to the Armenian Massacre, another instance of ethnic cleansing and an atrocity still not fully condemned (or acknowledged) by the US government. This was, and will remain, our most ambitious Verba Mundi title. James Reidel brought the book to our attention, noting that a complete translation had never appeared in English. Viking was the original American publisher; the book had been optioned by Louis B. Mayer for a feature film; the reviews, when it appeared in 1934, had been uniformly positive; and the book, cut substantially to fit the requirements of Viking and The Book-of-the Month-Club, which had bravely made it a Main Selection, had caught the public's imagination. It sold 34,000 copies in the first two weeks and was among the Book-of-the-Month Club's best-selling selections ever. But the success had come at a price – about a third of the book had been omitted in the Geoffrey Dunlop translation. These restored pages, translated and with an extended note on the book's history by James Reidel; a Preface by Vartan Gregorian, then President of the Carnegie Corporation, tracing the history of genocide, the rise of fascism (the book's appearance in 1934 coincided with the rise of Hitler in Germany); and the cooperation of S. Fischer Verlag, allowed us to provide the public with a complete version for the first time. The plot of the novel centers on how the inhabitants of several Armenian villages disobeyed the deportation orders of the occupying Turkish forces and fortified a plateau on the slopes of Musa Dagh – Mount Moses. During the summer of 1915, they managed to hold out for forty days in the hope of relief from the Allies. Werfel portrays their plight and relays their fate in what the *New York Times* proclaimed "a story which it is almost one's duty as an intelligent human being to read. And one's duty here becomes one's pleasure also."

Romain Gary: *The Roots of Heaven*
Introduction by David Bellos
Author's Note by Romain Gary
2018. 400 PP, 5½ × 8½″ $19.00 SC ⬤

In 1956, Gary's novel exploded into the world. A huge bestseller in France, the winner of its most prestigious literary award, the Prix Goncourt, it spent weeks on the US bestseller list. Why? Gary was hardly a household name; French novels rarely translated into popular US success stories. But the subject – the deliberate, systematic, and relentless hunting and killing of elephants for their ivory in post-colonial Africa – came as a shock. Gary brings it to life through his characters: Morel, a Nazi concentration camp survivor and former dentist who sees the animals as symbols of freedom and is willing to risk his life to save them; Forsythe, a disgraced American from the Korean War; and Minna, a former call girl, sign on to his cause. The stakes are large, and the forces stacked against them – political, social, and economic – appear impregnable. Morel takes action. A notorious elephant hunter is shot in the buttocks; a female trophy hunter is stripped and publicly whipped. Morel gains a following. The novel plays out against a background of decolonization which, to my mind, was as politically significant as the Cold War during the fifties and sixties. As these colonizers began slowly but inexorably divesting themselves, some of these transfers went smoothly, but others devolved into ruthless dictatorships, partisan squabbling, and outright chaos. By the time Mussolini invaded Ethiopia in 1935, nearly all of the continent had been colonized by seven European powers: the British, the Germans, the Dutch, the French, the Italians, and the Belgians. In 1939, 10% of the world's inhabited land mass, with a population of 150 million people, was under French sovereignty. Gary captures the infighting and political posturing into which so many countries descended, but the foreground is always the fate of the elephants, and the climax is played against the immense and lonely stretches of French equatorial Africa. Morel and his followers make their last stand, the vast elephant herds come to drink, and ivory hunters are there waiting for them with loaded guns.

The novel and Gary's curious career (he won the Prix Goncourt under two different names) are detailed in an Introduction by David Bellos, his biographer and the acclaimed translator of Georges Perec. He calls this effort "the first identifiably ecological novel in the literature of France, and perhaps the world." It's also a darn good story.

Aleksandra Lun: *The Palimpsests*
Translated by Elizabeth Bryer
2019. 112 PP, 5½ × 8½″ $17.00 SC ⬤

Aleksandra Lun was born in Poland, wrote this novel in Spanish, and translates from English, French, Spanish,

Italian, Catalan, and Romanian into Polish. That might give you some idea of the territorial ambitions of this bizarre, funny, cleverly allusive, and darkly comic novel that asks at least one central question: what is meant by one's "native" language? Who owns it and what is our relationship to it? The novel opens with our hero, one Czesław Prześnicki, languishing in a Belgian asylum undergoing Bartlebian therapy intended to eradicate from his memory any language that is not his native Polish. He has survived the long toilet paper lines of Poland, the loss of his lover Ernest Hemingway, and the abuse of the Antarctic literary community for his efforts to write novels in their native tongue. From there the reader goes on a long, and endearingly absurd, wild ride, one full of allusions to authors and literature of all nationalities and that raises real questions about "ownership," both personal and intellectual, and the relationships we have with the languages we are destined, solely by an accident of birth, to speak.

OPPOSITE: Just after graduating Dartmouth, the spring I left to enter basic training at Fort Leonard Wood in Missouri, I printed up this small brochure to advertise my Senior Fellowship project, *Lyric Verse: A Printer's Choice*. You can see the fun I was having with ornaments as well as early signs that the company to come was going to have no little trouble in the world of commercial publishing.

A Pleiades

# of Poetry

David R. Godine
1967

Poetry Chapbooks

The idea behind this series, which eventually numbered twenty titles, was to present contemporary poetry in a format that was accessible and affordable. A series of editors selected the authors, but the first five books clearly reflect the taste of Jan Schreiber, who worked as an editor at Godine for some years. All chapbooks were 48 pages, 5½ × 8½," printed letterpress in Baskerville and bound in patterned papers over boards. The list was impressive, eventually containing such heavy hitters as X. J. Kennedy, Thom Gunn, N. Scott Momaday, Donald Hall, John Peck, Gail Mazur, Gertrude Schnackenberg, William Logan and others. The second series was awarded the Carey-Thomas Award by the American Booksellers Association. The third and fourth series were printed and bound at The Stinehour Press, and Rocky Stinehour rashly offered to print the third series for $1/book, which doubtless represented a loss for the company and enabled us to price them at $5.00, still low but well above the $3.00/book we had charged for the first series. By the fourth series, he had regained his senses and there we were forced to sell them at $9 each, exactly three times the original price. Many of even the later titles are now selling for many multiples of the original list price. And others, unfortunately, still seem to be entirely invisible.

FIRST CHAPBOOK SERIES: 1974. $3.00 each
X.J. Kennedy: *Emily Dickinson in Southern California*
Kenneth Fields: *Sunbelly*
John Hollander: *The Head of the Bed*
Mary Baron: *Letters for the New England Dead*
N. Scott Momaday: *Angle of Geese and Other Poems*
Thomas Gunn: *To the Air*

SECOND CHAPBOOK SERIES: 1976. $4.00 each
Rachel Hadas: *Starting from Troy*
Donald Hall: *The Town of Hill*
Larry Rubin: *All My Mirrors Lie*
Barry Spacks: *Teaching the Penguins to Fly*
Nancy Sullivan: *Telling It*

THIRD CHAPBOOK SERIES: 1978. $5.00 each
Ann Deagon: *There is No Balm in Birmingham*
Alvin Greenberg: *In/Direction*
Gail Mazur: *Nightfire*
John Peck: *The Broken Blockhouse Wall*
George Starbuck: *Desperate Measures*

FOURTH CHAPBOOK SERIES: 1982. $9.00 each
Gjertrud Schnackenberg: *Portraits and Elegies*
Charles O. Hartman: *The Pigfoot Rebellion*
William Logan: *Sad-Faced Men*
Raymond Oliver: *Entries*
Ira Sadoff: *A Northern Calendar*

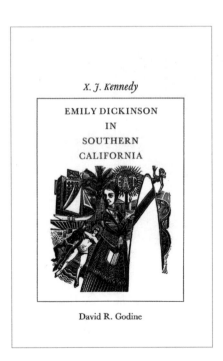

LEFT: Title page for X.J. Kennedy's *Emily Dickinson in Southern California* with a wood engraving by Michael McCurdy
RIGHT: Samples of some of the Chapbook Series covers Stephen Harvard designed, each printed in different colors and patterns

Charles Causley: *Selected Poems: 1951–1975*

1975. 292 PP, 5½ × 8½" $12.50 HC

I was a Causley fan since my days in college. He was then (and remains today) virtually unknown in the US, but he was, in some ways, the UK's Robinson Jeffers, a poet unafraid of tackling large subjects in a way that both told a story and managed to remain "poetic." Like Jeffers, he was a conservative, writing in traditional forms – usually quatrains that managed to rhyme, sometimes a poem of a single page, occasionally ones that ran on for pages and had a real narrative presence. With real compassion, he speaks, often in just a few stanzas, to larger issues, but his vision remains fixed in Cornwall, where he lived his whole life and served as a school teacher. Through it, he celebrates his fascination with the sea, Cornish daily life, the concerns of children, and the experience of war. When I learned that Macmillan UK was planning a volume containing a perfected version of every poem he wished to preserve and a group of twenty-three new ones – what would be, in effect, a comprehensive introduction to his work – I chimed in for a US edition. The result, printed in the UK on groundwood paper, is not among the best pieces of design and production to bear the Godine imprint, but the poetry is timeless and should have been read and applauded by a far larger audience than we were able to muster.

Yannis Ritsos: *The Fourth Dimension*

Translated by Rae Dalven

1977. 184 PP, 7 × 8⅜" $15.00 HC

When the translator Rae Dalven brought us the manuscript in our very first decade, Ritsos was the most widely published and widely read poet in modern Greece, yet his work was virtually unknown in this country. Ritsos was politically engaged, spending much of his life either in exile or in prison. He was active in the Greek resistance to Hitler, and equally outspoken when a right-wing military junta seized control of Greece in 1967. He was arrested, his books were banned, and he was confined to the prison island of Yiaros. Dalven knew him personally and had worked with him for fifteen years to put together a selection of his poetry that spanned almost four decades. Her efforts, the first honest and eloquent translations of his work to appear, served to bring his poetry before an English-speaking public and introduced American readers to a poet equal to the better-known work of Constantine Cavafy and George Seferis.

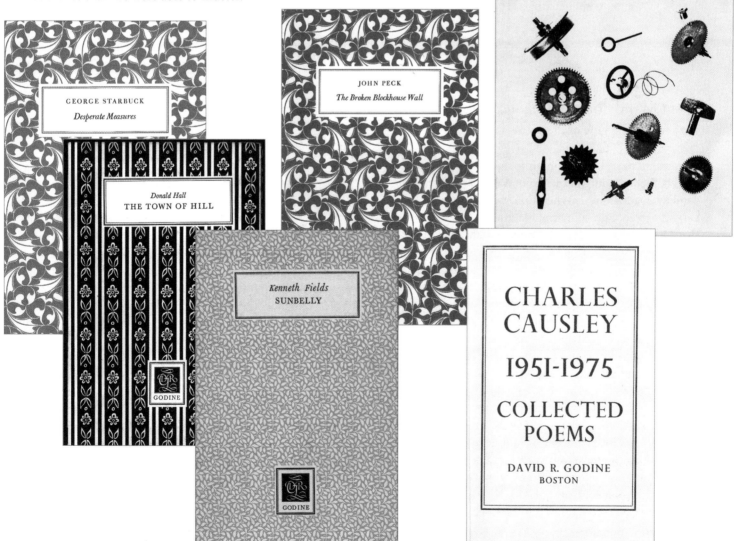

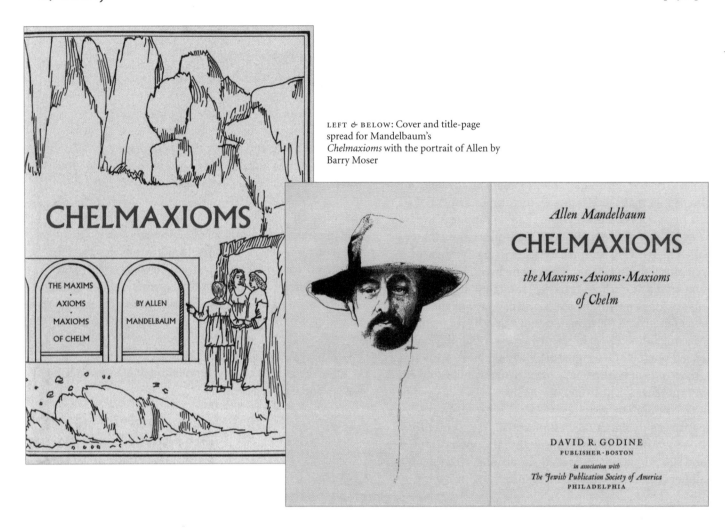

Allen Mandelbaum: *Chelmaxioms*

1977. 176 PP, 6½ × 9¾″ $10.00 HC

Introduced to us by our longtime supporter and friend, Robert Richardson, Mandelbaum was clearly a genius, if a somewhat addled one. When Bob suggested I look at his verse, I agreed with some trepidation, knowing full well that I would understand very little of it and that any effort to extract explanations or elucidations from Allen would involve a two-hour phone call. We were greatly helped by our friends at the Jewish Publication Society of America, who agreed to underwrite 1,500 copies. I called on Mike Bixler to set, design, and print the book, and Barry Moser agreed to draw a frontispiece which we printed from a line cut. Purely as printing, the book, set in Monotype Van Dijck and printed on a lovely laid paper from the Monadnock Mill, was as fine as anything we published. The text, in its learning, its references, its reach, and its demands (including what is surely the most extensive and erudite *scholia* in the history of American verse) is certainly among the most quirky and original books we ever issued. Praised by everyone from Irving Howe to James Wright, the book sold out quickly.

Guillaume Apollinaire: *Bestiary or The Parade of Orpheus*

Translated by Pepe Karmel
Woodcuts by Raoul Dufy

1980. 80 PP, 5½ × 8″ $13.00 HC, $6.00 SC

"Modern poetry" really begins in France with Apollinaire, but his *Bestiary* is probably the most traditional of his works, each poem a strictly rhymed quatrain. And Pepe Karmel's challenge, which I think he met brilliantly, was "to recreate Apollinaire's delicate balance between traditional, simple lyricism and modernist liberty." Karmel's solution was to translate the stanzas into free verse, thereby preserving a voice that would at once "mingle lyric imagery with a bawdy sense of humor" (after all, Apollinaire made a good part of his living writing pornography). The original edition, combining the verse with the bold and vigorous woodcuts of Raoul Dufy that recall his brief association with the Fauves, was first published in 1911 and was in Philip Hofer's words, not only "Dufy's first published and most important illustrations," but also the "first monumental French illustrated book of the twentieth-century." Like all too many books ahead of their time, it sold very poorly. Ours, in a greatly reduced (almost pocket) format, sold better and has been in print ever since.

GUILLAUME APOLLINAIRE

BESTIARY

or The Parade of Orpheus

Woodcuts by Raoul Dufy

Translated by Pepe Karmel

DAVID R. GODINE · PUBLISHER · BOSTON

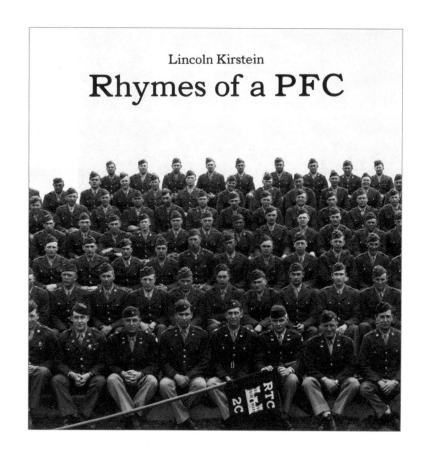

Lincoln Kirstein: *Rhymes of a PFC*

1981. 240 PP, 7¾ × 8″ $20.00 HC

Kirstein was easily, far and away, the most difficult, fractious, opinionated and stubborn author we ever published. But he was indisputably brilliant, a star at Harvard who in 1927 founded the literary magazine *Hound & Horn,* closely modeled on T. S. Eliot's *The Criterion,* and that published early work by (among many others) Gertrude Stein, Katherine Anne Porter, Elizabeth Bishop, and Walker Evans. He enlisted in the US Army in 1943, in 1944 was called to London for preliminary training, and was then sent to Europe as a member of the "Monuments Men," charged with rescuing and preserving artwork looted, and often hidden, by the Nazis. In January 1945, he was promoted to PFC, joined Patton's Third Army, and was assigned to retrieving artwork around Munich. He was discharged in 1945. This was his only book of verse and recalls that year-end liberation of Europe. I doubt this re-edition of his classic sequence of WWII poems, first published in 1964 by New Directions, later reissued again with further poems, and here once again expanded with extensive footnotes and annotations, would have proceeded far without the patient intervention and conciliatory counsel of Leslie Katz, then the editor of the beloved and much-admired Eakins Press, and his loyal assistant Harvey Simmonds.

We had the good sense to give the design over to Howard Gralla, who did a splendid job of fitting the poems, designing a handsome book around the longest line. Kirstein insisted on no line breaks, so Howard proposed a squarish format and setting the verse in the clunky and totally American Bookman. The book was published in both hard and softcover to considerable acclaim and has been unavailable for years. I don't think Kirstein was happy with us, the book, or the typography; this, the definitive edition, is not even mentioned in his bibliography. But I don't think Lincoln, despite his significant contribution to American arts, letters, culture, and dance, was very happy with himself either. Still, this remains one of the few great verse sequences to emerge from that brutal and necessary war. Kirstein saw himself (or I think he did) as a latter-day T.E. Lawrence, another hero with a genius for backing into the limelight who also deliberately placed himself among the "enlisted men" but whose parallel intelligence, ambition and political acuity quickly catapulted him into a higher sphere of action. Like the first edition, ours is now rare and expensive. It taught me to make wide allowances for geniuses and give them plenty of room to maneuver.

ABOVE & OPPOSITE: Cover and interior opening spread for Baudelaire's *Les Fleurs du Mal*, displaying the monotype prints created especially for this edition by Michael Mazur, and the fine calligraphy by G.G. Laurens

Charles Baudelaire: *Les Fleurs du Mal*
Translated by Richard Howard
Monotypes by Michael Mazur
1982. 398 PP, 5⅜ × 9″ $22.50 HC

I am not sure who came up with the idea for a new edition of this cornerstone of the modernist canon, but I suspect the credit goes to Sarah St. Onge, who was our persnickety managing editor and a French major. We had the good sense to approach Pulitzer Prize-winner Richard Howard for the translation and had the inspired idea of asking Michael Mazur, a superb printmaker/artist from neighboring Cambridge, to provide the monotype illustrations. These were the first illustrations for a trade book Michael had been asked to create, and he answered graciously and brilliantly with dense, velvety black prints that caught the brooding, festering voice of Baudelaire perfectly. The decision to print the entire French text at the back, to let Baudelaire's strikingly modern imagery and text speak for themselves, rather than *en face* with translations, was deliberate and, I think, wise, for the sequence needs to be read as a coherent whole, without interruption or distraction. Howard's translation made no attempt (wisely, again) to try to create a line-by-line translation of the verse qua verse. He realized that would be hopeless and instead provided a thoroughly readable, and equally modern, prose equivalent. To our amazement, the book was nominated for, and then won, the 1983 National Book Award for Translation, and it was reviewed on the third page of the *New York Times Book Review*. I suspect it remains one of Richard's favorite texts, and he certainly poured his heart and soul into it. The book remains in print to this day, among our perennial bestsellers, some ten printings later.

REVOLTE

Donald Hall: *The Man Who Lived Alone*
Illustrated by Mary Azarian
1984. 36 PP, 7¼ × 9″ $12.50 HC

Pairing Donald Hall, whose *String Too Short to be Saved* we had published, with Mary Azarian seemed a natural fit. Donald produced this charming story of an unnamed gentle soul who had been abused as a child and chooses to live by himself. Although hardly a hermit, he keeps his animals, faithfully visits his aunt and uncle, and lives peacefully alone. Through this story, Hall makes the point that there is a difference between living alone and loneliness, and that some people deliberately choose a solitary life and are not necessarily strange or abnormal. The language is pure northern New England, and so are the scenes Mary cut in pine. The original jacket had our bearded hero feeding his pet owl a dead mouse, but the librarians were so alarmed (although I strongly doubt children would be) that we modified it in later editions.

Andalusian Poems
Translated by Christopher Middleton and Leticia Garza-Falcon
1993. 116 PP, 6¼ × 10¾″ $30.00 HC

I have long admired the translations of Christopher Middleton and when the opportunity came our way to do this selection of thirteenth-century Arabian Andalusian poetry that had later been translated into Spanish and was much admired by the likes of Rafael Alberti and Federico García Lorca, we jumped at it. After all, who but Middleton would attempt something this complex: taking thirteenth-century Arabic poetry preserved in an eighteenth-century manuscript, then transcribing and translating it into Spanish in the early twentieth century, and converting it into an accessible English translation? We were especially fortunate that Tom Taylor was still presiding over his press in Austin, Texas with Bradley Hutchinson in charge of the Monotype

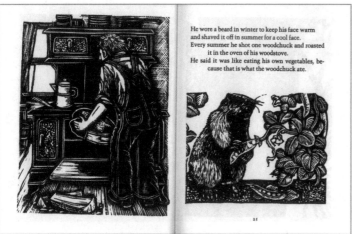

ABOVE: Mary Azarian's bold and sympathetic woodcuts accompany Hall's touching story of his Ragged Mountain neighbor. Everyone else in this book has a name, the aunt and uncle, their daughter Nan, her husband Amos, their daughter, the stubborn mule Old Beauty, even the pet owl Grover Cleveland. But the hermit has no name and dies, much as the author who celebrates him, staying at his camp, as Hall did in his house on Eagle Pond, alone, and where, like Hall, "He kept his beard in winter and summer now, because it was easier, and as he got older and older and older it grew so long that it covered the darns of his shirt."

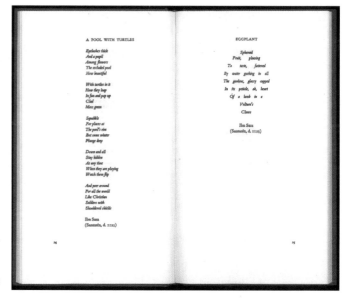

ABOVE: Interior spreads from *Andalusian Poems*

and printing machinery. This is, as I recall, one of only a few books we ever set in Blado and Poliphilus – not, to my mind, the most successful of the Monotype revivals, but quite successful in its smaller sizes and well suited to the spirit and style of the poems. The book was well received and widely reviewed, and I think the tall, narrow format is seductive. We published this, as well as a few other titles, for a small cadre of devoted bibliophiles, in an imprint I called "Hoc Volo" (or "This I wish"). By selling direct, we were able to invest a little more in the production, as demonstrated in the paper, presswork, and the title's attractive full-cloth binding.

Kate Barnes: *Where the Deer Were*
Illustrated by Mary Azarian
1994. 96 PP, 6 × 9″ $21.00 HC

At the time this was published, Kate Barnes was the first Poet Laureate of Maine, and I knew her in an indirect way because her mother, Elizabeth Coatsworth, was a favorite author and a close friend of Ray Nash's wife, Hope Nash, who was also her godmother. Kate's father, Henry Beston, had written the classic *The Outermost House,* as well as two books that we had reissued. She has retained possession of the classic shingled Cape house described in *Northern Farm* and her poetry reflects her love of the land, her affection for nature in all its manifestations, and her profound sympathy for animals, both wild and domestic. The poems are pastoral, refreshingly narrative, deliberately lyrical, and set solidly in the Maine countryside and the literary tradition in which she was raised. We cajoled Mary Azarian, our favorite woodcut artist, into providing the illustrations, which she did brilliantly, for this as well as Kate's second book, *Kneeling Orion.* The first hardcover was handsomely set in Waverly and printed letterpress by Scott Vile at his Ascensius Press.

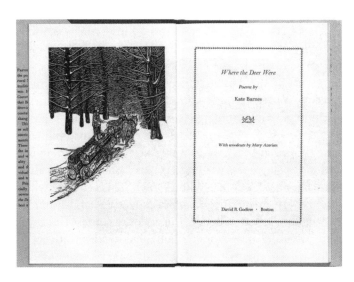

Wesley McNair: *Town of No & My Brother Running*
1997. 178 PP, 5½ × 8¼″ $16.00 SC

As of 2020, we have now published nine volumes of the poetry of Wesley McNair, a stubbornly loyal fixture of the house and a writer guaranteed to generate at least one book every eighteen months. I could choose any one of them, but this is my favorite – it combines his sense of New England, its lovable eccentrics and rugged topography, its flinty history and crusty characters. He brings it to life with stories that probably only a New Englander can fully appreciate, tales of the fat and thin, the wounded and the challenged, the hard-up and the genuinely poor. All told with both a sense of distance and compassion. *My Brother Running* is especially moving and personal, a memorial to a brother dead too soon and for reasons that can never be understood or reconciled. If any living poet's body of work continues to bear the mantle and recall the glory of Donald Hall's New Hampshire, it is Wesley McNair's evocation of Maine.

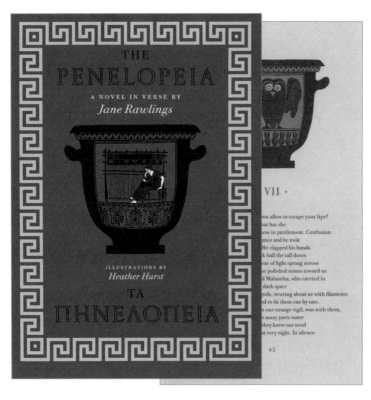

Jane Rawlings: *The Penelopeia: A Novel in Verse*
Illustrated by Heather Hurst
2003. 264 PP, 7 × 10″ $35.00 HC

Very few books that come to a publisher unsolicited and "over the transom" find their way into print, but this was one of them, suggested by an intern who read it and was its stubborn, enthusiastic champion. We came to love it as well—a title on which we lavished considerable attention. The poem takes as its premise that Penelope, who languished in Ithaka for some twenty years waiting for her husband Odysseus to return and flicking off suitors like flies, has given birth to twin daughters in his absence. Rawlings richly depicts her inner life, imagining she had made a promise to herself to set off on her own adventures should he ever reappear. Rawlings, in short, places women as central characters in Homer's world and, in the same cadences as translator Richmond Lattimore, creates a story relevant to a modern world. To Penelope's, and everyone else's, astonishment Odysseus does return, and after a very brief reunion, she announces her intention to set off, with her two daughters, on a journey to the Sibyl, a trip that the reader soon realizes will entangle her with as many challenges and adventures as those encountered by her husband. The book was set in Bodoni and handsomely printed with Greek vases designed by Heather Hurst and printed in terra-cotta and black. It is still in print, an early avatar of the women's movement and an articulate plea for independence that, like many of our unheralded classics, will be collected and treasured long after its shelf life at the warehouse expires.

Henry Wadsworth Longfellow: *The Song of Hiawatha*
Illustrated by Frederic Remington
Publisher's Afterword by David R. Godine
2004. 304 PP, 5½ × 8½″ $24.00 HC

In the summer of 1854, Longfellow would write in his diary "I have at length hit upon a plan for a poem on the American Indians, which seems to me the right one and the only. It is to weave together their beautiful traditions as a whole." What emerged the following year was *The Song of Hiawatha*, a compilation and conflation of legends, myths, and characters that present, in short, lilting trochees, the life story of Hiawatha, from birth to death. Here is a book-length epic, which goes far beyond the well-known and oft repeated "By the shore of Gitchee Gumee / By the shining Big-Sea-Water," of a real Native American who is at the center of a drama of high adventure, conflict, and tragedy. Longfellow's aim was not to tell a particular story, but to weave together the strands of myriad American Indian legend into a single fabric, and to provide Native Americans with an epic they could call their own. This at a time when both government policies and an expanding land-hungry population, firmly believing the cry of "Manifest Destiny," were initiating an inexorable campaign to strip Native Americans of their land and annihilate them as required.

Who would think that the owner of a bicycle store in California would come to us with a suggestion to republish Longfellow's great epic, and then promise to buy at least

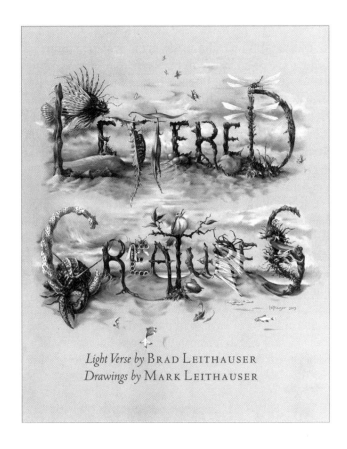

Brad Leithauser: *Lettered Creatures*
Drawings by Mark Leithauser
2004. 64 PP, 8 × 10″ $20.00 HC

Light verse, in any form, has never been taken seriously in this country. A few children read Edward Lear or Lewis Carroll or recite "Jabberwocky" by heart, but for the most part, critics ignore it and bookstores don't know where to shelve it. Humor? Poetry? Gags?

Brad Leithauser is a serious author but with a lighter side, and his brother Mark, who directs design at the National Gallery in Washington, is a true genius with both an etching needle and a drawing pencil. Together, the two brothers conspired to create this confection. Well printed on a fine uncoated paper, both verse and image really have lives of their own, and placing the book in the art section would be just as appropriate as poetry. Arranged as an Abecedarium beginning with "Anteater" and ending with the critters that form "The Zodiac" (a welcome relief from Zebra), the "creatures" include just about every form of living organism in between, from Emus to Pangolins, from the Damselfly to the Striped-Face Unicorn Fish. We published a second, and equally delightful, collaboration between the two brothers in 2007, *Toad to a Nightingale*, another witty gathering of light verse centering mostly on creatures, but with a few plants and objects thrown in for good measure.

one hundred copies annually? But this is precisely what occurred and how this book came to be. To our amazement, we confirmed that there was no complete edition of the poem available. When first published in 1885, the book was an immediate success, although the reviews were mixed. Our own *Boston Traveller* commented, "We cannot help but express our regret that our own pet national poet should not have selected as a theme something better and higher than the silly legends of the savage aborigines." It seemed inconceivable that this noble, if misunderstood, attempt to present a sympathetic portrait of Native American life should have gone entirely out of print, and when we reissued it, we incorporated the 400 pen-and-ink drawings that Houghton Mifflin had commissioned from Frederic Remington for their reissue in 1891. Most of them were totally unrelated to the text; Longfellow was primarily familiar with the Eastern tribes, especially the Onondaga. Remington's sympathies lay squarely with the tribes of the Dakotas – the Sioux, Cheyenne, and especially the Blackfeet. Still, it is a pity that Longfellow, who died in 1882, the first American whose bust would grace the Poet's Corner of Westminster Cathedral, didn't live to see their results. Or ours. Remington died in 1909 from a ruptured appendix. He was only 56, at the height of his career. The history of the Native American people is still being written.

Alexander Pushkin: *The Gypsies & Other Narrative Poems*
Translated by Antony Wood
Engravings by Simon Brett
2006. 160 PP, 5½ × 8″ $15.00 SC

Antony Wood was generally acknowledged among the very best of Pushkin's translators into English. This was no easy task, for these are five long narrative poems – one a comedy, one a tragedy, and three deliberately close to folk tales – that provide little room to hide in a few lines. Pushkin's language is often ironic, born out of everyday life, and always surprising. Wood manages to capture his tone, vocabulary, and style in translations that every reviewer conceded were remarkably close to Pushkin's originals. Handsomely designed in a small format, the book is definitely enhanced by the inclusion of five full-page wood engravings by Wood's brother-in-law, Simon Brett, a leading figure then and now in the modern movement to revive and celebrate wood engraving in the UK.

Rainer Maria Rilke: *The Inner Sky*
Selected and translated by Damion Searls
2010. 192 PP, 5½ × 8½″ $18.00 SC *with flaps*

These translations by Damion Searls, presented without introduction and en face with the German originals, present another side of Rilke. In poems and prose pieces, all of them appearing here in English for the first time, they are not arranged in chronological order or by themes. But they do, in the translator's words, "make a strong if implicit claim to be a whole, a coherent aspect of Rilke's creativity, not a grab bag of scraps." What sutures them together is the concentration on the intimate rather than the oracular. Here is Rilke, not participating in his usual preoccupation of channeling the Gods but looking up from a book and musing on the girls from his Czech boyhood, sharing his hallucinatory dreams of the olfactory pleasures of lemons kept on his writing desk in winter. The selections revolve around a cluster of images and ideas – birds and trees, giving and receiving, working, watching, and waiting. Entire segments of his work have been brought into the light, and Searls's original and deft translations, combined with the original German and French texts, provide the reader with a new language to approach and understand him.

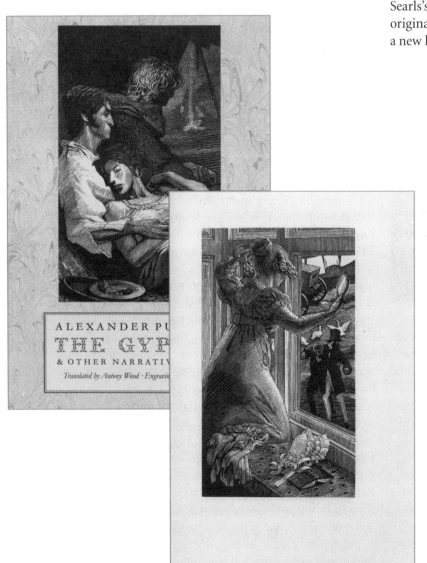

LEFT: Cover and an interior engraving by Simon Brett for Antony Wood's translations of Pushkin's narrative poems

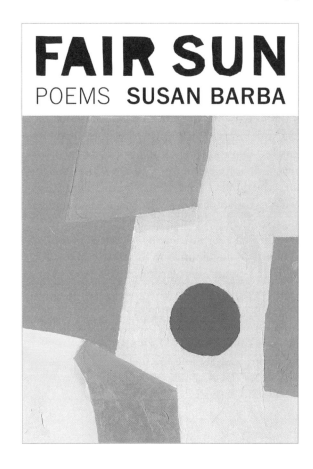

Mark Doty: *Paragon Park*
2012. 192 PP, 5½ × 8½″ $19.00 SC *with flaps*

We had published Mark Doty's first collection of verse, *Turtle, Swan*, in 1987 and his second, *Bethlehem in Broad Daylight*, in 1991. By the time 2010 rolled around, we were fast running out of stock with each, and Doty was being increasingly recognized as a fearless, risk-taking master of the form. W.S. Merwin had it right: "The precision, daring, scope, elegance of his compassion and of the language in which he embodies it are a reassuring pleasure." We suggested that we combine both volumes into one and that he consider including any unpublished early material he thought appropriate. He submitted to the latter task with some reluctance, observing that "This Spring I read through lots of this old work with an eye towards finding some early poems to include here, and I have to report it wasn't a lot of fun to do so." Nonetheless, he managed to come up with eight new poems "from the early eighties, at a time when I had just moved out of a heterosexual marriage and was discovering the terms of a more authentic life." He lightly revised them, "throwing out extra words and weak lines [he] didn't notice at the time" but retaining their core as well as the "hope there's pleasure in it and perhaps something intriguing about watching a younger poet building foundations for inquiries and outpourings to come." A vindication of those foundations can be seen in the recognition and awards Doty's work was to subsequently receive and the affection in which he is held by his peers.

Susan Barba: *Fair Sun*
2017. 86 PP, 6 × 9″ $18.00 SC

Susan Barba, a fellow Dartmouth College graduate, had worked as our very savvy editor for a few years before moving on to work for New York Review Books. But in her heart, I think she was always a poet, and it was a real privilege and pleasure to publish her first, and in 2020 her second, volume of verse. The poems here are carefully placed and carefully written. The first section explores the primacy of connection, between humans and the natural world and between each other. They are poems that explore the acquisition of language and its influence on how we perceive the world, the possibilities that language presents and the complexities of translation. The second cuts closer to home, a series of prose poems in which a child speaks to a grandfather about the details of his survival during the Armenian Genocide, the murder of his father, the suicide of his sister, the death of his best friend, and finally his (narrow) escape. The last section is set squarely in New England, shorter lyric poems exploring the proximity of life and death and the redemptive power of sympathy. In this first collection, in Robert Pinsky's words, "the great themes of suffering and immigration, identity and loss, take new forms."

William Wordsworth: *The Prelude*
Edited by James Engell and Michael Raymond
2018. 304 PP, 12 × 9½″ $40.00 HC

Composed in blank verse and generally considered at the heart of the Romantic movement, Wordsworth's *Prelude* is what Sir Frank Kermode considers "the greatest and most original of English autobiographies." Inspired by his friend, Samuel Taylor Coleridge, this masterful confessional epic charts the development of the author's mind, from his childhood to his youth in Cambridge and London and then through his travels through the Alps and the Continent. It touches on subjects ranging from leisure to literature, from nature to imagination (and pretty much everything in between). Scrupulously edited by Harvard's James Engell, it is complemented and enhanced by 200 color plates selected by Michael Raymond that both illuminate and elucidate the text. The complex design challenge of integrating type, captions and color images with uneven lines in this major undertaking was met triumphantly by Howard Gralla. As Helen Vendler would write in the NYRB,

"These [illustrations] offer to the American reader's eyes an array of scenes indispensable to an understanding of Wordsworth's world. At last—with Engell's eloquent and succinct introduction, helpful marginal glosses, notes, a chronology and maps—American readers and students have a *Prelude* of their own."

■ *... and it impresses itself on the young inhabitant more perhaps than some exotic scene or famous garden.*

■ *True shepherds of his day hold more of worth and authenticity than storied ones of old.*

8.5 Francis Towne (1740–1816). *Ambleside*, 1786. Yale Center for British Art, Paul Mellon Collection. With its "common haunts of the green earth," Ambleside, three miles southeast of Grasmere, was in Wordsworth's time one of the most picturesque locations in Great Britain.

Would leave behind a dance of images
That shall break in upon his sleep for weeks;
Even then the common haunts of the green earth
With the ordinary human interests
■ Which they embosom, all without regard
As both may seem, are fastening on the heart
Insensibly, each with the other's help,   170
So that we love, not knowing that we love,
And feel, not knowing whence our feeling comes.

Such league have these two principles of joy
In our affections. I have singled out
Some moments, the earliest that I could, in which
Their several currents blended into one,
Weak yet, and gathering imperceptibly,
Flowed in by gushes. My first human love,
As hath been mentioned, did incline to those
Whose occupations and concerns were most   180
Illustrated by Nature and adorned,
And Shepherds were the Men who pleased me first.
■ Not such as in Arcadian Fastnesses°
Sequestered, handed down among themselves,
So ancient Poets sing, the golden Age;
Nor such, a second Race, allied to these,
As Shakespeare in the Wood of Arden placed
Where Phoebe sighed for the false Ganymede,
Or there where Florizel and Perdita°

FASTNESSES: remote areas, strongholds
PHOEBE ... PERDITA: characters in Shakespeare's pastoral settings

144 | BOOK EIGHTH

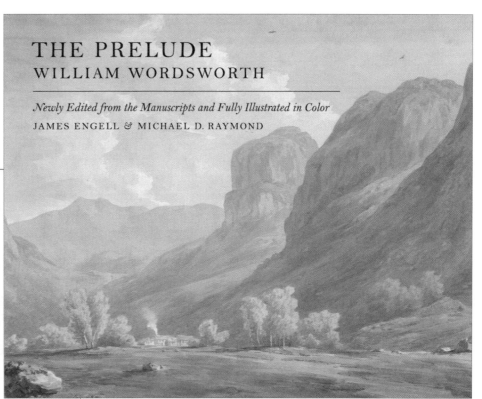

THE PRELUDE
WILLIAM WORDSWORTH

Newly Edited from the Manuscripts and Fully Illustrated in Color

JAMES ENGELL & MICHAEL D. RAYMOND

THE PRELUDE
1805

WILLIAM WORDSWORTH

Newly Edited from the Manuscripts and Fully Illustrated in Color
with Paintings and Drawings Contemporaneous with the Composition of the Poem

JAMES ENGELL & MICHAEL D. RAYMOND

with an Introduction, Maps, Notes, Glosses, and Chronology

DAVID R. GODINE · PUBLISHER · BOSTON

8.6 Joshua Cristall (1768–1847). *Arcadian Landscape with Shepherds*, 1814. Yale Center for British Art, Paul Mellon Collection. "And Shepherds were the Men who pleased me first. / Not such as in Arcadian Fastnesses / Sequestered . . . So ancient Poets sing, the golden Age." Wordsworth questioned such older accounts of pastoral life.

Together danced, Queen of the Feast and King;	190	Of maids at sunrise bringing in from far
Nor such as Spenser fabled. True it is		Their May-bush,* and along the Streets, in flocks,
That I had heard what he perhaps had seen,		Parading with a Song of taunting rhymes,

MAY-BUSH: hawthorn

ORWELL

AN AGE LIKE THIS

ORWELL

MY COUNTRY RIGHT OR L

ORWELL

AS I PLEASE

ORWELL

IN FRONT OF YOUR NOSE

Essays & Criticism

VOL. 1

1920
1940

VOL. 2

1940
1943

VOL. 3

1943
1945

VOL. 4

1945
1950

NONPAREIL
BOOKS

NONPAREIL
BOOKS

NONPAREIL
BOOKS

NONPAREIL
BOOKS

GODINE

GODINE

GODINE

GODINE

William Gass: *On Being Blue*

1976. 96 PP, 5⅝ × 8¾" $10.00 HC, $30 DELUXE

One afternoon, after we had opened our offices in downtown Boston, I took a call from Robert Gottlieb, the brilliant publisher of Alfred A. Knopf, and probably the best literary editor that publishing ever produced. He said he had in hand a short manuscript from William Gass that was too brief for their consideration but might make a handsome limited edition. I had never heard of Gass, but on reading the manuscript – a lengthy and brilliant meditation on the color blue that begins with a sentence of twenty-six lines and ends with "blue bottles, bank accounts and compliments, for instance, or, when the sky's turned turtle, the blue-green bleat of ocean (both the same), and, when in Hell, its neatly landscaped rows of concrete huts and gas-blue flames; social registers, examination booklets, blue bloods, balls, and bonnets, beards, coats, collars, chips, and cheese. . . the pedantic, indecent, censorious. . . watered twilight, soured sea: through a scrambling of accidents, blue has become their color, just as it's stood for fidelity" – I knew we had something rare, something original, something occasionally brilliant. For Gass, "Color is consciousness itself" and in this exposition he infuses color, but especially blue, with a life of its own. Bob gave us permission to print five hundred copies, but by the time we went to press, we already had in hand orders for 2,000, so we pleaded with him to allow us to increase the print run. He graciously acceded, and we printed 3,000 copies with a signed deluxe edition in a slipcase. Mike Bixler, who had set up his shop in Somerville, undertook the design and production. The first edition, printed letterpress in Dante on a lovely Ticonderoga Text Laid, sold out before publication. With Gottlieb's generous permission, we went back for a second hardcover printing, which was followed by eight softcover editions. The book has become something of a cult title, certainly the only Godine title ever found cradled in the arms of a naked playmate in a *Playboy* centerfold. Despite the occasionally raunchy language and vivid imagery, the typography is chaste and pure.

Howard Nemerov: *Figures of Thought*

1977. 224 PP, 6 × 9" $10.00 HC

Since we had previously issued a collection of Nemerov's short stories, I thought it appropriate to extend the canon with an equivalent collection of his prose, one he had subtitled "Speculations on the Meaning of Poetry and the Essays." As someone who considered poetry his primary passion, Nemerov had a lot to say on the subject – not only considerations of the meaning and mission of verse but also a wide range of eclectic pieces on everything from art to music. He was, for example, the first to publish a notice on the strange and original work of the artist M.C. Escher, but the essays range widely: an analysis of the structure of Dante's cosmology, the metaphors we use to describe the passage of time, "Thoughts on First Passing the Hundredth Page of *Finnegans Wake*." In all of them he is consistently intelligent, interesting, and often very funny, an academic whose voice speaks to the fundamental act of creation and does so with a delicious sense of humor, one guaranteed to generate a wide smile on almost every page. An essayist of range and perfect pitch, he is capable of making the reader actually *enjoy* what he is considering. There is more condensed energy in each of these essays than there is in most books.

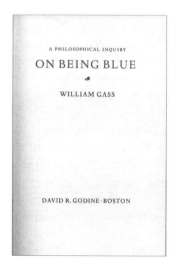

ABOVE: An early mockup of a poster to announce the publication of Nemerov's *Figures of Thought* showing a youthful Howard in a photo by Elsa Dorfman and exhibiting the fine calligraphy of Tim Girvin
OPPOSITE: A composite portrait of Orwell's face, created by the designer Lucinda Hitchcock for the spines of our four-volume collection of Orwell's nonfiction
LEFT: The simple letterpress title and interior page of William Gass's provocative *On Being Blue* set in Monotype Dante, designed and printed by Michael Bixler

William Gass: *Fiction and the Figures of Life*
1978. 204 PP, 5½ × 8¼" $7.00 SC

The World Within the Word
1980. 352 PP, 5⅛ × 8¼" $7.00 SC

A description of Gass's books always presents a challenge; he was a trained philosopher, his entire career spent teaching the subject at Washington University in St. Louis, but his obvious passion was writing – in all its manifestations. And he didn't hesitate to take them all on, as both a critic and a creator. Originally published by Knopf, we reissued two collections of his essays, one of his short stories and our own first edition of his meditation, *On Being Blue. Fiction and the Figures of Life* contains twenty-four essays divided into four chapters ranging from discussions of Gertrude Stein (a particular interest) to Jorge Luis Borges; some are book reviews, thinly disguised as vehicles to present his own opinions of the subjects at hand (Bertrand Russell's *Autobiography* and William Thompson's *The Imagination of an Insurrection*), but most are concerned with larger issues including the four lead essays of the first chapter exploring "Philosophy and the Form of Fiction," "The Medium of Fiction," "The Concept of Character in Fiction," and the titular "Fiction and the Figures of Life."

In *The World Within the Word*, he resumes his re-examinations and re-evaluations – Proust on the hundredth anniversary of his birth; Gertrude Stein, again (the "Mother Goose of Montparnasse"); Malcolm Lowry (whose "love is as murderous as the simpleminded"); a brief but resonant memoir of Nabokov; plus appraisals of Valery, Henry Miller, Sarte, Faulkner and Freud. And beyond books and writers, he explores and expands on ideas circulating in the flux of his mind, one that routinely managed to combine philosophy, literature, metaphor, and metaphysics in equal parts. His approach to literature – as well as writing – was unique in its originality, eclecticism, wit, and passion. If there was ever a defender of poesy in our time, he was it. His death in 2017 was a serious loss to American letters.

Noel Perrin: *First Person Rural*
Pen and ink illustrations by Stephen Harvard
1978. 142 PP, 6 × 9" $15.00 HC

This was the first, and just possibly the best, collection of the five "Rural" titles we published by the beloved Noel Perrin. Ned was teaching in Dartmouth's English Department while I was there, but it was clear that his real love was living on the land and protecting it. He was instrumental in initiating the college's Department of Environmental Studies. But here he sticks close to his home on Bill Hill in Thetford, Vermont, according to some the last active theocracy in New England. We were fortunate on two counts: first, the extremely talented Steve Harvard undertook both designing the book and providing it with his illustrations and calligraphy; and second that the *New York Times* picked it as one of the best books of that year. The succeeding four volumes, ending with the posthumous *Best Person Rural*, all followed the same format, albeit with different illustrators. I got to know Ned fairly well through a succession of four of his five wives and dearly loved him. He was among the first environmentalists in Vermont to drive an electric car, and I remember setting off with him to Hanover one morning when he forgot to unplug the charging cable. I think his happiest hours were spent on his tractor mowing Bill Hill and resetting the fence posts.

LEFT: Covers for Gass's *Fiction and the Figures of Life & The World Within the Word* designed by Sara Eisenman
RIGHT: Cover and an interior drawing by Stephen Harvard, who not only designed the book but also provided a sequence of humorous and appropriate drawings for every chapter as well as calligraphy for the cover and title page

Janet Malcolm: *Diana & Nikon: Essays on the Aesthetics of Photography*
1980. 176 PP, 6 × 8¾″ $12.50 HC

Malcolm, who is best known today for her probes into the history of psychoanalysis, first began as an essayist and reviewer for *The New Yorker* on photography. A quintessential New York intellectual, acute, fiercely intelligent, observant, she came to photography as an outsider with an intuitive grasp of what makes a good picture, and an instinctive take on the personality that lurked behind the lens. This was her first published book and is interesting because instead of concentrating on a single photographer or a particular body of work, she instead investigates larger themes—color, landscapes, portraits, death and blight in black and white—or examines and juxtaposes two opposing takes on the same subject—East (Stieglitz) and West (Weston), the simple plastic lens of the Diana camera versus the sophisticated apparatus of a Nikon, or the Great Depression as interpreted by both Robert Frank and Walker Evans. I can't recall how we managed to assemble all the permissions necessary for the many images that were reproduced, but I suspect Janet did the heavy lifting. Set in Zapf's Palatino, it was handsomely designed by Katy Homans, Godine pressman turned book designer, who selected the striking and dramatic verso images that precede every chapter while providing provocative and effective leads to the essays that follow.

ABOVE: Katy Homans designed one of our more striking title-page spreads, juxtaposing St. Gauden's statue of Diana with the elegant letters of Zapf's Palatino

Leslie Fiedler: *Fiedler of the Roof: Essays on Literature and Jewish Identity*

1991. 184 PP, 5½ × 8¼" $20.00 HC

Leslie Fiedler, the perennial bad boy of American criticism, shot across my horizon in high school. His *Love and Death in the American Novel*, published in 1960 while I was a junior reading the likes of Edmund Wilson, Lionel Trilling, W.K.Wimsatt, and the tribe of West Side Jewish intellectuals, hit my overly refined sensibilities like a rocket. What teenager could not be seduced by a critic who could write that "every classic American male writer was stunted… writing the same book over and over again until he lapses into silence or self parody." Fiedler didn't whisper, correspond, or politely converse with his fellow critics; he loathed them. If the elderly Jewish critical establishment was trying to appropriate the Anglo-American Wasp tradition represented in every staid American newspaper and journal of the sixties, Fiedler was the loud, outspoken rebel with a megaphone—the *New York Daily News*, not the *New York Times*, reporter. He was the irrepressible tabloid critic on steroids. Born in Newark (a youth much akin to Philip Roth's, and born in the same city), he encountered its racism and anti-semitism first-hand (but always gave the city credit for its fine museum and public library). He moved to Montana, probably one of five Jewish professors in the entire state, and taught there for twenty-three years, among the few academics who would dare write fiction, short stories, love stories, essays, even a book on being busted for possession of pot. The OED says he was the first to apply the term "postmodern" to literature. For this book, he assembled twelve provocative and penetrating new essays from the eighties and, like much of his work, it covers a lot of ground. The common theme, sometimes oblique, sometimes grand, is: How do Jews, who comprise only a small percentage of the population but a large territory when it comes to culture and its transmission, cope with an increasingly "post-Jewish" country? Fiedler looks for answers in literature, especially the work of Joyce, Singer, Styron, and Malamud, but much comes from his own experience. He recalls the Montana Legislature's attempt to drum him out of the state after teaching at the state university for a quarter century. Moving to Buffalo, he taught at SUNY for the remainder of his life. We published a second collection *Tyranny of the Normal: Essays on Bioethics, Theology and Myth* in 1996. He died in 2003, and I doubt quietly. "I have, I admit, a low tolerance for detailed chronicling and cool analysis," he wrote. "I long for the raised voice, the howl of rage or love." In our two books, his final collections, we gave him some small measure of audibility.

Andre Dubus: *Broken Vessels: Essays*
Introduction by Tobias Wolff

1991. 224 PP, 5½ × 8¼" $20.00 HC

This was Andre's first collection of nonfiction and his ninth book. Written between 1977 and 1990, the pieces explore much of the same territory as his fiction–his childhood, his Catholicism, the relationships between children and their parents, the tricky business of making a living as a writer, and dealing with his unswerving and futile devotion to the (then) reliably hapless Boston Red Sox. Especially moving is his account of the near fatal 1986 automobile accident that cost him one leg and the use of the other. It marked the end of life as he knew it and initiated a struggle, both emotional and physical, for survival. As Tobias Wolff would write in his fine Introduction, "[For Andre Dubus] the quotidian and the spiritual don't exist on separate planes but infuse each other. His is an unapologetically sacramental vision of life in which ordinary things participate in the miraculous, the miraculous in ordinary things." It was always this combination of apparently simple language and insight into the human complexities of everyday life that would spool out, to be invariably resolved by a broad generosity of vision that make both his fiction, and these essays, so unforgettable.

Nicolas Freeling: *Criminal Convictions: Errant Essays on Perpetrators of Literary License*
1994. 178 PP, 5½ × 8¼″ $23.00 HC

Prolific author Nicolas Freeling was not only a premier writer of crime fiction but also an informed and passionate critic of the genre. To abuse a metaphor, he knew where all the bodies were hidden, and this decalogue of ten essays, covering some of the expected suspects – Dorothy Sayers, Raymond Chandler and Georges Simenon – also extends the boundaries of the field to embrace writers like Conrad, Stendahl, Kipling, and Dickens who were probably unlikely to consider themselves first-class members of a criminal portfolio. But Freeling sees crime, in all its manifestations, as nothing more than an extension of life and therefore of literature *tout court*. As he says, "The nature of crime is also the nature of art."

Guy Davenport: *Geography of the Imagination*
1997. 398 PP, 6 × 9″ $18.00 SC

Guy Davenport, who died in 2005, was most likely America's last genuine autodidact. He knew everything – literature, natural history, languages, music, art – and he was able to make connections between them that no one had seen before. This book, originally published by North Point Press, had a huge influence on me, not only for its erudition, but for its insistence that we "re-educate our eyes," that those independent shards of culture and information that are presented to us in college as separate disciplines with discrete boundaries are in fact all interconnected. Life and culture do not come as discrete courses or subjects; they are all of one piece. The trick is to track down the ideas to their original sources. The people and the work that make life and the inquiring mind the most interesting are the true originals – and these are Davenport's heroes: Whitman, Pound, Olson, Welty, Berry, Melville and Tolkien, among others. I was so impressed by the collection, Davenport's own selections, that I actually wrote and told him that if the book ever went out of print I wanted to be first in line to reissue it. It did; that's how we added this jewel to our list.

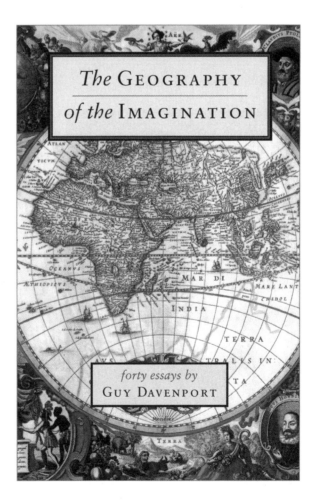

A Johnson Sampler
Edited by Henry Darcy Curwen
2000. 336 PP, 5½ × 8¼″ $18.00 SC   ᪷

Samuel Johnson is today far too little read, appreciated,
and enjoyed. Ironically, Boswell, his biographer, is probably more famous than the man he set out to immortalize.
But Johnson himself, who Dr. MacLean of Mull declared
was "just a hogshead of common sense" has far more to say
than Boswell, especially about things now pressing upon
us in the twenty-first century. His talent was his preternatural ability to get to the significant nub of a subject, to
clear our minds of cant, and to perceive what he called, in
a typically telling phrase, "the stability of truth." (One can
only imagine the fun he would have had with the concept
of "fake news.") Curwen, a Johnson aficionado since youth,
has sifted through everything Johnson wrote, as well as his
recorded conversations, to present the Great Cham in all
his moods and in a wide range of subjects. Reading and
writing, youth and age, wooing and wedding, the government and law, religion, education, business, and the antics
of his fellow man are all grist for Johnson's mill. And no
one, with the possible exception of Shakespeare, touched
on a wider variety of experience (because Johnson himself had endured them all). Sources for each quotation, a
suggested reading list, and an excellent index are included.
Pulitzer Prize-winner Walter Jackson Bate called it "The
finest collection, by far, of the wit and wisdom of the most
quotable of writers. Time and again, in whatever direction
we go, we meet Johnson on the way back."

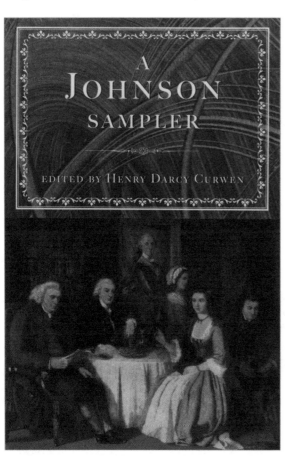

George Orwell: *The Collected Essays, Journalism, and Letters of George Orwell*
Edited by Sonia Orwell and Ian Angus
2000. VOL. 1 600 PP, VOL. 2 496 PP, VOL. 3 454 PP,
VOL. 4 576 PP, 5½ × 8¼″ $18.00 SC   ᪷

A major four-volume effort on the part of this small company, we issued this Nonpareil collection first on a license
from Harcourt Brace, the original US publisher. When
Harcourt was incorporated into Houghton Mifflin and
our license had expired, we fought for years to reissue it
and failed until the English agent representing the Orwell
estate stepped in. Here, starting in 1920 and continuing
for fifty years, in the best prose – book reviews, letters,
essays, weekly newspaper columns – is a record of a man
who could, and who loved to *write*. In his most famous

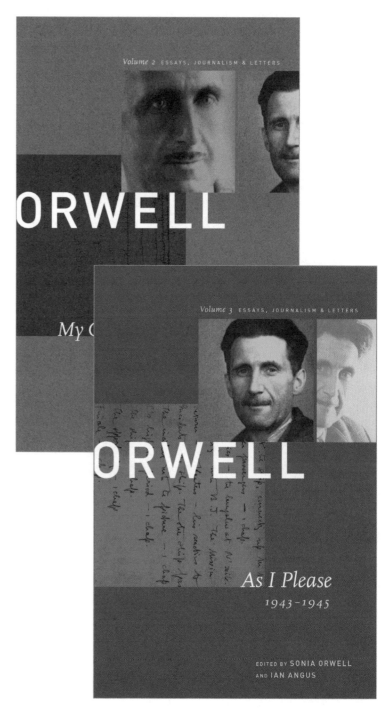

essay "Why I Write," he observes, "From a very early age, perhaps the age of five or six, I knew that when I grew up I should be a writer." And considering his prodigious output in a life that lasted only 46 years, many of them struggling to make a living and find enough food to keep his body alive. This collection of his nonfiction, scrupulously edited by his wife, Sonia Orwell, and scholar Ian Angus, contains the best selection, arranged in chronological order of his nonfiction available, a supercargo of opinion, speculation, reportage, and analysis that is breathtaking in its scope and eclectic passions. Where else could one find essays on the addiction of coffee and cigarettes (not to mention one on how to prepare a proper cup of tea), evaluations of Kipling, Dickens, Henry Miller, and P.G. Wodehouse, a first-hand account of the Spanish Civil War, a review of Hitler's *Mein Kampf,* and the poems of T.S. Eliot, and his famous analysis of the English character (which he knew from first-hand experience) "The Lion and the Unicorn"? This collection is among the few titles we published in fifty years that I can claim with complete if unbecoming confidence as "belonging on the bookshelf of any self-respecting bookstore."

David Travis: *At the Edge of the Light: Thoughts on Photography & Photographers, Talent & Genius*

2002. 192 PP, 6 × 8⅜″ $30.00 HC

For over four decades, David Travis was the leading light, the chief curator and beloved *primum mobile* of the Chicago Art Institute's photography collection. Like other curators (Beaumont Newhall, Robert Sobieszek, Richard Benson, John Szarkowski), his eye and mind went well beyond the image. I always thought the prefaces he had written to the volumes and shows he had curated deserved a permanent and coherent edition. Bright, personable and approachable, he was on first-name terms with photography dealers and curators throughout the world, and, more important, not only thoroughly conversant with their work but often a close personal friend of the artists as well. His warmth, enthusiasm, and intelligence shine through in every one of these essays – from considerations of the influence and contributions of photographers of the past to those of the present, like Brassaï, Kertész, and Karsh, all of whom he knew well and held close.

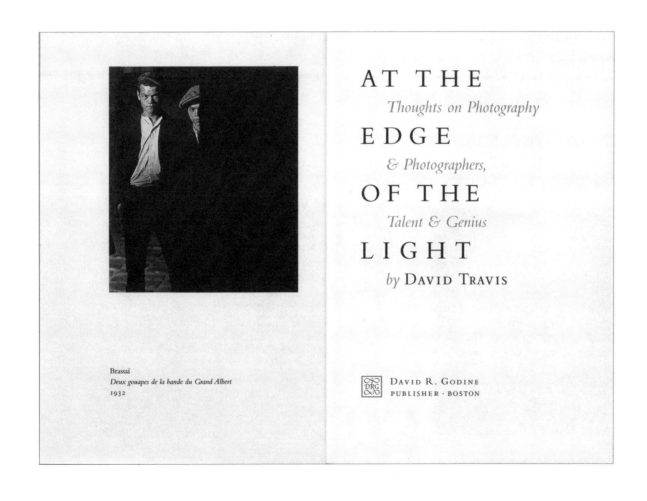

Brassaï
Deux gouapes de la bande du Grand Albert
1932

AT THE
Thoughts on Photography
EDGE
& Photographers,
OF THE
Talent & Genius
LIGHT
by DAVID TRAVIS

DAVID R. GODINE
PUBLISHER · BOSTON

Ralph Waldo Emerson: *A Year with Emerson*
Selected and edited by Richard Grossman
Illustrations by Barry Moser
2003. 256 PP, 5 × 9″ $27.00 HC

While I was working in New York, Richard Grossman, the
founder and moving spirit behind the small but mighty
Grossman Publishers, was among my heroes. And with
good reason. Here was the man who published Ralph
Nader's *Unsafe at Any Speed*, reprinted Robert Frank's *The
Americans*, and had issued *The Blues Line*, probably the
best anthology then, or ever, in print of these lyrics. On
retirement, he moved to a small town in northwest Connecticut, and when his former wife, the respected literary
agent Jill Kneerim, presented us with this title, it was impossible to decline. As a book it is probably neither "Essay"
nor "Criticism" but there's something of both resonating
in each one of the daily lessons and admonitions he assembled to celebrate the bicentenary of "The Sage of Con-
cord." Here is a delightful display of his range and genius
in almanac form – one for every day of the year, and not a
few written on the very day Richard cites them here in his
"book of days." Emerson's thoughts and musings cascade
around the universe even as he himself traveled the length
and breadth of the United States and Europe. Here he
serves as a companion and guide, and through him we
meet everyone from John Muir to Lincoln, from Carlyle
to Montaigne and the New England luminaries who were
part of his inner circle: Thoreau, Margaret Fuller, and the
Alcotts. Every month is illustrated with a new wood engraving by Barry Moser who, as an artist, has more than a
little in common with this surprisingly modern mind.

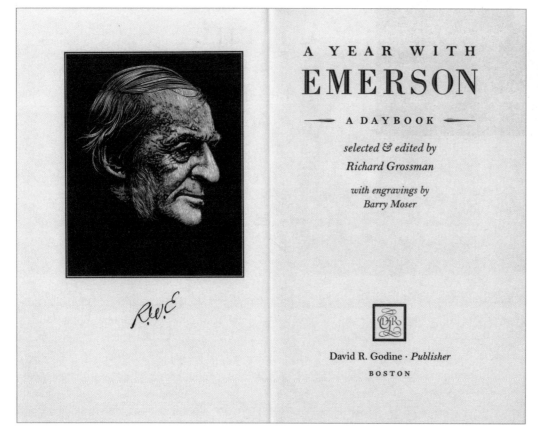

ABOVE & LEFT: Pages showing the
engraved frontispiece and monthly
chapter openings by Barry Moser, a
spiritual descendent of Emerson if
there ever was one

Steven Gilbar & Dean Stewart: *Not Forgotten*
2006. 240 PP, 5¼ × 8¼" $18.00 SC

Occasionally we issue books that are interesting, important, well written, nicely designed and regretfully ignored. This was one of them. Gilbar was a retired lawyer living in Santa Barbara and we had issued a number of his collections before. This seemed a perfectly sound commercial idea – to collect contemporary reviews, memorials, and speeches of deceased authors as observed by their contemporaries. The texts are as revealing of the authors who wrote them as those written about and some are classics. The writings Gilbar collected are neither obituaries (daily journalism) nor eulogies (formal speeches delivered from the graveside) but instead "commemorative essays" – pieces written after a subject's death, frequently by a friend or peer, in an effort to capture the personality and define the achievements of the departed. And what a list it is: Emerson on Thoreau, Howells on Twain, Cather on Crane, Baldwin on Wright, Bellow on Cheever. Morrison on Baldwin, Hoagland on Abbey, Di Prima on Ginsberg. We issued it first in hardcover with the perhaps offputtingly morbid title of "Published and Perished." That failed, so we decided on a new title and cover, seen here. Not much of an improvement. It appears there are times when I fall in love with a text for which no popular interest exists. As I said, this was one of them.

Jeanne Braham: *The Light Within the Light: Portraits of Donald Hall, Richard Wilbur, Maxime Kumin, and Stanley Kunitz*
Illustrations by Barry Moser
2007. 106 PP, 5¾ × 9" $25.00 HC

It was Jeanne's dream, but Barry Moser's encouragement, that finally sent both of them to interview and collate for posterity the four poets who Braham most admired: The New England quartet of Donald Hall, Richard Wilbur, Maxine Kumin, and Stanley Kunitz. Books like this have been done before, but in none of them have I heard the voice of the actual *subject* speak so clearly, so distinctly. You read these pages and you can really hear them talking to you in their own voices – and if that isn't sufficient, Jeanne always found exactly the right passages within their actual work to illuminate her points. Barry graciously contributed nine engravings to the effort, including four full-page portraits of the poets celebrated. The title comes from a line by Jeanne in her Introduction and is worth repeating, "If the act of creating a poem makes a clearing in the dark, there is another glow embedded within the poem, the light within the light, the long half-life of the poem's impact on the reader." When we published this in 2007, only Stanley Kunitz had left us. As I write this, in 2020, all four are gone. The lights that lit New England for decades.

LEFT & ABOVE: Jeanne Braham's *The Light Within the Light* with a watercolor cover and sample wood engraving by Barry Moser

Donald Hall: *On Eagle Pond*
2016. 272 PP, 6 × 9″ $17.00 SC

When Donald Hall first published this collection of short prose pieces in 2007 with Houghton Mifflin, he had lived in the same expanded farmhouse in New Hampshire that his great-great-grandparents had bought in 1878, and where his grandmother and mother were also born, for thirty years. Built in 1803 or thereabouts, nothing that had entered it had ever been thrown away, the attic stuffed with old chairs and broken-down bedsteads, postcards, letters, string, butter churns, and cranks for machines of inscrutable purposes. For decades this had been home for Hall, and for an all too short time also home to his wife Jane Kenyon. It was as dear to him as Lamb House was to Henry James, Sissinghurst to the Nicolsons, and Orchard House to the Alcotts. From here he could look out on the barn that once housed the herd tended by his grandfather, Ragged Mountain, and the road that leads down to the body of water that gives the book its name and its cover image. In it you'll find among the best essays ever written about New England and what it means to be a New Englander, collected in their entirety from two previously published books, including in this new edition unpublished pieces and even a few pertinent poems. Many of these read like extended letters, and this is no wonder: Hall's grandmother stopped reading after graduating high school but wrote postcards every day to her three daughters for fifty years. Hall was unstoppable; to be among his publishers was to receive at least a letter a week, some encouraging, some scolding, some just giving news from the farm. He was a man who loathed the telephone. In his last years he estimated he was writing (or dictating) over 4,000 letters and postcards a year. I visited him six months before he died. He was still sitting in exactly the same chair in which I had found him two years before, looking even more like a grizzled Old Man of the Mountain. Nothing in the house had changed. Jane's room was exactly the same as she left it when she died. But Hall's genius was to connect that place to people, and he did it tirelessly and unselfishly. He would write, "Reader, believe me: I know I am lucky. Every day, I know that my intimate connection with the family past, in this place, depends upon a series of accidents and not upon my virtue. Also I know that we do not require ancestors to connect, joyously, with a place and a culture." But if you come at it from the other end, if *you* want to connect with a place, a history and a culture, that of rural New England, you can look to no better source than this book by Donald Hall.

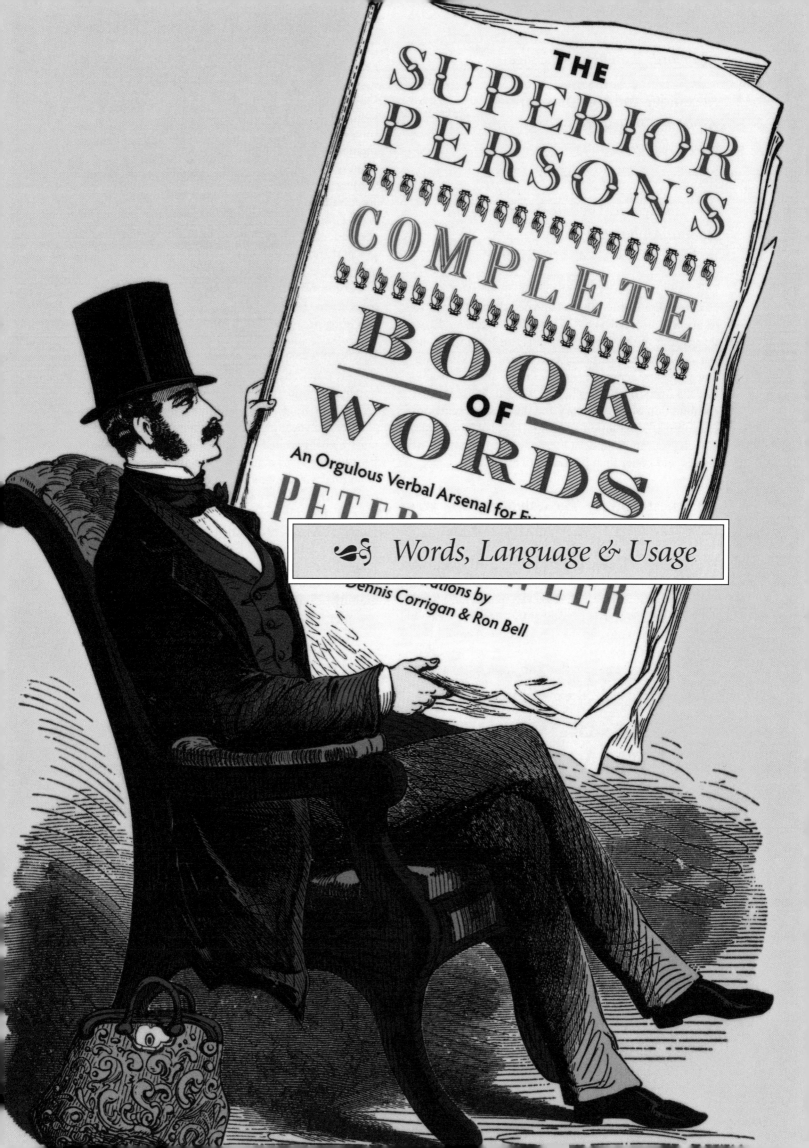

THE
SUPERIOR
PERSON'S
COMPLETE
BOOK
OF
WORDS

An Orgulous Verbal Arsenal for E...

PETER ...

...ations by
Dennis Corrigan & Ron Bell

Words, Language & Usage

Alexander and Nicholas Humez:
Alpha to Omega: The Life & Times of the Greek Alphabet
1981. 240 PP, 5¾ × 9¼″ $17.50 HC

ABC Et Cetera: The Life & Times of the Roman Alphabet
1985. 224 PP, 5¾ × 9¼″ $17.00 HC

Following their dissection of the roman alphabet in *ABC Et Cetera*, the Humez brothers turned their attention to introducing readers to the wonders, origins, and divagations of the Greek alphabet. I was fortunate to have Jan van Krimpen's Antigone Greek in my cases and was able to set and repro the shoulder notes and title page directly from the metal. The text is a delight, their usual combination of witty history and meaty side excursions examining the evolution and importance of Greek culture and civilization in modern life. For some reason, this title always sold better than its roman twin *ABC Etc.*

Sir Ernest Gowers: *The Complete Plain Words*
1988. 214 PP, 5½ × 8⅛″ $19.00 HC

In 1948, Ernest Gowers, a senior British civil servant, was asked by the Treasury to write a book to improve the work of government workers. The idea was to provide a handbook of usage and style to combat the often unintelligible "officialese" that bloated the argot of official employees that more often obscured the meaning and intent of a communication than revealed it. Gowers understood his mission. In the Prologue's opening paragraph, he comments, "Writing is an instrument for conveying ideas from one mind to another; the writer's job is to make the readers apprehend the meaning readily and precisely." Joseph Epstein continues in his Introduction, "All [Gowers's] efforts in this useful volume are bent towards helping his readers achieve that end. So subtle is Gowers's tact, so graceful and becalming his manner, that one soon reads along in this book quite forgetting that one is in the hands of a consummate teacher." For anyone putting sentences together to clarify a set of facts, requirements, or proposals this book provides divine guidance. The nine chapters on choice, style, and handling of words, will energize anyone faced with a writing assignment. Gowers views English, that great mongrel of a language, as a flowing river, not a stagnant pond, one constantly adding to its treasure. His lucid writing bears repeating: "English is not static –neither in vocabulary nor in grammar, nor yet on that elusive quality called style. The fashion in prose alternates between the ornate and the plain, the periodic and the colloquial. Grammar and punctuation defy all efforts of grammarians to force them into the mould of a permanent code of rules. Old words drop out or change their meanings; new words are admitted." First published in 1951, revised by Sidney Greenbaum and Janet Whitcut in 1986, it's both a pleasure to read and provides solid advice. More congenial than Fowler, correctly labeled as an "instinctive grammatical moralizer," it belongs on bookshelves of both accomplished and aspiring writers.

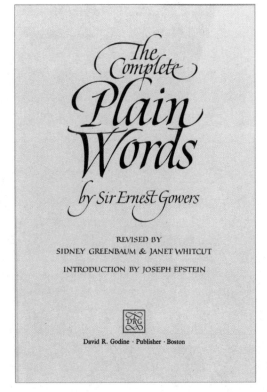

ABOVE: The jacket and title-page calligraphy of John Stevens for Gowers's *The Complete Plain Words* provides an almost playful touch to some stern injunctions.

Peter Bowler: *The Superior Person's Book of Words*

1985. 128 PP, 5¼ × 8¼″ $12.00 HC

For many years I faithfully attended the Frankfurt Book Fair, looking for gems we could publish in the States that would not cost a small fortune. The easiest books were, of course, those written in English that demanded little or no editorial attention. The collection of "weird and wondrous" words chosen and elegantly defined by the Australian Peter Bowler and discovered by my clever fellow traveller George Gibson on the floor, seemed a logical candidate, and we bought it for the munificent sum of $500. Some twenty-eight printings and 500,000 copies later, the book is still in print and remains among our strongest backlist titles. Bowler's genius was not only to pick out weird (but useful) words and provide the reader with an often hysterical (but always comprehensible) definition, but also to use the word in a sentence. Two other fortunate decisions were to publish the book inexpensively in hardcover rather than take the easier softcover route, and to have it illustrated, with great success, by Dennis Corrigan. We followed it with two subsequent editions along the same lines and later collected and reset all three and issued them as a single volume.

LEFT & BELOW: The appeal of Bowler's bestsellers was enhanced by the decision to illustrate the words, here handled deftly by Dennis Corrigan.

R. L. Trask: *Say What You Mean!: A Troubleshooter's Guide to English Style and Usage*

2005. 289 PP, 6 × 9″ $26.00 HC

Well before Lynne Truss and the *New Yorker*'s "comma queen" Mary Norris made news by reviving our interest in punctuation, the Anglo-American linguist R.L. Trask was fighting his own delightfully opinionated battle for good usage and standard practice. In this book, first issued in the UK, he lays down the law for writing simple, effective, and unambiguous sentences – the kind of sentence that delivers the facts. He aims to provide what every English-speaking grown-up needs to know if they want to compose a paragraph that can be understood by others. "If your readers cannot realize at once what you mean, then you have failed as a writer," Trask insists in one of many refreshingly blunt imperatives. "Use plain words. Avoid jargon. Read what you have written. Edit it and polish it. Work hard to make your meaning clear." He addresses all the essentials: the confusion between less and fewer; the inability to distinguish between "its" the possessive and "it's" the contraction; disinterested and uninterested; rent, hire, and charter; infer and imply; scratch and itch. It's true: Strunk and White cover much the same ground, and with equal humor and no-nonsense advice. But Trask brings them up to date. Here's a good example: "*artiste*: this pretentious word commonly means 'fraud pretending to be an artist.' Don't use it unless you mean to be insulting." These are rules for modern times, a style guide belonging on the shelf next to Fowler, Gowers, and "the little book."

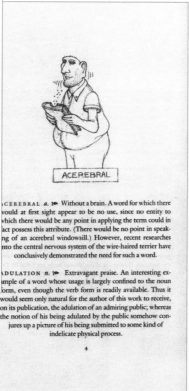

Ward Farnsworth: *Farnsworth's Classical English Rhetoric*

2011. 264 PP, 6 × 9″ $27.00 HC

We published this when Ward Farnsworth, who has been as devoted and loyal an author as any publisher could wish, approached us in 2010 while he was a law professor at Boston University and before he became the Dean of the Law School at the University of Texas. His hope: we'd publish his book devoted to rhetorical devices. As a graduate of Roxbury Latin, which requires six years of Latin and three of Greek, I actually knew a few of these terms: anaphora, chiasmus, zeugma, praeteritio. But a whole book devoted to them? We admired his approach: find the best examples of the various devices as delivered by the best orators and writers of the past millennium, organize them by their unpronounceable rhetorical names, and (above all) give examples from writers whose names the average reader would instantly recognize – Lincoln, Churchill, Shaw, Burke, Shakespeare, Chesterton – to demonstrate their use. We had no idea this approach would be so appealing to so many reviewers, but once the floodgates were opened by Michael Dirda at the *Washington Post*, the reviews just kept flooding in. George Will: "If you seek edification about the craft of writing, rarely has instruction been administered so delightfully." Simon Winchester: "A treasure trove of the liquid magic of words." Carlin Romano: "Get this book! No, really, *get this book!* Read clever Farnsworth and read him again." We had no idea that Ward was as ingenious a salesman as he was an author – or that he knew more strings to pull than we had ever dreamed of. He would go on to follow this success with *Farnsworth's Classical English*

Metaphor, The Practicing Stoic, and *Farnsworth's Classical English Style*. All of them follow the same model: define the need, explain the methodology used to explore it, provide specific examples that illustrate how it has been met by past masters. The mind of a consummate legal scholar at work. Much credit goes to the designer, Carl W. Scarbrough, for his elegant Grandvillean jackets and for hashing out the various design challenges.

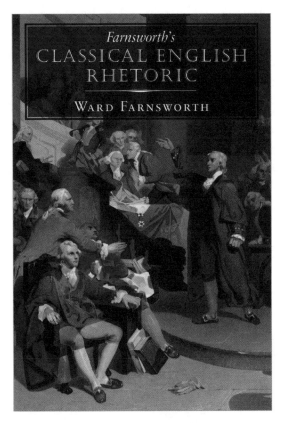

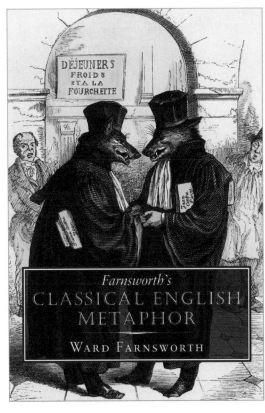

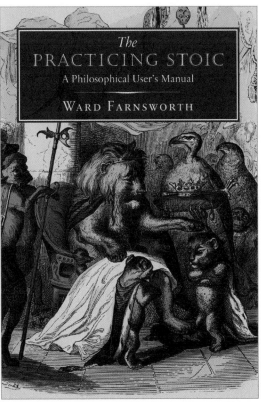

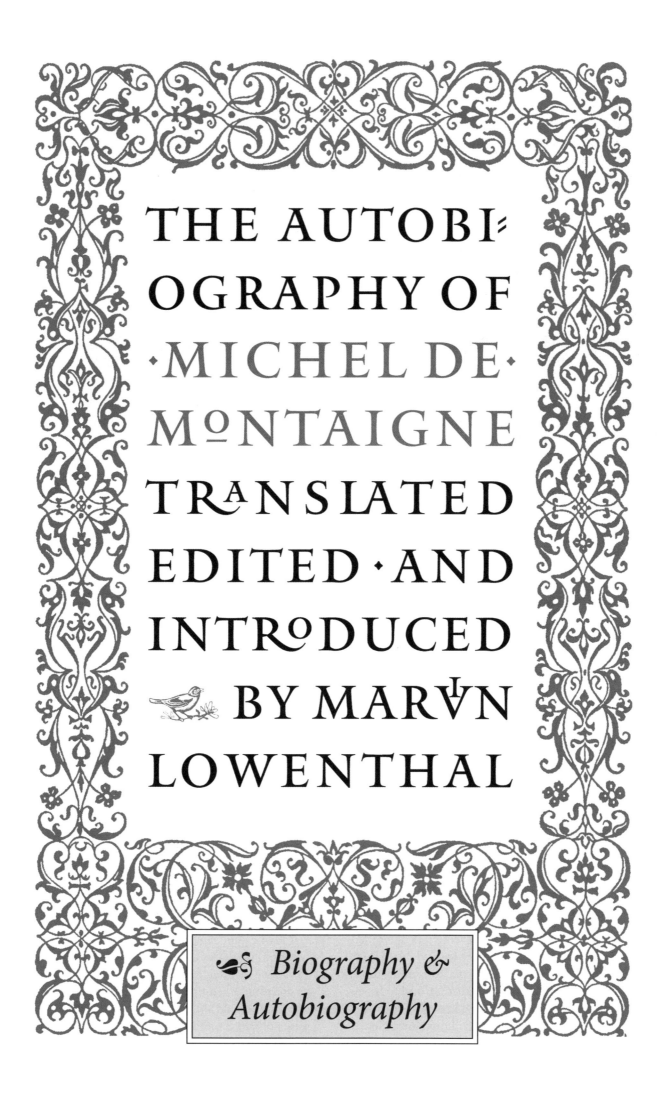

THE AUTOBI-OGRAPHY OF ·MICHEL DE· MONTAIGNE

TRANSLATED EDITED · AND INTRODUCED BY MARVIN LOWENTHAL

Biography & Autobiography

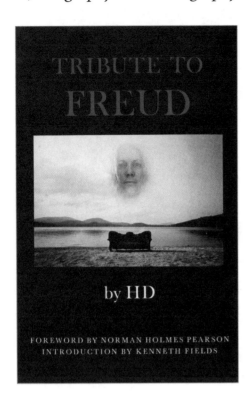

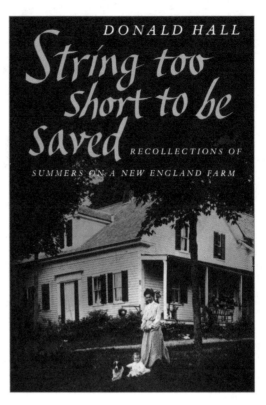

H.D.: *Tribute to Freud*

Foreword by Norman Holmes Pearson
Introduction by Kenneth Fields
1975. 240 PP, 5½ × 8″ $10.00 HC

This is the complete version of the book that Ernest Jones, Freud's biographer, called "surely the most delightful and precious appreciation of Freud's personality that is likely to be written," and probably it required a writer with the sensitivity of a poet to write it. And what a poet and what sensitivities. As a girl, Hilda Doolittle had worshipped William Morris. In her second year at Bryn Mawr she was briefly engaged to Ezra Pound. Moving to England she briefly married Richard Aldington and became close to D.H. Lawrence. In 1915, her first child was stillborn. In 1918, her older brother was killed in France and her father died of a stroke a year later. In the same year, she was pregnant with her second child, sick with pneumonia, separated from her husband, and about to leave England for the Scilly Isles, off Cornwall. She had visions; she saw figures and "writing on the wall." It was no surprise that in 1933 she turns to Freud in an attempt to restore some sort of mental equilibrium. Gradually he taught her to accept and deal with her confusions, urging her to examine the root causes of her fantasies. As the encounters intensified, the relationship between them deepened and Freud began to consider her more a pupil than a patient, among the few sensitive enough to understand his theories and techniques. Opaque with others, he would reveal himself to her, and H.D. repaid his trust in this illuminating, almost unique, tribute to his humanity.

Donald Hall: *String Too Short to be Saved*

1979. 176 PP, 6 × 9″ $6.00 SC

I think this was always Don's favorite book, although he never claimed it. It recounts his visits as a young boy to the old Keniston homestead that had been in his mother's family for generations and was still operating as a dairy farm in south central New Hampshire, much as it had for a century. In the revised edition, Hall gives a fascinating account of the history of the book. As a book it is more a sequence of vignettes; the daily life and routines of a barely subsisting dairy farm as seen through the lens of a young suburbanite from Connecticut whose summers with his grandparents were clearly the anticipated highlights of his year. He gives the complete backstory to the book; how the various parts were submitted to the *New Yorker*, only to be rejected and later, after his return from Oxford, accepted. The gallery of photographs forming the front matter were all family members and the eccentric and lovable Eagle Farm cast of characters who appear repeatedly in his wishful *Christmas at Eagle Pond*. I first encountered this book while working at the Stinehour Press in Lunenburg, VT. Viking, the original publisher, had decided to print the edition in hot metal with charming line cuts and a copy was lying around the shop. I took it back to my hotel room, read it in one night, and was enchanted. Later, it went out of print and we managed to buy the rights from a delighted Mr. Hall. We maintained the same format and typography through countless editions, using for the front cover a photo of young Donald sitting in the foreground, dressed in the requisite pinafore, on the front lawn of the family house to which he would eventually return to live and finally die.

Brendan Behan: *Borstal Boy*
Afterword by Benedict Kiely
1982. 400 PP, 5½ × 8¼" $9.00 SC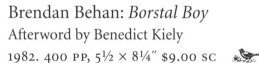

This miracle of autobiography and prison literature begins, "Friday, in the evening, the landlady shouted up the stairs, 'Oh God, O Jesue, oh Sacred Heart. Boy, there's two gentlemen here to see you.' I knew by the screeches of her that these gentlemen were not calling to inquire after my health, or to know if I'd had a good trip. I grabbed my suitcase, containing Pot, Chlor, Sulph, Ac, Gelignite detonators, electrical and ignition, and the rest of my Sinn Fein conjurer's outfit, and carried it out the window. Then the gentlemen arrived." These were, of course, the police, who knew Behan for what he was and arrested him. This occurred in Liverpool in 1939, within days of his arrival in England. He was just seventeen and a terrorist, filled with ideas of glory and determined to blast imperialist Britain. He was to spend three years in a prison and later a "borstal," a reform school, before returning to Ireland as a changed but hardly defeated rebel. As Benedict Kiely made clear in his Afterword, Behan was neither the familiar writer in the making, nor the typical IRA recruit, but something far more idiosyncratic and interesting. This, his great memoir, once banned in the Irish Republic, beautifully demonstrates that difference.

Richard Rodriguez: *Hunger of Memory*
1982. 208 PP, 5⅝ × 8¾" $15.00 HC

Of all the unillustrated nonfiction we have published, this still remains our most popular and influential title. Rodriguez was a "scholarship boy" who grew up in a

poor, Spanish-speaking family but with encouragement and ambition attended and excelled at Berkeley. In this poignant memoir of coming of age in America, he bravely makes the argument that English is, and should be the first, second, and third language of choice. I have no idea how Rodriguez found Godine, but I do remember meeting him in San Francisco while I was teaching at Stanford. Earnest, young, handsome, extremely articulate, and convinced that his book was important, he had no trouble persuading me. Bill Goodman was his perfect editor – sensitive, receptive, and loyal. When we heard that the book was not only going to receive a front-page review in the *New York Times*, but also reviews in the *Washington Post*, the *Chicago Tribune* and the *Los Angeles Times*, we knew we were tracking a small meteor. Part of the reason behind the book's success was its argument in favor of English as the primary, and necessary, language for success in this country. And the pain that often accompanies its acquisition. As he would write, "What I needed to know in school was that I had the right – and the obligation – to speak the public language of *los gringos*." It was a position that was especially powerful and poignant coming from an academic whose upbringing and family life were conducted entirely in Spanish, and it spoke eloquently to the power and importance of language in establishing a public, as well as maintaining a private, identity. Richard was no idealogue; he saw the flaws on all sides of an argument, including those espoused by his peers. He regarded the far-left academic multiculturalists as "the most sectarian people I know." He had little patience with the theory or practice of "affirmative action." This position was embraced by both right and left, and for different reasons. The book went through five printings in two months, selling over 20,000 copies. We'd never experienced anything like it before, nor have we since.

Francis Steegmuller: *Cocteau*
New Afterword by Francis Steegmuller
1986. 606 PP, 6 × 9¼″ $16.00 SC

In a book the *New York Times* called "surely a model of the biographer's art," Francis Steegmuller, who had previously tackled Flaubert, Maupassant and Apollinaire, takes on Cocteau, a major twentieth-century artist in a variety of fields whose life was a deliberate (and carefully orchestrated) scandal. The astonishing variety of his work as a poet, novelist, playwright, filmmaker (*The Blood of a Poet, Beauty and the Beast*) and artist all come into play in this award-winning biography. Steegmuller opens the door on the contradictions and paradoxes of his private life, the charm or nastiness he could turn on and off like a faucet, his generosity and selfishness, and the self-imposed poise and internal anguish of an opium-addicted homosexual man in the twentieth century. Cocteau was a man who knew, and often interacted with, everyone of note in the avant-garde life of France (his two favorites were Picasso and Stravinsky: "I feel at home with them"), but who also managed to be elected, and apparently without much opposition, to the inherently conservative Académie Française. For our Nonpareil, Steegmuller provided a new Afterword. The year 1983 marked the twentieth anniversary of Cocteau's death; celebrations occurred throughout France, new autobiographical material had been released (Cocteau would write, rewrite, and "rediscover" his autobiography throughout his life), and Steegmuller felt corrections and amplifications to the original interpretations were required. His biography still stands as the best existing account of the astonishing accomplishments of a man only France could have produced.

Patrick O'Brian: *Joseph Banks: A Life*
1993. 328 PP, 6 × 9″ $30.00 HC

Patrick O'Brian is, of course, best known in this country for his superb Jack Aubrey series of nautical classics, books our resident Wellesley College reader advised against (as did so many others) as examples of "arcane English maritime lore" (she never lived this down). But why no one had stepped forward to pick up this superb biography is a mystery to me. Sir Joseph Banks (1743–1821) was a naturalist, an intrepid explorer, and for more than forty years the president of the Royal Society, Britain's oldest scientific institution. He was instrumental in the founding of Australia, having accompanied Captain James Cook on his circumnavigation of the globe that recorded the existence of the continent. But a complete picture of his fascinating life had never been written, and O'Brian—historian, sailor, and an expert on the Napoleonic era—was the perfect man to undertake it. Making full use of his letters and journals, he brings from the shadows a forthright and hospitable man whose real genius was identifying, and then promoting, the genius of others. In his position at the Royal Society, he presided over a vast enterprise of scientific inquiry and exploration, setting the stage for a century when England not only ruled the waves, but also dominated scientific advancement. An indefatigable correspondent, Banks's wide circle of friends included Georges Cuvier, James Watt, Samuel Johnson, and Charles Gibbon. O'Brian provides a thorough and gracefully written biography of a full and important life. I had the pleasure of meeting him once, at The Somerset Club in Boston, the guest of his publisher at Norton. Both were exceedingly well behaved and thoroughly overwhelmed by the noisy and self-important guests from Harvard. I don't think O'Brian managed to get out more than a few sentences all night, and, as his hosts, I felt we had completely let him down.

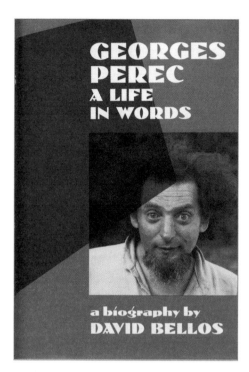

David Bellos: *Georges Perec: A Life in Words*
1993. 832 PP, 6⅛ × 9¼″ $45.00 HC

Georges Perec was a singular literary personality, a unicum. Italo Calvino called his *Life A User's Manual* "the last real 'event' in the history of the novel." Robert Taylor (in the days when great newspapers actually employed great book reviewers) wrote in the *Boston Globe*, "This is one of the great novels of the century. Even in an age of literary bombast, one might well qualify that assertion, but it's true – suddenly and unexpectedly, the late twentieth century has produced a novel on the level of Joyce, Proust, Mann, Kafka, and Nabokov." To step up and write about his life required dedication, a thorough knowledge of French and the author's extensive oeuvre, and the culture in which he grew up and worked. Perec's novels are rightly considered modern classics, but his linguistic curiosity and mastery extended to a number of forms: autobiography, drama and criticism, even crossword puzzles and palindromes (he would create literature's longest). There was only one possible choice for a biographer: David Bellos, then a Professor of French Studies at the University of Manchester, the world-class authority on the man and his work and his award-winning English translator. Bellos carefully and systematically introduces the enigmatic figure behind the remarkable literary trail, traces how his life experiences found their way into his novels, leading to books like *Things* or the harrowing *W, or the Memory of Childhood*, inspired by his mother's death in WWII at Auschwitz, and by his own sense of guilt as a survivor. Using unpublished documents and firsthand interviews, Bellos traces Perec's tragic childhood, his difficult apprenticeship, his emergence from obscurity, his central role in French intellectual life during the 60s and 70s, and his tragic death from cancer at the young age of 46. He discloses the story of his Polish-Jewish background and his friendships, through his alliance with the Oulipo group with such figures as Italo Calvino, Raymond Queneau, Harry Mathews, and others that helped shape, and offered support for, his extraordinary life. In more than 800 pages, a doorstop of a biography, Bellos chronicles the painstaking process by which a phenomenally gifted writer, suffering from a shattered past and crippling emotional baggage, reconstructed his life in the only way he knew how – in words.

Benedetta Craveri: *Madame du Deffand and Her World*
Translated by Teresa Waugh
1995. 486 PP, 6 × 9″ $35.00 HC

Possessing "a definite taste for defiance," the Marquise du Deffand (1697–1780) shocked even the most progressive and immoral of French society by flouting decorum and blatantly disregarding women's traditional roles. Her story, told by the granddaughter of the noted philosopher Benedetto Croce and professor of French literature, provides the first full-length portrait of a remarkable woman who played a major role in the turbulent decades leading up to the French Revolution. Married to a colorless nobleman ten years her senior, she approached, and engaged in, love and sex with a frank openness centuries ahead of her time. But she was far more than a libertine; her keen intelligence, wit, and spirit made her a close correspondent with the most prominent figures of the Enlightenment – Voltaire, Montesquieu, and Horace Walpole among others. Her salon, over which she reigned for forty years, remained command central for the French intelligentsia. Thoroughly researched (a full 88 pages of closely packed notes and references), Craveri's biography gives a tough-minded portrait of an intellectual who always had a cabinet minister up her sleeve, but also of an era and society in which conversation was an art form, and civility a pragmatic and social necessity.

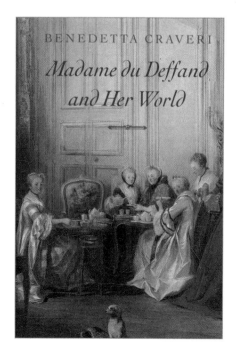

The Autobiography of Michel de Montaigne
Selected, edited and translated by Marvin Lowenthal
1998. 408 pp, 5⅝ × 8¼″ $17.00 sc

John Aubrey: *Aubrey's Brief Lives*
Edited from the original manuscript and with a life
of John Aubrey by Oliver Lawson Dick
Foreword by Edmund Wilson
1999. 544 pp, 6 × 9″ $18.00 sc

Everyone acknowledges that Montaigne's essays, a form he virtually invented *de novo,* are among the glories of civilized thought. In this thoughtfully arranged and carefully researched volume, Lowenthal has drawn from his letters, essays, travel writings and manuscripts to give us a readable and sequential biography of his life. And here it is told in Montaigne's own words, fulfilling his intention of presenting his self-image to the world through his writing: "My books and I are one." Into those books he would pour the accumulated and amazing variety of his perceptions, his extraordinary power of observation and analysis and his deeply felt love for humanity in all its messy contrariness. Above his desk he had inscribed a motto he took seriously: *Nihil humani alieni mihi puto*– nothing human is alien to me. He was, in many ways, the first modern writer, the first willing to look inwards at himself instead of outwards, the first to prove that originality and charm are the equal of scholarship and hogsheads of facts. He was, as Voltaire observed, "a wise man in a century of ignorance, a philosopher in an age of fanatics, who painted, in the guise of himself, our own flies and frailties… a man who will be loved forever." Marvin Lowenthal, defending his approach, notes in his Introduction, "I have long been tempted to give an account of [Montaigne's] life, thought and time. But as I drew near the project, I realized it would be folly and impertinence to write the life of a man who had spent his genius writing it himself, and who did it incomparably well." The book's handsome design reflects the talents of Scott Kosofsky, something of a polymath himself, who devised a new typeface, Montaigne Sabon, in which to set it.

The entire ferment of the lively Elizabethan age and the vigor of the following century come alive in this immortal trove of "brief portraits" that have been plundered and quoted by scholars for centuries. John Aubrey, the foremost gossip columnist of the seventeenth century, a louche country gentleman of lively and somewhat dubious character, left posterity not an organized book but a sprawling collection of notes, scribbles, and morsels of gossip. A brave and scrupulous Lawson Dick assembled, edited, and selected 134 that had something important to say, arranging them alphabetically, and restoring those passages expurgated by nineteenth-century editors. All of this while providing an extended essay on Aubrey's life and times and an extensive bibliography. They are all here: the flowers of Elizabethan England – Raleigh, Wolsey, Sydney, More, Shakespeare, and Milton – along with a galaxy of soldiers, scholars, imposters, and whores who all became, through Aubrey's jottings, and Dick's careful and accessible arrangement, not abstract figures from a history book, but alive in flesh and blood. We managed to include and reset

ABOVE: The typesetting of this book demonstrates how important typography and choice of type can be to a book's attractiveness and readability. For Montaigne Sabon, Scott Kosofsky created an entirely new font, based on the seminal designs of Garamond and Granjon that provided the foundations for Tschichold's original Sabon as well as most of the text types we read today.

Wilson's fine essay on Aubrey as a Foreword to our redesigned edition. It reads, in part, "I have never read anything else that makes me feel in quite the same way what it must have been like to live then, to find oneself a part of an England that was venturesome, unsettled, and eager, that was opening new horizons. John Aubrey, not one of its giants, brings its heroes down to human scale. He becomes, with Mr. Lawson Dick's edition, an unmistakable and manageable classic."

Iris Origo: *Images and Shadows*
1999. 288 PP, 5⅜ × 8¼" $16.00 SC

Born a Cutting in 1902 to a wealthy and patrician Long Island family, Iris Origo arrived with a silver spoon in her mouth and was instantly catapulted into a life, in her words, "of unfair advantages of birth, education, money, environment and opportunity." But her beloved father died tragically while she was a child, and her mother decided the family would be better served by ambitious travel and private tutors than conventional schooling. So, although Iris would spend considerable intervals at the family's ancestral estate on Long Island and her grandfather's castle in Ireland, her youth was peripatetic—Ireland, Greece, Egypt, and finally Florence with Bernard Berenson. At age 22, she married Antonio, a young landowner, and in 1923, they bought La Foce, an entire valley, still feudal in its organization, in southern Tuscany where for fifty years they reforested the barren valley, improving the land and the lot of the peasants. During WWII, they saved endangered children and downed Allied airmen from the brutal incursions of the Nazis, an ordeal she describes in *War in Val D'Orcia*. She was a prodigious worker, writing history, biography, and two memoirs of her life—this one, from her birth until her marriage, and the second, *War in Val D'Orcia*, an account of the valley during the Nazi invasion.

Garret Keizer: *A Dresser of Sycamore Trees*
2001. 212 PP, 5½ × 7½" $18.00 SC

The company seems to have an affinity for authors and artists from Vermont's Northeast Kingdom. Richard Brown connects with it through his photographs, Frank Howard Mosher through his fiction, and Garret Keizer through his empathetic spiritual engagement. The ostensible purpose of this book is to tell the story of how he "came to be the lay minister of a small Episcopal parish in an old railroad junction town in the northeast corner of Vermont." Like the prophet Amos, a herdsman and dresser of sycamore trees, Keizer has a parallel, and more challenging, calling as a shepherd of human souls. Of course, he was, in real life, far more than a "Lay minister," serving equally as a high school English teacher, husband, and father, and, reading between the lines, the Father Confessor to the entire isolated community. But there is nothing remote or isolated about this book or the issues and concerns that Keizer struggles to address. Key among them are reconciling a life of faith with the demands of daily existence, while providing some evidence that "grace" exists in the lives and actions beyond its reaches, perhaps beyond the boundaries of formal religion. Here Keizer excels, never talking down or preaching to his audience, taking the parries and thrust of daily life and trying to imbue them with a sense of the holy. And unlike most preachers, he understands that he has as much to learn from his parishioners as he has to teach them, "All I can hope to do is remind them of what they know, to enliven what they know—that is, to make it more accessible to their imaginations, and thus to their faith." With an eye attuned to both the pleasures and pratfalls that make life on earth so rich, he presents a pragmatic and often hilarious blueprint of the work required to maintain a parish, negotiating your way through it to the kingdom of heaven.

OPPOSITE: *Aubrey's Brief Lives* is set in the seventeenth-century letters of Christoffel van Dijck, who Lance Hidy discovered was born and died within fifty days and a few city blocks of his Amsterdam contemporary Rembrandt van Rijn. Although they apparently never met, Lance, in this masterful broadside, presents his engraving of the artist and a synopsis of the van Dijck roman & italic and allows that Rembrandt "showed not the slightest talent for type design" but that his "fame among typographers is insured by the coincidence of dates which forever associates his name with that of Christoffel van Dijck." It seems almost criminal to bury this information in a caption.

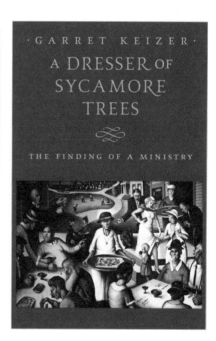

Richard Watson: *Cogito Ergo Sum: The Life of René Descartes*
2002. 344 PP, 6 × 9″ $35.00 HC

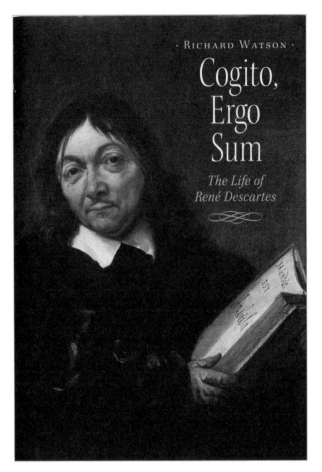

Descartes is the philosophical architect of the modern world. In metaphysics, he established the view that mind and body are distinct substances, a fundamental position if one is to believe the human soul is immortal. In mathematics, he invented analytic geometry – the basis of calculus, which makes physics as we know it possible. He perfected methods for proposing and testing hypotheses through experiments that were repeatable and verifiable, the basis of modern science. In optics, he discovered and described the law of refraction and reflection. In medicine and physiology, his analyses of the relationship between the sense organs, nerves, and the brain is still taught today. He didn't see the point of refuting Aristotelian Scholasticism; he just wanted to show a better way. Our twenty-first-century world – from mind-body dualism to heart pumps, from pop psychology to the personal computer and iPhones – are thoroughly Cartesian. He could land in a spaceship and feel right at home; nothing would surprise him. We live in a world in which deductive reasoning guides and controls not only our science, technology, and daily actions, but most of our moral decisions as well. For forty years, Richard Watson, a professor of philosophy at Washington University in St. Louis, made Descartes his life study, pursuing him in libraries, and tracing his steps through Europe where Descartes wrote, studied, lived, and died. The result is as much a meditation on the differences between America and Europe as a biography. Where else could you find an extended discussion of the forty or fifty varieties of licorice to be had in the Netherlands. We offer one option: Switzer. In Watson's hands, Descartes comes alive for the modern reader, his theories are made comprehensible through defensible, and sometimes outrageous, analogies and occasionally wild conjectures. You get to tour rural Holland, the old districts of Paris, and the convoluted streets of Stockholm with the author, and what emerges is not only a window into the world of Descartes, but a life that comes alive, as does that of a crusty, opinionated, and idiosyncratic scholar who has a lot to say on the subject he knows and loves best – and much besides.

ABOVE: Booker Telleterro Ervin & Kenneth Patchen

LEFT: Robert Duncan

Jonathan Williams: *A Palpable Elysium*
Introduction by Guy Davenport
2002. 176 PP, 8 × 10" $30.00 SC *with flaps*

Jonathan Williams was among the many distinguished graduates of Black Mountain College, that little factory near Asheville, NC that churned out an entire generation of modernist poets, writers, artists, and photographers. Gropius, Motherwell, Rauschenberg, Penn, Creeley, Kazin, Dahlberg, Cage – they all came out of that fecund little nursery. Williams, a writer, editor, publisher, and agent provocateur, followed in the same tradition, and this is his pantheon of heroes. In this book, with its impossible title, he tries to record his cultural heroes in both his memorable words and his photographs, which were less so – he would take only one shot with a cheap camera and it was hit or miss. What is so memorable is his range of passionate acquaintances – not just the living: Dahlberg, Pound, Williams, Siskind, Niedecker, Miller and Merton, but also the tombs and gravestones of e.e. cummings, Charlie Parker, Rachmaninoff, Wallace Stevens, Erik Satie, Kenneth Grahame, and (not to be missed) the Mausoleum of Walt Whitman. All the Black Mountaineers are here, or most of them (and what a list that is!). He would go on to found The Jargon Society, a publisher that championed a number of his friends who had never been properly recognized. His press deserved an award for its outstanding contribution to American letters. Like Melville's *Moby-Dick*, Thoreau's *Walden*, Apollinaire's *Bestiary*, and Blake, Hopkins, and Emily Dickinson, who had to wait years for proper recognition, the book was a sales disaster. It should have sold on the anecdotes alone; James Wright asks the poet Kenneth Rexroth why he writes, to which KR shoots back "To overthrow the capitalist system and to get laid – in that order." We put the great publisher James Laughlin of *New Directions* on the front cover. No one recognized him. In fifty years, most of my list may well be forgotten. This, *A Palpable Elysium*, I predict, will be among the few survivors.

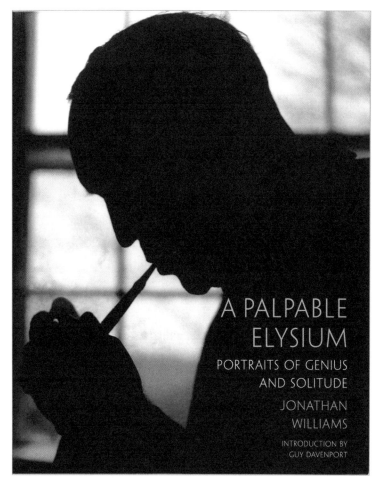

A PALPABLE ELYSIUM
PORTRAITS OF GENIUS
AND SOLITUDE
JONATHAN WILLIAMS
INTRODUCTION BY
GUY DAVENPORT

ABOVE: James Laughlin, founder and publisher of *New Directions* in his Norfolk, CT studio

LEFT: Kenneth Rexroth

ABOVE: Robert Kelly   RIGHT: Harry Partch   ABOVE: Henry Miller

Caroline Moorehead: *Iris Origo*

2002. 84 PP, 6 × 9″ $35.00 HC

Until Moorehead's biography, the world had come to know and embrace Iris Origo primarily through her own writing. Written with circumspection and the prerequisite distance of a historian, Origo reveals very little of her childhood: the early death of her father, her peripatetic wanderings with her eccentric and self-centered mother, her entrée into the circle of privileged and wealthy society at the Villa Medici at Fiesole where she was introduced to the world of politics and art at the feet of Bernard Berenson, Harold Acton, and Edith Wharton, whose petty bickering and conservative politics had a profound influence on how she would spend her life. With total access to the family papers, archives, and documents, Moorehead reveals her world, painting a fair, and not altogether flattering, portrait of one of the great writers and scholars of the last century and a life that was hardly free of tragedy and conflict: the tragic loss of her son and the conflicts, both political and personal, she endured with her husband, Antonio. Hers was a career made all the more remarkable by her lack of any formal education. But through travel, exposure to some of the great minds of Italy and England, and an undeniable, indefatigable energy, Iris emerges from these pages as a woman of formidable strength, courage, and probity. If she hadn't written a single word, her acts of generosity and solicitude, sheltering downed Allied airmen and feeding the children of her domain in Val D'Orcia during the brutal German retreat through Italy in WWII, would be enough to ensure her admission into heaven.

Dialogues of Alfred North Whitehead

Recorded by Lucien Price
Foreword by Caldwell Titcomb
Introduction by Sir David Ross

2002. 412 PP, 5½ × 8¼″ $18.00 SC   🐦

First issued in hardcover in 1954 by Boston's Atlantic Monthly Press, no doubt under the inspired leadership of Edward Weeks. I read this in college and believed then, as now, that it provides just about the only accessible window into the mind and thought of one of the most influential (and inscrutable) philosophers and mathematicians of the twentieth century. Whitehead's career began at Trinity College, Cambridge, where he was a member of the Apostles and author, along with his student Bertrand Russell, of the three volume *Principia Mathematica*, the seminal text on how to apply mathematics to logic (or maybe logic to mathematics). He stayed there, a legend, primarily keeping his focus on mathematics, logic, and physics until 1910 when he moved to London – with no prospect of employment. By 1918 he was dean of the Faculty of Science at the University of London and in 1924, at the invitation of Henry Osborn Taylor and aged 63, he was invited to Lowell's Harvard to join the Philosophy Department, taking over from its founders William James and George Santayana. By this time his interests had shifted from mathematics to philosophy (in which he had no formal training) and finally to metaphysics. I tried reading his book *Process and Reality* based on the Gifford Lectures of 1927–28, and with sentences

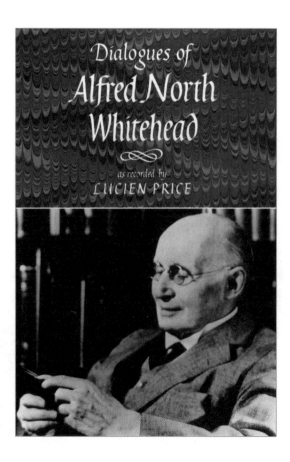

like "Sometimes we see an elephant and sometimes we do not. The result is that an elephant, when present, is noticed." found it totally incomprehensible. In classes and seminars, he was a distracted and often distant presence, cherubic with his white hair and bright blue eyes, amiable, somewhat opaque. Partly, this was probably due to age, and partly to his posture as an intensely private individual. He instructed that his entire archive be burned on his death. His biographer, Victor Lowe, observed that "No professional biographer in his right mind would touch him." Nonetheless, Lowe responded with two volumes. Where Whitehead really shone was at the teas, the "in-house symposia," that he and his wife provided for undergraduates, graduates and visitors in their Cambridge home. To these came not only young Harvard students with their dates, but also a procession of eminent intellectuals. And it wasn't for the food; this was strictly a tea and cake affair. Among them was Lucien Price, then an editorial writer for the *Boston Globe*, a Phi Beta Kappa Harvard graduate, a reporter who, in Louis Lyons's words "made literature of journalism," and apparently a man with a formidable memory. He would transcribe and arrange Whitehead's thoughts and conversations verbatim. There are throughout clear references to Plato (the model). But there is something in these conversations for everyone; they are as clear, thought-provoking, and original today as a century ago. Every page has some kernel of revelation. Who but Whitehead would have observed that among the primary reasons Christianity endured and triumphed is the fact that what is first heard on entering, and the last on leaving, a church is music?

Irene Tichenor: *No Art without Craft: The Life of Theodore Low De Vinne*
2005. 342 PP, 6 × 9″ $35.00 HC

While it is true that Theodore Low De Vinne will not go down in history among the world's best designers, he was an extraordinary man and an exemplary employer and printer. He was the first in a line of scholar printers who never attended college (D.B. Updike, Stanley Morison, Henry Bullen), a founder of the Grolier Club, a man respected by his peers and synonymous with technical skill and mechanical innovation. A pioneer in the methods required to print delicate wood engravings, he was an early advocate of tight word spacing, and a perfectionist when it came to even impression and consistent presswork. Upon his death in 1914 he was the leading practitioner of an industry that was among the largest in America, one now largely abandoned. It is impossible to conceive of the accomplishments of Updike, Rogers, Blumenthal, and others without what De Vinne brought to the craft in the late 1890s. Irene Tichenor covers his entire life fairly and comprehensively, making clear what Updike and others observed, that the entire sense of "fine printing" or bibliographical scholarship in this country originated with TLD.

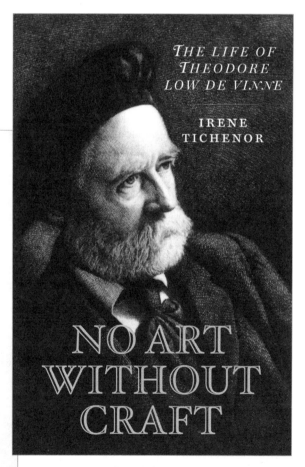

LEFT: A typical De Vinne title page, printed five years after The Grolier Club of New York was founded and featuring its seal, which is still in use today

Kate Colquhoun: *The Busiest Man in England: A Life of Joseph Paxton, Gardener, Architect & Victorian Visionary*

2006. 314 PP, 6 × 9″ $35.00 HC

It has always seemed to me that in Victorian England you could walk down any street, throw a stone, and hit a genius. But even in that era of multiple polymaths, it was generally agreed that Joseph Paxton and his career stood high among the Victorian greats. He was the indispensable man, the self-taught polymath and "can do" pragmatist who, it seemed, could solve any problem and deal with any issue. At 23, he was named the Chief Gardener of Chatsworth and transformed it into the greatest garden in England. His experience with the glass and steel of greenhouses led him to propose "The Crystal Palace" for the Great Exhibition of 1851, a "fairy palace" that encompassed eighteen acres, required 2,000 workmen to build, and entertained six million visitors. A spectacular success, it led to an endless stream of commissions: designing parks and public buildings, suggesting ways to ease congestion, pollution and filth in what was then the most populous city in the world. Colquhoun brings the man and his time to life. Drawing on personal papers and historical archives, she gives us not only Paxton the public persona but also an admirable portrait of a loving husband, indulgent father and generous friend. He was a man who truly personified the Victorian idea of self-improvement, resourcefulness, civic service, and breathtaking energy. It was no wonder that the second busiest man in England, Charles Dickens, recognized him as the first.

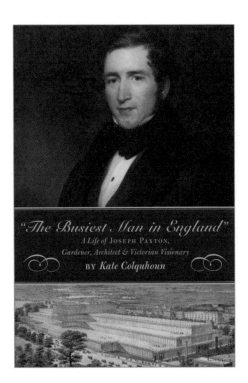

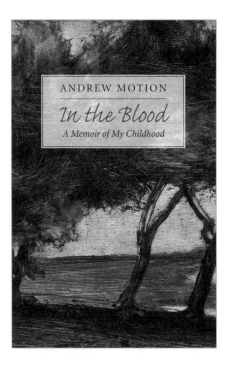

Andrew Motion: *In the Blood*
A Memoir of My Childhood

2007. 328 PP, 6 × 8½″ $25.00 HC

For some reason, Andrew Motion, who had been the Poet Laureate of England for a decade, had never been published in the United States. Our editor, Susan Barba, read this extraordinary memoir in the Faber & Faber edition and persuaded me to publish it. His life, forever changed by the accident his mother suffered while riding, is told in the most moving and deliberate prose, at once accurate and evocative.

Laurie Lee: *Cider with Rosie*

2008. 224 PP, 5½ × 8½″ $16.00 SC

As I Walked Out One Midsummer Morning

2011. 216 PP, 5½ × 8½″ $16.00 SC

A Moment of War: A Memoir of the Spanish Civil War

2015. 144 PP, 5½ × 8½″ $16.00 SC

I belonged to that generation which saw, by chance, the end of a thousand years' life … a world of hard work, of villages like ships in the empty landscape, of white narrow roads, rutted by horses and cartwheels, innocent of oil or petrol …

Lee was born in 1914, in Gloucestershire, the sole male among a gaggle of doting sisters, and miraculously raised by a single mother. He opens the book with himself, age three, just a baby, and continues through his first kiss with Rosie at sixteen. His is a young life infused in equal parts with raw intensity and innocence and conveyed in a lush, expressive prose that magically spotlights the child's side of the journey between infancy and adulthood. He reports on the cadences and challenges of family and village life while suffering all the agonies and awkwardness of adolescence. It may be another time and another place, but we have all been there before, a journey we know and recognize. First published in 1959 and instantly acclaimed as a classic, it was followed by *As I Walked Out One Midsummer Morning*. Lee, looking for adventure and eager to see the world leaves the UK for Spain in 1938 with his violin strapped to his back, just before the Civil War (to read this narrative is to completely understand why that war was predetermined, inevitable, and endlessly bloody), and his return to Spain to fight against the Franco regime was recounted in *A Moment of War*. All the books in this trilogy are masterpieces of biography, but also of history. In reading them you pass from an idyllic and isolated English country village, through the threadbare remains of feudal pre-Franco Spain, into the bloodbath of its Civil War and the fight against fascism. Reading this last book of the trilogy, you hope you'll then pass into the light of what you presume will be the dawn of a new era. But this, you realize in hindsight, was only a hope, one still waiting to be realized.

Glenna Lang & Marjory Wunsch: *Genius of Common Sense: Jane Jacobs and the Story of The Death and Life of Great American Cities*
2009. 128 PP, 7½ × 10″ $18.00 HC

Jane Jacobs's far-sighted 60s polemic *The Death and Life of Great American Cities* radically altered the way we thought about urban development. It had an immediate impact on city planning, architecture, and how we understand the way life is sustained and works (or doesn't) in neighborhoods. Appearing at the height of the "urban renewal craze," when razing entire neighborhoods seemed the righteous road to progress, Jacobs correctly perceived that the new structures being built were often far inferior to the ones being replaced, and that the fabric of neighborhoods that had held them together was being destroyed. The result was both architectural and societal sterility, yet another signal of the post-war efforts to standardize and consumerize America. She was predictably ridiculed and pilloried by the establishment, but her ideas quickly took hold. The book was a game changer. It was to urban planning what Carson's *Silent Spring* was to pesticides and Friedan's *The Feminine Mystique* was to women's emancipation. No one ever looked at what sustained viable neighborhoods the same way again. Born in Scranton, never attending college, her life story is one of determination and independence. She followed the trail of evidence, no matter where it led. Lang and Wunsch distilled mountains of documents, interviews, and contemporary press clippings to sugar her story down to 128 pages. Illustrated with over a hundred images, many never published, it was a brave effort to get her story out to young readers, many growing up in neighborhoods she was instrumental in saving. Among the *New York Times* best books of 2009, it showed we learn from data and thinking, not by accepting what passes as "conventional wisdom."

Gerald Durrell: *Fauna and Family*
2011. 192 PP, 5½ × 8½″ $16.00 SC 🐦

Beasts in My Belfry
2016. 216 PP, 5½ × 8½″ $17.00 SC 🐦

Fillets of Plaice
2008. 192 PP, 5½ × 8½″ $16.00 SC 🐦

There is much to commend the three books that comprise the "Corfu trilogy," written by the youngest of the Durrell children during their stay in Corfu. But it is only fair to take Gerry, who comes across as an entirely trustworthy writer and benevolent observer, to task for some of the facts. His older brother Larry, the writer, and twenty-one years older than Gerry, was born in India where their father died and the family chose to return to England. It was not an easy transition. The mother comes across as a devoted, if slightly dotty, doting parent in both the books and the ensuing BBC series. Larry was the motivating force that removed the family from the UK to Corfu, partially to protect her from further institutionalization, partially to keep the family intact, and partially because they could afford it. He probably was a bit pompous, but in the books he comes across as insufferable. I tend to doubt this; I think Gerry, younger, probably jealous, is simply playing for effect, exaggerates his idiosyncrasies, as well as others in the family, for a good story. And they remained close friends throughout their lives. What does come across is his abiding love for animals, in all shapes, sizes and sexes. This was to serve him well in his capacity as zookeeper, animal gatherer, and a spokesman for the preservation and protection of species. But in fact, the family was probably no more dysfunctional, or bizarre, than countless others, and the lines between fact and fiction are deliberately (if often hilariously) blurred and broken. *Fauna and Family* is the third of the trilogy he wrote while the family made its home on Corfu, introduced with his beloved *My Family and Other Animals*; *Fillets of Plaice* contains five zoological vignettes centered on extrafamilial "other animals" while *Beasts in My Belfry* concentrates on his early passion for pets and strays of all stripes that eventually led to the world famous zoo he created at Whipsnade.

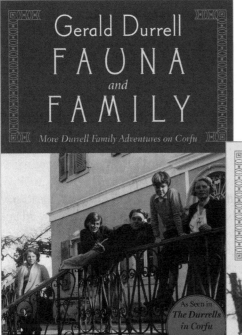

BELOW: We tried to portray Gerry Durrell from youth to relative old age in these covers, with designs that unite them as relatives. The shot on *Fauna and Family* shows the entire family on the balcony of their Corfu retreat with the beleaguered mother on the far right and Gerry beside her on the railing. This was the scene of the most famous book of the trilogy, *My Family & Other Animals*.

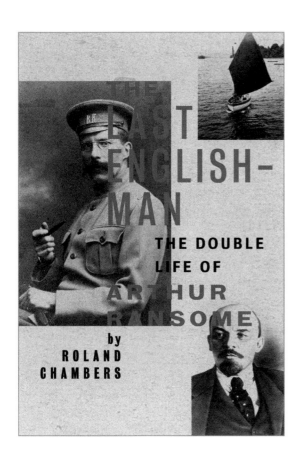

mocracy if just given enough time and breathing room. His undisguised sympathy for the Revolution and the Bolshevik party gave him unparalleled access to its leaders, policies, promises, and plots. Only an author like Chambers, whose deep understanding of the multiple currents and crosscurrents of Russian politics in the late teens and twenties, could have reconciled Ransome's movements and connections with the moving target of Russian politics in an ever-changing bureaucratic landscape. And what emerges is not an amiable English gentleman, but a confused, tortured, and ultimately conflicted figure, a writer who produced over thirty-five books but a personality unable to embrace either country or ideology fully. He died in 1967, two years before Neil Armstrong put foot on the moon. He probably would have been as offended by it as he was by the invention and invasion of television. It is little wonder that in almost all his *Swallows and Amazons* books, parents, and parental controls, disappear within the first few pages and children are left to their own devices. Ransome could sympathize with that, and gain some relief and control seeing life through the eyes of the six children (only two of them boys). They became his surrogates, his vehicles for speaking to the world because he could never find, in himself, a voice he truly believed in.

Roland Chambers: *The Last Englishman: The Double Life of Arthur Ransome*

2012. 410 PP, 6 × 9″ $30.00 HC

As publishers of Arthur Ransome's beloved *Swallows and Amazons* series, it's no wonder we'd be interested in a new biography of this elusive, adventuresome, and enigmatic author. People assume from the subject matter, topography, and characters of the twelve books in the series, first issued in 1930 and continuing almost annually for thirteen years, that he must have been a sweet-tempered and lovable old salt whose main passion in life was messing around with boats. Nothing could be further from the truth. The series was written after he had returned home in 1928, and been told to *stay* home, from Russia where he had been, between 1917 and 1924, the Russian correspondent for the *Daily News* and the *Manchester Guardian.* He returned to England convinced his active life was behind him. And politically at least, he was right. The government made that perfectly clear, and for good reason. His loyalties were always divided. He spoke fluent Russian, would marry Trotsky's private secretary, and was as beguiled by the Russian steppes as by the Coniston waters. Despite all the evidence before him, he somehow could never manage to see Stalin for the butcher he was or that the Revolution had gone horribly wrong. He thought (probably until he died) that somehow Russia would see the light and transform itself into a Parliamentary de-

Barbara Paul Robinson: *Rosemary Verey: The Life & Lessons of a Legendary Gardener*

2012. 270 PP, 5½ × 8⅜″ $30.00 HC

Why, one might well wonder, would an extremely successful New York attorney, the former head of the New York bar, abandon a lucrative practice and beloved husband to spend a year as an intern (overworked, underpaid, and rarely appreciated) to Rosemary Verey, the acknowledged queen of the perennial border and gardening successor to both Gertrude Jekyll and William Robinson. Well, if you have the mind of a lawyer and want to learn something quickly, from the ground up, thorns and all, pulling up stakes in Manhattan and travelling to work as a volunteer provides a certain and quick route to success. Barbara took advantage of the opportunity with grim determination. We tend to forget the enthusiasm with which Americans were embracing English gardens, gardeners, and garden style in the seventies. Verey was the rock star of the British crop, engaging, convincingly patrician, and able to seduce American audiences with her wit and knowledge. Robinson clearly gained her trust and late in her life spoke with her every week by phone. It was probably inevitable that she would finally decide to write a biography to cover her life, her "must see" garden at Barnsley House, her advice to and entanglements with the rich and famous, and, above all, her determined advocacy for the "English Style." Like Jekyll, Verey came to gardening late in life, the result of a riding accident. She published her first book at 62, followed by seventeen more in twenty years. She was also a firm believer that America could, and should, develop its own native horticultural vernacular, and she brought to that not only her own practical experience but a rich repository of garden history and literature. She managed to develop a language that was at once classical and contemporary. She was, much like her American biographer, a genuine original. At least one legacy she left to America can be seen clearly today in the garden Barbara Robinson and her husband created (from scratch) at Brush Hill in northwestern Connecticut.

Robert D. Richardson: *Splendor of the Heart: Walter Jackson Bate and the Teaching of Literature*

2013. 132 PP, 5 × 8″ $20.00 HC

Bob Richardson entered my life quite unexpectedly one summer day in the late 70s while we were still in the basement at Dartmouth Street. He was the head of the English Department at the University of Denver, not someone who would be expected to come out and ask, quite plainly, if we might possibly need some financial help. Boy, did we ever. He was the first of five investors who over the next decade did as much as my father and Dean Paul Siskind to save us from extinction. His memorable biographies of Thoreau, Emerson and William James had been published by the University of California Press and Houghton Mifflin. A

revered figure in the literary firmament and a fine saltwater sailor, and he became a close friend, one who actually attended my wedding in 1986 and left that evening to meet Annie Dillard, who had written him an admiring letter about his take on Thoreau. Three weeks later, I got a phone call that began, "Sit down. We're getting married."

This little confection of a memoir is about his teacher at Harvard, Walter Jackson Bate–brilliant, funny, encouraging, and loyal, clearly the man who set Bob on his life's work. But the book is, at its core, about the joys, and the importance, of *teaching*. He takes the reader back to Harvard of the fifties where a teacher like Bate could hold a classroom of undergraduates spellbound by making literature seem "achingly human, and real, and important." Above all, Bate managed to instill in his students the notion that literature meant nothing unless it led to action, that simply understanding the text was a dead end unless it affected behavior. Bate also believed, and made his students believe, that "Education is impossible without the habitual vision of greatness." Richardson convincingly transmits that vision and passion–for Johnson and Burke, the Romantic poets, Dickens and Arnold, Hopkins and Eliot–making it palpable and contagious. The result is a lucid, vivid, even thrilling, tribute to a writer and teacher who clearly changed the life and dictated the destiny of the author and countless others, but who also confirms Goethe's conversation with Eckermann: "Everywhere, we learn only from those whom we love."

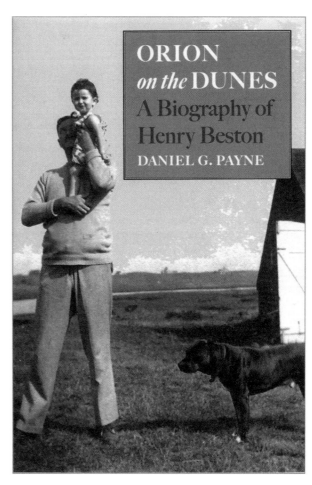

Daniel G. Payne: *Orion on the Dunes: A Biography of Henry Beston*

2015. 500 PP, 6 × 9″ $30.00 HC

When war broke out in Europe in 1914, a twenty-six-year-old Harvard writing instructor named Henry Sheahan volunteered for service with the American Field Service. After serving as an ambulance driver in France and witnessing the carnage at Verdun, he returned to America, changed his name to Henry Beston, and began writing children's stories (much admired by his friend Teddy Roosevelt). In September of 1926, he would take a two-week rental on a shack overlooking an isolated stretch of dunes on the outer beaches of Cape Cod. There, with only the Coast Guardsmen who patrolled the shore as his companions, he would muse, "the fortnight ending, I lingered on, as the year lengthened into autumn, the beauty and mystery of this earth and outer sea so possessed and held me that I could not go." He would spend a year there, writing in his shack on the Nauset beach. The resulting book, *The Outermost House*, is universally considered a foundational classic of American nature writing, often compared with the writing of Thoreau, Burroughs, and Muir. He would later move, with his wife, the children's author Elizabeth Coatsworth, to Maine and settle on a farm on the shores of Damariscotta Lake. Payne's is the first biography devoted to the man and his work. Drawing on unrestricted access to Beston's archives and interviews with family and friends, he limns a masterful portrait of this underrated prose stylist, one who Rachel Carson claimed was the only writer who had any influence on her work. Beston would last visit his shack on the Nauset marsh in 1984 when it was dedicated as a National Literary Landmark. He would die two years later and be buried with his wife in a small graveyard adjoining their home, Chimney Farm, in Nobleboro. His work, as a writer as well as a naturalist, has continued to exert a tremendous influence on poets, naturalists, and novelists alike, and in this long-anticipated biography, tracing the arc of his eventful life, Payne brings the man to life and does him justice.

SPECIMEN DAYS
BY WALT WHITMAN

Walt Whitman: *Specimen Days*

Introduction by Alfred Kazin
Designed, Researched & Edited by Lance Hidy
1971. 224 PP, 8¼ × 11½″ $25.00 HC

This was a very early and quite audacious attempt for a firm not even a year old. I had asked Alfred Kazin to choose an American text that he considered important and neglected and provide us with an Introduction. His choice was Whitman's *Specimen Days*, a day-by-day account of the poet's life, first in his hometown of Camden, New Jersey, then in Brooklyn, and later, and more revealingly, as a nurse in Washington during the height of the Civil War. Far more than a diary or random jottings, *Specimen Days* is Whitman's most personal and most extensive prose statement. It provides contact with a poet's mind at its source, through youth, middle, and old age, with intense, lyric observations of a nation at war and at peace, a vista of a vigorous people and an expanding continent. Lance Hidy fell in love with the book, and we were fortunate that Alan Fern, then the curator of prints and photographs at the Library of Congress took pity on us and gave us full access to the Library's Feinberg Collection of Whitman photographs. These, supplemented in part by other rarely seen images, including the penetrating portraits of the aging poet by Thomas Eakins, formed a portfolio at the back of the book portraying Whitman from youth to a few days before he died. Even today, his daily entries from the war-torn embattled capital

have real resonance and credibility, an immediacy that could only be conveyed by someone participating on the front lines, seeing the results of war firsthand, and treating, as Whitman did, both sides with equal consideration. Not, I think, as a political gesture, but rather a moral one, although, as Kazin observes, "*Specimen Days* is the one book about the Civil War by a first-rate writer of the time that reflects the national fervor of the North."

Stinehour Press set the type and Harold Hugo of the Meriden Gravure Company prevailed on us (doubtless anticipating a likely and imminent bankruptcy) to print the book entirely in duotone offset. Offset was then, for us, a totally unknown process, but with Harold's help, we soon learned that it could be, in its own way, as satisfactory and as appealing as letterpress. In all, we printed a total of 6,250 copies: 3,000 in hardcover, 3,000 as a sewn paperback using the same sheets, and a special edition, ludicrously priced at $35.00 with a slipcase and printed on a specially made paper containing a Bram de Does watermark. In the happy days when libraries had budgets to buy books and a review in the *New York Times Book Review* really sold them, we were saved by a page six review by Leo Marx.

There was a certain life lesson buried here that was to follow us and surface throughout the next fifty years. Baldly, it was "Act, then think." If we had measured the odds of the book issued by an unknown press in an edition of 6,250 copies, with no resources for promotion or advertising, actually succeeding, we would never have attempted it. This was not, after all, the typical product of a "private press." The contents were important but hardly unknown, the introduction was passionate and scholarly, the number of copies represented a large risk, the production standards were intemperately high, and the list prices of all three editions were, even in retrospect, more than reasonable. We were lucky to have succeeded and luck in this case was *not*, as Branch Rickey used to observe, "the residue of design." It was the residue of luck. But it confirmed, at least in our own minds, that we could play in the big leagues and occasionally hit a home run. Additionally, once convinced of a book's substance and importance, we would more often than not take the plunge, often not entirely clear where or how the adventure would end. Talent, occasionally genius, was everywhere. It was our job to identify it and then to make it public. This book was entirely the result of one such genius, Lance Hidy.

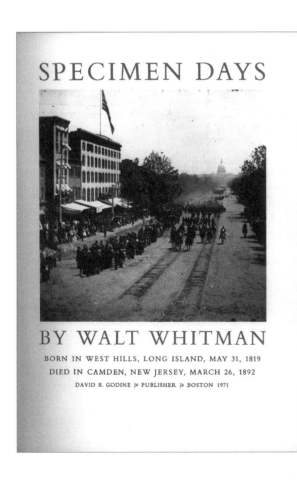

SPECIMEN DAYS

BY WALT WHITMAN

BORN IN WEST HILLS, LONG ISLAND, MAY 31, 1819
DIED IN CAMDEN, NEW JERSEY, MARCH 26, 1892

DAVID R. GODINE ❧ PUBLISHER ❧ BOSTON 1971

OPPOSITE, LEFT: A duotone inset on the red buckram binding for Whitman's *Specimen Days* showing wounded soldiers outside the hospital after the Battle of Fredericksburg, among the bloodiest of the war. Whitman visits for the week over Christmas, tending the wounded of both sides, writing letters for the dying. He records "... the results of the late battle are exhibited everywhere about here in the thousands... the wounded lying on the ground, frozen hard, and the occasional snow." His note of December 21st could have described a scene within their sight, "Outdoors, at the foot of a tree, within ten yards of the front of the hospital, I notice a heap of amputated feet, legs, arms, hands, etc., a full load for a one-horse class." Beneath a portrait of Whitman, age 35, just before the publication of *Leaves of Grass*, and finally, in 1891, by his friend Thomas Eakins, just a year before his death in March 1892.

Selected Prose of John Wesley Powell
Edited and Introduced by George Crossette
1971. 136 PP, 6¼ × 9⅝″ $12.50 HC

Powell, a giant of the late nineteenth century, has too often been overlooked by historians. He was a leader of the scientific community in Washington when Washington was the scientific as well as the political capital of the country, instrumental in establishing such national institutions as The Smithsonian Institution, The National Geographic Society, The Bureau of Ethnology, and The Cosmos Club. He was the force behind the establishment of the Geographical and Geological Surveys of the American West for which he served as director from 1881 to 1894. Late in his life, he devoted his full-time energies to the study of the Native American tribes of the West and especially their mythology and language. Most astonishingly, his was the first party to successfully run the full length of the Colorado River through the entirety of the Grand Canyon, embarking at Green River Station, Wyoming and emerging 100 days later at the mouth of the Virgin in Nevada. As Crossette, the Chief of Geographic Research at the National Geographic Society, pointed out, "Certainly, this was one of the most dangerous and exciting trips ever attempted in the American West; there were no records of earlier visitors, no turning back, and no escape past the high canyon walls." The Colorado was then completely unknown and unexplored, a run of river that even the Native Americans, who warned him against attempting it, had never navigated. And he did it – with ten men and only one arm. But his greatest love was science, and he embraced it with a passion peculiar to the nineteenth century, for in it and through it he saw our future as a nation. As Crossette concludes in his Introduction, "We admire a man for his various talents or deeds, be he a scholar, philosopher, scientist, soldier, explorer, organizer, or public servant. Powell was all of these, and in addition he had the gift of vision, an ability to look into the future – and to plan for that future."

This edition of his selected prose contains his major as well as a fine selection of his lesser-known writing. All of them, even today, are eminently readable and relevant, for Powell had, in Crossette's words, "an ability to simplify scientific facts for all – the scholar, the layman, and the unschooled" with "a descriptive style that gave life to otherwise dull and prosaic accounts." Equally valuable was the inclusion of unpublished photographs by John Karl (aka Jack) Hillers, the photographer who accompanied Powell down the Colorado.

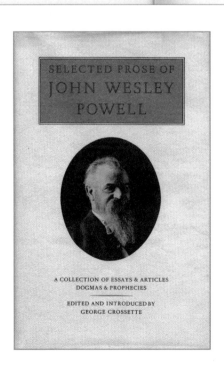

ABOVE: Jack Hiller photographed Powell and his crew on the then-unexplored and uncharted Colorado River. Their 100-day journey was the first to navigate this wild and untamed river gorge, a journey from which there was no turning back. Repairs were frequent and here you see a Canyon boat in 1871, well above the river, being worked on and, on the recto, Powell's boat with his famous chair and (take my word for it) a life preserver under the seat.

Sarah Kemble Knight: *The Journal of Madam Knight*
Introduction by Malcolm Freiberg
1972. 60 PP, 6 × 9″ $10.00 HC

First published in 1825, this journal kept, as Malcolm Freiberg puts it in his Introduction, by "that plump, keen-eyed, and sharp-tongued observer of colonial New England" has been a reliable mirror into the manners, characters, and topography of southern New England since she first set out from Boston to New York. Following what is now the roadbed of the former Pennsy/New Haven, now Amtrak, line, she leaves Boston in 1704, midway into her 39th year, heading for New Haven for vague family and business reasons and finally making it as far as New York. The book, which had been reprinted often, although the whereabouts of the original manuscript remains unknown, was initiated at the suggestion of Freiberg, then the beloved editor of publications at the Massachusetts Historical Society. He saw Kemble as "a female endowed with qualities enabling her not merely to compete easily but to survive nicely in a man's world." Enterprising, thrifty, and ultimately land rich, she died in New London in 1727 leaving an estate of more than £1,800. But it is this journal, personal, perky, and plucky, that presents her impressions of a pristine, emerging New England for which she will always be remembered. The book was set in Baskerville, but enlivened by five fine wood engravings by Michael McCurdy printed directly from the blocks in a second color.

Gerald Gottlieb: *Early Children's Books and Their Illustrations*
1975. 302 PP, 9 × 12″ $35.00 HC

In our early days we were very close to the beloved Charles Ryskamp, then the director of The Pierpont Morgan Library in New York. He had the vision and the funds to arrange exhibitions showcasing their extensive collections, and we had the pleasure of publishing many of them. But two stand out: Joseph Blumenthal's *Art of the Printed Book* (see Typography) and Gottlieb's. Gerry was then curator of early children's books at an institution that had (among other superlatives) "one of the most important and comprehensive collections of its kind in the world" of early children's books. His aim was "to suggest sources and influences that may have played a part in their long development." It was a very large playing field starting with a late-tenth-century *Aesop's Fables* from southern Italy and ending with the holograph manuscript of Munro Leaf's *The Story of Ferdinand* with the inspired drawings by Robert Lawson, and finally, the autograph manuscript, with original illustrations, of de Saint-Exupéry's *The Little Prince* – and pretty much anything of importance in between. Selling exhibition catalogues is always a challenge; people see them tied to a particular time and place, and they are usually a series of dry numbered entries with no connective tissue. This, however, was superbly designed and produced in color by The Stinehour Press and the prose descriptions really caught the spirit of all the 225 entries. In Ryskamp's words, "Not a history of children's literature, it is a selection of masterpieces or milestones from the past two thousand years of books and pictures that either were intended for children or ultimately became their special property." The title won the 1975 Carey-Thomas Award.

THE JOURNAL *of*
Madam Knight

Including an introductory note
by Malcolm Freiberg *and* wood
engravings *by* Michael McCurdy

DAVID R. GODINE · BOSTON · 1972

Early Children's Books

and Their Illustration

Engravings on Wood by *Rudolph Ruzicka*
With Text by *Walter Muir Whitehill*

LEFT, RIGHT: The jacket and title page from Whitehill's *Boston* displays the multi-color engravings on wood by Rudolph Ruzicka. This book brought together a constellation of stars, not only Whitehill for the text, Ruzicka for the illustrations and Harold Hugo for the printing but also P. J. Conkwright for the typographic layout and John Anderson of the Pickering Press for the title-page design. The image of Boston's State House was taken from the garden of the editor of *The Atlantic Monthly*, Ellery Sedgwick. Built in 1789, to the design of Charles Bulfinch, the gold was added in 1861. By the time of Ruzicka's 1931 engraving, it was, in Whitehill's enchanting metaphor "A bird with a red body, gold dome, white wings and a yellow tail."

BOSTON

Distinguished Buildings & Sites
Within the City and its Orbit
as Engraved on Wood by
RUDOLPH RUZICKA
With a Commentary by
WALTER MUIR WHITEHILL

...VID R. GODINE · PUBLISHER
Boston

RIGHT: This engraving shows the ancient homestead of the Quincy family, which first came to Boston in 1633.

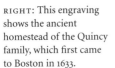

LEFT: A four-color engraving of the Old House, the stately mansion in Braintree (now Quincy) Massachusetts bought by John Adams in 1787 while he was still in London as Minister to the Court of St. James. Serving two terms as Washington's Vice President and one as President didn't allow him much time to use it, but from the end of his presidency until his death on July 4, 1826, he lived there continuously, the only one of four generations of Adams to live there year round. Today it and its contents are under the administration of the National Park Service and open to the public. Updike's choice of a Latin quotation from Ecclesiasticus was entirely apposite, "Let us now praise famous men."

Walter Muir Whitehill: *Boston*

1975. 133 PP, 5⅝ × 8⅝″ $12.50 HC

Walter was, in the latter years of his life, "Mr. Boston," presiding over the Boston Athenaeum with a grace and authority only equaled in my experience by Charles Ryskamp at the Morgan Library. Walter had been for decades the great connector of Boston society. Working from his office at 10½ Beacon Street, he introduced us to talent wherever he saw it – and that included printers, writers, historians, and artists. When I approached him to do a book with us, he immediately suggested collecting the twenty-nine color wood engravings Rudolph Ruzicka had created for D.B. Updike, who sent them from the Merrymount Press to his customers as Christmas cards from 1911 to 1941, and for which the Athenaeum held the progressives.

He would write brief essays of almost exactly 750 words (and when it came to Boston history and topography, there could not have been a better candidate) and we would print them *en face* with the engravings. These had been printed in flat colors, in some cases as many as six, by Updike, each with their appropriate Latin inscriptions. The issue was how to reproduce them. This was solved, I'm sure with no little effort, by Harold Hugo at the Meriden Gravure Company, who was able to figure out an imposition scheme that allowed us to print them in flat colors as well, and on a very inviting Warren's Olde Style Laid special making of paper. Meriden in those days had only single-color presses, and some of these engravings entailed as many as six separate runs. It was a labor of love for all involved. The binding was full cloth with a color plate of Bulfinch's State House set within a debossed panel. In his essay on Admiral Morison, Whitehill observes, "Readable history is only written by men who have some strong personal enthusiasm for their subjects." His enthusiasm for Boston, its history, its architecture, and its personalities is on full display in this, among our most satisfying, close to perfect books.

Steve Dunwell: *The Run of the Mill:
A Pictorial Narrative of the Expansion,
Dominion, Decline and Enduring Impact of
the New England Textile Industry*
1978. 312 PP, 8¾ × 11″ $25.00 HC

Like many of our best books, this was not the work of a
professional writer, but rather a talented, energetic, young,
local amateur photographer who had become intrigued
by the rise and fall of the New England textile industry. He
had, throughout the 1970s, visited the last surviving mills,
capturing on film the faces, machinery, and buildings that
had made fortunes for New Englanders, had supplied the
Union troops with uniforms and blankets, and which were
now on the brink of extinction. But Dunwell's text, beginning with the earliest harnessing of waterpower in Rhode
Island by Samuel Slater in the 1790s and climaxing with
the rise of the giant industrial complexes in Lowell and
Lawrence, was written simply, declaratively, and eloquently. The facts he amassed, organized, and marshaled for his
story themselves made for a dramatic narrative. He was a
rare combination – a gifted writer and a talented photographer. His last paragraph gives some idea of the power of
his prose: "The Industrial Revolution haunts New England.

The carcass of its greatness, its parts, is picked clean to the
skeleton, yet still shows the last isolated twitches of life. It
is no surprise that the creature died; it was too big and too
old to adapt. The surprise is that so much of its legacy can
still be seen." The final signatures of the book contain his
photographs of those skeletal remains, and in the faces of
the factory workers you can still detect the sense of pride
that went into their work.

Designed by Robert Dothard, set in Dwiggins's Electra
and containing scores of engravings and original drawings,
this was history come alive. And these were the days before
a computer could accommodate text and image, so the text
and captions were set first in hot metal, the artwork photographed and reduced to size, and the whole assembled with
scissors, a T-square, and rubber cement on matte board,
to be shot and printed at nearby Halliday Lithograph. To
our amazement, the *New York Times Book Review* gave it a
front-page notice (those were the days) and the print run
of 4,000 copies was sold out in six months.

BELOW: The title-page spread of Dunwell's comprehensive examination of
the rise and fall of New England's mill towns, this showing a bird's eye view
of Putnam, Connecticut bisected by the flow of the Quinebaug River, the
water-powered factories it spawned along its bank, and the industry and
prosperity water power provided for every New England state. The flow of
water-created fortunes, especially in textile manufacturing, as quickly in the
nineteenth century as the industries disappeared in the twentieth.

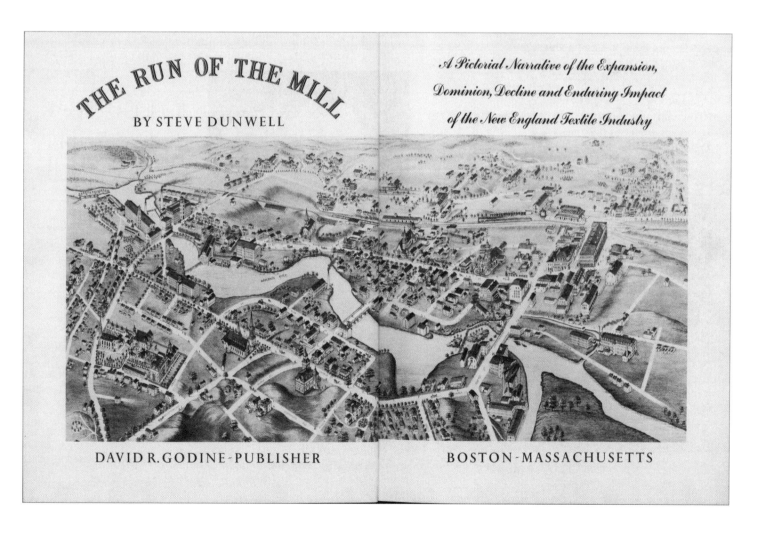

Noel Perrin: *Giving Up the Gun: Japan's Reversion to the Sword, 1543–1879*

1979. 134 PP, 6 × 8" $9.00 HC

The bulk of this fascinating narrative, without the illustrations, first appeared in the *New Yorker* in 1965. It presented a case study that still stands as a deliberate debunking of that old saw, "You can't turn back the clock." For that is exactly what Japan did between 1543 and 1879; it effectively outlawed the use or manufacture of firearms of any kind and in the process isolated itself from the rest of the world until finally opened to Western culture in 1853 by Commodore Perry. Before 1543, the gun culture was fully developed in Japan; they had guns that were every bit as technologically advanced – and just as deadly – as those in the West. It was simply that the idea of an anonymous gunman being able to kill an enemy from a distance a few hundred feet, with no human contact, was contrary to the samurai culture, and, for once, culture trumped technology. In retelling this, Perrin produced an altogether fascinating book, spellbinding not only because he was a reliably good storyteller who could make even the footnotes fascinating, but also because he took on our commitment to "progress" as a major tenet of the modern world and dismembered it. Here was a civilization that did indeed "turn back the clock" and a story that really has few, if any, parallels in modern history.

Julius Caesar: *The Battle for Gaul*
Translated by Anne and Peter Wiseman
Illustrations selected by Barry Cunliffe
1980. 208 PP, 6¼ × 9⅜" $16.00 HC

Every decade or so, someone will invariably come forward with a new translation of Caesar's commentaries on his decade-long campaign, not only against the Gauls, but pretty much all of Europe. Told with the directness and uncluttered factual style of a ruthless military commander, he recounts his crossing the Rhine to wage punitive excursions into Germany, his two invasions of Britain, the annihilation of two legions lured into an ambush and the heroic last stand of Vercingetorix. Part history, part propaganda to insure his continued support back in Rome, and part unwitting self-portrait, the unvarnished prose reveals the mind of a clever and relentless military strategist. What makes the Wiseman edition special, and why it was adopted as a Main Selection of the History Book Club, is first that the text is translated into the first person, giving it a vivid and personal immediacy, and second that Barry Cunliffe, a professor of archaeology at Oxford, provided illustrations to the text, along with the captions. The maps and drawings, the color plates of the jewelry and statuary, the diagrams of the fortifications and campaign maneuvers, make the text and the tactics come alive. You feel as though you are fighting alongside Caesar, watching history as it unfolds. And, like Caesar, you invariably triumph.

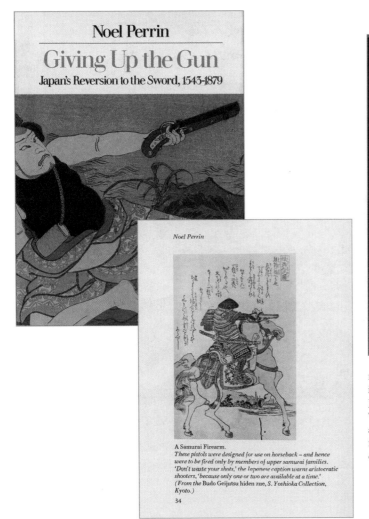

A Samurai Firearm.
These pistols were designed for use on horseback – and hence were to be fired only by members of upper samurai families. 'Don't waste your shots,' the Japanese caption warns aristocratic shooters, 'because only one or two are available at a time.' (From the Budo Geijutsu hiden zue, S. Yoshioka Collection, Kyoto.)
34

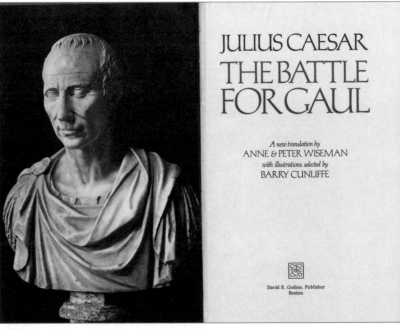

LEFT: In addition to his convincing text, Perrin was assiduous in finding illustrations, generally woodcuts in manuals, that confirmed his case that the Japanese were well acquainted with firearms. His caption for this one reads, "*Shooting While You Retreat.*" This print shows a special technique for shooting at enemies behind you. "Lean well to the left," the caption says. "Take your right foot out of the stirrups and prop it on top. Now turn your head and aim back over the horse's rump."

Iris Origo: *The Merchant of Prato*
Introduction by Barbara Tuchman
1986. 456 PP, 6 × 9″ $19.00 HC

In her introduction, Barbara Tuchman asks "Why is *The Merchant of Prato* one of the great works of historical writing of the twentieth century?" She answers, "Iris Origo's success in resurrecting not only a personality (the fourteenth-century merchant Francesco di Marco Datini), whom we can recognize, but also his times, his town, his marriage, his household, his country home, his friends and associates, and his business dealings, makes a work of extraordinary interest with that quality to grip and take hold of a reader that makes a book everlasting." This was yet another of Origo's excursions into biography, with her other great excavation being the life of Giacomo Leopardi. But here she brings us back to fourteenth-century Florence, to a wool merchant who left intact a mass of letters, documents and business data that only a master with Origo's grasp of history, language, and business could untangle. Tuchman quotes the British critic Arthur Marwick's observation that "History is a finished product, not raw material." And she goes on to add that "What Iris Origo has done with superb skill is to present a finished product fashioned entirely from authentic raw material of real life, taken from the remarkable archive that was Datini's gift to posterity." In this book, a wonder of primary research, she reveals not only one of the great success stories of the Middle Ages but also the very energy of the age.

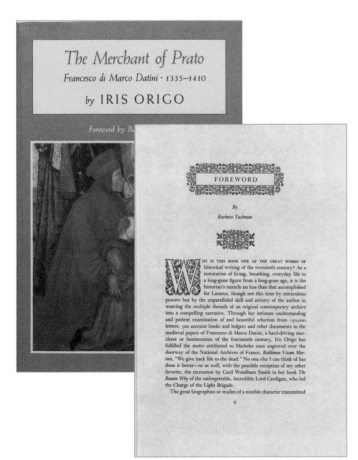

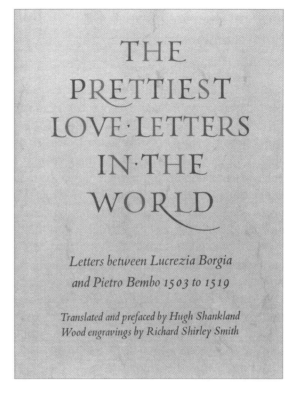

The Prettiest Love Letters in the World: Letters between Lucrezia Borgia and Pietro Bembo 1503–1509
Translation and Preface by Hugh Shankland
Illustrated by Richard Shirley Smith
1987. 112 PP, 7 × 10″ $25.00 HC

We brought this title in and issued it in offset from the letterpress edition printed by the Libanus Press in England and containing wood engravings by Richard Shirley Smith, among the most talented of a great generation of British engravers. The title was conferred by Lord Byron on a stash of late fifteenth-century letters between a high-born Venetian scholar with poetic ambitions and the young political bride whose father, the Pope, wielded absolute power. There is a constant, nervous tension between the explosive flames of young romance and the constant danger of having them quelled, likely ruthlessly, if discovered and exposed. The text was admirably translated by Hugh Shankland, who manages to explain the subtleties contained in the metaphors and abstruse allusions that were conventionally contained in Renaissance letters and literature. The translations are set in Arrighi italic, while the originals are transcribed in Roman, set in (what else?) Bembo, among the finest of the Old Style Venetian faces cut at Monotype under Stanley Morison. The wood engravings by Shirley Smith are sometimes purely decorative but often provide a real clue to the tensions residing in the lovers' texts, as well as current social and political events, including Lucrezia's grief at the demise of her father, Alexander VI, after his reign of eleven years.

Walt Whitman: *The Sacrificial Years*
Edited by John Harmon McElroy
1999. 192 PP, 6 × 9″ $30.00 HC

In December 1862, at the height of the Civil War, the poet and newspaperman Walt Whitman traveled to a Virginia base camp in search of his wounded brother. The unattended misery he saw there–rows and rows of unburied corpses, piles of amputated limbs, wounded men lying on the frozen ground–moved him, as he would write, to "a profound conviction of necessity" that he do *something* to help relieve it. He was the only one of the literati of his generation to actually actively participate in that national tragedy, to personally attempt to allay the suffering the war would impose on both sides. He would spend the next four years working at the military hospitals of Washington, D.C. at considerable risk, tending the sick and wounded until well past the war's end. He recorded some of this in *Specimen Days*, which we had published in 1971, and although he never kept a formal diary, the hundreds of letters he sent, the articles he wrote, and other "memoranda" were collected and chronologically arranged here by John McElroy, a professor at the University of Arizona. By arranging the material sequentially–including extracts from his previously unpublished Civil War notebook–he reconstructs a continuous narrative of month-to-month experiences expressed in Whitman's own words. Poignant and powerful, capturing the full extent and horror of that immense and unending conflict, these are essential documents of those crucial years. Along with the 300 entries are over 50 duotone photographs of the places, people, and events so vividly captured in Whitman's prose.

V. S. Pritchett: *London Perceived*
Photographs by Evelyn Hofer
2000. 256 PP, 6½ × 8½″ $20.00 SC

Originally published in a larger format by Harcourt, Brace in 1962, this has always been among my favorites. To visit London and not read it is to miss a singularly human and lucid take on the city, accompanied by sensitive and evocative photographs of monuments and scenes, many still visible today. London of the mind, heart, and eye is displayed and dissected in this classic collaboration that provides a panorama of the city's history, art, literature, and daily life. Here is the city so many love and know well, a paradox of grandeur and grime, bustling markets surrounded by tranquil parks, a mixture of ancient and modern palaces, pubs, docks, and railway depots. As Pritchett observes, "If Paris suggests intelligence, if Rome suggests the world, if New York suggests activity, the word for London is experience. This points to the awful fact that London has been the most powerful and richest capital of the largest world empire since the Roman and, even now, is the focal point of a vague Commonwealth. It is the capital source of a language now dominant in the world. Great Britain invented the language. London printed it and made it presentable." Great Londoners stalk the pages–Wren, Pepys, Defoe, Hogarth, Dickens, and, of course, that consummate Londoner, Samuel Johnson, who commented, "No, Sir, when a man is tired of London, he is tired of life; for there is in London all that life can afford." Our sewn paperback of the original 1962 edition contains duotone reproductions of all Hofer's evocative photographs, offering a loving tribute to a great city, a combination of text and image, writer and artist, that has rarely been equaled.

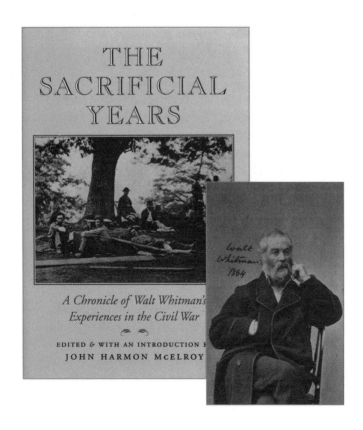

Belinda Rathbone: *The Boston Raphael*
2014. 338 PP, 6 × 9″ $30.00 HC

Belinda's father, Perry Rathbone, was the Director of Boston's Museum of Fine Arts from 1955 to 1972. A product of the little nursery conducted by Paul Sachs at Harvard's Fogg Art Museum, a course in connoisseurship and museum management that produced an entire generation of museum directors, he was both ambitious and charming. In 1970, the Museum was to celebrate its 100th anniversary – the same year as the Metropolitan. The latter had captured the media's attention with Rembrandt's *Aristotle Contemplating a Bust of Homer*, and Rathbone was determined to do them one better. So he bought what he (and others) considered a genuine Raphael in Italy and unwisely brought it through Boston customs without declaring it. The Italian government got wind of this and set a bulldog on the case. The story gradually and unhappily unfolds with Rathbone unceremoniously dismissed by a craven and alarmed Board and the painting returned to the Italian government (among the earliest examples of repatriated art) only to be deemed a fake and consigned to the basement of the Uffizi Gallery. Rathbone recounts the events with unfailing objectivity combined with unavoidable sympathy. She doesn't have to fabricate anything; the story is riveting enough, from the battles with the Board, the efforts to justify the painting's illegal entry, the social and political challenges of running what was, in essence, a private and privately funded institution. The personal drama provides the scaffolding, but this is more than just about her father. In a larger sense, it is about the changes that every public Boston institution experienced in the sixties and seventies, the slow but inexorable transition from what were essentially closed and insular Brahmin strongholds into organizations overseen by, and capable of serving, a broad and diverse public.

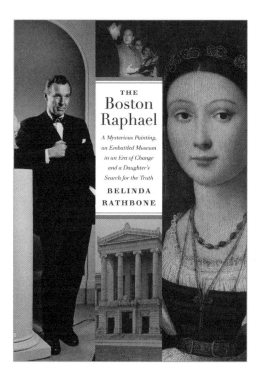

Thomas E. Bator *&* Heidi A. Seely: *The Boston Trustee*
2015. 176 PP, 5 × 8½″ $30.00 HC

When approached by Tim Knowlton, our old friend and the principal at the venerable Curtis Brown agency, about the likelihood of our doing a book on what seemed to me a hopelessly narrow subject, I was dubious. But the more I learned, most especially that the "Boston Trustee," as he or she is collectively known, had $32 *billion* in assets under their control and were an institution unique to the Commonwealth, the more my interest grew. This was, for many of us growing up in Boston, not fanciful history but a quotidian reality. For the first thirty years, the press had been built and kept alive by a combination of family trusts and unaccountably sympathetic trustees, and like most beneficiaries I knew less than nothing about how they operated or how their tradition had evolved. Bator and Seely fill in the gaps handsomely and with no little drama, for this was the device whereby the enormous fortunes that nineteenth-century Bostonians accumulated, and more specifically how a closely knit and interconnected cultural elite passed on their wealth from one generation to another, predictably, legally, safely, and prudently. Here we see the court decisions, the social and political forces, and the growing necessity of a separate institution specifically created to meet a real need. It lived up to its subtitle, meticulously and compellingly presenting *The Lives, Laws & Legacy of a Vital Institution*. It touched home and remains a book from which much can be learned.

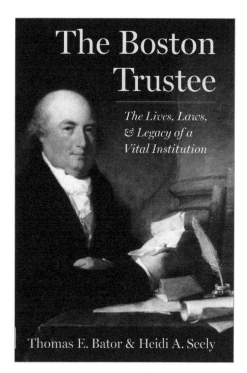

ABOVE: A Gilbert Stuart portrait of John McLean, whose trust, contained in his will, and the law case arising from its interpretation, "gave us the standards by which all trust investments are measured."

Daphne Geismar: *Invisible Years: A Family's Collected Account of Separation and Survival during the Holocaust in the Netherlands*

2020. 248 PP, 8¼ × 11¾″ $40.00 HC

In 2018 Daphne Geismar gave a talk at Boston's Society of Printers about a book she was engaged in writing, an effort that had occupied her for over a decade. It was an attempt to provide an account of nine members from three related families, all of them part of her own, who suffered through, or perished in, the Nazi occupation of the Netherlands. I had never heard of Daphne Geismar, had no notion of her distinguished career as a book designer and, like much of the audience, was hardly prepared for the harrowing tale she had to tell. I think everyone left the room that evening in a state of shock. I called her agent the

next week and after a series of cordial delays, we acquired the book.

In 1940, when the German Wehrmacht invaded the Netherlands unopposed, the Jewish population was about 2% of the country, mostly fully assimilated and largely apolitical. Within months, the noose began to tighten. Jewish businesses began to close, their owners stripped of their titles and assets or replaced by Christian executives. Everything from having a job to riding bikes was forbidden. School children were called out and forced to wear stars, trains left the central station regularly, bound East to unknown destinations and, as it turned out, to almost certain death. Geismar's family, seeing what was happening, realizing that to submit to deportation was a death sentence, went into hiding. Along with thousands of other Jews, they were sheltered and hidden by their countrymen, shuttled from one hiding place to another, always sepa-

Invisible Years A Family's Collected Account of Separation and Survival during the Holocaust in the Netherlands **Daphne Geismar**

LEFT TO RIGHT: The printed cover, sample spread, endpapers and an opening from Daphne Geismar's harrowing and memorable *Invisible Years*

rated so that none knew the whereabouts of the others. Parents and their children were torn apart, often out of touch for months, sometimes years. The history of Dutch resistance is not comforting. Despite no history of anti-Semitism, its Jewish population well integrated in both businesses and the government, the Jewish mortality rate was twice that of neighboring Belgium and three times that of France, which by comparison has a long history of anti-Semitism. The Dutch Reform Church was helpful and supportive, hiding many Jews, including Daphne's grandparents, in the attic of a church. But seventy percent of its Jewish population perished in the camps; fewer than 50,000 out of 155,000 Dutch Jews survived, of these roughly 15,000 who had been in hiding. Next door, almost all Danish Jews were saved.

Through some miracle, the evidence and the memo-ries of the Geismar family during these fateful years were preserved – in letters, in diaries, in small mementoes that told larger stories. Combing through the scattered archive, through interviews and dogged research, Daphne was able to reconstruct the story of the nine family members – her parents, her grandparents, her aunts and uncles – recording and reconstructing their stories in their own words. Using a trove of photographs and artifacts, she brings her family's stories back from the dead. In Daphne's hands, they come to life as part of the human fabric, part of *our* fabric; she sheds a new light on the brutality of the Holocaust and the experience of those who suffered and survived it. She challenges us to follow the threads of their fates, hopeful that their stories, in resisting and ultimately outlasting inhumanity, will somehow become ours. In every way and on every level, one of our great books.

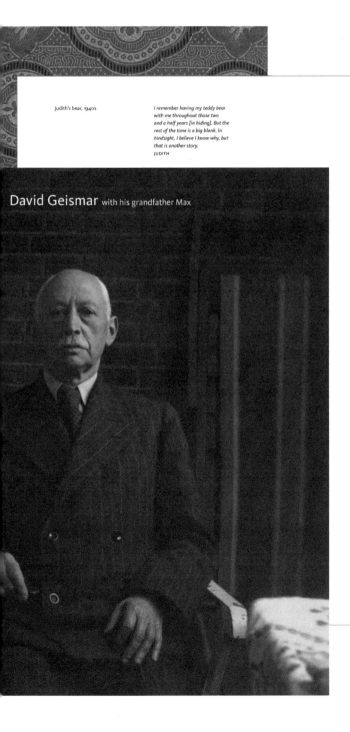

Judith's bear, 1940s

I remember having my teddy bear with me throughout those two and a half years [in hiding]. But the rest of the time is a big blank. In hindsight, I believe I know why, but that is another story.
JUDITH

David Geismar with his grandfather Max

LEFT, BELOW: Two spreads from Chris Loker's *Shimmer*, a book that convincingly confronts and defines what is meant by a "children's picture book" and then proceeds to select a hundred convincing examples, some well known and beloved, like Ludwig Bemelmans's *Madeline*, and others refreshingly and unjustly uncelebrated, like Joseph Low's *Mother Goose Riddle Rhymes*. Far more than a picture book, Loker defends her choices with eclectic data, facts and invariably good taste. You are guaranteed to enjoy the pictures, but the text is a revelation.

Chris Loker: *A Shimmer of Joy: One Hundred Children's Picture Books*

2020. 256 PP, 8½ × 11" $35.00 HC

This book has a focus that is concisely expressed by the author in her first paragraph: "A picture book is composed of words, pictures and the dramatically paced rhythm of pages turning together in a reader's hand. When these elements come together with creative mastery, a surge of mind or heart can occur, as with any form of fine art. At its most inspirational, a picture book can provide a transporting reading experience – punctuated by shimmering moments of joy." I suspect the enthusiasm of Ms. Loker for her subject is more than evident in this proclamation, but her book backs up and confirms that enthusiasm with a hundred stellar examples of the art she celebrates. Yes, there are old chestnuts, ones we all know and read (or have had read to us) as children: Potter's *Peter Rabbit*, de Brunhoff's *Babar*, Wise Brown's *Goodnight Moon*, McCloskey's *Make Way for Ducklings*, Sendak's *Where the Wild Things Are*. But there are many among the hundred that will come

as (hopefully welcome) surprises. Who still remembers Elizabeth Morrow's *The Painted Pig* or Taro Yashima's *Umbrella* or Esphyr Slobodkina's *Caps for Sale*?

Each title is illustrated with at least two images, often of the cover, always of an interior page, and in full and faithful color. But the real treasure is in the text, for in the extended and detailed back stories of authors, artists, and even publishers, agents and awards, Loker provides the real drama, the stories hiding untold behind the great stories. There is information here that no one who ever loved, collected, stayed awake at night to listen to, or searched the internet for a copy of these books should miss. No one can say any "selection" is definitive. And people will always quibble with choices; one reader's primrose is another's poison ivy. But this title comes as close to defining an art form, explaining its mission and selecting its very best examples published over the past 115 years, as any book can. Great tribute is due to the author and the book's designer, Jerry Kelly, for their patience and good humor over what was a nearly three-year journey, and one with plenty of bumps along the way.

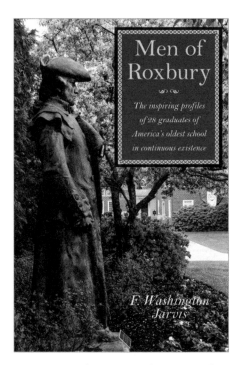

ABOVE: Dr. Joseph Warren, Revolutionary War hero, sternly greets students entering the quadrangle of the Roxbury Latin School, founded in 1740, the oldest school in continuous operation in North America.

F. Washington Jarvis: *Men of Roxbury*

2020. 480 PP, 6 × 9″ $35.00 HC

Founded in 1645 by John Eliot, called by some the "Apostle to the Indians," the Roxbury Latin School is the oldest secondary school in continuous operation in North America. I entered it in the sixth form and stayed there for six years, graduating in 1962. Our class began with forty-six students and graduated twenty-three, a drop-out rate of precisely 50%. It was, when founded, a preparatory school for Harvard College (back then also a tiny institution with a student body of under fifty, and for which a reading fluency in Latin and Greek were primary entry requirements). Of my twenty-three classmates, nine attended Harvard. There were few electives. Six years of compulsory Latin and three of Greek. The tuition in my day was next to free and the academic standards high, but it was a dying institution. There was no college counselling, no help if you were failing, no real empathy for any emotional issues that might arise, and little sympathy for failure. If you survived, your future was assured, but the attrition rate was appalling and wasteful. Tony Jarvis was brought in as the headmaster in 1974 and served for thirty years. It is no understatement to say he saved the school, making it a place where boys were genuinely loved, where they were expected to participate in everything from field sports to the glee club, and where the school motto, *Mortui Vivos Docent* ("The Dead Teach the Living"), was taken seriously. Among the few schools with a royal charter from George III, it was certainly the *only* school, under Tony's Anglophilic reign, where a full-length

cut-out of Queen Elizabeth II greeted you on entry and the Union Jack flew side by side with the stars and stripes.

You might expect a book like this, exploring as it does the life history of twenty-eight of the school's most distinguished graduates (all deceased) to be nothing better than an assembly of soporific panegyrics. It is nothing of the sort. In Tony's hands, these men come alive on the page, as does history. You are there in Boston on the eve of the Revolution with Dr. Joseph Warren as he stokes the radical fires with Sam Adams and goads Boston to make a clean break with England. And you are there with him on Bunker Hill, the first hero to die in the cause of liberty. You are with Admiral Clifton Sprague, and his motley task force, Taffy 3, as he outsmarts and outmaneuvers Admiral Kurita's immeasurably greater force at the Battle of Leyte Gulf, an encounter that Wilfred Deac would call "the greatest sea fight in history…" You are there with the Shakespeare scholar, George Lyman Kittredge at Harvard; with Arthur Vining Davis as he perfects, and revolutionizes the production of aluminum; with Frederick Law Olmsted, Jr. as he single-handedly radically redefines the professions of landscape architecture and city planning; with Paul Dudley White who invents the discipline of cardiology and writes the pioneering textbook defining heart disease; with James Conant, the frosty and distant scientist who led Harvard into a new era of relevance while advocating the abolition of small independent private and public schools; and finally, and perhaps most endearingly, with Albert H. Gordon, the legendary founder of Kidder Peabody, a staunch Republican who made it a point to walk from every major airport into its attendant city; an athlete who, at 81, ran the London Marathon; a philanthropist who bought for Tony's "one true school" the best surviving copy of the founder's Eliot Bible for $330,000; and who was, in his 69 years as a trustee, a stubborn supporter of Tony's ambitions. I recite all this (conveniently ignoring the equally gripping lives of twenty other graduates) because the school did instill a sense of purpose in me and others – the salient take-away being "From those to whom much is given, much is to be expected." RLS disciplined my scatter-brained approach to life and learning, providing a loose but practical framework – for study, for time management, for assessing priorities, and, probably most importantly, for recognizing talent and excellence. It gave students confidence in their own ability to think through problems and come up with solutions. It made it safe to say something was "good" or "bad" without hovering squeamishly in some middle ground. And it made it emphatically clear that, as Blake observed, "Execution is the chariot of genius." It doesn't matter very much what or how much you know; what matters is what you do with it. Tony died after a prolonged battle with cancer in October of 2018. When historians look back in fifty years for the men who made the most difference to John Eliot's "little nursery," Tony Jarvis, its Moses, will head the list.

Thomas W. Gilbert: *How Baseball Happened:
Outrageous Lies Exposed!
The True Story Revealed*
Introduction by John Thorn
2020. 384 PP, 6 × 9″ $28.00 HC

The origins of baseball are as shrouded in myth—and untruth—as the founding of our nation. Once a folk game native to the island of Manhattan, it offered camaraderie, exercise and fresh air in a time when American city dwellers were notorious for their dreary pursuit of the almighty dollar and their indifference to physical fitness. For reasons that lie well outside the playing field, pre-Civil War New Yorkers launched a national movement to transform their casual game into a tool for unifying and improving a disjointed nation. It was a wholly amateur effort; the early baseball pioneers were unpaid, part-time athletes with rich lives outside of sports and no interest in exploiting the game to make money. They practiced law and medicine, built railroad and telegraph systems, published newspapers and fought the Civil War. The baseball movement succeeded spectacularly. In fifteen short years, it spread the game from coast to coast, blazing paths that other American sports have followed. Two of its key victories were accidental—fans and professionalism. When baseball reached the open fields of the then-independent city of Brooklyn, it sparked the sport's first and most enduring rivalry.

Baseball as a spectator sport caught the popular imagination and fandom was born. An 1858 all-star game between New York and Brooklyn drew an unheard-of crowd of ca. 10,000 and was the first game any Americans had ever paid to see. The Civil War spread the sport by mixing New Yorkers with men from Massachusetts, Ohio and Illinois; soldiers played in campgrounds and in southern prison camps. In the late 1860s a war-weary country embraced the sport as entertainment and the top players and clubs became valuable commodities. The first professional league debuted in 1871. But why are baseball's own origin stories so demonstrably false? How and why did baseball really happen? In a masterpiece of research, Gilbert unearths the true, largely untold story of baseball's origins —who played it, exactly how it spread, and its connections to larger social and cultural trends. He fills in longstanding gaps in our understanding of race, class, and sex in early baseball. The Amateur Era is little-remembered today, but the sport of baseball did not begin with professionalism any more than with Abner Doubleday in Cooperstown or Alexander Cartwright in Hoboken. This is the backstory, in full and enhanced with vintage photographs, of how baseball's amazing amateurs created the first American sport. It is, in the words of John Thorn, Major League Baseball's official historian, "a brilliant new approach to our game, and its author tells a hundred stories you have never heard before."

An 1865 portrayal of baseball as a house divided between New York and Brooklyn. The principal clubs are divided into two categories: Brooklyn (banner on right) and New York City et al. (banner on left). The small full figures along the top and bottom are key members of each of the prominent clubs. The playing field at center is Brooklyn's Union Grounds, the first ballpark. The larger busts on either side are journalist Henry Chadwick and Thomas G. Voorhis, president of the National Association of Base Ball Players. Above and framed in black crepe is the martyred James Creighton, baseball's first national star, who had died three years earlier.

CHAPTER SIX
A Ballplayer's Tale

J AMES CREIGHTON's baseball career was like a nuclear explosion. It didn't last long, but afterward the world was never the same. Pre-Creighton baseball was a hitter's dream. Early baseball rules required pitchers to deliver the ball deadunderhand with no wrist snap. The result was pitches that were slow, straight and easy to hit; pitchers tossed the ball over the plate and ducked. In the 1850s scores in double figures were the norm. Around 1860 Creighton figured out a legal or apparently legal way to throw very hard with movement and command. Widely imitated, his maximum-effort fast pitching changed the game more than a hundred Babe Ruths. The Babe may have hit a lot of home runs, but he did not invent the home run and he did not change the basic structure of the game. Creighton's new style of pitching so upset the balance of power between offense and defense that it led to the creation of the strike zone, which has been the center of the action of a baseball game ever since. Before the strike zone, baseball games were decided by which defense did a better job of controlling balls put in play; ever since, they have been decided by who wins control of the imaginary box hovering over home plate. This is the single biggest

[183

ABOVE: A spread that shows a poster illustrating the split between the teams that grew and prospered in patrician New York and those hailing from a grittier Brooklyn. The small figures at the bottom display the key players from the various clubs as well as the first ballpark, Brooklyn's Union Grounds. The black draped figure at the top center is a bust of the martyred pitcher James Creighton whose prowess on the mound led to the creation of the strike zone. The first national star of the game, still unacknowledged in the Baseball Hall of Fame, he had died three years earlier in 1862 of a "strangulation of (the) intestine."

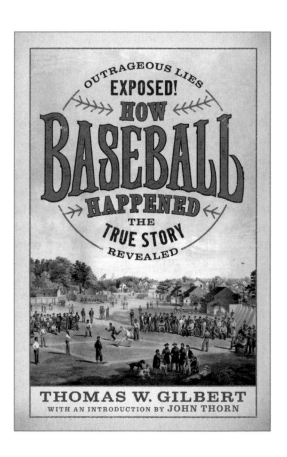

OPPOSITE: Everything that needs to be said about the poverty, pride, resilience and physical beauty of Vermont's Northeast Kingdom is contained in this haunting photograph from Richard Brown's *The Last of the Hill Farms.*

BELOW: This portrait of Alfred, Lord Tennyson, which she called "The Dirty Monk," was among the artist's favorites.

Julia Margaret Cameron: *Victorian Photographs of Famous Men & Fair Women*
Preface and Notes by Tristram Powell
Introductions by Roger Fry and Virginia Woolf
1973. 128 PP, 10¼ × 12¾″ $22.50 HC

Originally published in 1926 by Leonard and Virginia Woolf at their Hogarth Press and rightfully considered a landmark in the canon of photographic books, it seemed inconceivable to me that this title was no longer available. So, in 1972, I wrote the formidable Norah Smallwood of the Hogarth Press asking if they would consider a reprint. She saw the potential immediately and engaged Tristram Powell, a documentary film director and devotee of Cameron, to write a new preface and notes to the various personalities Cameron had captured (visually, literally, and in real time) at her studio on the Isle of Wight. The result was a reasonable facsimile of the first edition with new notes on the plates by Powell and including an additional twenty-three new studies and commentary that reflected the current scholarship. Many luminaries of British literature and science are, of course, included: Longfellow, Tennyson, Browning, and Carlisle, as well as Herschel, Darwin, and Hooker. Cameron is often considered something of a "talented amateur" who more or less stumbled into photography and by dint of charm and perseverance

managed to corral the Victorian greats into her studio and hold them captive. I don't buy this; she was a cultured and sophisticated student of art, history, literature, and science. At 48, she may have come to photography late – she was given a camera by her daughter with the note "It may amuse you, Mother, to try to photograph during your solitude at Freshwater," and although technically challenged by the process, the soft focus of the images, the dress, the close-ups of the faces, were all original. She produced 900 plates in her twelve-year career there, and although her portraits of male sitters may border on idol worship, she took them seriously, seeing it as her "duty towards them in recording faithfully the greatness of the inner as well as the features of the outer man."

The first paragraph of Roger Fry's original Introduction bears repeating, although many of these questions (judging by the prices Cameron portraits now command and the literature available) have been answered. He wrote: "The position of photography is uncertain and uncomfortable. No one denies its immense services of all kinds, but its status as an independent art has always been disputed. It has never managed to get its Muse or any proper representation on Parnassus, and yet will not give up its pretensions altogether. Mrs. Cameron's photographs posed the question long ago, before it was shelved. The present publication affords perhaps a favourable opportunity to reopen the discussion." It was among our very first books on photography as an art – one intended to "reopen the discussion." Our reissue of this brave effort of the Woolfs', released only three years after our founding, threw our hat early into that ring and made its mark.

Arnold Newman: *One Mind's Eye: The Portraits and Other Photographs of Arnold Newman*
Foreword by Beaumont Newhall
Introduction by Robert Sobieszek
1974. 224 PP, 11 × 9″ $27.50 HC

I cannot recall whether Newman approached us for this collection or we him. But it was the first serious photography book we attempted entirely on our own, and I think the collaboration between Newman, the artist, and Lance Hidy, the designer (and no mean artist himself), resulted in what was a groundbreaking book. Like *Specimen Days*, it represented a real risk, for to afford the duotone printing and the full-cloth binding, while keeping the list price affordable, we had to print a minimum of 5,000 copies. We were fortuitously joined in this by Tom Rosenthal of Secker and Warburg, who took an additional 3,000 copies for the UK. Although many of the images presented in the pages have become iconic – Stravinsky hunkered under the eighth note of his piano lid, Henry Luce in the boardroom of *Time-Life*, Ben Shahn grasping a clarinet before his easel, Dr. James Watson in front of his formula-filled chalkboard at Harvard, Robert Moses posed on a girder with the Manhattan skyline in the background – this was Newman's first major book. His work at the time was not all that well known in the US or beyond.

Although we had issued a few photographic books before this, Newman's *One Mind's Eye* was, and remains, among our singular contributions to the field. Newman was superficially ebullient, but, like most professionals, a thorough perfectionist. He knew little about fine printing, but he had a very clear idea of how the book should fit together and how the images should look on the page. Lance, the perfect collaborator, spent days in Newman's New York studio figuring out which images to include, and how to size and sequence them. There are many aspects

to the design that are worth comment – the reproduction of the shots of Newman on location and annotated test sheets (the sample of Igor Stravinsky's shows 12 of the 26 exposures Arnold made during the sitting) in the Sobieszek Introduction, the carefully letterspaced Optima of the title page, the thoroughly "modern" appearance of the two-column unjustified text, the careful and deliberate sequencing and juxtapositions of the 192 images. But it is really the quality of Newman's skill as a portraitist that shines through most distinctly, and like all great portraitists from Penn to Beaton, from McBean to Karsh, he developed his own signature style of "environmental portraiture" – posing his subjects in their particular and personal settings with backgrounds that define their professions – that is unmistakable.

ABOVE LEFT: The jacket, with the type set in carefully letterspaced Optima and portraits showing the interesting personal relationship between Georgia O'Keeffe and Alfred Stieglitz (1942), David Ben-Gurion seated before the Israeli Declaration of Statehood (1967), and thoughtful Pablo Picasso in France (1954)
ABOVE: O'Keeffe, again, before her easel at Ghost Ranch, New Mexico, in 1968
LEFT: A test sheet of 13 shots of Igor Stravinsky in New York interacting with the lid of his grand piano, one of 26 exposures

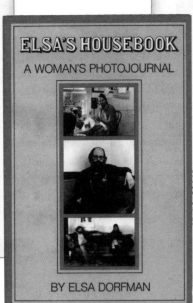

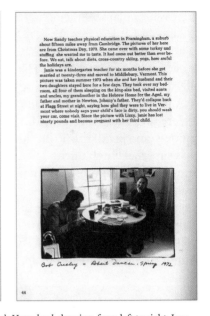

RIGHT: Lance Hidy, the book's designer, had learned that Kodak had conducted research showing that orange and yellow were the most effective colors for marketing purposes, so that explains the cover.

ABOVE & LEFT: Pages from *Elsa's Housebook* showing, from left to right, Lawrence Ferlinghetti, poet and the *primum mobile* of San Francisco's renowned City Lights Bookstore standing with Gordon Cairnie, the proprietor of Harvard Square's equally famous Grolier Book Shop, Ferlinghetti in one of Elsa's chairs, and Robert Creeley and Robert Duncan with their coffee in her kitchen. The cover stacks from top to bottom: Robert Creeley, Allen Ginsberg and, on the couch, David and Patricia O'Connell.

Elsa Dorfman: *Elsa's Housebook: A Woman's Photojournal*
1974. 80 PP, 6 × 9″ $6.00 SC

"My camera shapes my life and the way I approach it. It makes the occasion, Let's take a picture I say. We sit on a couch. I get out the tripod. Of course we pose. The camera reinforces our high." This, of course, was the opposite of our usual approach, or that of our photographers, which tended to be formal, technically precise, and carefully planned. Elsa, who had spent some time in New York working at the Grove Press, was the opposite–easy-going, hospitable, a confirmed habitué of Cambridge who welcomed visitors (for whatever reason and at all hours) to her home and loved talking. Her book is sort of an informal visual gallery of the Beat generation, a record of the familiar faces of contemporary American letters (mostly avant-garde) as they posed on her couch, stayed in her spare bedrooms, and ricocheted around her small house in Cambridge. Unposed and at ease, we see Allen Ginsberg, Peter Orlovsky, and Gregory Corso lounging on her couch, Robert Creeley and Robert Duncan relaxing over coffee, Robert Bly and Lawrence Ferlinghetti ("He was very serious, proud of his work, and very polite. Soothing almost.") at work on their manuscripts, and a very young Andrew Wiley looking like a pre-Raphaelite cherub with a beret. The camera gave Elsa a role and a rationale, and she exploited it brilliantly, if somewhat eccentrically. My fondest memories are of her selling her prints from a pushcart in Harvard Square at Christmas for $15.00 each. But, as Elsa points out here, "Portrait photographs aren't the whole

person, the real person. They are only one mini second, an instant that has an authority of its own." But this was the Cambridge of the seventies, the intellectual lodestone of Boston, then a bubbling mix of class and race, scholars, musicians, poets, and artists, with Elsa at the center of it.

Michael Hiley: *Frank Sutcliffe: Photographer of Whitby*
1974. 224 PP, 8⅞ × 11⅛″ $27.50 HC

Peter Turner and Richard Wood: *P.H. Emerson: Photographer of Norfolk*
1974. 112 PP, 8⅞ × 11⅛″ $20.00 HC

John Hannavy: *Roger Fenton of Crimble Hall*
1976. 184 PP, 8⅞ × 11⅛″ $27.50 HC

In the mid-seventies, when we had really abandoned any idea of surviving as printers and had turned our attention, and modest resources, toward publishing, we found two major allies in the UK. The first was John Ryder, the noted typographer, designer, and typographic historian at the Bodley Head, who published almost every one of our early typographic titles under their imprint, and the second was Gordon Fraser, an elderly gentleman who had made his fortune with greeting cards and decided to quickly dissipate it by starting a publishing company. To run it he hired two very able protegees, James Fraser, who served as the acquiring editor, and Peter Guy, given free hand in terms of production and design. Like ours, this was a small

Photographs

ABOVE: Images from Hiley's *Frank Sutcliffe* and Turner & Wood, *P.H. Emerson*

shop, devoted to quality and not afraid to take on major projects of a decidedly non-commercial nature. Following up on our initial publication of the Victorian incunable by Cameron, we co-published a set of three major books on nineteenth-century British photographers Sutcliffe, Emerson, and Fenton. All were pioneers in the field whose work was little known in the US. These were the first major monographs devoted to their lives and work.

Sutcliffe devoted his entire life and creative energy to photography. His career spans the late nineteenth and well into the twentieth century, covering techniques from wet plates requiring long development times to the advent of the Kodak and the instantaneous snapshot. Most of his work was done in and around Whitby, and his images capture water rats, the last days of sail, fishermen and their wives, as well as the broader canvas of an England still "regional" in the best sense. Emerson, our stereotype of an English gentleman, was a medical doctor, a naturalist, a writer of real scope and importance (he was an early enthusiast of both Stieglitz and Julia Margaret Cameron), a photographer, and a superb billiard player. His real influence, beyond his talents as a photographer, lay in his insistence that photography be regarded as an independent art, with its own unique techniques and attributes. Fenton will always be remembered as the photographer who made the Crimean War visible, but his talents went far beyond this. He travelled widely, to the Crimea and Russia, and his photography is far more embracing than his peers, fascinating museum shots of plaster casts and marble busts, portraits, landscapes, architectural studies. Of the three, his career was by far the shortest, only eleven years. He took up the camera in 1851 and abandoned it in 1862 to resume his legal practice. The reproductions for all three, printed at Rowley Atterbury's Westerham Press in Kent, were as good as fine-line offset technology allowed

at the time. Subsequent books on all three have, of course, appeared, but these were the first studies of three Victorian gentlemen who left their footsteps in the sands of time.

Kipton Kumler: *Photographs*
Introduction by Deac Rossell
1975. 72 PP, 10½ × 12¼″ $20.00 HC

Kip Kumler was not then, and is not now, a household name, but the photographs he took of trees, landscapes, architecture and, especially, the leaves of plants, greatly moved me. They reminded me of the beautiful studies, printed as wood engravings, that Benjamin Fawcett made in the nineteenth century. Kip was then an employee at the Cambridge consulting firm Arthur D. Little and, being an engineer by training, he left nothing to chance. He came with the book fully laid out and the costs detailed, even with samples of the binding material. Although the number of plates are small, 57 in all, they were chosen very deliberately. As Deac Rossell wrote in his Introduction, "This book exists for more than casual browsing. It is not just a record of specific locations. It is more than a discrete collection of images. It is a book for thoughtful eyes. A book for reading with the eyes." My kind of photographer.

Following in the tradition of Weston, Atget Stieglitz, and Adams, Kip had taken most of the photographs with a large format camera and 8 × 10″ film and developed them himself. At this point we had only two printers who could handle material of this tonal range – Meriden Gravure and Rapoport Printing. We chose for this the latter one and bound it in full buckram. In terms of square inches, it is among the largest photographic books we ever published. And among the most beautiful.

Robert A. Sobieszek and Odette M. Appel:
The Spirit of Fact: The Daguerreotypes of Southworth and Hawes, 1843–1862
1976. 176 PP, 12 × 10½" $27.50 HC

This was among the early books we published with institutional financial and editorial support, in this case from George Eastman House, which was then under the energetic leadership of Robert Doherty, and along with Boston's Museum of Fine Arts and New York's Metropolitan, one of the primary beneficiaries of the Josiah Hawes collection. The exhibition, which travelled to all three sites, featured daguerreotypes, those delicate, fugitive, and exquisitely defined images captured on silverplate and here developed by the Boston team of Southworth and Hawes. They were among its earliest exponents in America and the principals of a studio that recorded personalities representing the cultural core of America in the nineteenth century: Emerson, Longfellow, Daniel Webster, Harriet Beecher Stowe, Lemuel Shaw, and Zachary Taylor, and the famous "branded hand" of Jonathan Walker, the Cape Cod seaman sympathetic to slaves whose attempt to free them resulted in a year's solitary confinement, a $600 fine, and an S.S. burned into his palm for "slave stealer." Printed on a reflective metal surface, a daguerreotype is notoriously difficult to successfully photograph for reproduction, and Eastman House took particular care in giving us splendid glossies of the originals. The book was designed by Clint Anglin, set in Linotype, and splendidly printed by Thomas Todd Company of Boston. It was the first, and remains the best and most definitive monograph on the firm, and one of the more beautiful books we produced in the early days of fine-line duotone offset.

Olivia Parker: *Signs of Life*
1978. 72 PP, 10 × 9½" $15.00 HC

I still love this book, the first of Libby Parker's many, and one of the technical marvels we managed to squeeze out in the years when fine-line printing was in its infancy. The problem was that the photographs were selenium tinted, not really black and whites, but subtle combinations of deep blacks and reddish browns. Normally, this would require four-color process printing, which we knew we could not afford. The problem was solved by Fran Canzano of Acme Printing, who worked closely with Dr. Edwin Land of Polaroid over a number of years, perfecting their presses to handle the demands of his annual reports. He was able to separate the images into two colors with a filter and to print them using a two-color press on a lovely cream sheet. Designed by Katy Homans, set by Mike Bixler in Dante, bound in an imported orange cloth, I know everyone was thrilled (and not a little surprised) by the results.

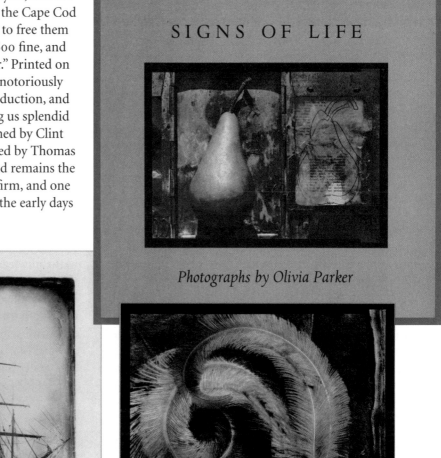

86. "CHAMPION OF THE SEAS," EAST BOSTON

When the "Champion of the Seas" was launched from her East Boston pier in May of 1854, she ranked as the world's largest sailing vessel, registering 2,447 tons. Built by Donald McKay (Plate 8), she was the second in a quartet of clippers constructed for James Baine and Company of Liverpool and Australia. According to *The Boston Daily Atlas* (May 20, 1954), the "Champion of the Seas" was a marked improvement over the "Lightning," the first of the four clippers:

Her ends are as long, though not as sharp or concave, and are even more beautiful in their form. She is 238 feet long on the keel, and 259 feet on the deck between perpendiculars. ...The run is long and clean, and blends in perfect harmony with the general outline of the model. Broadside on she has all the imposing majesty of a ship of war, combined with the airy grace of a clipper.

This daguerreotype is thought to be the only existing photographic image taken shortly before the "Champion of the Seas" was towed from the Grand Junction Wharf where she was loaded for her maiden voyage to Liverpool.

LEFT: *Champion of the Seas*, the largest of the clippers built at the East Boston yard of the great designer, shipwright and entrepreneur Donald McKay whose portrait was said to hang over her transom sofa. When she was launched in May 1854, she was ranked as the largest sailing vessel in the world. This daguerreotype is the only existing likeness of her before her maiden voyage to Liverpool.

71
La buena fama durmiendo
Good reputation sleeping

52. [Curly-headed youth with lyre]

ABOVE: One of a series of typically soft focus, romantic photographs
of the same nude boy by Fred Holland Day and simply labeled in
Jussim's *Slave to Beauty* as "Curly Headed Boy with Lyre"

Jane Livingston: *M. Álvarez Bravo*
1978. 132 PP, 8½ × 11″ $32.50 HC

With his friends Orozco, Siqueiros, and Rivera, Álvarez
Bravo was a member of the revolutionary movement that
shook Mexico in the 1930s. But unlike theirs, his work was
never political, but rather, in his words, "the work of talent
nourished by personal experience" and, as such, a challenge to pinhole. In this, the first monograph in English
devoted solely to his work, we see landscapes and still
lives, shop fronts and laborers. Many of the images are
unsettling, as are his captions, "Set Trap," "Striking worker
murdered," "Slaughtering Day." The iconography is elusive,
the juxtapositions often startling, but there's no doubt the
vision is deliberate and original. The 82 duotone plates in
the book represent the entire spectrum of his work from
palladium prints to color. Accompanying a major exhibition of his work at the Corcoran Gallery of Art in Washington, DC, it helped cement his place among the master
photographers of the last century.

Estelle Jussim: *Slave to Beauty: The Eccentric Life and Controversial Career of F. Holland Day, Photographer, Publisher, Aesthete*
1981. 326 PP, 7¼ × 10″ $35.00 HC

Although not particularly beautiful, this remains among
the more important texts we published in the field, the
first to explore the life and work of the talented (and at
this time relatively unknown) Fred Holland Day. His
Boston, at the turn of the century, was the center of
avant-garde publishing and a printing revival – inspired
by Morris's Kelmscott Press example. With personalities
as strong and talented as Bertram Goodhue, D.B. Updike,

Bruce Rogers (then working at Riverside), and others, it is
little wonder that Day, a generous eccentric, could flourish. A photographer in the photo-secessionist camp, book
collector, and from 1895 to 1905 the moving spirit behind
the Boston's Copeland and Day, he was responsible for
bringing many of the UK's "Yellow Book" authors and
artists to a continent more attuned (at least in Boston) to
the Medieval sensibilities of Morris than the risqué lines
of Beardsley. But above all, he was a man of multiple and
varied talents, a genuine pioneer in every field he touched.
Jussim's opening paragraph is worth quoting in full "He
was a most unusual human being, an extraordinary genius
with his camera, an eccentric in dress and habits, generous
to poets, impoverished women writers, Boston bohemians,
and young immigrant boys, especially his protégé Kahlil
Gibran. Proud of his affiliation with the Decadents – a
term of vastly different meanings to his generation than
to ours – he worshipped John Keats and Honoré de Balzac,
collected one of the most impressive private libraries in
the United States, and was the confidant of the English
and French aesthetes." Jussim, a scholar who would have fit
right into the Boston of Isabella Stewart Gardner, was the
perfect author. She lived near his primary archive and left
no stone unturned in pursuing her research into the various strands of his multiple careers. Coming to grips with
Day in his multiple personalities was, as she wrote, "The
most fascinating project of my career." Fully illustrated and
including a 48-page duotone portfolio of Day's photographs, extensive notes, and a full index, the book was
warmly received and was followed in the present century
by numerous further monographs on this seminal figure.

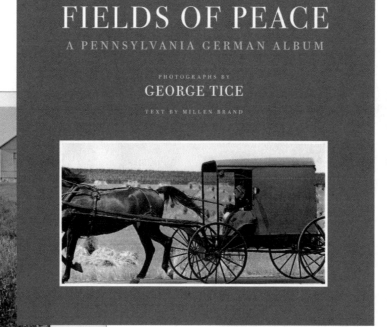

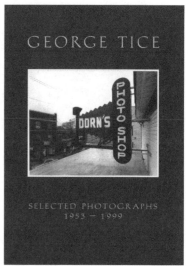

TWO AMISH BOYS · *Lancaster, Pennsylvania, 1962*

| 40 |

George Tice: *Urban Romantic:*
The Photographs of George Tice
1982. 132 PP, 12 × 11½″ $40.00 HC

Selected Photographs
2000. 96 PP, 5⅝ × 8″ $17.00 HC ℗℗

Fields of Peace
1998. 180 PP, 9⅝ × 8¾″ $45.00 HC

Seacoast Maine
2009. 144 PP, 9⅝ × 8¾″ $40.00 HC

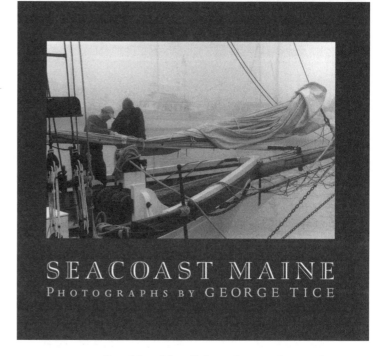

We have collaborated with George Tice, a photographer I count as among the major talents of his generation, on four titles. And all of them are as extraordinary, in their particular way, as anything we published in the field. Tice had a sixth sense for the perfect photograph – for the right frame, the right light, the right constituent parts all naturally engaged and arranged. In this, he was the opposite of Newman, Parker and Purcell, who carefully arranged and manipulated their settings and their subjects. Like Caponigro, his genius lay in *plein air* photography; whether it was the icons of Manhattan, a water tower brooding over his beloved New Jersey landscape, the Pennsylvania Amish, or Maine rockbound coastline, he had a gift for seeing just the right image in just the right light. A dedicated and meticulous technician, developing his own negatives to exacting standards. As we published more books, he be-

came more comfortable with collaboration; we knew what he wanted and he knew what we could deliver. In *Urban Romantic*, one sees the full spectrum of his work until that time: the haunting images of New Jersey, his native state, in all its diverse cacophony; the majestic views of Manhattan from the Jersey shore and atop the Chrysler Building. *Seacoast Maine* captures the craggy coves, rugged personalities, and placid light of the northeast coast.

In *Fields of Peace* we were fortunate to be able to reuse the Millen Brand text that originally appeared in the Doubleday edition. Combined with the Tice images, it travels back in time to a primarily agricultural America, rural and simple, a sympathetic panegyric to the (even then) fast-disappearing life and lifestyle of the Amish who had settled in the fertile farmland and forgiving political landscape of Lancaster, Pennsylvania.

SECOND SIGHT

THE PHOTOGRAPHS OF
SALLY MANN

Introduction by Jane Livingston

DAVID R. GODINE · PUBLISHER · BOSTON

Sally Mann: *Second Sight*

1983. 72 PP, 12 × 11½″ $25.00 FLEXIBOUND

Sally Mann went on to become a famous photographer for reasons quite different than the talents she displays in this relatively quiet and conventional first publication of her photographs. The challenge was to reproduce the images she had developed on a high-gloss paper in the same book as her collotypes, printed on an uncoated sheet, more ethereal and abstract. We solved this, to some degree successfully, by printing the book on two different sheets, a medium gloss and a smooth uncoated. Gary Gurwitz of Mercantile Printing, then an independent firm and one we had worked with on a number of projects, supervised the project, and we had the book bound in a new "flexible bound" format developed by Alan Horowitz. Mann was, for all her formidable intelligence and relentless ambition, essentially a Gothic southerner at heart, the visual equivalent of Poe – dark, brooding, deeply enamored of and fascinated by life's more disturbing and upsetting manifestations. When she approached us with her next project, our option, a collection of photographs of thirteen-year-old girls (including her daughter), I was squeamish and uncomfortable. The book seemed somehow intrusive, voyeuristic, and opportunistic. I suspected it would sell, but the blatant sexuality of the prepubescent poses, the knowing expressions on faces that should have been innocent, appeared to me prematurely coquettish and often

[31]

forced. I declined the option, and Aperture brought out the book to enormous success. My favorite Mann images remain not the ones that try to make a point, however subtly, but the quiet and evocative landscapes near her home in Lexington, Virginia, and the character studies that suggest a release from her often morbid preoccupations.

Carl Chiarenza: *Landscapes of the Mind*
Introduction by Estelle Jussim
1988. 160 PP, 11¾ × 11½" $40.00 HC

Polaroid under the leadership of Dr. Edwin Land bore no resemblance to any corporation in America. A technologically driven firm, it valued and rewarded technical advances and put scientists well ahead of salesmen in its hierarchy. Land was famous for many memorable quotes, but my favorites is "The size of a marketing department at any corporation is always in inverse proportion to the quality of its product." He therefore built an infrastructure that rewarded quality and encouraged innovation, consulted with and listened to artists. Clarence Kennedy from Smith College and Ansel Adams were part of the team, and their advice was taken seriously. The company supported photography as an art, funded a publishing program that made the work available and lent their large format instant cameras to artists, not only to promote the brand but also to see how far the technology could influence the art, and vice versa. When the SX-70 appeared, they made film available to a fleet of photographers, Marie Cosindas, Arnold Newman, David Hockney, Joel Sternfeld, William Eggleston, and Olivia Parker, among others, to demonstrate that "Polaroid color photography is more than an alternative to conventional techniques, it is an artistic idiom that occupies its own place in contemporary photography."

Among their favorites was Carl Chiarenza, a native of Rochester (home of their chief rival, Kodak), an RIT student, but hardly a disciple, of Minor White, who was then affiliated with the University and George Eastman House. After graduation, he came to Boston to study journalism, established a small gallery in the basement of the photo lab, and, along with Paul Caponigro, Nicholas Dean, Minor White, and Carl Siembab, was instrumental in dragging Boston into the modern era. During the early 60s, Chiarenza decided his future lay with images, not words, and was encouraged by Polaroid to begin experimenting with their film. White would print his articles, and his abstracts would appear on the back covers of *Aperture*. In 1963, he was asked by BU's Fine Arts Department to teach courses, but his road was blocked, predictably, foolishly, later when the Dean of the College informed him he'd need a PhD. His thesis (controversial as it involved a living artist) was on Aaron Siskind, probably the strongest influence on his career and aesthetic vision. He received his PhD from Harvard in 1973 and remained at BU for over a decade, before returning to Rochester in 1986 as an endowed professor at the University. His work is almost entirely abstract. It can be seen to real effect in this, one of the largest format books we published, designed by Carl Zahn and printed by Fran Canzano at Acme Printing from tritones by Richard Benson. The elegant Eelco Wolf was the prime mover behind the book; Estelle Jussim and Charles Millard contribute essays reviewing his life but little to explain his work.

Behind him (and many other Godine photographic initiatives) was Dr. Land, for whom we designed and oversaw a number of annual reports. Land was the Steve Jobs, and Polaroid the Apple, of the sixties and seventies. The annual meetings were media events, eagerly awaited by the press, Wall Street analysts, and a loyal crowd of stockholders. A man of infinite generosity and vision, Land was among the great leaders of American enterprise. I remember sitting in his office early one morning and looking at the Carleton Watkins print on his wall. Computers were just making their presence felt, and I asked him if they might ever have an effect on Polaroid. Land was a chemist. His answer, briefly edited, was "No, because the computer will never provide enough memory to capture the same detail as a square inch of silver halide." He had bet the company on the wrong horse.

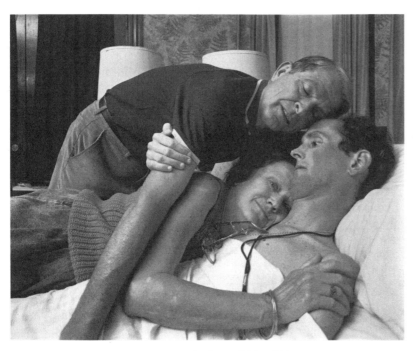

Robert, Ginny, and Bob Sappenfield, Dorchester, Massachusetts, August 1988

Photographs by NICHOLAS NIXON · Text by BEBE NIXON

PEOPLE WITH AIDS

Tom Petchkiss   Paul Fowler   Joey Brandon   Tom Moran   Mark Pfetsch

Laverne Colebut   Tony Mastrorilli   Linda Black   Dean Madere

Bob Sappenfield   Keith McMahan   Donald Perham

George Gannett   Elizabeth Ramos

Sara Paueto

PEOPLE WITH AIDS

PHOTOGRAPHS BY NICHOLAS NIXON

TEXT BY BEBE NIXON

DAVID R. GODINE · PUBLISHER

BOSTON

Nicholas and Bebe Nixon: *People with* AIDS
1991. 168 PP, 9⅝ × 8¾″ $40.00 HC

This is a book about fifteen people. Very little of it is about their everyday lives. Most of it is about their sickness, their dying and their deaths.

So begins the Nixons' stark and moving visual and verbal document recording fifteen victims of a disease that had swept across the planet in the 1980s, about which very little was known and that almost always ended in death. Today, as I write this, we have the coronavirus, perhaps even more frightening in its scope and, as the mechanisms of its dispersal are more varied and in some cases still unknown, potentially even more deadly. But AIDS was equally frightening, and by no means solely restricted to the gay community. The medical establishment provided little hope, and certainly no promises of a cure, as the magnitude of the disease became apparent. The loss of life was staggering, and both sympathy and justice for the victims were

in short supply. The Nixons, hoping to document this, managed to find fifteen volunteers who knew they were going to die but were willing to have the progress of the disease, and its effects on themselves, their family, and their friends, recorded and published. Nicholas's straightforward, powerful photographs combined with his wife's careful rendering of countless conversations take the reader to a place of shadows not often encountered. They merge to make this an arguably groundbreaking book, a testament to a terrible cultural and physical phenomenon that exploded on a global stage, but also one of fear, hope, rage and impotence, experienced on a smaller and more intimate scale. Each of the subjects had contracted AIDS, a disease that introduced them to illness, and finally death, far earlier than any of them expected. In these pages, it was our hope that their voices and stories would be heard. The book was printed with contributions in kind from every one of the manufacturers, from the paper merchant to the binder. By the time the book was finally published, all but one of the subjects had died.

Barbara Norfleet: *Looking at Death*

1993. 142 PP, 9⅝ × 8¾″ $40.00 HC

In centuries past, death was a close companion, an expected visitor. Disease and war, infant mortality and natural disasters, eliminated life routinely. Death was real and close, not viewed with terror or astonishment but resignation and compassion. It was an event celebrated communally, in the presence of family and friends. And more often than not in the home. In the past century, this attitude changed; we assumed that medicine would eradicate disease, that civil order would prevail, that wars would cease. Life could probably be extended indefinitely. But in the past few years, death has come back to life; wars still rage, pandemics carry off thousands, random shootings massacre scores of innocents. Assembled from the vast photographic archives of Harvard University, more than four million images residing in libraries, archives, museums, offices, and closets, Curator of Photography Barbara Norfleet assembled images from every corner, portrayals of shootings and disease from the medical school, mummies and headhunters from ethnology, the carnage at Gettysburg from Gardner's *Photographic Sketch Book*, Angus McBean's "Death of Caesar" from an Old Vic production of 1939 in the theatre collection. Together they provide a panorama of every variety of death and dying, from around the globe, from every possible camera angle. Strangely, much of it is not disturbing; the ash-coated figures from Pompeii, Eugene Smith's portrait of Spanish women grieving over a dead patriarch, the countless shots of stillborn infants dressed to the nines and lying placidly, almost serenely, in their caskets, all assume a grave and silent dignity. But as an event we must endure, there is no reason why it should not be explored and given its rightful due. As Montaigne inscribed on his rafter *Humani nihil a me alienum puto*: I consider nothing human alien to me. And what could be more human than death?

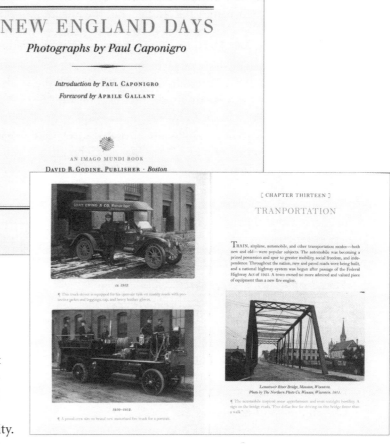

Paul Caponigro: *New England Days*
Preface by Aprile Gallant
2002. 80 PP, 9⅝ × 8¾″ $35.00 HC

For many years, ever since I met and worked with him at
the Maine Photographic Workshop, I had hoped to publish a book with Paul Caponigro, and when the Portland
Art Museum approached him for an exhibition and set
funds aside for a catalogue, we finally had our opportunity.
Like most of our photographers, Caponigro was a perfectionist; he developed his own images the old-fashioned
way, by hand, in a darkroom in his basement. Like many
artists, he was never completely satisfied with the results
– not even with his own work. He wasn't entirely sure
we would do right by him either, but he did trust Robert
Hennessey to make the duotones and was on press to
supervise the sheets at The Studley Press when the book
was printed. While the images are limited to those taken
in New England, they do give a broad overview of his life
as a master photographer, from the early images taken in
his native Massachusetts in the late 1950s through the still
lives recording features near his home in Cushing, Maine.
The natural world predominates: trees, flowers, rocks. He
would write in his Preface: "Photography is a medium,
a language, through which I might come to experience
directly, live more closely with, the interaction between
myself and nature." This is one title in which I wish we had
been able to go with a larger format; Caponigro's images,
with their careful attention to the details and subtleties of a
landscape, need space. Still, this was very well printed and
affordable. And I will always be grateful to Aprile Gallant,
who was then working at the Museum as a Curator, for
helping us pull it off and writing the fine Introduction.

Rosamond Vaule: *As We Were: American Photographic Postcards, 1905-1930*
Foreword by Richard Benson
2004. 216 PP, 7 × 9¾″ $45.00 HC

For decades Rosamond Vaule had been collecting "full
tone" postcards – that is, postcards printed directly from
the negatives and not as half-tone or collotype reproductions. They are, in every way, "original" photographs, and
although some were issued in relatively large editions,
most of "these little visual miracles produced in editions as
small as one or as large as a few hundred" were issued by
small-time operators in small towns and village scattered
across America. Photography, by the turn of the last century, had worked its way into the fabric of American life.
It touched everything, as necessary as today's computer.
The ubiquitous photographic postcard brought it to the
masses – small, affordable, and topical, it could be mailed
anywhere for a penny. The variety of imagery, much of
it shot and developed anonymously in small studios by
inspired amateurs, is probably the most comprehensive
visual record we have of a country exploding with energy,
invention, and confidence. Taken together, they celebrate
early twentieth-century America in all its vitality and variety. In a charming and scholarly book, Ms. Vaule selects
the best of them from across the country, discussing their
social and historical context and explaining the mysteries
of their manufacture and dissemination. She identifies and

describes the idiosyncrasies and characteristics of their makers and lists their names and studios. But the images themselves are really what captures us: the homey store and shop fronts, the frisky children and oblivious pets, the sober grownups trying desperately to appear adult, the airships, and barn raisings, and tradesmen. We shot all the postcards directly from the originals and the book, beautifully set and designed by Dean Bornstein, was superbly printed in duotone on a fine, offwhite uncoated sheet. Our previous book, *Prairie Fires and Paper Moons*, highlighted the postcard collection of Andreas Brown that subsequently made its way to the Getty. It was the first serious and scholarly book devoted to this variety of widely collected but sparsely documented ephemera.

Frederic Woodbridge Wilson: *The Theatrical World of Angus McBean*
2009. 192 PP, 9⅝ × 8¾″ $40.00 HC

Angus McBean is almost totally unknown, and certainly unsung, here in America, but in England only Cecil Beaton (who accurately called him the best portrait photographer of his era) was his equal recording the British stage between the 1940s and 1960s. His entire enormous archive resides at Harvard's Theatre Collection – eight tons of glass plate negatives, index prints, programs, and copyrights, where Fred Wilson, its curator, long wished for a book documenting its range and quality. The choices were endless; the production records of the Old Vic, now known as the Royal Shakespeare Company, the opera productions of Glyndebourne and the Royal Opera House, of Covent Garden, the ballets and operas of Sadler's Wells, and a complete range of West End productions, from comedies to tragedies, plays to musicals. He was the favorite photographer of Vivien Leigh, Laurence Olivier, and Edith Evans, he recorded countless plays starring John Gielgud, Ralph Richardson, and Alec Guinness, not to mention younger stars like Audrey Hepburn, Richard Burton, and Elizabeth Taylor, great photographs of the greatest actors of what

were arguably the greatest decades of British theatre. The photos, with their dramatic, signature McBean lighting and long exposure times, are riveting, but equally valuable and fascinating are the extended notes by Frederic Wilson on the performers and performances, the backstories on the larger-than-life personalities and intractable egos; he brings the English theatre to life for the reader, providing a window into a world America experienced only second-hand. McBean's own career was varied; his specialty was the theatrical work, but he was also a pioneer of surrealist photography, the montage, and multiple exposure images, all displayed here with long captions. The book was a sales disappointment; it should have been recognized as an invaluable resource for anyone interested in the history of twentieth-century theatre. The public idolized many of these figures. Why didn't they want to learn more about their backgrounds, lives, and careers? And you could hardly do it more painlessly or entertainingly than through the images and text presented in this book.

LEFT: Paul Scofield as Lear hovering over Diana Rigg as Cordelia in the 1963 Royal Shakespeare production
BELOW: Richard Burton donning his crown as Henry IV in the Shakespeare Memorial Theatre production of 1951

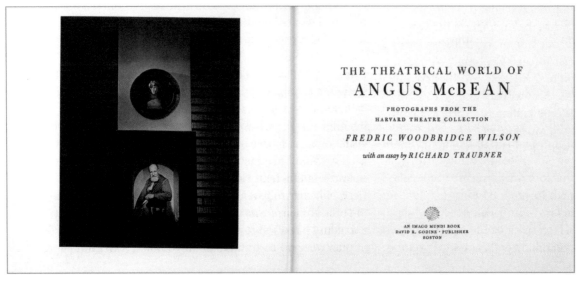

ABOVE: Cyril Ritchard, Katharine Hepburn, and Robert Helpmann, surrounded by five pound notes in Shaw's 1952 play *The Millionaires*

Yousuf Karsh: *Regarding Heroes*
Selected, with an essay by David Travis
Biographical sketches by Patricia Koura
2009. 192 PP, 9¾ × 12½″ $50.00 HC

This was surely our photographic magnum opus of the first decade of the new millennium. Karsh, the photographer of choice to kings and queens, presidents, artists, and musicians, had an extraordinary gift for capturing their characters and displaying their best characteristics in his closely observed headshots. He captured them with their dignity, often nobility, intact, at their best. David Travis, our longtime friend from the Art Institute of Chicago, steered the book in our direction, and with the generous support of Karsh's wife, the diminutive but determined Estrellita, we were able to do the prints justice. Five thousand copies were printed and bound in Switzerland by his longtime friend and collaborator, the Lucerne printer Genoud, and the results were better than we hoped, in every way spectacular. Designed by Sara Eisenman, printed on a lovely uncoated cartridge paper, and bound in full black cloth, it is perhaps the last book of this quality we will ever issue and certainly the last we will be able to print in Switzerland. We began shipping the book in June of 2009 and were sold out of it in a year.

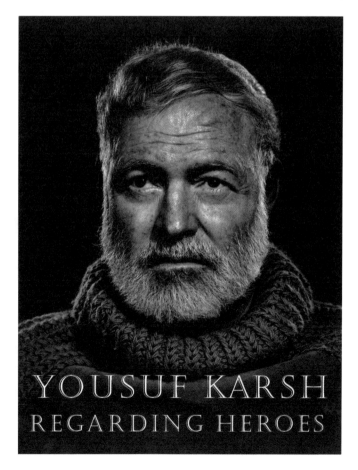

Stu Cohen: *The Likes of Us: America in the Eyes of the Farm Security Administration*
2009. 214 PP, 9 × 12" $50.00 HC

The whole purpose behind Resettlement Administration photography has been a simple and unspectacular attempt to give information. The task has been to confront the people with each other, the urban with the rural, the inhabitants of one section with those of other sections of the country, in order to promote a wider and more sympathetic understanding of one for the other. – Roy Stryker in a memo, ca. 1937

Housed in the Library of Congress, the archives of the Farm Security Administration contain an essential, and endlessly fascinating, mirror of American life from the late 1920s to the onset of the Second World War. Guided by the adroit hands and watchful eyes of Roy Stryker, it includes the work of dozens of photographers funded by the program – among them giants like Walker Evans, Ben Shahn, Marion Post Wolcott, and Russell Lee. Working like a spider at the center of an intricate and complex bureaucratic web, Stryker would arrange their assignments, sending them throughout the country on road trips with "shooting scripts" – laundry lists of possible subjects and situations – while also leaving them free to explore the locales and inhabitants from their own perspectives. Cohen's book collects and arranges the best of nine of these expeditions into the American heartland: Walker Evans to Pennsylvania, Alabama, and Louisiana with side trips to Mississippi and Georgia; Ben Shahn in Ohio, Kentucky, Arkansas, and West Virginia; Dorothea Lange to the migrant workers of California; Russell Lee in New Mexico; Marion Post Wolcott in Florida, and five of them, including Carl Mydans,

documenting New Orleans between 1935 and 1941. Uniting the often iconic images with the shooting scripts, letters, and other archival documents, Cohen gives a picture that goes beyond the glory of the photographs themselves. He focuses a revealing spotlight on the FSA at work – not just the work itself, but how it evolved and matured under Stryker's guidance and direction. It is sometimes forgotten that this was a program forged in the 1930s, at the height of the Depression, and with a political purpose: to document the crisis of poverty that was gripping much of rural America. Stryker chose the photographers because they were *artists,* and they were given a free hand to manipulate their subjects as they saw fit. One example: this book shows not only the famous "Migrant Mother" shot by Dorothea Lange at the Nipomo pea farm, but also the three ancillary images. As she later wrote, "I did not approach the tents or shelters of other stranded pea-pickers. It was not necessary. I knew that I had recorded the essence of my assignment." These were not photojournalists but artists on the government's payroll charged with making a point and changing public policy. It was federally supported propaganda to gain Congressional support to lift, in FDR's words, "one-third of a nation" out of misery. The trips Stryker orchestrated and images like Lange's were instrumental in securing the necessary relief.

Reproduced in duotone, the 175 photographs were all printed from the original negatives in the Library of Congress, providing an opportunity to see lesser-known images and understand the inner workings of one of the government's most original and creative Great Depression initiatives. Widely reprinted, the images allowed all America to see for itself the conditions of rural poverty pervading almost all 48 states. The program permanently shifted both political and social policies, alleviating real suffering.

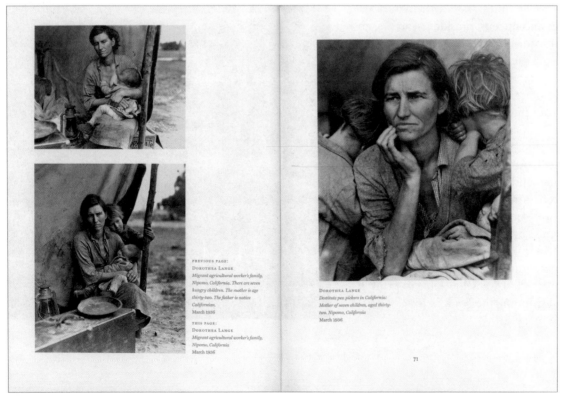

PREVIOUS PAGE:
DOROTHEA LANGE
Migrant agricultural worker's family, Nipomo, California. There are seven hungry children. The mother is age thirty-two. The father is native Californian.
March 1936
THIS PAGE:
DOROTHEA LANGE
Migrant agricultural worker's family, Nipomo, California
March 1936

DOROTHEA LANGE
Destitute pea pickers in California: Mother of seven children, aged thirty-two. Nipomo, California
March 1936

71

LEFT: Probably Dorothea Lange's most famous image is the "Migrant Mother," her 1936 shot of the 32-year-old pea-picker and mother of seven shot at the Nipomo farm in California. But it was by no means her only take on either the condition of migrant workers or the woman. Stu Cohen's fine book, *The Likes of Us,* gives the complete stories, not only of the photographers and their famous images, but also of how Roy Stryker's choice of artists, their assignments and the wide dissemination of their images changed the societal and governmental attitudes towards rural poverty in the United States. Great credit is due to Carl W. Scarbrough for his work pulling all the disparate pieces of this puzzle of a book together into a coherent and appealing whole.

Rosamond Purcell: *A Matter of Time*
1975. 80 PP, 7 × 7½″ $12.50 HC, $6.00 SC

Half-Life
1980. 62 PP, 10 × 9⅜″ $25.00 HC

When we published her first two books, Rosie was living in Cambridge, the daughter of the distinguished teacher and collector of Victorian literature, Robert Lee Wolff. So it should not be surprising that her images were often combinations of reality and imagination, of objects and reflections, of hybrid identities, belonging to, as she put it rather neatly, "states of mind rather than to reality." In the constructs that she builds and the visual furniture she manipulates, you can see a world-class visual archaeologist at work, artfully dressing, juxtaposing, and rearranging her objects to give them the appearance of "whole life." Like all the photographers we embraced, she was an expert technician in all media, understanding that "technique more loving than content never fails to impress," but it really is her content that catches and holds the eye's attention. Her first book, in black and white, *A Matter of Time*, was published five years earlier on an uncoated sheet.

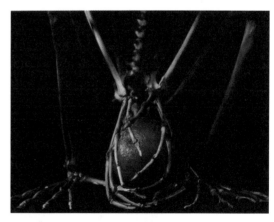

Gordon Dodds, Roger Hall, Stanley Triggs: *The World of William Notman*
1995. 240 PP, 9 × 12″ $50.00 HC

I had first encountered Notman in the Triggs/Harper collaboration: *Portrait of a Period: A Collection of Notman Photographs, 1856–1915* issued in folio by the McGill University Press. By any standard, this was a magnificent edition, concentrating primarily on his Montreal studio photographs. On reading it I realized the Notman empire stretched far afield, even including a studio in Boston. I hoped a book exploring his business and photographic activities in the northeastern United States, as well as his broader reach throughout Canada, might be of value. All three authors labored mightily on the text, trying to suture together elusive evidence and assemble business records that were, in their words, "virtually nonexistent." What did exist were the 400,000 images in Montreal's Notman Photographic Archives, proving that the firm's activities in the US, and especially on the major campuses of the Eastern universities, were extensive. But little else. The Boston and Cambridge images were especially striking, including portraits of local and visiting dignitaries, such as Ralph Waldo Emerson, Lilly Langtry, Robert Louis Stevenson; the architecture of the city in the 1870s; and the campuses of Harvard, Princeton, Dartmouth, and Vassar, which would provide America's next generation of civic leaders and financiers. The printing was adequate, the binding extraordinary, and the sales disappointing.

Peter Moriarty: *Lotte Jacobi*
2003. 96 PP, 5⅝ × 8″ $19.00 SC ℘

We had missed an early opportunity to publish a monograph of Jacobi's work in the seventies, so when her former student came to us with the observation that no book remained in print that showcased her work and that she had spent the latter part of her long and active life in New Hampshire, we could hardly refuse. This small "Pocket Paragon" displays most of her memorable images, including Lotte Lenya, Albert Einstein, and Thomas Mann, but also provides a broad and generous selection of the work she produced in Germany before emigrating to the USA. Although she never considered herself a "style" photographer, she was, at her best, the equal of an Avedon or a Penn. She was always drawn to intellectual celebrities like Einstein, Buber, Kollwitz, May Sarton and Robert Frost, and her portraits, executed quickly, surely, and with deceptive simplicity, are masterful for their delineations of character, her probes for the lineaments of genius. This little book compressed the fifty years of her life, thought and work into one affordable volume.

Richard Brown: *The Last of the Hill Farms: Echoes of Vermont's Past*
2018. 136 PP, 9 × 11″ $40.00 HC

No one growing up in New England when I did with any eye for the landscape was unfamiliar with the work of Richard Brown. It appeared in books, as well as the now departed *Vermont Life*, easily spotted for both the remarkable technical skills he brought to it and the honest, but always tender, reality his images conveyed. This book was Vermont in the early seventies, a land of sheep, cattle, work horses, wood-burning stoves, and outhouses – far removed in time and space from the industrial Northeast. Determined to record it before it disappeared, Brown saw a pastoral and unspoiled corner where "for the briefest interval, a window opened and the spirit of Vermont's past – granite hills cleared and farmed, hard lives lived and lost, struggles and endurances, a harsh land made starkly beautiful by nature and by man – was made palpable." And Brown did record it, lugging a heavy 8 × 10″ large plate view camera that would have been at home in the hands of Mathew Brady. Not only the hauntingly beautiful landscape, but also the people whose "endless hours of backbreaking, monotonous work" were spent with a conviction that "their age-old labors were a struggle waged against time itself – labors that just might hold modernity at bay." This was a record of the last gasp of a life in the hill farms of the Northeast Kingdom as it had been lived for generations, a time when a farmer could make a living with a herd of thirty cows with a little sugaring or lumbering on the side. The faces of the people – grave, strong, resolute – bring to mind Walker Evans's photographs of the tenant farmers of Alabama. But this is unmistakably Vermont, preserved in glass plates that produced images of great clarity, tonal range, and depth of field. They were beautifully reproduced in China by Four Colour Print Group to a design by the author's wife Susan. The last truly great book of photographs of my tenancy, it is a tribute to the talents of

a singularly lovable photographer and a celebration of a way of life, and the people who lived it, that have all but disappeared. It deserved all the acclaim it received.

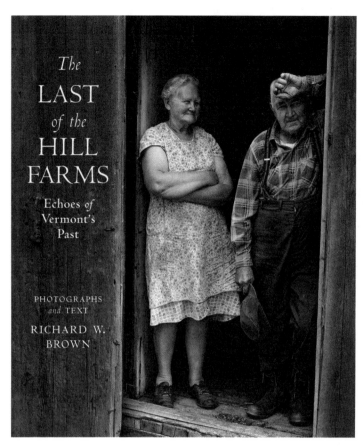

Learmonth Farm
KIRBY | 1974

EULOGY

W HEN I WAS A KID my family took trips to northern Vermont to see the leaves and camp on Burke Mountain. Winding up Route 5, I became aware of a profoundly different view passing by our car windows. Everything north of White River Junction was a foreign country.

People wore faded denim and weren't afraid of getting dirty. They spoke with an accent I barely understood. Their houses were old, in need of paint and dwarfed by immense barns. Wrecked cars and derelict tractors rusted away at the edges of fields and tethered goats grazed on lawns. I thought it was the most beautiful thing I had ever seen. I wished that one day I could live in one of those farmhouses and that this paradise would never change.

The first wish was granted. The second, of course, was not. Vermont's hill farm landscape evolved as much by fortuitous accident as intent. It was too good to last. But with my camera I could bear witness to this compelling world where it still lingered. Photographs capture moments that never change. For this I am truly grateful.

John Tancock: *The Sculpture of Auguste Rodin*

1976. 664 PP, 8¾ × 10⅞″ $40.00 HC

The Rodin Museum in Philadelphia contains the most extensive collection of Rodin sculpture outside of the Musée Rodin in Paris. Every major piece from every major period of his work is represented, as well as extensive auxiliary examples of all the media he employed in his work – plaster, bronze, marble, wax, and terracotta. In over six-hundred pages of text, almost 130 of his key pieces are here documented and fully described, often including early studies in plaster and multiple images from different angles. In the case of his larger pieces, like *The Burghers of Calais*, there are additional photographs of the studies he would often create to help define particular features – heads, hands, feet, and even drapery in plaster maquette studies. This could easily have been another drab exhibition catalogue, but it was elevated by four ingredients: the photography of the sculpture by Murray Weiss, the Clarence Kennedy of the Quaker State; the instinctively good judgment of the Editor of Publications, George Marcus, who had the sense and taste to have it designed and organized as a *book*; the design, printing, and binding of the entire volume, our first and last book produced entirely in gravure, by Conzett and Huber of Switzerland; and the excellent text and research provided by John Tancock, who assesses Rodin's achievements, techniques, and place in the history of art. He leaves no stone unturned in his research and references, and his text is at once scholarly and free of jargon. The book, the author, and the museum combined to do justice to this extraordinary gift of the sculpture by Jules Mastbaum to his beloved city of Philadelphia.

200 Years of American Sculpture

1976. 336 PP, 9⅛ × 11½″ $40.00 HC

I suspect it was Tom Armstrong, then the Director of the Whitney Museum of American Art, and David Rockefeller, the Chairman of the Board of Chase Manhattan Bank that served as its chief sponsor, who came up with the idea of celebrating the nation's bicentenary with a major exhibition of American sculpture. They were prescient in this, for this was indeed a subject they both rightfully perceived as "not fully surveyed previously" and one coming into its own as "a separate subject of serious study for art historians and museum specialists." I can't imagine what they were thinking when they approached us, only six years old, to undertake the design and production of a book that would have challenged the resources and stamina of a publisher ten times our size. This was a major undertaking, intended to cover the entire field, from aboriginal art through contemporary sculpture. There were over

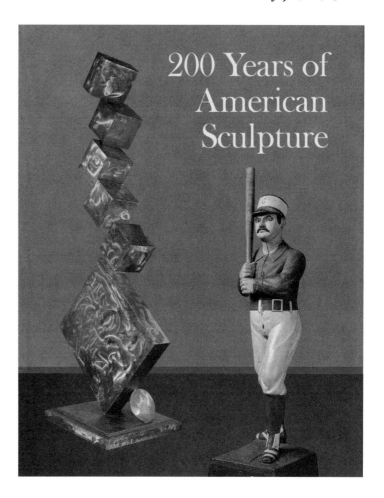

150 lenders to the exhibition from around the world, a complex and detailed mass of text and illustration, seven extensive essays on various periods with accompanying illustrations by heavy hitters Norman Feder, Wayne Craven, Daniel Robbins, Rosalind Krauss, and Marcia Tucker. The book features a selected bibliography, a thorough biographical survey of all the artists represented (with their photos, histories, and bibliographies appended), and an eight-page, three-column index set in 9-point type.

We were extremely fortunate that Lance Hidy was still on the staff and undertook the formidable job of the design, ably assisted by the young RISD graduate, Carol Goldenberg, all of it coordinated by Yong Hee Last, affectionately referred to as "The Iron Butterfly." The print run was an astounding (for us) 8,000 copies, split between hard and softcovers for the Museum. We were responsible for handling everything from ordering the bright white coated paper to supervising the printing by Rochester's Case-Hoyt on their six-color sheet-fed presses. The book remains a standard in the field, a testament to Armstrong and his staff who managed to pull off what would today, for insurance reasons alone, be totally impossible. I wrote, without the usual hyperbole, in our 1976 catalogue, "We think it among the finest books of the decade." I still think so. And to everyone's surprise, we all parted friends. Tom would write "We are all convinced that our joint endeavor could not have been more pleasant or successful." The book stands as a tribute to everyone involved.

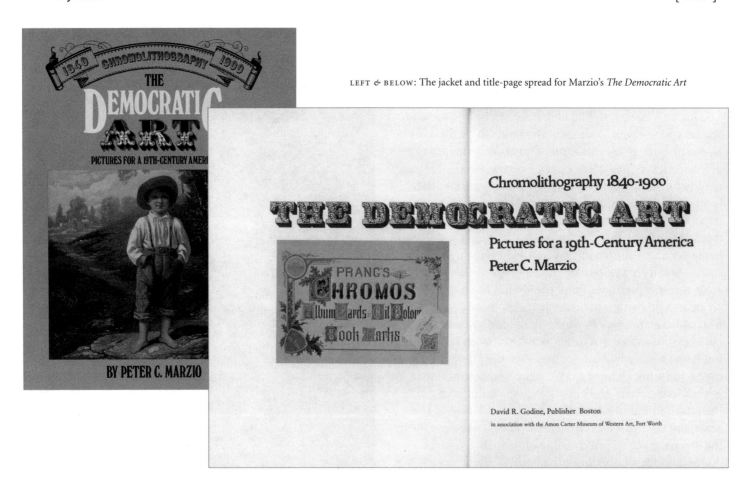

Peter C. Marzio: *The Democratic Art: Pictures for a 19th-Century America*

1979. 376 PP, 8 ½ × 11" $50.00 HC

I knew Peter from my trips to Washington where he was the director of the Corcoran Gallery. This book, the most important of the many he wrote, had its genesis as his doctoral dissertation at The University of Chicago with his two distinguished advisers Daniel Boorstin and Joshua Taylor. It was clearly a subject close to his populist heart, for it tells the story of how art reached, and ultimately enriched, the masses of post–Civil War America. The "chromo," essentially a color lithograph, required real skill to separate the subject into their component colors. But once the separations were made, one for each stone, the subject could be (and was) produced in the thousands. Carefully registered, the hues and colors of original art could be faithfully reproduced in huge numbers and sold for modest sums. Religious art, sporting scenes, fires, earthquakes and other natural disasters, landscapes, still lives, portraits, and posters – they were all fair game for an industry that found a home in every major American city and employed thousands of craftsmen. Marzio tells this story dramatically and thoroughly, covering every aspect of the colorful artwork that, through the efforts of impresarios like Louis Prang of Boston and Currier and Ives of New York, found its way onto the walls of every American home with a few pennies to spare. A legitimate objection to the book, hand-

somely designed by Rich Hendel, was that the color section was printed separately on a coated paper and located in the rear. A reader had to inconveniently flip back between print and image. As printing on uncoated paper improved and the cost of full-color presswork decreased, we were able to answer this objection in future titles. Issued in 1979 in conjunction with an exhibition at the newly opened Amon Carter Museum in Fort Worth, this was among our earliest efforts in the realm of art books and remains the standard reference for the subject.

S. Lane Faison, Jr: *The Art Museums of New England*

1984. 496 PP, 5½ × 10" $35.00 HC

When this was published, Faison was Art Professor Emeritus at Williams College, from which campus and under Faison's leadership an entire generation of art lovers had emerged in the sixties and seventies. He had very capably taken over the same role Paul Sachs had played at Harvard's Fogg Museum in the thirties and forties, training an entire generation of art historians, curators, and museum directors who had come to know him and love art (often at the "maison Faison") while studying at Williams College and its illustrious companion, the neighboring Clark Art Institute. He was already a legend when (according to him), he was approached "by David Godine" to revise and update a guide to the museums and institutions of New England that Harcourt Brace had published back in 1958. I suspect this was a false tribute. Bill Goodman, our savvy editor, was at Harcourt during those years, knew Faison well, and was almost certainly the *primum mobile* behind the book. And what a book it became, almost 500 pages with 550 images, covering in detail not only the purely procedural (hours of operation, phone numbers, addresses, etc.), but, more importantly, what of real importance was contained in each collection. Faison was a beloved fixture in the museum world (and knew everyone), but he was also a writer of real consequence – reading this book is like attending a master class with a first-rate art historian. The art comes alive on the page. You can read the book today, forget about the directions and admission charges, and get a first-rate education in art history, in all periods and epochs, from Egypt to America, from prehistory to modern. I look at this book today and marvel at what was involved and how we ever pulled it off. The type was hot metal Garamond; every page had to be laid out and set down with scissors and glue. The permissions costs alone must have been daunting, although I am sure Faison was able to obtain much of it for free. We were still a small outfit, just over a decade old. We should have gone out of business. We later simultaneously issued the book as three separate paperbacks, covering two states each.

John Rowlands: *Holbein: The Paintings of Hans Holbein the Younger*
1985. 288 PP, 9 × 12″ $75.00 HC

Holbein the Younger is acknowledged as a giant of Renaissance art. His paintings bridge a gap between the High Renaissance of Europe and the economic and social energy of sixteenth-century England and France. Many of his portraits, such as the full-length portrait of an arrogant and autocratic Henry VIII, are instantly recognizable and almost totemic. In this rich study, John Rowlands, the Keeper of Prints and Drawings at the British Museum, treats Holbein's entire career, tracing his beginnings working for his father in Augsburg, the banking capital and among the great commercial centers of the Empire, then to his role as the leading painter in Basel, thence to France and finally to England, where, under the patronage of Sir Thomas More, he fast became the primary artist of the Tudor court. He was a man who moved easily between countries and among civic and religious groups. His art provides a rich tableau of his own life and of personalities on both sides of the Channel, including the endless procession of queens, and potential queens, of Henry VIII. But above all, his ability to convey the characters of his sitters sets him apart from his contemporaries, a striving for perfection that is most evident in his portrait paintings and drawings. This "critical faculty . . . and his perception of its

LEFT & ABOVE: The jacket and an interior spread for Lane Faison's comprehensive *The Art Museums of New England*
RIGHT: Holbein's iconic portrait of the imperious Henry VIII

potency in communicating decisively the sitter's character" was, in Rowland's words, "a true measure of Holbein's supreme genius as a portrait painter." This volume presents a new assessment of both his life and his art. It reconsiders dubious attributions, presents all of his paintings, 37 of them in full color, and provides an extensive bibliography, an index, a fully illustrated list of his miniatures, and a catalogue of both his lost and rejected paintings. Published in association with Phaidon Press in London, it stands high among the most handsome art books on our list.

Bascove: *Stone and Steel: Paintings & Writings Celebrating the Bridges of New York City*
Introduction by Mary Gordon
1999. 112 PP, 8⅝ × 9″ $30.00 HC

Nothing is more sacred or more central to the iconography of New York City than the bridges by which it is accessed. For countless artists and writers, photographers and poets, these enduring structures, some of them beautiful and some merely workmanlike, have not only provided a link to the outside world but a means through which the great metropolis is introduced to countless visitors. As Alfred Kazin

observed, "All bridges, if they are well built, have their own beauty. They recall the passageway that is perhaps the most enduring symbol of life. They speak of the journey across, and they mark the limits within which we must live." This lovely book contains fourteen striking full-page paintings of the bridges that lead into the city, accompanied by the writings of poets and authors. There are the well-known classics by Hart Crane and William Carlos Williams, but also a host of entries by contemporary celebrants including Gay Talese, Helen Keller, Octavio Paz, Richard Wilbur, and Derek Walcott among them. As Mary Gordon says in her Introduction, "This is a New York book, a book of promise and of life, a life of hope and danger and stability, a vessel that contains within itself the possible and the impossible, and the mutations and transformation of one to the other." We went on to publish more books illustrated by Bascove, including a lovely collection of food writing enhanced by her paintings, and a similar one on the joys of reading. I love them all, but this remains my favorite as it seems to me her most varied, with the style ranging from the visionary to the descriptive to the abstract, as well as her most personal. Here the writing seems a riff on her painting, rather than the other way around. But they are all special, as she was to us for many years.

WILLIAMSBURG BRIDGE

LEFT: The Williamsburg Bridge is probably most inspiring from underneath and once provided the fastest route to LaGuardia.
BELOW: The cover quite rightly shows the Brooklyn Bridge by moonlight.

Adam Van Doren: *An Artist in Venice*
Preface by Theodore K. Rabb
Foreword by Simon Winchester
2013. 128 PP, 6⅛ × 9″ $27.00 HC

Venice has always been a magnet for artists, probably exerting a greater attraction than any city in the West. Canaletto, Guardi, Turner, Whistler, and Sargent were all seduced by its ambiance, a place where colorful historical architecture interacts with suffused natural light, and history seems to float much in the present as the past. Van Doren's twenty-three full-color watercolors are his love letter to its beauty, and his fresh, personal commentary provides a background that lifts this beyond an art book. For Venice was the little nursery to which writers, poets, and musicians – among them Ruskin, Pound, Byron, Brown, and Brodsky – all retreated when they needed shelter. It's a high bar, but Van Doren rises to it in his charming memoir of his visits to *la serenissima*. He provides both a verbal and visual tribute to a city that he sees with his own eyes and wanders through with his own Baedeker, one that recognizes the genius of the past while providing new angles of sight. Ruskin single-handedly saved the city with his *The Stones of Venice*; Van Doren continues the tradition, celebrating it in real style.

Dave H. Williams: *Small Victories: One couple's surprising adventures building an unrivaled collection of American prints*
2015. 328 PP, 7 × 10″ $40.00 HC

This beautifully designed, printed, and illustrated book is a guide through one couple's adventures assembling what was probably the finest collection of American prints in private hands (now residing at the National Gallery). You follow their adventures as they experience victories and defeats, gain knowledge, cover old and well-tilled soil and break new ground. In a collection of 6,000 prints, they manage to assemble the iconic names and also venture into new and unexplored territory: the regionalists who worked in Cape Cod and northern California, the small workshops that sprang up in Dallas and Charleston, SC, New York's Ashcan School, Hayter's Atelier 17, the prints by African American artists in the 1930s, and the hundreds of WPA artists working in small towns across the country during the Depression. They open new doors to techniques like the screenprint, shed light on little-known connections: the artists of the Mexican Revolution, how the WPA introduced so many artists to the challenges of printmaking, the influence of the Vorticists. By structuring the book primarily as a memoir Dave presents their saga as an adventure. You read it and think, "This couple knows every bit as much about prints as any academic. And they are breaking new ground with every step they take." Most collectors are amateurs and every one of them (including professionals, curators, and academics) could learn more than they could imagine reading this book. My old math teacher used to say, "As the area of your knowledge increases, the circumference of your ignorance grows accordingly." The Williamses' taste, knowledge, and savvy expanded with that circumference.

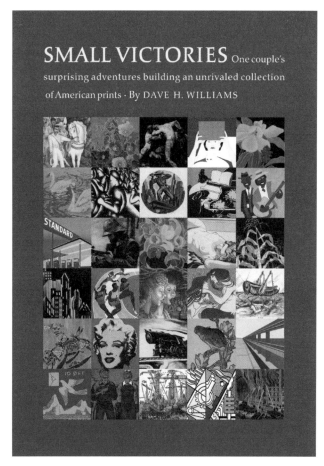

Christine Hadsel: *Suspended Worlds: Historic Theater Scenery in Northern New England*

2015. 196 PP, 12 × 9″ $40.00 HC

Talk about esoteric. When Chris Hadsel first approached me with her proposal for a book on what seemed to be a hopelessly remote corner of the art world, I was less than enthusiastic. But when she came to the office, showed us the photos, and told us the backstory of what she and her organization, *Curtains Without Borders*, had done to

preserve and protect these fragile, wonderful, and often bizarre canvas backdrops, I couldn't resist. This was a look back to small town America–before there was radio, and TV, movies, and the internet–where every community had to provide most of its own entertainment. They would gather in town, opera, and grange halls to enjoy locally sourced variety shows. Anything would pass: recitations from Shakespeare, temperance lectures, young ladies' poetry recitals, and amateur theatre productions, often followed by a communal supper. Behind the stage, some-

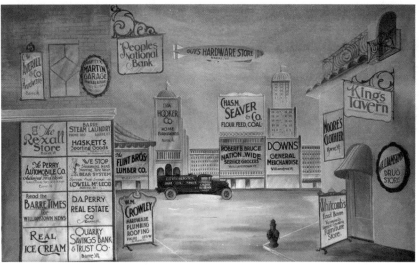

NEW HAMPSHIRE
WITH HISTORIC S1

MT. MAJOR GRANGE #310, NOW THE WEST ALT
MOUNT HOPE GRANGE #7 AND
DORCHESTER GRANGE #280 AND 7

See Postscript for thirty-nine more curtains from

Advertising Curtain, attributed to Arthur Ives, Plymouth, NH, c.1930
Williamstown Elementary School, from the former Williamstown Grange #81, Williamstown, VT

 134

times created for a specific performance, but more often as a general backdrop for whatever action was occurring onstage, were huge, hand-painted stage curtains, of which Chris and her cohorts had managed to locate over 500 examples in northern New England alone. They include grand drapes graced by totally imaginary and improbable scenery – European castles, romantic landscapes, Roman gods and goddesses (always of the better sort), and even chariot races from *Ben-Hur*. There are urban scenes to serve vaudeville acts, parlor scenes for Victorian melodra-

mas, and rustic interiors, in case a version of *Uncle Tom's Cabin* was coming to town. And most interesting were the ads for local stores and industries, incorporated right into the artwork. She goes on to identify and provide brief biographies of all the major artists, as well as a postscript listing the locations for every one of the known curtains in New England. Yes, it's a small corner of the art world, but, with the possible exception of our book on the duck decoys of Martha's Vineyard, never has a small corner been more thoroughly, thoughtfully, and beautifully explored.

NEW HAMPSHIRE SCENIC ARTISTS

FRANKLIN P. CARPENTER (1852-1914)

WILLIAM W. CULVER (1834-1927)

EGBERT L. FOSTER (1866-1947)

JAMES BARTHOLOMEW DUFFY (1872-1953)

MARION RHOADES FRACHER (1911-1972)

ROBERT WILLS NAVES (1916-1944)

ARTHUR STRATTON IVES (1896-1955)

MAXFIELD PARRISH (1870-1966)

FRED GEORGE QUIMBY (1863-1923)

EVERETT LONGLEY WARNER (1877-1963)

LUCRETIA ROGERS (1910-1977)

GEORGE A. THOMPSON (1905-1983)

A series of typical canvas theatre curtains from the "Live Free or Die" state of New Hampshire.

CLOCKWISE FROM LEFT TOP TO BOTTOM: An advertising screen promoting local businesses attributed to Arthur Ives, Plymouth, NH; a car advertisement from Northwood Ridge, NH; a jacket displaying the Grand Drape of Lake Memphremagog by an unknown artist, Irasburg, NH; signature of Arthur Stratton Ives of North Woodstock, NH; the Grand Drape "Naumkeag" by Franklin P. Carpenter of Londonderry in Litchfield, NH

Allen Blagden: *Marking the Moment*
Introduction by John Wilmerding
2017. 164 PP, 10 × 11″ $50.00 HC

"There was a long bench in the living room of our house. And it was full of paper, crayons, watercolors—all the essential ingredients for creating art." So began Bladgden's long career as an artist, beginning as a pupil of his father then teaching, as Allen would later, at the Hotchkiss School in Lakeville, CT. This book spans from his early days in rural Connecticut, to his college career at Cornell, to his trips to paint wildlife of Africa, wilderness in the Adirondacks, the coastline of Maine. And then there are the portraits of Egyptian women, Native American chiefs, Maasai warriors, and favored celebrities, in various stages of dress and undress. Allen was incorrigibly modest, his own worst promoter, but I found his art consistently arresting, interesting, and revealing, American realism set squarely in the traditions of Audubon, Eakins, Homer, and Wyeth. But always his own. As John Russell wrote of him in the *New York Times* in 1986, "Allen Blagden comes across as a case of multiple identity. He can do portraits. He can do veiled women in Egypt. He can do still life. He can do a sandhill crane, and many another strange bird, and he can do the Metropolitan Museum in a snowstorm… In each capacity, he comes on as a true soldier of art." Like Peter Beard, he believed in firsthand encounters with wildlife. And the

resulting portraits, of even the wildest adimals, are intimate and empathetic, painted with sensitivity combined with superb skill. It was a tribute to an artist whose work deserved a book, and I think we performed that service.

Robert D. Mussey, Jr. & Clark Pearce:
Rather Elegant than Showy: The Classical Furniture of Isaac Vose

2018. 310 PP, 9½ × 11⅞" $50.00 HC

At the turn of the seventeenth century, Boston was among the three richest cities in America. Money was flowing in from lumber, ice, granite, the cod fishery, and manufacturing. The wealthy could, and did, display their wealth — in portraits, in architecture, and in furniture for their homes. No one provided them with the then-trendy classical style better than Isaac Vose and his workshop, whose superb workmanship and creative interpretations rivalled those of his far-better-known contemporary, Duncan Phyfe of New York. Published to coincide with an exhibition by the Massachusetts Historical Society, and handsomely supported by them, this large format, lavishly illustrated study gives the man and the team of workmen he assembled from all over Europe the credit they have so long deserved. The photography, the printing, and the design by Sara Eisenman did the subject proud, and the book and authors were awarded the New England Historical Society's Historic New England Book Prize for 2019. And much of the credit goes to the MHS, whose team encouraged the authors to write a *book*, not an exhibition catalogue. This is also the only instance I know in which Isaac Vose (the subject of the book), the authors, the publisher, and the designer all resided in the same town of Milton, Massachusetts.

OPPOSITE: Maggie Dirrane, star of Robert Flahertys 1930s documentary film of the bleak lives of the islands off Ireland's west coast "Men of Aran." Allen found her "in her small stone cottage, because I learned she was still alive. She posed for me for two full days before revealing that she was totally blind, thus I tried to capture the knowing brilliance of her pale blue eyes."
OPPOSITE BELOW: A typical Blagden exotic, an Egyptian vulture
BELOW & RIGHT: The jacket and an interior page from the Mussey/Pearce book on the furniture of Isaac Vose, *Rather Elegant Than Showy*, displaying the elegant classical curves, fine craftsmanship and flashy finish that made these products of the Vose workshop the favorites of Boston aristocracy at the turn of the seventeenth century.

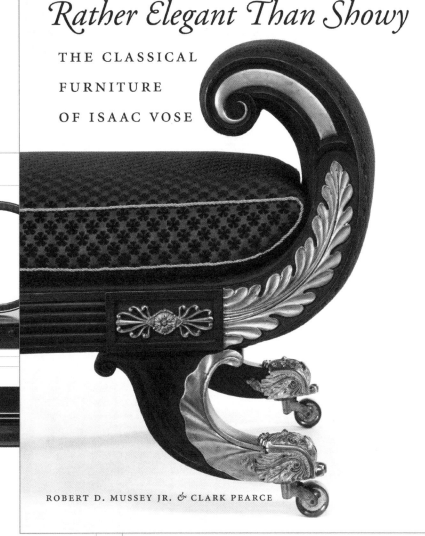

(above) FIG. 308 Detail of dressing table with mirror in figure 154, attributed to Isaac Vose & Son, Boston, 1819–22. Museum of Fine Arts, Boston, Gift of Miss Aimée and Miss Rosamond Lamb (1977.567). Photograph © 2018 Museum of Fine Arts, Boston. (above right) FIG. 309 Dressing mirror, attributed to Isaac Vose & Son, Boston, 1819–24. Mahogany, Honduras mahogany, white pine, brass, mirror glass; H 30½, W 35⅝, D 12⁷⁄₁₆. Deveikis and Barkentin Collection; photo, David Bohl. (right) FIG. 310 Card table, attributed to Isaac Vose & Son, 1819–22. Mahogany, Honduras mahogany, chestnut, brass (casters replaced), iron; H 30¾, W 36¼, D 18. Deveikis and Barkentin Collection; photo, David Bohl.

By These Signs You Will Know Them: Connoisseurship and Construction of Vose Furniture [251]

John Wilmerding: *American Masterpieces: Singular Expressions of National Genius*
Foreword by Eric Gibson
2019. 116 PP, 11 × 9″ $40.00 HC

Anyone who reads the Saturday edition of the *Wall Street Journal* and turns to the Art Review section recognizes in it the best writing by the best critics on the most interesting subjects that American journalism has to offer. Premier among the contributors is John Wilmerding, former deputy director of The National Gallery and later chair of the Department of Art and Archaeology at Princeton University. Collected here is a selection of his best twenty-five essays that appeared on the newspaper's "Masterpieces" pages between 2006 and 2019, an entire course in American art – painting, sculpture, architecture, and photography, illustrated with full-color plates and then close examinations of pertinent details. To read any one of them, from the earliest Copley portrait of Mr. *&* Mrs. Thomas Mifflin of 1773 to Wyeth's *Snow Hill* of 1989, is to understand the particularity and individuality of American art, how each of the media were all, in their own unique ways, integral to the formation of a distinctively American artistic idiom. This book was a signal contribution to the field, and a book that, in the words of the WSJ's Arts Editor Eric Gibson, showcased Wilmerding's "ability to take readers to the heart of a work of art or an artist's intention in the most succinct yet penetrating prose."

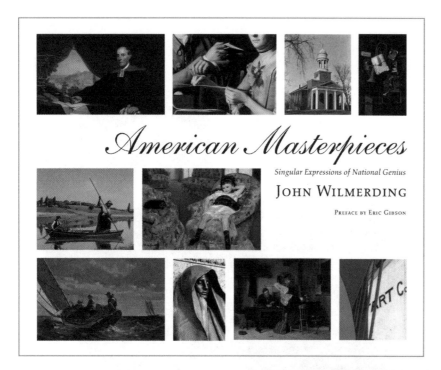

RIGHT: "Second Story Sunlight," a 1960 painting by Edward Hopper, in which Wilmerding, as in his other entries, points out both the obvious and the hidden, the probably deliberate emphasis on duality, of the two dormers each with two windows, the two women, even the title of the painting, but also the more subtle; the differences between the elderly woman in black evidently reading a paper and the buxom blond in the bathing suit with "her chest thrust out as if to catch attention." Why are they there? How are they related? What are they thinking? As he points out, moving from the obvious to the obscure, "Often simplicity of designs shields a complexity of emotions, and an impending narrative yields only to inexplicability."

OPPOSITE: A classic example of a small, two-story Queen Anne residence in the Bronx, the last of a row of two-story houses on Anthony Avenue that "held out" as developers bought the land and built the apartment houses now flanking it on either side. These, and even more dramatic stories of greed, stupidity and cupidity, are revealed in Alpern and Durst's *Holdouts! The Buildings That Got in the Way.*

Nigel Nicolson: *Great Houses of Britain*
1978. 288 PP, 8½ × 11″ $30.00 HC

This title, published in conjunction with England's National Trust, was a revised and expanded edition of the original published in 1963. We are all now familiar with many of the characters and social formulae from exposure to Downton Abbey. The English country home was a peculiarly British institution, set in what looks like a country park and resembling something between a palace, a country estate, and a villa; it was generally an ancestral property, often going back generations, sometimes centuries, each one with its own particular history, architectural style, interior furnishings, works of art, and fine furniture. And what better guide than Nigel Nicolson, superb writer, heir to the celebrated Sissinghurst Castle in Kent and its historic gardens designed by his father Harold and his mother Vita Sackville-West, and already the author of several books on politics, social history, architecture, and my personal favorite, *Portrait of a Marriage*. If any man could find instant, cordial, and trusted access to these homes and describe them eloquently, it was Nigel Nicolson.

This book selects and describes thirty-nine of the finest, in England, Scotland, and Wales, all but two of them open to the general public, ranging from Medieval manor houses and Tudor Halls, from classical Palladian mansions to elegant Georgian villas. The choice ranges from the familiar – Knole, Chatsworth, Blenheim, and Petworth – to lesser-known, but no less beautiful, examples like Ightham Mote, Blicking, Felbrigg, and Holkham Hall, Weston and Ditchley Park, and Easton Neston. Each is a masterpiece of its period, many are associated with the great names of English architecture – Inigo Jones, Sir John Vanbrugh, Robert Adam, John Nash, and Joseph Paxton – but each, too, is singular for the families associated with it: their taste, their feuds, their acquisitions and dispersals, and their choices of how their homes would be set in the landscape. It contains all the well-known facts, but also any number of backstories that only someone with Mr. Nicolson's background and sense of history could have unearthed and so lucidly expressed. I had the pleasure of visiting Sissinghurst with my family shortly after the book was published. Nigel was there, greeted us warmly, and graciously spent several hours giving us a personal tour of the home and the legendary gardens. I strongly suspect this was the first time my father actually took my career as a publisher seriously and thought his son might possibly have a future.

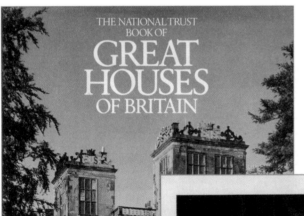

LEFT & BELOW: The jacket showing Hardwick Hall and a spread from Nicolson's *Great Houses of Britain* showing the vast edifice of Blenheim Palace, designed by Vanbrugh and the birthplace of Winston Churchill. The color plate displays the architectural grandeur of one of the many marble doorways that separated the various state rooms. The sheer massive scale of the buildings, what Nicolson called a "backdrop to a Wagnerian opera" has always been controversial. Robert Adam thought it "so crowded with barbarisms and absurdities, and so borne down by their own preposterous weight, that none but the discerning can separate their merits from the defects" while Sir John Soane said it stamped Vanbrugh "the Shakespeare of architects."

William C. Brumfield: *Gold in Azure: One Thousand Years of Russian Architecture*
1983. 444 PP, 8⅜ × 10⅞" $60.00 HC

This title was a very ambitious undertaking for a small press, even in 1983 when library funds were still being used primarily to buy books. Bill Brumfield, a professor at Tulane University, had spent three long sabbaticals travelling through Russia in the seventies and photographing its architecture, most particularly the monumental examples of cathedrals, churches, and palaces found in both the major cities as well as the vastly varied countryside. Designed

by Richard Hendel and set in Trump by Roy McCoy, it was a massive undertaking, over 400 pages of scholarly text, 300 black and white and 80 color images. But in the end, it was recognized as the first modern attempt to trace the Russian architectural aesthetic from the Byzantine-influenced churches of tenth-century Kiev through the transformations of Peter the Great and the twentieth century's hodgepodge of conflicting styles. Brumfield, who had a doctorate in Slavic languages and spoke Russian fluently, was able to interweave social history with architectural narrative in a way that made for a very readable, as well as beautiful, book. This was certainly our most ambitious foray in the field and will always be counted as a singular and original contribution to scholarship.

214. Cathedral of the Intercession. Detail.

25. Cathedral of the Transfiguration of the Savior.

26. Cathedral of Saints Boris and Gleb. Chernigov.

27. Cathedral of Saints Boris and Gleb. Plan.

28. Cathedral of Saints Boris and Gleb.

ABOVE: The front cover of Brumfied's *Gold in Azure* shows the Church of Saint Andrews in Kiev, a shot of what are probably the most famous cupulas in all of Russia on Moscow's Cathedral of the Intercession (Saint Basil's), and the entries to the late-twelfth-century Cathedral of Saints Boris and Gleb in Chernigov.

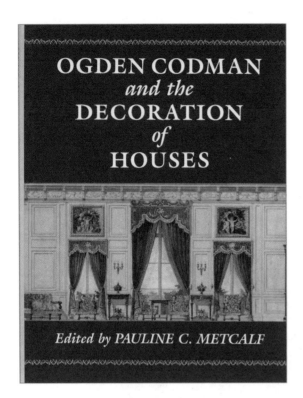

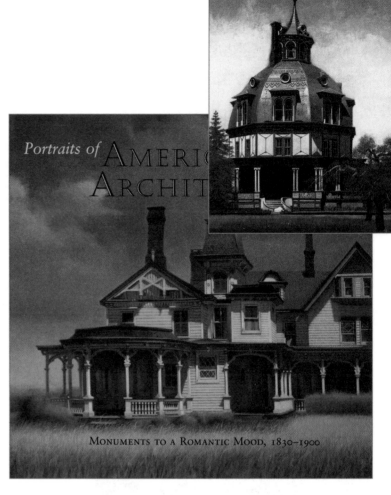

Pauline Metcalf: *Ogden Codman and the Decoration of Houses*
Edited by Pauline C. Metcalf
1988. 224 PP, 8½ × 11″ $40.00 HC

Codman's influential career as both an architect and interior designer is fully explored in this nicely illustrated monograph that documents his career as the foremost exponent of what we now call "The Classical Revival." Codman is perhaps best known for his collaboration with Edith Wharton in the seminal book *The Decoration of Houses.* Since its first publication in 1897, the book has served as a primer for the more tasteful participants in America's "Gilded Age." Embodying his mantra of "suitability, simplicity and proportion," it remains, even today, something of a Bible for classical, elegant taste in interior design. His influence can be seen everywhere, from The Breakers of Newport (anything but simple) to fashionable town houses designed for the merchant princes of New York. Designed by Richard Bartlett and appropriately set in Carter's lively Galliard typeface, it was published in conjunction with The Boston Athenaeum to accompany a major exhibition of Codman's drawings, documents for each commission, and modern and contemporary photographs of his rooms and buildings. Compiled and organized by architectural historian Pauline Metcalf, the book gives a full picture of his New England roots, the milieu in which he worked and, above all, the variety and elegance of the designs he provided for the wealthy pre-Depression families of Boston, Newport, and New York. Its publication went far to confirm his place among the premier architects of our past.

Harry Devlin: *Portraits of American Architecture: Monuments to a Romantic Mood, 1830–1900*
1989. 196 PP, 14 × 11″ $50.00 HC

This book is a paean to the nineteenth century, probably the last time in our history when materials were abundant, skilled labor was affordable, architectural styles changed as often as hem lines, and the average middle-class American could not only afford to own a home but often have a direct influence on its appearance. Harry Devlin was essentially a painter, but his real passion was for the architecture of the years between 1830 and 1900, the so-called Victorian era when the reigning mood was Romanticism and the choice of styles was eclectic and almost infinite. I had been aware of his work through his childrens' books, most notably *To Grandfather's House We Go,* but had no idea that he had spent the better part of forty years selecting the most significant examples from a period when America would build, borrow, and invent the most dazzling array of architectural styles in its history. He would travel along the Eastern seaboard to record these, creating paintings that are as detailed, dramatic, and revealing as any portraits, for these were *his* beloved models. He was also a writer whose style sparkled with information, opinion, and outspoken digression – my kind of author. In the book you'll find his paintings of seventy structures, from octagonal barns to

Cape May cottages, from elegant New York townhouses to the New Hope railway depot, from the Whalers' Egyptianate Church in Sag Harbor to Harvard's Hasty Pudding Club in Harvard Square. You look at these structures, compare them with what's being built today in the name of "new housing" and you have to say out loud, "Wasn't that a time!"

OPPOSITE: Jacket from Devlin's *Portraits of American Architecture* showing "Roselawn," a Victorian eclectic displaying a fascinating jumble of styles; a ca. 1870 Italianate porch, 1880s stick style elements, a twentieth-century mansard roof, and a Second Empire Tower. Located in Flemington, New Jersey, it was, according to legend, built as a fresh-air infirmary for the owner's ailing wife. INSET, OPPOSITE: The Armour-Stiner House, more popularly known as "The Bonnet House" is an over-the-top example of many octagonal homes constructed following an enthusiastic endorsement. This entry in the "Survey of Historic American Buildings" quoted by Devlin is interesting: "In addition to eclectically incorporating Gothic, Stick Style, Second Empire and Eastlake detail, this house is one of two domed octagon residences in the United States. Its siting, design, heating-plumbing systems reflect the mid-nineteenth-century architectural philosophies of Orson Squire Fowler, noted phrenologist, sexologist, amateur architect and author of the popular *The Octagon House: A Home for All.*"

Bryant F. Tolles, Jr.: *The Grand Resort Hotels of the White Mountains: A Vanishing Architectural Legacy*

1995. 276 PP, 9 × 11¼″ $50.00 HC

tourist trade. Tolles's carefully researched and profusely illustrated volume identifies and explores some thirty outstanding examples explaining their architectural details, their social histories, and the often surprising stories behind their lovely, white-painted wooden façades. The book also explains the dramatic evolution of the building types themselves, from the first rural highway inns of the Rosebrooks, Crawfords, and Fabyans in the 1820s to the initial railroad hostelries and the grand hotels of the 1850s, to the era culminating in the expansive resort complexes at the end of the nineteenth century.

Bryant researched the book for over three years, culling valuable records, information, and visual materials from libraries, archives, and private collections throughout New England and beyond. He places the buildings in a broad national and historical context, explains the origins and development of a highly specialized industry, and discusses the symbiotic relationship between the railroads and the hotels. The concluding sections offer a comprehensive bibliography and a valuable listing of the names and locations of all the major hotels, including the many that have succumbed to the ravages of age and fire. Illustrated with over 200 black-and-white and twenty color images, the book is a definitive history, a delightful, vastly entertaining social document of a New England phenomenon that has now all but disappeared.

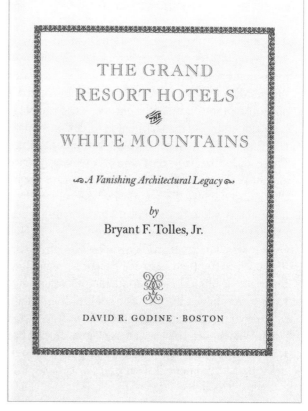

LEFT: The photograph shows but one part of the sprawling Mt. Washington Hotel in Bretton Woods, NH. The Spanish Renaissance Revival–style buildings, mostly miraculously still standing, are in Tolles's words, "the survivors of a prolonged and agonizing attrition that has all but eliminated their competition."

THE GRAND
RESORT HOTELS
of the
WHITE MOUNTAINS

A Vanishing Architectural Legacy

by

Bryant F. Tolles, Jr.

DAVID R. GODINE · BOSTON

This was the first book to fully explore the architecture, as well as the related economic, social, and cultural history, of the grand resort hotels of New Hampshire's White Mountains. These beautiful buildings, situated in what have always been among America's oldest and most frequently visited vacation and recreational locales, were the first structures in the country to be exclusively designed for the

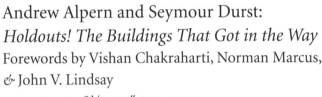

Andrew Alpern and Seymour Durst:
Holdouts! The Buildings That Got in the Way
Forewords by Vishan Chakraharti, Norman Marcus,
& John V. Lindsay
2011. 194 PP, 8¼ × 11″ $40.00 HC

A strip of land 5 inches wide and 78 feet deep owned by a taxi driver whose asking price foiled a developer's dreams for a huge apartment house. An empty 8 × 20′ site in the middle of a Wall Street office building created for an outhouse in the eighteenth century. A two-story building surrounded by a tall apartment complex on upper Broadway that owed its existence to the timing of Prohibition. These and more, stories of almost unbelievable cupidity and stupidity on both sides, are snapshots of the holdouts that got in the way. They appear whenever development makes land valuable and a profit motive intervenes. These urban battles are often portrayed as David and Goliath encounters. The small homeowner who refuses to abandon his hearth pitted against a heartless, venal developer, invariably millionaire real estate moguls intent on ousting hapless families or businesses from buildings they have inhabited for generations. But there's another side to the story. What about the harried, well-intentioned builder, who has invested huge sums to buy up land for a development that would benefit thousands, only to see his plans thwarted by a solitary landowner? This book, often side-splitting, sometimes gut-wrenching, recounts the colorful personalities and outrageous actions that often emerged from these stark confrontations. More than 200 illustrations show the holdouts, before, during, and after the construction they delayed. Holdouts. Yes, they all happened in New York (where else?), and they continue to happen. Everywhere. For anyone interested in the sometimes hectic, sometimes pathetic, sometimes downright hilarious struggles of individuals against developers and vice versa, this book contains lessons for everyone.

Alex Karmel: *A Corner in the Marais:*
Memoir of a Paris Neighborhood
1997. 160 PP, 6 × 9″ $25.00 HC

For anyone who loves old houses, and Paris before the city was completely rebuilt in the nineteenth century, the old, unspoiled, district of the Marais holds a special appeal. In a knowledgeable and conversational tone that nonetheless gives the reader confidence that the author really knows (and lives) his subject, Karmel traces the social and architectural development of this corner of the City of Lights from its time as a Roman settlement, through the major restructuring brought about by Henry IV and Baron Haussmann, to the present conservation and renovations of older, and still untouched, neighborhoods like this. The book concludes with a "walking tour" of the district in which the principal buildings are discussed with brisk au-

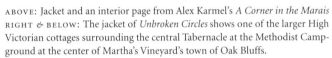

PASSAGE DES SINGES, BY ATGET
"...a nest of criminals..."

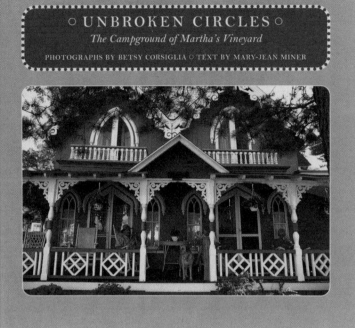

ABOVE: Jacket and an interior page from Alex Karmel's *A Corner in the Marais*
RIGHT & BELOW: The jacket of *Unbroken Circles* shows one of the larger High Victorian cottages surrounding the central Tabernacle at the Methodist Campground at the center of Martha's Vineyard's town of Oak Bluffs.

thority. Karmel never loses sight of the fascinating human details – the waves of settlement, its rich ethnic diversity, the royal feuding and family chicanery – that have all played such a role in shaping Paris as we know it, and especially this fascinating and still original corner, as we know it. The book was orchestrated by our resident Francophile, editor, and wizard, Mark Polizzotti, and is illustrated throughout with photographs and period engravings.

Mary-Jean Miner: *Unbroken Circles: The Campground of Martha's Vineyard*
Photographs by Betsy Corsiglia
2000. 142 PP, 9½ × 8⅝″ $35.00 HC

Anyone who has travelled by ferry to Martha's Vineyard and disembarked at Oak Bluffs has hopefully made time to visit to former Methodist Campground, perhaps to attend a concert or lecture at the Tabernacle, and to marvel at the small wonders of vernacular architecture, still lovingly maintained, that surround it. It was here, in the years of the Civil War, that the first clusters of High Victorian bungalows were constructed to replace the temporary tent platforms that had provided space and shelter for the faithful who had journeyed from the mainland to listen to the teaching, preaching, and music emanating from the central Tabernacle. These makeshift cottages have survived, transformed into Victorian cottages of almost infinite variety, a colorful necklace of fretted woodwork, bright, improbable color, and eclectic architectural ornaments

of every possible variety. Lovingly tended, sometimes by families extending back generations, they are splendid examples of the architectural style known as "Carpenter Gothic." Adorned with protruding porches, eccentric furniture, flowers, and lanterns, they are reminders of a time when family life was close, faith was straightforward and uncomplicated, and the summer twilights lasted forever. They are well represented here, 120 photographs with a fine text describing the history, folklore, customs, and characters of a unique and devoted American community.

BELOW: Originally built to an 1888 design by Peabody & Stearns, Leighton House was later redesigned in 1979 by Robert A.M. Stern at the recommendation of Yale architectural historian Vincent Scully.

ABOVE: An interior spread from Doris Doane's book on the development of the Cape Cod house showing the delicate pencil drawing by Howard Rich
RIGHT: Sky Hill, resembling an eighteenth-century tidewater Virginia plantation house with its double-column palladian entry, was allegedly designed by the noted New York architect Charles Adams Platt.

Doris Doane: *A Book of Cape Cod Houses*
Drawings by Howard Rich
2000. 96 PP, 9½ × 8¾" $15.00 SC

I was calling on a Cape Cod bookstore and asked the knowledgeable owner what book needed reprinting. He immediately suggested Doris Doane's chaste study of what every child comes up with when asked to draw a home: The Cape Cod. Everyone knows them but as the author notes "Few people are aware of its origins, its well-defined types, and the characteristic features that have made the Cape Cod house an enduring form of our native domestic architecture." The features are easily defined: a symmetrical, one-and-a-half story home with the chimney in the middle, a centered front door between two matching windows, and siding of either clapboard, or cedar shingles. Built across New England, homes to fishermen and farmers, city dwellers and shipwrights, the style defined our vernacular between the mid-1600s and roughly 1850. Their low-slung design was economical, easy to build and generally impervious to the weather. Modified after WWII by Royal Barry Wills, they became the design of choice for the burgeoning suburbs. In short, the "Cape" was our national design, one that worked its way into people's psyches and hearts. This book provides the history of these homes enhanced by Rich's exquisite pencil drawings–clear representations of exteriors, floor plans, interior rooms, and details like chimneys, fireplaces, overmantels, staircases, even wallpaper. Fortunately the original drawings survived and with these and Carl W. Scarbrough at the helm, we reset and reconstructed the book from scratch.

William Morgan: *Monadnock Summer: The Architectural Legacy of Dublin, New Hampshire*
2011. 160 PP, 10 × 7" $25.00 SC *with flaps*

The high mountain town of Dublin, NH, nestled in the Mount Monadnock foothills, attracted a wave of distinguished visitors in the late nineteenth and early twentieth century. Mark Twain spent two summers there, calling it "the one place I have always longed for, but never knew it existed in fact until now." Its climate, unpretentious lifestyle, and dramatic scenery attracted artists as diverse as Joseph Lindon Smith, George de Forest Brush, the young Frank Benson, and Rockwell Kent. Literary lights included Henry and Brooks Adams, Irving Babbitt, the historian Hendrik Willem van Loon, the poet Amy Lowell, and even Ethel Barrymore. Its other claim to fame is that it's home to just about every architectural style, providing a playground for almost every major architect and architectural firm of the late 1800s: Charles A. Platt, Peabody and Stearns, Shepley, Rutan and Coolidge, Rotch and Tilden, Henry Vaughan, Louis Lilly Howe, and John Lawrence Mauran. From small boathouses to imposing mansions, Dublin was ideal for a clientele that had the money and discrimination to indulge architects of all stripes and styles. The results, mostly still standing, are engagingly described in the delightful prose of architectural historian Will Morgan, who spent his youth summering in the town. Yes, a small subject, but one that gives a real sense of what happened in New England when taste, talent, and money intersected.

Camp Liberty, Great Pond,
Belgrade Lakes, Maine.

ABOVE: Main room. Here the
camp's framing is covered in
beadboard with minimal disrup-
tion by trim. The continuous
windows facing the lake slide in
wooden tracks to open. The open
partition in the foreground may
have been remodeled from an
earlier complete partition. Note
breaks at the ends of the beadboard strip immediately above the
central header; cuts like these are
evidence of later alteration.

LEFT: Boathouse. Boathouses,
perhaps more than any other
building or architectural feature,
symbolize summer life on the
inland lakes.

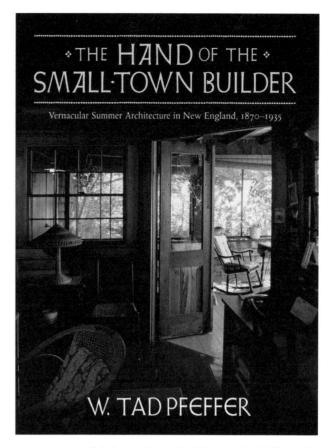

LEFT & ABOVE: All the houses described and illustrated in Pfeffer's study
of northern New England vernacular architecture were designed and generally constructed by "small town builders." The one to the left shows Camp
Liberty on Great Pond, a lakeside cottage and one of many that dotted the
Belgrade Lakes region of Maine. The cover shows a typical interior of the
many seasonal camps built as vacation retreats throughout northern New
England in the years before WWII.

W. Tad Pfeffer: *The Hand of the Small-Town Builder: Vernacular Summer Architecture in New England, 1870–1935*

2014. 200 PP, 8 × 11″ $40.00 HC

It might well appear strange that a book about the summer homes of northern New England should be written
by a world-class glaciologist living outside Boulder and
teaching at the University of Colorado. But every year Tad
Pfeffer spends his vacations in Randolph, NH, and it was
there that his interest was piqued by the summer homes
constructed from scratch by local builders. The building boom started soon after the mountains, and later the
shoreline, were opened to rusticators by the railroads. It
was an era when professionals from the cities – teachers,
doctors, lawyers, businessmen – routinely devoted the
summer months to their families and frequently looked
north for fresher air, cleaner lakes, higher mountains, and
undeveloped coastlines. Mostly middle-class, they had
neither the means nor the desire to hire a professional
architect. Instead they turned to local builders, often
beginning with a rental and then pointing to a structure
they liked, suggesting a few modifications, and leaving in
September with the instruction, "Try to have this ready
for me and my family when we return next June." The

local builders, talented craftsmen, familiar with the local
supply chains and materials, would comply, sketching out
the basic lines, supervising construction and serving as the
liaisons and house-sitters for, "A far cry from the 'cottages'
of Newport and Bar Harbor, they were perfect for comfortable summer living, complete with porches, multiple
bedrooms, a view, and simple wooden stud construction."
For a decade Pfeffer spent his summers travelling northern
New England, to the lakes of Vermont, the mountains of
New Hampshire and the seacoast of Maine, to track down
the names of the builders and ferret out what plans or
correspondence might survive. Sensitive to local topography and landscape, carefully sited, built with native
materials using local labor, these are small masterpieces
of vernacular design. And Pfeffer's research, text, captions,
and photographs provides rich primary sources for both
contemporary architects and builders.

LEFT: The cover for Van Doren's collection of presidents' homes shows Washington's beloved Mt. Vernon where, as he would write, "I had rather be on my farm than be emperor of the world."

ABOVE: Joe and Rose Kennedy's retreat in Hyannisport, MA showing the sitting room off JFK's bedroom and the library with shelves of Rose's annotated books

BELOW LEFT: Peacefield, the "quaint yet stately federal home of four generations of the Adams family" built by John and Abigail, it was home to two presidents, a Secretary of State and a preeminent historian. In David McCullough's words, "like a geological cross-cut whereby you see past times in layers."

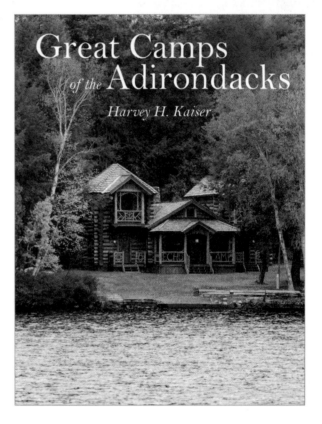

Adam Van Doren: *The House Tells the Story: Homes of the American Presidents*
Introduction by David McCullough
2015. 196 PP, 12 × 9″ $40.00 HC

We have published three books by the gifted artist/writer Adam Van Doren who comes from a bloodline that almost guarantees talent. This is my favorite: an illustrated excursion into the homes of fifteen US presidents, distant and recent past. The text is personal and unaffected, but it is quite amazing what Adam and his watercolors manage to reveal about each of the personalities. Here, in almost every instance, is personal as well as historical information you won't hear from the lips of the government tour guides. He personally visited each of the homes, sometimes as guests of living presidents, and his perceptions, both in words and images, provide real insight into their lives, their passions, their ways and priorities of arranging their lives. There is a world of difference between the genius of Jefferson's Monticello and the worn linoleum and simple furnishings of Harry Truman's kitchen. He misses very little. David McCullough puts the history of the homes—and their inhabitants—in perspective with his usual lucid prose. Adam's earlier book on the history and architecture of Venice and his more recent one on Yale, where he continues to teach. Both are filled with a palpable fondness for history as well as a congenial personality. But this is my favorite, the backstory of our leaders told through the places, the human environments, they called home.

Harvey H. Kaiser: *Great Camps of the Adirondacks*
1982. 256 PP, 8¼ × 11¼″ $45.00 HC
& 2020. 300 PP, 9¼ × 12″ $50.00 HC

Harvey's 1982 book was our first serious assay into the world of color printing, and, at least on that level, not especially successful. But as a text, it captured, at precisely the right time, America's growing fascination with vernacular architecture, with our increasing interest in using local materials to build homes that were intended to be more a part of the landscape than imposed upon it. Harvey lived in upstate New York and was in charge of facilities management for Syracuse University, which at that time owned Sagamore, one of the original "Great Camps." Like others built in the Adirondacks by the tycoons of the Gilded Age, these "camps" were to the peaks and lakes of the Adirondacks what the "cottages" were to Newport and the sea. There, in the wilderness, were grand and extended building clusters inhabited for one month by the captains of American industry and society (with plenty of servants and staff stashed away in adjoining cabins) and with just enough adjoining wilderness (often thousands of acres) for the native guides to take the "sports" fishing and hunting, thereby convincing them that they were roughing it. By the 1980s, the larger camps had been mostly deserted by the original families, many were facing demolition or decay, and the conservation movement to save them from the "forever wild" statute implanted in the Park's founding documents was still in its infancy. This book was the catalyst that started that preservation revolution. It's among the very few books we have published that have had a direct and profound social and political impact.

In the late nineties, it seemed time for a reappraisal. What had been the fate of the original camps? What new ones had been built and older ones restored? What new architectural firms and forces had been brought in to not only restore the older ones to their former glory, but to design and build new ones? Although it contains a few repeats of the older camps, the 2020 revised and expanded edition is an entirely new book; it features new photographs (many from the air this time), a new and far more detailed text, and a fresh new design by Wynne Patterson. It's interesting to contrast the two editions and see how much they differ. Set in hot metal, with an allusive "rustic" design, the earlier book was plainly a product of the eighties in terms of both its character and production. Wynne's 2020 version is clean, fresh, and appealing to a modern aesthetic. Harvey passed away just before the latest edition was printed, but he got to work through and see all the pages. I can still hear his voice on the telephone. He was a good friend and faithful author. And he loved those camps and was gratified to see the effect his books had on their revival and survival. I miss him.

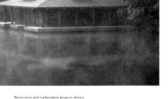

LEFT *&* ABOVE : Pages showing newly built two-slip boathouse of Camp Cobblestone on Spitfire Lake, the Japanese-inspired boathouse and main lodge of Pine Tree Camp of Upper St. Regent Lake and, on the cover, owner Tim Mullins's and the architect Michael Bird's careful 2018 reconstruction of Durant's original twin tower main lodge at Echo Camp on Raquette Lake

This is the last in a long series of letters James
Rufus Agee wrote to James Harold Flye,
a priest and teacher at St. Andrew's,
an Episcopal school near Sewanee,
Tennessee. Father Flye first met
Agee the summer of 1919.
Their correspondence
begins with a letter
Agee wrote from
Phillips Exeter Academy
in 1925. It ends with this
letter found by Father Flye
sealed but unmailed on the mantel
of Agee's living room. James Agee
died of a heart attack in New York City,
May 16, 1955. He was forty-five years of age.

The text of the letter has been reprinted with
the kind permission of the publisher, George
Braziller, Inc. from the book, 'Letters of
James Agee to Father Flye'. Copyright
(c) 1962 by James Harold Flye
& The James Agee Trust.

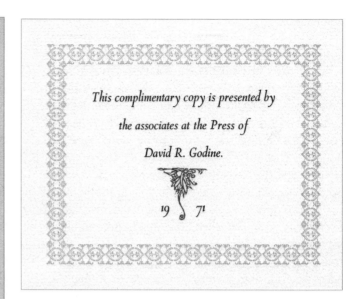

This complimentary copy is presented by

the associates at the Press of

David R. Godine.

19 71

THE LAST LETTER
OF JAMES AGEE
TO FATHER FLYE

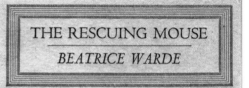

THE RESCUING MOUSE
BEATRICE WARDE

CLOCKWISE FROM ABOVE: An early pamphlet reprinting the last letter James Agee wrote to his old friend, mentor and priest, Father Flye,
his teacher from St Andrew's school near Sewanee, TN. It was found
unopened on the mantle of Agee's New York apartment upon his death
on May 26th, 1955, at the age of 45; two labels, for this and Beatrice Warde's
talk at the opening of a fine printing exhibition in London; a "compliments card" we would send out with review copies; Browning's classic
versification of the Pied Piper myth; title page for Gassendi's tribute to the
humanist scholar, book collector, correspondent and collaborator Nicole
Claude Fabri de Peiresc, with an Introduction by Arthur Freeman.

PIERRE GASSENDI

Peiresc
&
His Books

N·C·F·P

David Godine
Publisher
Boston · Mcmlxx

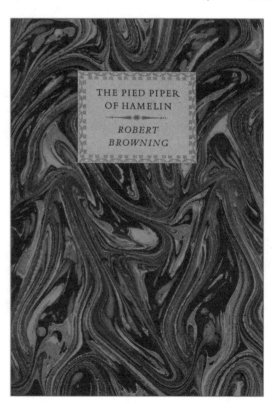

THE PIED PIPER
OF HAMELIN

ROBERT
BROWNING

OPPOSITE: A page from William Steig's *Rotten Island* that
displays one page of his parade of multi-footed, pimpled,
tentacled, and toothsome monsters

tails, and even heads, all in ridiculous arrangements. Some had armour-plating full of tacks and rusty nails, and some had wheels for legs. No two were ever alike.

Dylan Thomas: *A Child's Christmas in Wales*
Illustrated by Edward Ardizzone
1980. 42 PP, 7¼ × 9½″ $13.00 HC

In the days when we were acting like a corporation and had regular board meetings, it was clear that being a primarily "literary" publisher would probably take us down the road to ruin. Quickly. Roger Straus, then active in sales at Farrar, Straus and Giroux, mildly and presciently suggested that if we wanted to survive, we had better start a children's list. I replied that I knew nothing about children's books, to which Roger replied that it didn't matter; design them nicely and pick out a few good stories and we'd sell them. At least better than poetry. This was among the first four we published. It had been published in the UK by J.M. Dent, and the printing, on a

soft, absorbent uncoated paper, was so listless and lifeless that no one had noticed it. I figured that if we could get our hands on Ardizzone's original artwork and print it on an off-white coated sheet, we'd have a winner. We did, and we did. The story of Thomas's Christmas in the Welsh seaside town of Cardiff is immortal, now often performed on stage, read aloud in countless homes, a solid part of the yuletide tradition. We also made a tough decision; we substituted the handsome calligraphy of George Laws for Ardizzone's somewhat illegible hand. But the book didn't need much help beyond decent printing and design. After all, who could resist a book that begins, "One Christmas day was so much like another, in those years around the sea town corner now and out of all sound except the distant speaking of the voices I sometimes hear a moment before sleep, that I can never remember whether it snowed for six days and six nights when I was twelve or whether it snowed for twelve days and twelve nights when I was six."

LEFT & BELOW: The calligraphy by George Laws and the printing on an ivory semi-coated sheet really helped the appearance and sales of this book. The snowball fight may have only occurred in Thomas's mind, but the topography is real; Ardizzone actually visited Cardiff to ensure his architectural details rang true.

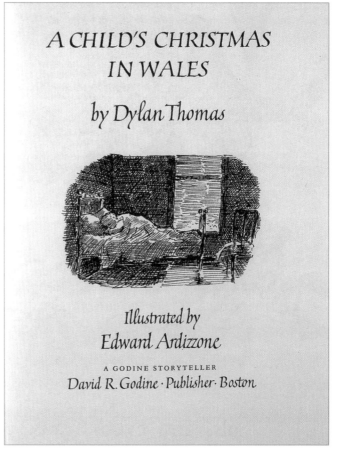

Sergei Prokofiev: *Peter and the Wolf*
Illustrated by Erna Voigt
1980. 32 PP, 10 × 9½″ $11.00 HC

This, along with Dylan Thomas's *A Child's Christmas in Wales*, was among the first four books I bought in 1979 on one of my first trips to the Frankfurt Book Fair. Like many, I had grown up listening to Prokofiev's music, and probably listening to the story as well, but I had never seen an illustrated version, one that displayed as the very first plate all the heroic characters of the drama, along with the instruments that reflected their personality – plucky Peter with the violin, the chirpy little bird with the flute, the duck with the oboe, the cat with the clarinet, the grumpy grandfather with the bassoon, and, of course, the "large gray wolf" with the French horn and the hunters with their kettle drums. Voigt conveys the various stages of the story in a series of full-plate folk paintings, but ups the ante somewhat by also including a few bars of their signature themes and an image of the instrument. In other words, pedagogy combined with artistry. We were shocked that year when the *New York Times* chose both this and *Child's Christmas* as among the ten best children's books of the year. "Wow," I thought "This is easy. I could almost do this blindfolded." A vain hope and one that quickly faded.

LEFT & BELOW: We again used George Laws's calligraphy to provide an elegant touch to this jacket. Each spread, in addition to the story, contained both the instrument and the musical themes that provided the signatures for the leading characters. Here a clearly ravenous, emaciated wolf is on the prowl on the recto page with his French horn and musical notation calling cards opposite on the verso.

No sooner had Peter left the meadow than a large grey wolf did come creeping out of the forest. The cat ran quickly up into a tree.

French Horn

Thomas Keneally: *Ned Kelly and the City of the Bees*
Illustrated by Stephen Ryan
1981. 128 PP, 5½ × 8¼″ $12.00 HC

To the best of my knowledge, this is the only children's book written by Thomas Keneally, most famous for his *Schindler's List*. I encountered the book on a visit to the London offices of the formidable Tom Maschler at Jonathan Cape. Maschler was to Cape what Robert Gottlieb was to Knopf, and their publishing programs often overlapped and intersected. But this little confection had somehow been overlooked by US publishers. It presents the tale of Ned Kelly, the Jesse James of Australia, who lies delusional in a hospital struck down by appendicitis and is offered a drop of golden liquid that shrinks him down to apian dimensions. Together with Nancy Clancy (who speaks only in irritating rhymed couplets), Ned rides off on the bee's back into the hive where he encounters Romeo, the lovesick drone; Basil, the political activist; and the haughty queen, Selma. The book is instructional as well as witty, and the fetching scratchboard engravings by Stephen Ryan add considerably to the story. Life inside a beehive was a natural fit for our nascent children's list. And it seemed no one else was interested, so Maschler kindly let us have it for publication in the US.

Ilse Plume: *The Story of Befana: An Italian Christmas Tale*
1981. 32 PP, 10¾ × 8⅝″ $12.00 HC

We have published over a half-dozen books with Ilse Plume, but this, her first with us, remains my favorite. It retells the old folktale of Befana, the Christmas Witch, who is to an Italian Christmas what Santa Claus is to ours. Befana just misses the Wise Men to visit the Christ Child with her bag of toys and spends much of her life traveling to catch up with them. But she finally gives up and contents herself traveling from the Alps to Sicily, creeping into bedrooms and leaving toys for all the boys and girls, or, had they been naughty, only a lump of coal. Plume worked with hard pencils and her sensibility always led her to the colors and the countryside of Italy. By this time, we had almost abandoned hot metal, and this was probably its last gasp in a Godine title. The Centaur was set by our old friends at MacKenzie and Harris in San Francisco and looks glorious in its large size. Bound in full red cloth, the stamping features Ilse's ever-present signature stars.

LEFT: Stephen Ryan's fine black-and-white scratchboard illustrations provided a fine counterpoint to Keneally's apian saga.

ABOVE & ABOVE RIGHT & OPPOSITE: We published many fine books with Ilse Plume, all showing her masterly use of colored pencils. But this, her first, with its consistently blue skies (both night and day) and Befana dressed in red, I consider her best.

Andrew Lang: *The Chronicles of Pantouflia*
Illustrated by Jeanne Titherington
1981. 208 PP, 5½ × 8¼″ $11.00 HC

Lang is best known for his twelve "colored" Fairy Books that started in blue in 1899 and ran through eleven sequels of various colors. But he was no mean storyteller in his own right, and here you have two tales "made up altogether out of his own head by the author, of course with the help of the Historical Papers in the kingdom on Pantouflia." At his christening, Lang reveals, the poor Prince of Pantouflia was saddled with the ultimate curse. A bitter, ill-tempered fairy doomed him with the terrible words, "You will always be smarter than everyone else." His fate is sealed. Being smarter than everyone doesn't necessarily generate a lot of friends (especially when you remind them of it incessantly), and one day the prince, awakening to find himself totally deserted, realizes that intelligence is no substitute for friendship. By saving the kingdom from two very nasty monsters (and suppressing his all-too-wise

opinions), he manages to be embraced again by his family, wins the heart of a modest and lovely wife, and becomes a beloved ruler. In the second tale, his son Ricardo is another story. His father's love was for books, Ricardo's is for adventures, often dangerous, sometimes foolhardy. So Prigio uses his curse to engineer an accident that forces Ricardo to use *his* brains rather than his brawn. The succession is assured, and it's obvious the next king will be every bit as clever as his predecessor. Lang tells both stories with real charm, and although they're certainly a spoof on an old trope, he never talks down to his audience. He clearly believes in fairies. Titherington's carefully rendered and perfectly imagined pencil drawings provide the perfect droll accompaniment.

LEFT & BELOW: Titherington was an equivalent master with black and white pencil. She also manages to capture the fertile imagination and sense of humor of Lang's somewhat tongue-in-cheek spoof on the traditional fairy tale.

'Hi! page, my chain-armour, helmet, lance, and buckler!
A Molinda! A Molinda!' (which was his *war cry*).

Mary Azarian: *A Farmer's Alphabet*

1981. 60 PP, 8½ × 13″ $13.00 HC

Back in the seventies, my family bought a fine 1804 brick Federal on a dirt road in Vermont. Across from us, and still working a dairy farm, lived Kendall and Gladys Adams. Gladys was still teaching in a one-room schoolhouse, K-5th grade, just down the road. On Thanksgiving Friday, she came across the road to say hello and show me a set of flashcards she was using to teach her second-graders. These were not your usual flashcards; they had been commissioned by the State of Vermont in an effort to engage Vermont's younger rural population with the virtues and attractions of country living. She said they were working "wicked good." The artist who had cut them in soft pine was one Mary Azarian, then living on a farm in Plainfield, VT. She had learned the technique from Leon-

ard Baskin while a student at Smith College, and she was clearly a master. I went up to pay her a visit and found her at work, cutting pine furiously in a small shed adjoining her house while her then-husband was out plowing the fields with oxen. It could have been a hundred years ago. In her work you can really see the difference between a woodcut, cut on the plank with a knife, and wood engraving, cut on the end grain with a burin. Her imagery brings to mind the masculine, vigorous, no-nonsense woodcut art of Northern Europe in the fifteenth and early sixteenth century. Printed in two colors, in a size large enough for framing, the images of Apples, Gardens, Neighbors, Stoves, and Underwear, accompanied by the upper- and lower-case letters, are big, bold, full of life, amusing and engaging. Shortlisted for the Caldecott Medal (which she eventually won), it has remained in print ever since.

LEFT & ABOVE: Produced in a very large format with the upper- and lower-case letters printed in red, the bold, strong woodcuts of Mary Azarian grace the walls of many a New England home. They provided Vermont's second graders a painless and effective way to learn the alphabet while celebrating the virtues and benefits that accompany growing up in the country.

Saki: *The Story-Teller*
Illustrated by Jeanne Titherington
1982. 112 PP, 5¾ × 8¾″ $9.00 SC

Saki, born Hector Hugh Munro in Burma and living out
his unhappy childhood with two impossible maiden aunts,
is more of an addiction than an author. When I read him,
I was seduced, along with many others, by his piquant,
champagne-dry, and morbidly funny tales that first appeared at the beginning of the last century. Long out of
copyright, we were free to select thirteen of the best and
couple them with the delicate, almost ethereal drawings of
Jeanne Titherington, then an immensely talented young
graduate of the Portland School of Art. In Saki's world, the
war is between the children and adults, with Saki clearly on
the side of the kids. Children man the barricades against
their predictable, prudish, and petty elders, pitting their
agile wits against their slower, but considerably larger and
more powerful, opponents. There is never much doubt of
the outcome. This wasn't a deathless contribution to literature, but it was a handsome example of typography, book
design, and illustration. And it managed to get an author I
loved on our list.

Daniel C. Beard: *The American Boy's Handy Book*
Foreword by Noel Perrin
1983. 468 PP, 5½ × 7¾″ $10.00 SC

Lina & Adelia Beard: *The American Girl's Handy Book*
Foreword by Anne M. Boylan
1987. 496 PP, 5½″ × 7½″ $10.00 SC

Daniel C. Beard: *The Field & Forest Handybook*
2001. 448 PP, 5½″ × 7½″ $15.00 SC

The books authored by Daniel Beard and his sister Adelia
were staples of the Boy Scout movement when published
late in the nineteenth century. When Bill Goodman suggested we reissue *The American Boy's Handy Book* on the
hundredth anniversary of its first publication in 1882, I
had my doubts. Time had moved on. Movies and TV (and
later video games and Facebook) had supplanted books
as the preferred entertainment for children. The book
itself was as ugly as anything we had ever reissued, fairly
shouting its nineteenth-century heritage. How wrong I
was. Here we are, over 650,000 copies later, with close to
fifty printings behind us. You have to ask yourself (well,
at least I do): what did I miss here? What accounts for the

RIGHT: The busy, crowded, dated, retro
covers for the Beard titles defy all conventional marketing wisdom. With over
650,000 copies of just his *American Boy's
Handy Book* in print, they are at once
the most typographically primitive and
unstoppably popular of any softcovers
we've issued in fifty years.

continued fascination with a title that is now almost 140 years old, and many of whose activities are presently either illegal, ill-advised, or impossible? I think Ned Perrin hits on one answer in his fine Foreword. He makes the case that children love to be *free*. Many really *do* want to go off and make slingshots, and small boats and tree houses and they are perfectly happy to do this without parental supervision or electronic guidance. Huck was free, and your heart was with him. But he was also innocent, and there is a part of every parent that looks back on those years, before sexual awareness, or social competition, or a fixation on grades and accomplishments, as a period close to an innocent paradise, a period every parent wants for their children. Beard was among the founders of the Boy Scout movement in America, a highly organized group affair with rules, awards, and hierarchies. It's always been interesting to me that this book offers the exact opposite; these projects are not for boys, they are for *a boy*, for a boy probably between ten and twelve still in a state of natural savagery. This put him instantly in a state of war with his parents and probably his sister, who was certainly already wiser. This brief interlude of innocence and wildness was probably viewed as natural and healthy, an expected rite of passage. Beard gave the country its activity Bible – solo initiatives and projects that would occupy any enterprising boy for days. And he made it a point to urge parents to "let boys make their own kites and bows and arrows: they will find a double pleasure in them, and value them accordingly, to say nothing of the education involved in the successful construction of their home-made playthings." Our reissue also proved the ultimate anti-couch-potato weapon. When any youngster complained, "But Dad, I'm bored. There's *nothing to do*," the father could hurl a copy of Beard at him, and it almost always worked. We did three other books in the series. His *Field and Forest Handybook* runs a close second. Faltering in the rear has always been *The American Girl's Handybook*. I once asked a bookseller why. She answered, brightly, "Well, that's simple. Because girls don't want to learn how to knit and tat. They want to be like their brothers. They want to be out there hunting small furry animals with blowguns." Probably more than a little truth in this, but thank God I followed Bill Goodman's suggestion.

Mary Azarian: *The Tale of John Barleycorn or from Barley to Beer*

1982. 36 PP, 8½ × 9⅝″ $13.00 HC
2018. 36 PP, 8½ × 9⅝″ $19.00 HC

In 1982 we published the second book of the gifted and Caldecott-award-winning Mary Azarian. It was an ancient and beloved British ballad that anthropomorphically recounts how barley is converted into beer. In the Middle Ages, this was not a boutique activity for the idle rich but central to survival. We were young and naive, saw it as primarily a book for children and, inexplicably, included her fairly explicit instructions for brewing beer in a bathtub. Especially helpful was her note "It is somehow comforting to think that making beer in the home is an ancient tradition that has continued in an unbroken line to the present day. It is to be hoped that the singing of the song and the brewing of the beer will both survive as homely arts." Not surprisingly, the review establishment was not amused by this endorsement of the "homely arts." Evidently, they envisioned a wave of American children rushing to local supermarkets, buying ingredients, and then, unbeknownst to their parents, initiating the fermentation process in their bathtubs. We're pleased to report that, to the best of our knowledge, this degradation of our national character never occurred. Perhaps a few of the very children exposed to, and bravely resisting this temptation are now starting their own microbreweries across the land.

Seeing the error of our ways (and because this was always among Mary's favorites), we decided to reissue it, with the woodcuts hand-colored and transformed, much as John Barleycorn, into an adult title. Still sung in England today, the song celebrates the age-old story of barley, beer's essential component, from planting to harvesting, threshing, and brewing. And the words are calligraphed in an appropriately uncial hand by the talented George Laws. Finally, a book the world was waiting for: an intelligent toast to sophisticated beer drinkers.

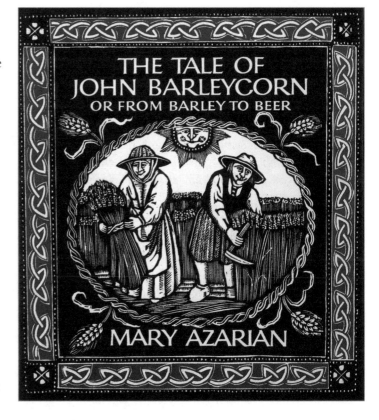

William Kotzwinkle: *Trouble in Bugland*
Illustrated by Joe Servello
1983. 160 PP, 6 × 8″ $13.00 HC

I knew this title had a bright future when both my children, who generally recoiled with horror from anything I published as too advanced and/or sophisticated for their taste, asked me to read these stories of the insectile underworld to them again and again. Addison, naked from the bathtub, even observed, "Dad, you've finally published a book someone might actually want to buy." Right on the money, for this is Kotzwinkle at his best and most artful, five stories, all told in a perfect Holmesian voice, but featuring an all-star cast of insects. Children, of course, found this icky but irresistible, and the colored drawings by Joe Servello rendered the creatures, especially the arachnids, frightening and commendably loathsome. Kotzwinkle deserves more attention than he receives as among the most versatile, literate, prolific, and talented writers this country has produced. But this title will always remain among my all-time favorites.

William Steig: *Rotten Island*
1984. 32 PP, 8⅞ × 11⅞″ $13.00 HC

This solitary, but marvelous, title by Steig came to us through the efforts of David Allender, then a youngster who decided to enter the world of publishing via Godine instead of finishing college. We were fortunate he chose us, working out of our Dartmouth Street offices. The book, originally entitled *The Bad Island*, was out of print, and no one was willing to tackle it because Steig insisted, quite rationally given the subject matter, that it be printed in day-glo inks. We had never heard of day-glo inks, but gave him what he demanded, and the result is surely one of the greatest monster books of all time. Not just one monster, but entire pages full of them, clawing and screaming, biting and scratching amidst erupting volcanoes. A real festival of flame and fury. And the only recorded instance in the English language where one can encounter the memorable juxtaposition "petrified sauerkraut."

ABOVE: Joe Servello's detailed drawing of the enterprising Holmes and Watson, their insectival contemporaries and a convincingly Victorian England are the perfect complements to Kotzwinkle's intricate plots and fiendish characters.
RIGHT: Here we see Steig unleashed, volcanoes exploding, insects engaged in mortal combat, beasts of all stripes running amok with fang and claw. No wonder kids love what is certainly his largest, brightest and most uninhibited title, one that satisfies every child's yearning for a little chaos and mayhem, all of it presented in day-glo color.

Mary Stolz: *Quentin Corn*
Illustrated by Pamela Johnson
1985. 128 PP, 6 × 9″ $13.00 HC

I think it was Noel Perrin, a man with considerable experience with pigs, who brought his friend, Mary Stolz, to our attention. She was then living in Florida taking care of her ailing husband, and although her books had been stars on the Harper & Row lists of the forties and fifties, she had faded into a modest obscurity and quiet retirement, her stories a little too old-fashioned for Harper's taste and her heroes a little too predictably quaint. But I loved *Quentin Corn*, the story of a pig who finds his horizons limited, his life dull, and his prospects unappealing. How to escape this unpromising reality? Run away, and assume the identity of a human being. And Quentin, being no ordinary pig, could *talk!* It's the talking that, of course, undoes him and his future as a money-making carnival freak talking pig was not entirely the future he had in mind. Quentin decides that reversion to a free-range boar is preferable. The fine typographer Barbara Knowles designed a lovely book around the exquisite and humorous drawings of Pam Johnson and the droll prose of Mary Stolz. The first of four totally satisfying books we were to do with them.

Susan Hill: *The Woman in Black*
Illustrated by John Lawrence
1986. 144 PP, 5½ × 8½″ $11.00 HC

We came to this more through the artwork of John Lawrence, whom we had previously published in *Good Babies, Bad Babies,* than any appreciation of the considerable writing skills of Susan Hill. But like Kotzwinkle, she was a literary chameleon of real genius, in this case setting a mystery, really a ghost story, on the obligatory English moor and leading the reader to relax while malignant forces are at work or else just biding their time. She was, in fact, so good that we published two of her novels in our Nonpareil line. It was interesting, and probably fortunate, that the book, which we published as an adult title, was immediately assumed to be a YA because of the drawings by Lawrence. American reviewers and librarians often make this assumption almost automatically; if the book contains artwork it must almost certainly be intended for children, a position most emphatically not observed in Europe, and most especially in France, where art and word have lived in peaceful adult harmony for centuries. But the plot and language carry the reader right through to the devastating climax. The book was converted into among the longest running plays on the West End and then a movie starring Daniel Radcliffe. It is a ghost story to remember, a roller coaster ride of terror and horror, when then, at the very end, *on the very last page,* just when you think you have come through safely…

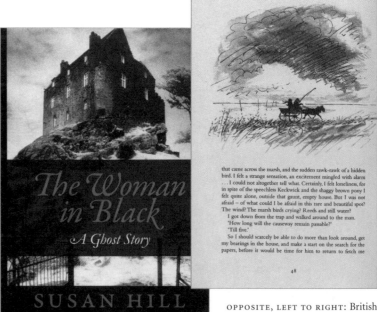

ABOVE: *Cover and a typically exquisite pencil drawing by Pamela Johnson*
RIGHT: *John Lawrence's illustrations seduced American reviewers into believing Hill's chilling horror story was somehow intended for younger audiences. I suspect any youngster who read it did not sleep well for a fortnight.*

OPPOSITE, LEFT TO RIGHT: British set designer Graham Rust proved the perfect artist to undertake the drawings for these two Burnett classics. Very much in the tradition of the English watercolor, they provide a comforting balance to the heroines' challenges and ultimate triumphs.

Frances Hodgson Burnett: *The Secret Garden*
Both illustrated by Graham Rust
1986. 224 PP, 7 × 9½″ $16.00 HC

A Little Princess
1987. 224 PP, 7½ × 9½″ $18.00 HC

These two beloved classics have been loved by generations of both grownups and children. Burnett had an undeniable genius for telling stories and creating plots that pull your heartstrings, inventing characters of unforgettable personality. In *The Secret Garden*, it's Mary Lennox, a spoiled, surly orphan "as tyrannical and selfish a little pig as ever lived," who is summarily orphaned after both parents die of cholera in India. Sent to live with her distant uncle on a desolate moor, implanted at forbidding Misselthwaite Manor with its hundred rooms and Yorkshire staff whose language she can barely understand and no friends, she meets, one by one, a hearty Yorkshire housekeeper, a secretive grounds-keeper, a cheerful robin, and Dickon, a boy her own age whose affinity for all things wild finally engages her. Between them, they bring Colin, the secret, sickly invalid back to life and give hope to his father, her uncle Archibald Craven, who had abandoned Colin and all hope upon the death of his wife. The key that releases Mary and the rest of the family is, of course, the secret garden, locked up and deserted for years, which they conspire to bring back to life.

Sara Crewe of *The Little Princess* has another problem: her father, Captain Crewe is exceedingly wealthy and, because he considers the Indian climate unhealthy, decides to plant her at an expensive London school for girls – rich and spoiled girls – which Sara, kind, forgiving, and generous, is decidedly not. She has her own parlor and even her own maid, extravagances warmly welcomed by the conniving and greedy Miss Minchin of the "The Select Seminary for Young Ladies and Gentlemen." But when the father dies unexpectedly and his fortune evaporates, the unscrupulous headmistress consigns Sarah to the cold, unfurnished attic, her food diminished, her contact with friends curtailed. Here she bravely relies on her imagination to keep her sane until her father's old friend moves next door, discovers Sara as his friend's long-lost daughter, and restores her to her position as an heiress. There is little doubt in the reader's mind she will continue on her generous road.

Burnett treats her characters with empathy, introducing them one by one, making sure that the plots and the situations are clear. She had suffered her own tragedies; her first son, Lionel, died of tuberculosis at age 16. Two marriages failed, and both were front-page news. But she was a fighter; the lawsuit she initiated in England in 1888 to protect the earnings accumulating from the 1886 stage success of *Little Lord Fauntleroy* was instrumental in establishing a precedent protecting both American and British authors. Both *A Little Princess* and *The Secret Garden*, which began their lives as plays, were rewritten and published as books in 1905 and 1911 respectively. Both, huge successes, have been rewritten and reworked for stage and screen continuously and appear regularly on any list of the most popular children's books of the last hundred years. Burnett, never once rejected by a publisher, would write a grand total of 52 books and 13 plays. *The Secret Garden* was written, appropriately, in the spacious rose garden of her extensive Long Island estate where she would spend the last seventeen years of an event-filled life, one that would make a fine novel in its own right – and not a few sequels. Unlike many available abridged versions, our editions include the full text of the originals. And English set designer Graham Rust's illustrations provide the perfect counterpoint to the text.

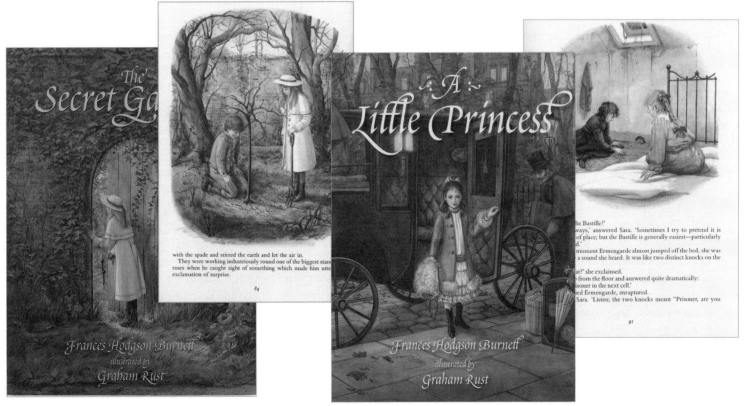

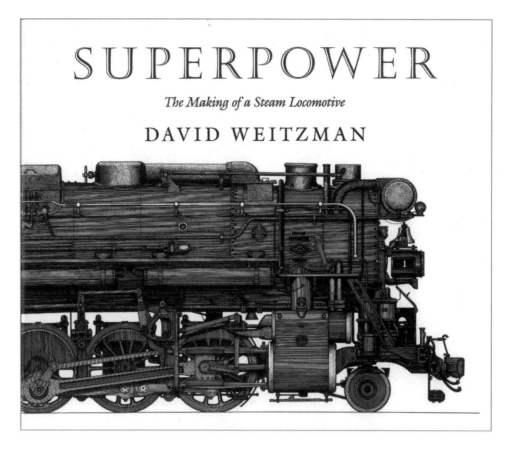

David Weitzman: *Superpower: The Making of a Steam Locomotive*

1987. 108 PP, 12¾ × 10¾" $20.00 HC

By 1900, one out of every ten Americans was somehow employed in a job relating to the railroads. They were our country's first great industry. And every boy, at least of my generation, was at some point in their youth fascinated by them, may have even seen the last of the grand steam engines as they inexorably transitioned to diesel. This is the most wonderful train book imaginable, certainly among the most technically challenging projects we ever attempted. It relates the story of Ben, who at eighteen follows in the footsteps of his father and reports for work at the great "Loco" plant in Lima, Ohio. Ben starts as an apprentice as the yard is engaged in building the prototype of the 1870 "Berkshire," a 2-8-2 (two small wheels in front, eight big driving wheels, and two under the cab) behemoth, the most powerful and efficient steam locomotive ever built. In his tour through the various departments of the plant you meet the designer, who must compromise and balance weight with strength, and see the blueprints drawn, revised, and refined. You follow Ben to fifty buildings spread over 65 acres, stopping at the foundry where the massive frames are poured into damp sand moulds, visiting the machine shop where the intricately detailed drawings are converted into equally precise parts. You see how wheels are made (not easy, they have to be perfectly round) and driving rods, and how rivets are driven and a boiler constructed. All this is conveyed not only in an engaging and technically accurate text but in line drawings of the most precise nature. The production presented problems we'd never encountered. The drawings were on mylar, drawn with an architect pen (so they could be easily erased and redrawn). But they were often close to four feet in length. No one in America had cameras large enough to shoot them in line. We had to send them to Japan. And the book had to be large. Very large. Any smaller and the tightly drawn lines would clog and lose their definition. It had to be printed on a dull-coated paper to hold the detail, and bound in full cloth to support the book block. All this we sold for $20.00. But for every kid who ever set out to assemble an American Flyer, Lionel, or HO scale train set, this was the ultimate book, the one they'd hoped for. It demanded attention and concentration. The text never condescends, simplifies, or sugar coats the difficult processes. It presents a short course in engineering, a tribute to the vision of designers, the painstaking drawings of draughtsmen, and the proud, often dangerous, labor of the workmen who make it all happen. True, the steam locomotive is no longer part of our lives, but none can look at this book without a rush of nostalgia. Like the work at the "Loco," it is a beautifully detailed and researched document, a product of craftsmanship and pride that reflects credit on everyone who was involved in its assembly. Pride of place definitely goes to author and artist, David Weitzman, a classy veteran who would do two more books with us, including *Thrashin' Time*, a similarly detailed account of the last days of steam harvesters on the Great Plains. Like this book, among our finest, he was, and remains, *sui generis.*

ABOVE & RIGHT: Jacket and interior page of *Anne of Green Gables*, illustrated by Lauren Mills with the lovely calligraphy by John Stevens

L.M. Montgomery: *Anne of Green Gables*
Illustrated by Lauren Mills
1989. 352 PP, 7 × 9½″ $20.00 HC

Hard as it is to believe, when we issued this new edition in 1989, there was not a single decent edition of Miss Anne (with an e, thank you very much) Shirley's adventures in print. Her charms are timeless and irrepressible–who could resist a tale of a precocious young orphan girl taken into the home–and soon the hearts–of an elderly and very set-in-their-ways couple and the tale of her growing up in rural Prince Edward Island? It provides not only a great story, but also a role model for generations of spunky and determined young women. Lauren Mills, who had previously illustrated George MacDonald's *At the Back of the North Wind* for us, provided the nearly Burne-Jones-like drawings, and John Stevens contributed the calligraphy.

Barbara McClintock: *The Heartaches of a French Cat*
1989. 48 PP, 8½ × 11″ $15.00 HC

Animal Fables from Aesop
1991. 48 PP, 7 × 10″ $18.00 HC

Audrey Bryant was the editor who discovered Barbara McClintock and published in 1989 her first (and quirki-

est) title, *The Heartaches of a French Cat*, the wrenching story of feline betrayal and ultimate redemption. Minette, poor but beautiful, is at first seduced by the charm and wealth of Count Bisquet, but, on learning of his philandering, abandons him to live alone and publish a best-selling memoir of their courtship and his desertion. The entire story is supplied with only a "Cast of Characters" as a guide, no words, the plot conveyed entirely through a series of (mostly) black-and-white Grandvillean line drawings with a very few guideposts for the reader. It was a virtuoso display, but, as a "children's book" very much in the sophisticated French tradition. It was followed two years later by her interpretations of Aesop's animal fables, a trope that has engaged artists since the fifteenth century. In McClintock's version, a series of nine acts, representing nine classic fables, are enacted by children in costume on the living stage. The drawings are, again, modern versions of the French genius Grandville with echoes of his English counterpart, Charles H. Bennett, who published his own interpretations of the fables ca. 1857 in London. Like theirs, hers are subtly colored, thoroughly alive with a blend of drama, charm, and droll wit in the tradition of La Fontaine. This is a title that has enjoyed a long shelf life, and when Barbara wins the Caldecott award, which she surely deserves, I trust readers will rediscover these early examples of her considerable talents.

W. Heath Robinson: *The Adventures of Uncle Lubin*

Afterword by David R. Godine

1992. 128 PP, 5⅝ × 8″ $10.00 SC

I had never encountered the work of the immensely talented and now unaccountably obscure W. Heath Robinson until Lucy Hitchcock, then working at the company as a designer and proofreader, brought in her battered copy of *Uncle Lubin* and urged us to publish it. Reading it, I could well understand her enthusiasm, for here was an author and an artist of genuine whimsy and a real talent for telling a story. In doing a little research for my Afterword, I found he was beloved in England as "The Gadget King," the equivalent of our own Rube Goldberg. He came from a distinguished family of equally talented illustrators and had himself provided the artwork for over sixty titles, the best known of which were the ones he wrote and illustrated himself. To quote myself, "These works contain none of the Medieval line of a Morris, the accentuated sensibility of a Rackham, or the repressed sexuality of a Beardsley; they are free, easy and totally (and innocently) whimsical." Robinson's facility for inventively depicting the absurd (of which his most endearing was a six-tiered communal baby carriage for beleaguered babysitters) is manifest in the adventures Uncle Lubin sustains in his determined, and ultimately successful, effort to recover his nephew Peter from the nefarious and elusive bag-bird. Working with Lucy, Scott Kosofsky set and designed the book in "Golden" modeled after Morris's "Golden" type.

Arthur Ransome: *Swallows and Amazons*

1995. 352 PP, 5½ × 8″ $8.00 SC

1 : *Swallows and Amazons*

2 : *Swallowdale*

3 : *Peter Duck*

4 : *Winter Holiday*

5 : *Coot Club*

6 : *Pigeon Post*

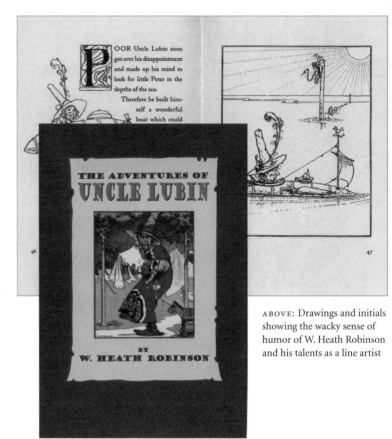

ABOVE: Drawings and initials showing the wacky sense of humor of W. Heath Robinson and his talents as a line artist

7 : *We Didn't Mean to Go to Sea*

8 : *Secret Water*

9 : *The Big Six*

10 : *Missee Lee*

11 : *The Picts and the Martyrs*

12 : *Great Northern?*

In 1929 Ransome retired from his life as a double agent for both England and Russia to retreat permanently to his beloved Coniston waters. Here he took to writing about the only place he ever thought of as home, a terrain he knew and loved. As has been demonstrated, most of the characters described, and many of the places depicted, in this twelve-volume series, are real, somewhat embellished and enlarged perhaps, but based on Ransome's actual experiences when, as a youth, he boarded a train to spend his summers in the Lake District. The attraction of the books, I believe, lies in their total lack of affectation, and the unusual, indeed unconventional, cast of characters, which featured the two Amazons (both girls) and the four Walker siblings (two of them female). Ransome also writes from experience; he was an excellent sailor and an experienced navigator. He had a fine ear for dialogue, and many of the adventures he describes he may well have first heard in his employment as a reporter for *The Guardian* and the British government. A long list of librarians predictably cautioned us against publication; the books were too long for children to handle (this was long before *Harry Potter* came on the scene), the type was too small, the characters were too English, one of the girls was called Titty, they were all out of step with the times, etc. But it turned out that Ransome had a large and loyal following in this country (the books had formerly been in print with Lippincott), and many were eager to pass along the adventures to the next generation. An attraction for the children, I am sure, is that parents, indeed all adults, disappear in the first few pages and don't reappear until the last. They stay in touch with

smoke signals or not at all. No email chains, no frantic cell phone calls, no visibly worried parents. The children live by their wits and off the land. As their father (a naval commander far off on the high seas) curtly replies to their mother when queried whether letting them stray is a good idea, BETTER DROWNED THAN DUFFERS IF NOT DUFFERS WONT DROWN. Eventually, we reissued all twelve volumes, each with a new cast of characters, a new challenge for the children, and often with settings in different locales.

BELOW, LEFT & RIGHT: Ten of the dozen Ransome titles reissued in his *Swallows and Amazons* series. The uniform format, interior design and title calligraphy by Julian Waters gave the series a unified appearance.

Joan Aiken: *Shadows & Moonshine*
Illustrated by Pamela Johnson
2000. 240 PP, 5½ × 8″ $19.00 HC

Born in 1924, Joan Aiken has long been considered among the more versatile and imaginative authors of books for young readers. Her novels, like *The Wolves of Willoughby Chase*, are praised for their wit, wordplay, and sly parody. She also has an uncanny ability to tell a really good story employing classic (and often challenging) English and presenting fascinating characters and compelling action. Like her father, the poet Conrad Aiken, she was adept at a number of forms, but a master of the short story. In this fetching baker's dozen of what she herself considers her best, she can be scary (everyone knows her fascination with wolves and witches) and poetic (as in "Moonshine in the Mustard Pot" and "The Lilac in the Lake"). But whatever she set her hands to reads like the work of a master. We were fortunate to engage Pam Johnson as the illustrator. Among the real talents we came to know and love, she had moved from Cape Cod to a sheep farm in Maine. Sheep require chemicals to keep them healthy, and whatever she used had so affected her hands that she could barely hold a pencil. It took her a year to complete the drawings for Joan's book and they are, I think, among her best. She was the first artist of *my* generation to pass away, and I miss her.

Anne Lindbergh: *The Worry Week*
Pictures by Kevin Hawkes
2003. 144 PP, 5½ × 8⅛″ $11.00 SC

If you cruise Penobscot Bay you are bound, at one point, to pass through "The Thoroughfare," which separates North Haven from Vinalhaven. This is where the old families and rusticators hang out, and where the two Lindbergh sisters, Anne and Reeve, daughters of Charles and Anne Morrow Lindbergh, have summered since childhood. Imagine the shock to three young girls, who have been looking forward to their vacation there all season, when their parents are forced to close their camp and return to Boston for a funeral. Not for a day, but a week. But these daughters of a Harvard professor and Longfellow scholar, are no slouches; they devise a surreptitious way to return on the ferry with plans to reopen the cabin and enjoy themselves. "Just think," quips eleven-year-old Allegra, "we'll be on the island and we won't have a worry in the world." It turns out their plan has a few holes in it. When they return to their cabin they find it locked and emptied of food. Allegra, ever practical, realizes it's up to her to provide for the bookish Alice and seven-year-old Edith (aka Minnow), who seems preoccupied with gluing seashells to canisters. Fending for themselves, the girls learn to live off the land, gathering berries, chanterelles, and mussels. And in the process, Allegra learns a more important lesson: being a parent can be *very* stressful. Lindbergh's seaside story, suffused with the carefree pleasures of childhood, summer heat, swimming, and finding a treasure that binds them closer to their family's history and New England's literary heritage, confirms her place as among the best storytellers the region. And can you figure out the connection between the children and Longfellow?

ABOVE & RIGHT: Covers and a sample page from Aiken's *Shadows and Moonshine* and Lindbergh's *The Worry Week*

François Place: *Old Man Mad about Drawing*
2004. 112 PP, 6 × 9″ $20.00 HC

I first encountered François Place at Frankfurt, where I fell in love with *The Last Giants.* We published it successfully in 1993. When the chance came to do his book centered on the life of the Japanese artist Hokusai, we lept. The French have a peculiar propensity for doing children's books as oversized folios, a format that emphatically fails in the US. Carl W. Scarbrough used the William Rodarmor translation and the Place illustrations to create an entirely new book: an octavo that preserved the charm and originality of the art and still read like a "typical" children's book. Of course, there was nothing typical about it – it presents Japan just opened to the West by Commodore Perry in 1853, a country still feudal and under the complete control of an hereditary monarch but where art was rewarded and the crafts encouraged. Place introduces the reader to the trades the Japanese had perfected to print books of great beauty and balance and all the processes involved: ink-making, woodcutting, printing. Above all, he pays homage to an artist he clearly worships and who was reputed to have commented, "From the age of six I had the habit of sketching from life. I became an artist and from 50 on began producing work that won some reputation, but nothing I did before the age of 70 was worthy of attention. At 73, I began to grasp the structures of birds & beasts, insects & fish, and the way plants grow. If I continue trying I will surely understand them better by the time I am 86 so that by 90 I will have penetrated their essential nature. At 100, I may well have a positively clear understanding of them, while at 130 or 140 or more I will have reached a stage where every dot & stroke I paint will be alive." We have very few living artists on our list who can genuinely be called geniuses. Place has a place of honor among them.

Joe McKendry: *Beneath the Streets of Boston*
2005. 48 PP, 9 × 11″ $19.00 HC

With this fine first book, the winner of the 2005 Massachusetts Book Award, Joe McKendry takes his place in a long line of brilliant artists/illustrators – David Macaulay, Chris Van Allsburg, and David Wiesner among many others – who graduated from the Rhode Island School of Design. Like them he conceived his book as a coherent whole, in his case examining the life beneath Boston streets during the building of America's first subway system. Both the narrative and the sepia watercolors, created with such accuracy that many mistook them for photographs, sweep the reader along as the tunnels expand from Park Street along the "elevated" track through Charlestown and Roxbury and ultimately beneath the river to Cambridge. In 1895, this was hardly routine work; it was new and dangerous and necessary. The burgeoning population of immigrants was making the streets impassable, and public transportation was the only rational answer. McKendry uses politics and newspaper accounts to give the story real immediacy and gets Charlie where he wants to go for only a nickel. In *Beneath the Streets of Boston* he gives lively, politically charged accounts of the country's first underground transportation system, doing for subways what Dunwell had for New England mills. Printed in color, in a large format, it represented discovery of another real talent.

LEFT: Interior page from Place's *Old Man Mad about Drawing*
BELOW & RIGHT: Sample spread showing the sepia watercolors and the cover from McKendry's *Beneath the Streets of Boston*

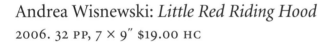

Tom got into the frog with Aunt Bundlejoy Cosysweet and started it up. The frog hopped over the fence and the next three gardens in one giant hop.

Andrea Wisnewski: *Little Red Riding Hood*
2006. 32 PP, 7 × 9″ $19.00 HC

Our second book with the talented papercut artist Andrea Wisnewski was the old chestnut of the girl in the red cloak, but here she is set in a New England winter and the characters are dressed like Old Sturbridge settlers. We noodled the storyline to make it fit properly and not disturb the dramatic two-page spreads. People generally mistake Andrea's papercuts for woodcuts, but in fact she uses same-size black sheets of paper and carefully cuts out the whites with an x-acto blade. Then she has a printing plate made, prints it as a relief block, and hand-colors it. Here's the classic tale of the girl, the grandmother and the wolf, all set in a countryside very reminiscent of colonial New England. Andrea's daughter, Allison, served as a model for the loyal granddaughter, and in this version, the grandmother is indeed eaten, but emerges moist, albeit intact.

Russell Hoban: *How Tom Beat Captain Najork and His Hired Sportsmen*
Illustrated by Quentin Blake

2006. 32 PP, 6¼ × 8″ $7.00 SC

A Near Thing for Captain Najork
Illustrated by Quentin Blake

2006. 32 PP, 6¼ × 8″ $7.00 SC

It would be hard to make a claim to being a children's book publisher of any merit and not have on the list at least a few of the books illustrated by Britain's resident genius, Quentin Blake. Best known for his drawings for the novels and stories of Roald Dahl, Blake's long career has extended over hundreds of titles plus these two, featuring the adventures of Tom, a memorable and lovable youth admirably and hilariously presented by Russell Hoban. In the first volume, Tom is living with his aunt, Miss Fidget Wonkham-Strong, who is anything but lovable. "She wore an iron hat, and took no nonsense from anybody. Where she walked the flowers drooped and when she sang the trees all shivered." Tom is her challenge, "a boy so good at fooling around that he does little else." To teach him a lesson, she calls in the formidable Captain Najork and his hired sportsmen, who challenge Tom to three rounds of womble, muck, and sneedball, certain they will win. But when it comes to fooling around, Tom doesn't fool around. His skills prove without limit and exceptional. Well, the second volume continues in the same vein. Tom has understandably advertised for a new aunt and is living happily with Bundlejoy Cosysweet. He fools around and invents a jam-powered frog that so provokes Captain Najork that he sets out after him in his five-person pedal-powered snake, intent on revenge, determined this time to

ABOVE & RIGHT: Kim's vivid hand-colored linoleum cuts provide a happy companion to her father's lively verse.

beat him. The chase is thrilling but the outcome is never in doubt. These books are the perfect marriage of art and text; zany, outrageous, action-filled, and replete with quirky juxtapositions of words and language that both challenge and entertain. Works of genuine genius.

Dennis Webster: *Absolutely Wild*
Illustrations by Kim Webster Cunningham
2009. 32 PP, 9½ × 8¾″ $18.00 HC

I saw a display of Kim's linoleum cuts at an exhibition in Peterborough, NH and was immediately struck by the vigor and color of her animals and the viscerally engaging and often hilarious verses by her father. This was Kim's first book and she could not have been more genial and cooperative. We worked hard on getting the type and borders to balance the art, and anyone who bothered to read the poems about animals made visible and lovable invariably ended up buying the book. I can think of few titles that would be more fun to read aloud to a child in bed than this one. Just try this deathless tribute to the moose.

THE MOOSE

The massive moose can meet his needs
By munching moss and twigs and weeds
He is a solitary fellow
All he does is stand and bellow.

A stranger thing you'll never meet
He's got big knees and bigger feet
His nose is huge, his hair is hopeless
He smells because his life is soapless.

But when a female wanders by
Her beauty makes him preen and sigh.
Both look as odd as all their kind
It must be true that love is blind.

Nowhere else in the English language will you find the words "hopeless" and "soapless" coupled in the same quatrain.

Edward Ardizzone: *Sarah and Simon and No Red Paint*

2011. 48 PP, 7½ × 9″ $18.00 HC

I confess to being a longtime and avid fan of anything illustrated by the genial and prolific English artist Edward Ardizzone. Over a career that spanned fifty years he illustrated literally hundreds of books, some 5,000 of his drawings appearing in adult novels, children's books, poetry, and his own stories. Our very first list of children's books contained an Ardizzone classic, his drawings for Thomas's *A Child's Christmas in Wales,* and we subsequently brought out editions of Noel Langley's *The Land of Green Ginger,* Eleanor Farjeon's *The Little Bookroom,* and a delightful compendium of his own *Letters to Friends* featuring his illustrations. But this is among my all-time favorites – who could resist a story about two children raised in the obligatory attic (optimistically known as "The Studio") by the starving artist of a father and the beleaguered mother? The story features Sarah and Simon, the two lovable children who apparently never go to school but learn all they need in life on the floor of "the shop they liked best of all, the old second-hand bookshop into which nobody

ever seemed to go." Trouble arises when the family, on the verge of starvation, is unable to buy the tube of red paint that will enable the father to finish his masterpiece, due to be delivered to the dealer the very next day for a confirmed sale. The story involves the requisite rich uncle who disapproves of the father's profession as an artist, cuts him off without a shilling, but in the end confesses, "I was wrong to be angry with you all those years ago. I have watched your two clever children at the bookshop and seen your lovely pictures. I know now that you were right to become a painter." And help them he does, and with his help they soon become rich and famous.

It's hard to read this and not connect some dots between the artist in the book and the artist who created him. Ardizzone was a dashingly fast illustrator. The expressions on the faces are little more than dots and dashes, the cross-hatching to define shape and volume put down at breakneck speed. Much of his work was single- or two-color, this one originally drawn in black outline and a sepia wash to produce a two-color effect, set down on some arcane substrate called Kodatrace. His work is almost unfailingly sunny, fresh, and immediate. He and Quentin Blake (who described Ardizzone's temperament as "Arcadian") are the two giants of British book illustration of my era.

LEFT & BELOW: Ardizzone's cover shows the father painting his masterpiece with a hungry family looking on and, in a right-hand page, the anxious mother reminding the beleaguered artist that there's no food in the larder and the children are hungry. "Their mother cried a lot, hugged the baby, and told her husband he must go to Uncle Robert and make it up." Matters were getting desperate.

Now there was nothing more to sell and no money to tide things over. Worse still he could not finish his masterpiece in time to sell it.

Their mother cried a lot, hugged the baby, and told her husband he must go to Uncle Robert and make it up.

Nan Parson Rossiter: *The Fo'c'sle: Henry Beston's "Outermost House"*

2011. 32 PP, 8 × 10″ $18.00 HC

Nan's hope, which I think she executed brilliantly, was to introduce young readers to the saga of the year Henry Beston spent in a 16 × 20′ shack on Cape Cod and to evoke the solitude and wonder that led to the writing of *The Outermost House*. He lived there alone, through the changing seasons, witnessing the migration of the birds, the wonder of stars in the night sky, the furious storms that pummeled the coast. During the days he would wander along the beach, take notes, and think. At night he would come home to write, occasionally entertaining visits from his only neighbors, the surfmen from the nearby Nauset Station. She tells his story in his own words, artfully woven together with her art, which glows with its own inner light and simplicity. Together they both present and amplify his natural world, making him, his year on the beach, and his life in the little shack he loved come convincingly and poignantly to life.

"Henry's house sat high on a dune overlooking the great rugged coastline and the vast and thundering ocean. It was a snug and sturdy little house built with straight strong timbers. The men who built it carried the lumber and bricks across two miles of marsh roads and sand dunes. Henry's neighbors called his house the "Outermost House" because it was farther out on the dunes than any other, but Henry called the little house the Fo'c'sle."

LEFT: Henry as a young man, awakening to nature and about to evoke it in his classic *The Outermost House*, his lyrical memoir describing the year he spent in that small shack and a book instrumental in protecting a large part of the Cape's fragile shoreline.

Richard Adams: *The Tyger Voyage*
Illustrated by Nicola Bayley
2013. 32 PP, 9½ × 11″ $16.00 HC

This title began its life as another Maschler/Gottlieb/Cape/ Knopf collaboration, and I'm sure no one in their right mind thought that when it was published in the US in 1976 it would climb onto the bestseller list. Richard Adams was years away from publishing his classic *Watership Down*, and this was the first book by Bayley, then a young and unknown English artist. But I was taken with the book and owned an original copy, and when Sue Ramin mentioned that the rights were free and the book was being reprinted by the Andersen Press, I jumped at the chance to put it on our list. Our brief flap copy gives the bones of the story, "A gentleman tyger and his son set sail in a rather dubi-

ous boat into the timeless unknown. Together they roam across the seas, through jungles, across ice-covered mountains, past erupting volcanoes to be rescued by a troupe of gypsies. Eventually they return to Victorian England with many an extraordinary tale to tell." In fact, the book is far more clever than this suggests. It seizes on the British tradition of fearless nautical exploration and reduces it to easy-to-digest rhyming quatrains, engaging for children and entertaining for adults. The artwork by Bayley, which could have easily been at home in a fifteenth-century vellum Book of Hours, is jewel-like in its precision and color. Printed full size on the rectos, it perfectly complements the verse. This was a book that gave real pleasure to both children and adults, a near-perfect collaboration between writer and artist. And our reissue, newly shot from the original art, holds up well against the original.

Peter Ackerman: *The Lonely Typewriter*
Illustrated by Max Dalton

2014. 40 PP, 10 × 8″ $17.00 HC

The "Lonely" series, conceived and executed by the Acker-man and Dalton team, started with *The Lonely Phonebooth*, the touching and true story of the square landmarks that once graced practically every street corner in New York City but which, by the early twenty-first century, had all but disappeared. Taking one of the last standing examples (now preserved as a city landmark), Ackerman and Dalton built a story around it. And in much the same vein, did the same for *The Lonely Typewriter*, a topic I find of consider-able interest as I still regularly use one. But mine is an IBM Selectric (with the correction ribbon) and theirs was a cross between Max's Remington and Peter's Smith Corona manual. And it's based on a true story.

It seems that Martin Luther King's secretary was a real wizard of the keys, and when she died she passed her beloved manual on to her daughter. The daughter (here Penelope) used it faithfully until the day she passed a store advertising the then-novel "personal computer" (with an amazing 144 MB of memory!). Penelope brings it home and is thrilled – no more correction ribbons – "It worked much faster than her typewriter and let Penelope fix her mistakes on the screen and look up everything she wanted to know." The typewriter was consigned to the attic. Skip ahead a few years to her son Pablo writing his paper on penguins and puffins. Suddenly the cursor freezes, the computer dies. But Mom has a solution (as Moms usually do). "Up in the attic, under dust and spiderwebs, sat the typewriter. Its pale yellow keys stood alert like soldiers. Its long silver arm stuck out like it would like to shake Pablo's hand. Pablo asked 'What's that?' 'A typewriter,' said his Mom." Well, you can finish the story. Pablo writes his essay on the typewriter and even brings it to his school where it is stared at in wide-eyed amazement by his classmates. No screen! No plugs! No electricity! This typewriter isn't lonely any longer.

It's a simple story, but all the mechanics are fully illus-trated and explained; the technical names of the parts that still sing in the ears of my generation: carriage return lever, platen, shift key, space bar, a saga of the primal animal whose DNA has somehow found its way its way into our digital world. The team followed up with *The Screaming Chef*, who is anything but lonely. All three of them charm-ing, and thoroughly modern, tales for our times.

Andrea Wisnewski: *Trio: The Tale of a Three-legged Cat*

2017. 40 PP, 10 × 8″ $18.00 HC

Meet Trio, the runt of the litter, born with only three legs, but very much the little cat that could. And meet, too, Andrea Wisnewski, a genuinely inspired artist with a sly sense of humor and a pitch-perfect instinct for color and design. This was the third book of hers we published, preceded by *A Cottage Garden Alphabet* and her version of *Little Red Riding Hood*, her reimagining of the beloved adventure. But this involves a fetching little kitten whose infirmity doesn't stop him from pouncing, sneaking, and jumping like other felines. Trio has particular affection for the eleven chickens (which, as the author observes, can be testy) that share his garage and garden, and he is game to engage in all their activities: digging up bugs, rolling in the dust, and most mysteriously and ambitiously, laying eggs. This challenge requires real effort, especially making it up to the nesting box. But once he's figured it out, he returns to it every day. And his persistence pays off. Sure enough, one day an egg starts to hatch beneath him, and little does he know that the chick that will emerge, with its own singular infirmity, will be his best friend. As a subtle story about diversity, mixed species, colorful images, a dramatic storyline, getting along with neighbors, and overcoming obstacles, it is a small wonder of integrated design, colorful images, and memorable characters.

The chickens did one thing that Trio could not do, no matter how hard he tried.

They laid eggs.

Trio knew [...] chicken [...] that [...] didn't st[...]

THE KING *of the* BIRDS

Written & Illustrated by
HELEN WARD

TRIO
The Tale of a Three-legged Cat

Written and Illustrated by
ANDREA WISNEWSKI

All together, the birds took to the sky.

They flapped, bounded, leapt and lumbered into the air like a rising roof of wings...

Helen Ward: *The King of the Birds*

2018. 40 PP, 10 × 8″ $18.00 HC

It's an ancient folktale. A gaggle of old (but not necessarily wise) birds decide they need a king. How to choose? And on what basis? After considerable discussion, they decide their monarch should be the bird that can fly the highest. The eagle takes on the challenge and appears to win the crown, but deep within his feathers hides a tiny wren who, "Beating his little wings furiously, rose into the cold, thin air… higher than the eagle, higher than all the other birds." Both fell back to the ground, and the elders had to decide on the winner. In the end, they agreed "Having the highest flyer for a king was one thing; having the cleverest was even better." The story is engaging, but what really carries the book are the spectacular, detailed, and artfully arranged ornithological drawings of the various species by Helen Ward, probably a few hundred in all. Sometimes one bird to a page, sometimes entire flocks of different species. Every spread a riot of color and inventive typography. The best feature, for devoted bird watchers, is the inclusion of detailed tables at the back of the book, displaying each spread in detail and providing keys to the common names for each of the birds, an ornithologist's dream come true.

Clifton Fadiman: *Wally the Wordworm*

Illustrated by Arnold Roth
Afterword by Anne Fadiman
2019. 64 PP, 7 × 8¼″ $18.00 HC

Wally is a worm who lives for words, but he's starved for inspiration. . . until one day he slithers into a magical book: the dictionary. There he finds the Mother Lode, plenty of fodder, for from the moment he embarks upon his logomaniacal odyssey he finds everything a hungry wordworm requires – from "auk" (which rhymes with "hawk" and also sounds a little like "yak") to really tasty ones like "mellifluous" and "ptarmigan" (Wally had a little trouble pronouncing this one, but the Dictionary told him to throw away the P and it went down nicely). This was, of course, Clifton Fadiman's device for introducing his indisputably brilliant children to uncommon words, to make them see the panoramic possibilities of the English language. The book had been originally published in 1964, but his daughter Anne kept getting queries about it at her talks and lectures. It was a fondly remembered favorite nowhere to be found. After an appearance at The Norwich Bookstore, the lovely and lively owner, Liza Bernard, passed on the tip and guaranteed an initial buy of five copies – a lot for her and enough for me. Arnold Roth had miraculously kept the art, and Michael Babcock was able to reconstruct the book from scratch from a used copy. Anne wrote her usual elegant Afterword, putting the book in its original context: stories her father used to tell her when she was a young, precocious girl on the receiving end. As she put it, "In the late 50s and early 60s when my father was telling me and Kim" (her brother) "about Bertram" (Wally's original name) "the book market for small children was dominated by easy-to-read stories based on the principle that young readers should never encounter words they didn't already know, lest they become discouraged. My father, by contrast, believed that children had a far greater appetite for difficulty than was commonly assumed; that they should read over their heads and beyond their years; and that children's literature should therefore not be dumbed down but smarted up." In another context he would write, "There is only one way to enlarge a rubber band and that is to stretch it."

Fadiman's theories on children's appetites fit very well with ours. I remember him fondly presiding over the panel of judges at the Book-of-the Month Club. Over the course of his career he was the editor-in-chief at Simon & Schuster, the book critic for *The New Yorker*, and the host of the popular radio quiz show *Information Please*. He was the author of books on wine, anecdotes, and the *New Lifetime Reading Plan*. Arnold Roth, who made certain Wally was invariably fitted out with a red necktie and baseball hat (its bill mostly forward but sometimes backward), is well known for his contributions to *The New Yorker* and *Esquire*. In all, it was a delightful collaboration.

James Whitcomb Riley: *When the Frost is on the Punkin*

Illustrated by Glenna Lang

1991. 32 PP, 8¾ × 11″ $16.00 HC

Glenna Lang, who has illustrated four successful children's poems for us, came across this well-loved Indiana classic, perfect for its fall colors and lilting language. I suppose it has been recited by generations of midwestern farmers, for it perfectly captures the brisk days of fall when "the frost is on the punkin." Like all Glenna's books, the artwork relies on strong, primal colors and easily recognizable shapes and digestible story lines. Simple, but in no way unsophisticated. It is often more difficult to illustrate a short, simple story or poem than a longer one, and Glenna had that gift. The books, produced in a uniform size, provided perfect read-alouds for parents and children alike.

OPPOSITE: The legendary yawl *Dorade,* flying the burgee of the Seattle Yacht Club, is drawing nicely with spinnaker and a mizzen staysail set on a broad reach in the Straight of Juan de Fuca in the Swiftsure Race. Photograph © Guy Hoppen.

Pamela A. Miller: *And The Whale is Ours: Creative Writing of American Whalemen*
1979. 216 PP, 6 × 9¼″ $15.00 HC

In 1979, before its merger with the New Bedford Whaling Museum, the Kendall Whaling Museum housed among the world's great whaling collections, and certainly the most extensive collection of books and manuscripts dealing with Yankee whalers and whalemen. This is a selection of their best, in the words of their director, a "hunt for diamonds – or rhinestones – in a woodpile of more than 3,500 whaling manuscripts." That search resulted in what is surely the best anthology ever collected between covers of poetry, prose, and even playwriting, found in the logbooks, journals, diaries, and occasional sketchbooks the whalemen kept on their multi-year voyages to distant oceans. It's all here: a whaling captain's tender poem to his wife, a fo'c'sle deckhand musing on the bane of bedbugs and fleas, the songs the crews would sing, and the verses they would recite to fill the long interstices of boredom between brief bouts of grueling work, excitement, and danger. What Miller has to say about their poetry, novellas, songs, and letters is a happy blend of literary criticism and social history. She adroitly humanizes that obscure figure, the Yankee whaleman, as she uncovers his most poignant statements of hope, fear, and joy. Designed by Howard Gralla, this was the last book we set in hot metal (Monotype Ehrhardt, composed and reproed at William Clowes in the UK) before converting to the short-lived expedient of photocomposition to be followed very quickly by the wonders of digital typesetting.

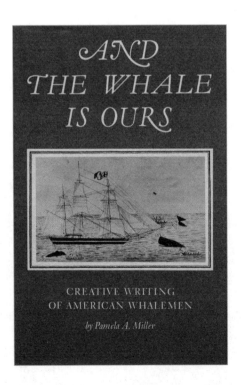

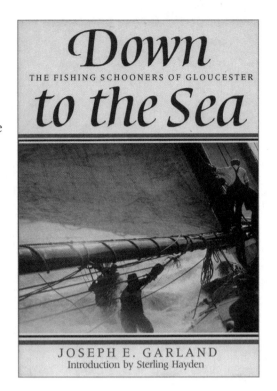

Joseph E. Garland: *Down to the Sea: The Fishing Schooners of Gloucester*
Introduction by Sterling Hayden
1983. 244 PP, 7¼ × 10½″ $25.00 HC

John N. Morris: *Alone at Sea: Gloucester in the Age of the Dorymen, 1623–1939*
2014. 476 PP, 7 × 10″ $28.00 SC

These two titles are two sides of the same coin, that coin being Gloucester, the legendary fishing port on the eastern shore of Massachusetts, home to a rich legacy of lore and legend, grief and glory. Garland, an old salt who made his home on Rocky Neck, that fortuitous protrusion that forms the harbor, was the acknowledged "voice of Gloucestermen" and no one conveyed the romance of the era of sail represented by the Gloucester schooner better than he did. Of the men he'd write "Their life was aroused by the sea and the wind and ended by them." Of the schooners, his passion, he wrote "They were of wood, metal, hemp and cotton, and sailed by flesh and blood idolatry… [They] evolved and were conceived and born, tested, trained and worked. They played, idled, and hibernated. They were vessels for all seasons. They triumphed, were wrecked, run down and drowned. They killed and they rescued. They fell into neglect, and old age and died." If Garland's romantic prose doesn't knock the wind out of your sails, try this from the Introduction by Sterling Hayden: "And is there no irony in the fact that, for some of us at least, no schooner yacht ever built could measure up, for sheer unvarnished beauty, to those great tall sparred, long boomed latter day fishing schooners with that homely word Gloucester emblazoned round their bulwarks." It was a short, glorious, and dangerous life, from roughly 1870 to 1935. Then it was over as quickly as it began.

For a longer historical sweep of the town's history, you have to read Morris's thorough and comprehensive account that begins in 1623 and ends in 1939. The grandson of a doryman who perished in 1935 while trawling for halibut, Morris was inspired by his loss to write what Garland himself called "a masterpiece that's been waiting generations to be told and the most complete and compelling history of Gloucester fishing ever written." In his historical overview you read a full panorama of the city's maritime history in almost 500 pages. When we think of Gloucester, we mostly think of cod, but cod was only part of the picture; halibut and mackerel, herring and haddock all played their part as well. Morris provides the documented detail – right down to every ship that sailed from 1693 to 1940, the size of the fleet and the names of the vessels, even the number of lives lost at sea. The romance is made real by the data – and through it the risks and rewards that made Gloucester synonymous with glory, guts, and danger. And if there's anything further you need to know, there's a complete glossary of terms and a seventeen-page double-column index. Both books come complete with photographs, charts, and data, rich in historical detail and

personal anecdotes. Both are the standards by which any future histories will be judged. What a town! What stories!

John Falconer: *Sail & Steam: A Century of Maritime Enterprise, 1840–1935*
1993. 192 PP, 9½ × 11¼" $50.00 HC

The century before World War II bore witness to the greatest ships ever built – or ever likely to be built. Whether graceful clippers, luxurious ocean liners, ponderous dreadnoughts, or elegant pleasure craft, this century of maritime ambition, coupled with execution, produced an era of men and ships that will never be equaled. During this period, England was the reigning queen, and housed in the archives of her National Maritime Museum in Greenwich is a vast and largely unknown collection of photographs that the author and curators culled to provide 200 outstanding examples, all of them reproduced in duotone in this fine folio volume. And what images they are, from the earliest photos of Fox Talbot, Bonfils, Fenton, and Frith to the gripping final documentaries of the last days of sail by Alan Villiers. All aspects are covered: the early glory decades of wooden spars and stiff canvas; the inexorable replacement of wood by iron, then steel and finally steam; the thrills of the last grain races; the introduction and challenges of yacht racing; the construction of enormous war ships and intimate pleasure craft. The design and printing were admirable, the writing thrilling, but what I personally hold most dear is the lettering on both the front jacket and title page by Michael Harvey – among the best lettering artists of our, or any, time.

ABOVE & RIGHT: The crew of the *Parma* is gathering canvas far out on her topgallant yardarm and high above the deck in 1933. The four-masted steel barque, built in 1902, was among the last of the big ships engaged in the grain trade between Australia and Great Britain, and on this voyage she made the voyage in eighty-three days, the fastest of any ship engaged in the Grain Races. The Australian Alan Villiers, who took the photo and co-owned her, tirelessly chronicled the final years of commercial sail. As Falconer would write, "To the end of his life, Villiers travelled, sailed and photographed the diminishing heritage of the world's sailing fleets, and he died in 1982, after a life immersed in all aspects of the sea.

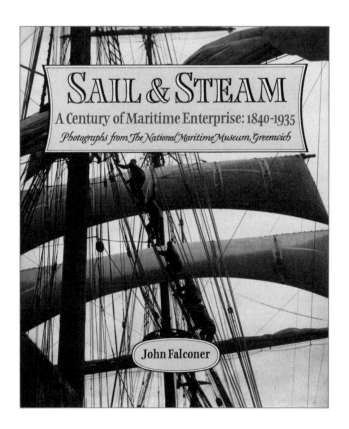

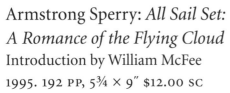

LEFT & ABOVE: Jacqueline Sakwa's calligraphy adds real life to Sperry's portrait of Donald McKay's *Flying Cloud* with every inch of sail drawing on her record-breaking 89-day passage from New York to San Francisco.

Armstrong Sperry: *All Sail Set: A Romance of the Flying Cloud*
Introduction by William McFee
1995. 192 PP, 5¾ × 9″ $12.00 SC

Armstrong Sperry, who won the Newbery Award for his YA novel *Call It Courage*, was a familiar and respected children's author at mid-nineteenth century. He both wrote and illustrated his texts, providing a coherence often lacking in young adult titles. In this case, young Enoch Thatcher tells the story from the vantage of old age. His father's merchantman had gone down off Cape Horn, and he promises his bereft mother that under no condition would he consider a life at sea. But the lure of Donald McKay's nearby shipyard and the construction of his masterpiece, the *Flying Cloud*, proves too much for both of them. He joins McKay, works in the drafting room, and soon learns the names of every line, spar and tackle. Almost inevitably he ships out aboard the *Cloud* on her maiden voyage from New York to Frisco, on which she sets the record of 89 days, a run only equalled twice, once by her in 1854 and once by Andrew Jackson in 1860. As Samuel Eliot Morison would write in *The Maritime History of Massachusetts*, "McKay built faster clippers and larger clippers, but for perfection of beauty and design, weatherliness and consistent speed under every condition, he nor anyone else surpassed *Flying Cloud*. She was the fastest vessel on long voyages that ever sailed under the American flag." These were the last great days of sail in the US, and the clippers were the last desperate attempts of sail to compete with steam. The span was short, just the two decades of 1845 to 1865, for as the saying went, 'Sail could make time, but steam could keep it.'

Sperry came from a line of Connecticut sea captains and he describes the ship, the rigging, and the routines of life and language onboard a full-rigged clipper in convincing detail. The book hits home precisely because it is never theatrical, although there is no love lost between Enoch and the sea lawyer or the belligerent, bullying first mate. The salty language, the diction of the nautical commands, even the personality of the captain, the legendary, hard-driving thirty-seven-year-old Josiah Perkins Creesy out of Marblehead, are authentic and credible. His story was hardly unusual: the lure of life at sea seduced many youngsters in maritime New England. They provided the muscle and sinew that made these over-canvassed vessels fly. As McFee writes, "It is a passion which for good or ill is born in many boys, even though they live far inland and have no immediate contact with the sea. When they grow up in a shipping community, the craving becomes irresistible. The sea calls and will not be denied." This is among our few books in which the design, typesetting, and illustration were just too good to improve; we took it as it was, adding only a new cover and title page with a calligraphic flair.

Olin J. Stephens II: *Lines: A Half-Century of Yacht Designs by Sparkman & Stephens, 1930–1980*
Foreword by J. Carter Brown
Preface by A. Knight Coolidge
2002. 192 PP, 14 × 11″ $125.00 HC

The profession of yacht design, at least as it was practiced in the sailing world through most of the last century, combined art, instinct, experience, and the beginning of mathematical modelling. It marked the end of an era when boats were designed by hand at a drawing board, or by feel using carved half models, an era when Herreshoff, Burgess, and Alden slowly began transforming it into something approaching a science. No one in the field made that transition more formidably, or had a more profound impact on design in general, than Olin Stephens. Beginning when he was barely out of his teens with the record-shattering *Dorade*, spanning designs from shoal draft-race winners like *Finisterre* to his unbroken streak of three consecutive America's Cup victories, he routinely brought home the gold while consistently producing yachts striking for the beauty of their lines. A design from the pen of Olin Stephens is as immediately identifiable as a drawing by Homer or a fugue by Bach.

But beyond, and often behind, the beauty was the beginning of yacht design as a science. Working with Kenneth Davidson at the Stevens Institute of Technology, he was able to develop tank testing using smaller models, heeled and upright, to predict performance. He would comment, "The ability to put numbers on sailing performance provided a yardstick that completely changed the role of statistical comparisons in yacht design." With his brother Rod, he perfected rigging and rigging materials. At his father's insistence he attended MIT for a few weeks as a freshman but determined, with good evidence, that he was probably a better problem-solver than any of his professors and left. John Carter Brown, the former director of the National Gallery for whose father Olin had designed the great *Bolero,* the first major American yacht launched after WWII, would write in his Foreword, "Olin J. Stephens was not an engineer, or even primarily a naval engineer – he was an artist." That's true, as far as it goes. But read this

description of what went through his head when reviewing finished drawings provided by the Sparkman *&* Stephens office: "What I was looking for was pretty simple. I was fussy about prismatic coefficient, or the relationship of mid-section area to length and displacement. I tried to be particular about balance between the ends and as far as possible, balance throughout, i.e. above and below water, freeboard versus displacement (necessarily taking beam into account), as well as sail area versus stability and wetted area." Here, as with Donald McKay, I discern both the eye of an artist and, equally, the mind of a scientist.

All the drawings for the nearly fifty designs selected resided at the S *&* S archive at the Mystic Museum in Connecticut. Knight Coolidge, who came up with the idea, worked with Olin selecting and dividing them into categories. The book was an entirely homegrown affair; Carl W. Scarbrough did a magnificent job with the design, the paper was specially manufactured at the Monadnock Mill in Bennington, NH, the printing at Thames Printing in Connecticut, and the book bound in full cloth by New Hampshire Bindery. A credit to all involved. The price of $125 scared off a number of bookstores – until they learned that Olin Stephens sat on the right hand of God. We printed 1,500 trade copies and 250 deluxe, signed and numbered by Olin and in a slipcase. All were gone in six months. Olin lived to 102. I met him a few times at Kendall, a Quaker retirement community above Dartmouth College. He was still getting up at six AM to run its radio station and driving his car at unbelievable speeds. His library included everything from Far Eastern religious tracts to modern poetry. Montaigne would have felt right at home. A genius in every way.

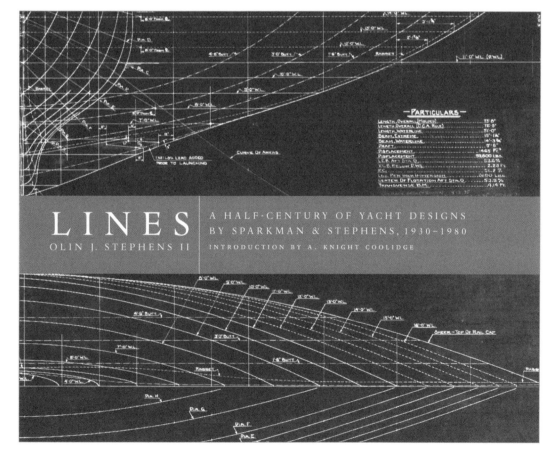

Alan Granby *&* Janice Hyland: *Maritime Maverick: The Collection of William I. Koch*
2006. 278 PP, 13 × 12″ $150.00 HC

As both sailor and collector, William Koch has always been a maverick. An outsider and Johnny-come-lately to the world of yacht racing, he brought the 1992 America's Cup back to these shores through scientific innovation, precision team-building, and a damn-the-odds attitude toward the competition. An equally quirky and opinionated collector, he has assembled a collection of marine masterworks that spoke profoundly to his love of the sea and all its traditions. It is a unique, historically significant treasure trove of art, artifacts, ship models, figureheads, even entire reproduction rooms. Koch, the sailor, connoisseur, and collector, is manifest on every page of this beautifully produced celebration of America's life at sea. One sterling, and not easily forgotten, example of the extent of his enthusiasm—he has commissioned models of not only every yacht that ever *won* the America's Cup, but every yacht that has ever *competed* in it. In addition, you encounter fully illustrated chapters devoted to shipboard furniture, navigational instruments, a magnificent collection of canvases depicting the naval battles of the War of 1812, and objects seldom celebrated or documented but that provide an unrivaled window into centuries of life below deck. No ordinary mortal would probably be able to afford any item on display in this sumptuous volume, but you can see them all, printed in six-color offset, with an excellent accompanying text by Granby and Hyland in a book that will provide weeks of pleasure to any art lover, antique collector, naval historian or blue-blooded sailor.

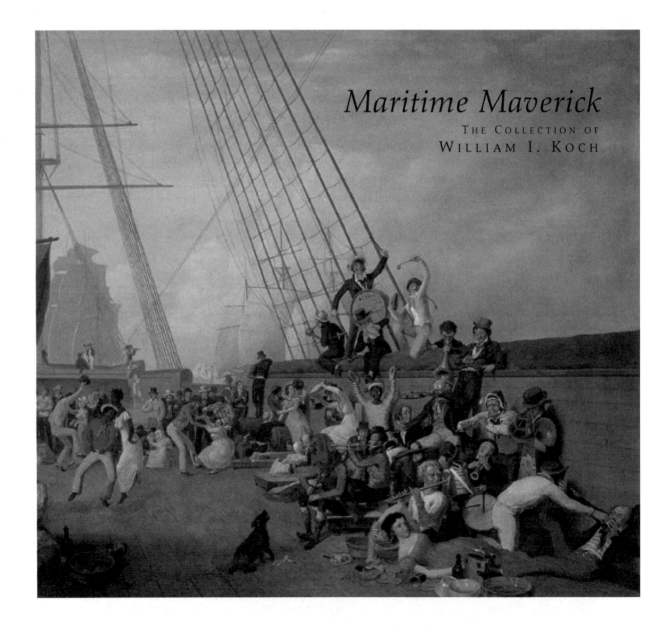

Maritime Maverick
THE COLLECTION OF
WILLIAM I. KOCH

Keith McLaren: *A Race for Real Sailors*

2006. 256 pp, 8½ × 10" $40.00 HC

In the summer of 1920, the crowds following the vagaries of the America's Cup series were frustrated. Every time the weather breezed up, the organizers called off the race. These might be races for men in white linens and tender hulls, but they hardly reflected the stuff of *real* men working in *real* time on *real* boats, the maritime reality of men still making a living off the sea. The mutterings traveled to the taverns of Lunenburg and Halifax; why not show these fancy yachtsmen what the last of the working schooners, manned by genuine salts in sea boots, could do? A trophy was donated, and a Nova Scotia newspaper put out the challenge to their rivals in Gloucester, America's main fishing port and home to her largest and fastest fleet of schooners, inviting them to engage in a "race for real sailors." The story of those schooners, those skippers, and the races they waged in *all* weather is masterfully, and equitably, explored in the Canadian author's definitive history. It is a story in which, for once, America does not often come out the winner; the star of the fleet is always the *Bluenose*,

the brute from Lunenburg, and her hard-driving, irascible, impossible skipper, Angus Walters, who consistently broke America's heart, but whose heart was itself broken by his country's refusal to come to the rescue of his beloved craft (although she still shines brightly on the obverse of the Canadian dime). The stirring, often poignant tales of every craft, skipper, and race are illustrated with contemporary photographs and five maps. The salt spray practically blows off the pages with the excitement McLaren brings to each contest. This is a book, a history, that we guaranteed would keep even landlubbers pegged to their seats. And it did.

BELOW & RIGHT: The Canadian *Bluenose* and *Columbia* out of Gloucester run before the wind carrying every available stitch of canvas at the start of the first race in 1923. The grey-hulled *Columbia*, the last of the all-sail schooners built for the American fishery, was probably the closest rival to the *Bluenose*, her ability to sail closer to the wind making her a real contender.

LEFT: Originally built by Fife, the Scottish master, in 1926 as a twelve meter, the 72' yawl *Cotton Blossom IV*, flying her mizzen staysail and spinnaker, scuds across Buzzards Bay with the rest of the New York Yacht Club fleet in 1956.

BELOW: *Beetle Cat 81* may heading for trouble as she plows into the fleet on a starboard tack and right of way. This 1949 photo shows how many blue water sailors were introduced to the stresses and strategies of serious ocean racing in gaff-rigged catboats sponsored by The New Bedford Yacht Club, which will probably be adjudicating a protest once this race is over.

On the Wind: The Marine Photographs of Norman Fortier
Introduction and captions by Calvin Siegal and Llewellyn Howland III
Selected by Michael Lapides
2007. 154 PP, 9½ × 8⅝" $40.00 HC

For five decades the photographer Norman Fortier recorded the work, the play, the yachts, and the industries of Buzzards Bay with devotion, attention, and affection. Beginning as a Navy aerial photographer in the Pacific, shooting islands, vessels, and planes during WWII, he returned home to New Bedford to open a photography studio. When Waldo Howland offered him a small space along the row shops fronting Elm Street, he made the move, remaining there from 1947 until 2005. I knew this territory well; I had bought my Concordia 39 yawl through the offices of Waldo Howland, and in those days, when Concordia maintained a large storage and repair facility just behind Fortier's studio, that yard was bustling with personalities larger than life and always ready to provide advice to a young, inexperienced skipper.

In this selection from the some 100,000 negatives deposited at New Bedford's Whaling Museum in 2004, we see a visual synopsis of an entire region: local factories and boat building shops, aerial photos of the islands, maritime photographs of every description—commercial fishing vessels, trawlers, lobster boats, tugs, sailors and master builders, and, most lovingly, sailboats of every kind, from mod-

est, small crafts to stately J-boats. They show the last days of wooden sail and the slow decline of New Bedford as a major port and manufacturing center. The text and captions by Howland and Siegal combine palpable affection for the man with total understanding of the landscape, yachts, and personalities he recorded. This was the first of five major titles co-published with the New Bedford Whaling Museum, and no small part of their success was due to the design skills of Carl W. Scarbrough and photographic wizardry of Michael Lapides.

Stuart M. Frank: *Ingenious Contrivances, Curiously Carved*

2012. 400 PP, 9 × 11″ $65.00 HC

The voyages of the whalemen were long, up to three years, and comprised of nine parts tedium, loneliness, and boredom and one part excitement and immediate danger. To fill the time, and make a little extra money on their return, the sailors would often turn to engraving the bone and teeth of the whales they captured. The resulting objects – practical, decorative, whimsical and sometimes unbelievably complex – were not just the engraved sperm whale teeth that the term "scrimshaw" most often evokes, but also canes and crimpers, umbrellas and swifts. Much of the fleet set out from New Bedford, then among the richest cities in America to provide whale oil, the "fossil fuel" that for a few short decades would provide the light and illumination for a burgeoning economy. So it is no surprise that The New Bedford Whaling Museum would house the most extensive and comprehensive collection in the world. From it, Stuart Frank, the acknowledged authority, selected the material he describes with a curator's eye and a storyteller's enthusiasm in this comprehensive study. The 700 detailed and dramatic photographs, cunningly and artfully photographed by Richard Donnelly, show this "art of the sea" as it has never been presented before, and the design by Sara Eisenman and the book's printing with its full-color spreads were equal to the challenge.

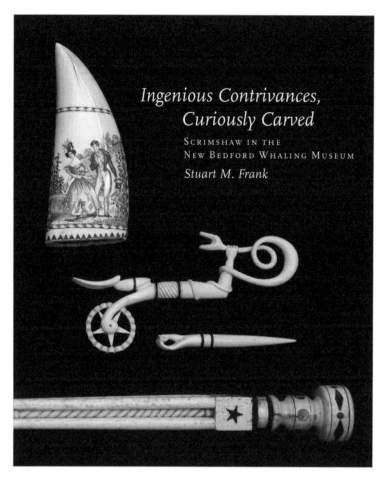

Ingenious Contrivances, Curiously Carved

SCRIMSHAW IN THE
NEW BEDFORD WHALING MUSEUM
Stuart M. Frank

BELOW: An array of whalemens' crimpers imaginatively carved of whale and walrus ivory from *Ingenious Contrivances, Curiously Carved*

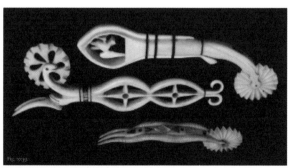

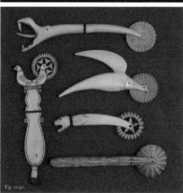

Fig. 10:39. **Three variant whale ivory serpent crimpers.** One has two snakes flanking a straight handle inlaid with abalone, baleen, and mother of pearl [Kendall]; one has two snakes and pierced-work trimmed with baleen and tortoise shell [Wood]; and the third has a pierced-work eagle with a snake looped around the edges [Wood]. Largest 8⅜″ (21.3 cm). 2001.100.704, 1923.7.27, 1923.7.81

Fig. 10:40. **Crimper Menagerie.** The alligator is panbone and may have been influenced by indigenous West African relief-carvings in elephant ivory; the others are whale ivory. The polar bear seems to have been influenced by Eskimo motifs (see Chapter 13), the dragon is a rare motif (a kind of exaggerated serpent), and the seagull is cleverly carved so the wings can function as a fork. There is a wheel missing from the two doves crimper; several others are known by this same hand. Largest: 8½″ (21.6 cm). [Wood (4) and Hinsdale (1)] 1923.7.36, 1923.7.33, 1923.7.48, 1923.7.1, 1959.8.16

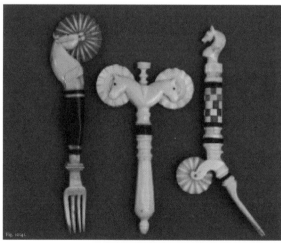

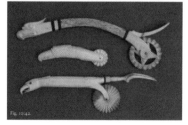

Fig. 10:41. **Equestrian crimpers.** One has a single horse's head, rendered in whale ivory with a wood handle [Hinsdale]; one has double horses' heads, carved out of whale ivory and trimmed with baleen [Kendall]; and the third takes the form of a chess knight elegantly treated in walrus ivory, wood, and baleen. Largest: 9½″ (23.5 cm). 1959.8.15, 2001.100.1257, 2001.100.1422

Fig. 10:42. **Eagle crimpers.** On two of these the entire handle is carved out of whale ivory in quite different images of an eagle [Snow and Wood]; on the third the eagle effigy appears on the tip of a panbone shaft [Kendall]. The longest is oversize at 10¼″ (26 cm). 1919.31.49, 2001.100.1653, 1923.7.44

LEFT & ABOVE: After her decisive win in the 1931 Transatlantic and later the same year the stormy Fastnet race, both *Dorade* and her crew returned to the US national celebrities. The first maritime media stars. They arrived at New York harbor to a heroes' welcome, leaving Battery Pier with *Dorade's* crew in a convoy of limos to join a motorcade down Broad Street to attend a City Hall reception with the mayor. As Adkins observes, "They would remain so for the rest of their lives, not entirely because of the two races but because of what those two races had started. Olin Stephens II would ultimately be considered the greatest yacht designer of racing yachts of the twentieth century." Olin, still in his early twenties and a college dropout, would write with typical modesty "It was an experience, fun, but the best was getting back to normal family life and work."

Douglas D. Adkins: *Dorade*
Foreword by Llewellyn Howland III
2012. 240 PP, 8½ × 10½" $65.00 HC

At 5:45 the morning of Tuesday, July 1931, a small, narrow yawl touches the Isles of Scilly and ghosts into the English Channel, past the Lizard Lighthouse with its signal tower set on a high green headland. There are no telephones, much less cell reception. The signalman hoists a flag, asking "What ship is this?" The little yawl answers immediately with the code flag "*Dorade*." Then the signalman sees a second flag "Which am I?" He hoists the answer "You are first." The yacht was *Dorade*; it was the Transatlantic Race, and there was no second. Taking the northerly route, she had blown the fleet out of the water, winning by a full two days, over four on corrected time. It was an astonishing and unexpected victory for Olin Stephens II, her twenty-one-year-old designer and navigator; his brother Rod, responsible for her deck hardware and rigging; and a young and appealing crew that was fêted by the King and adored by the British press. Later the same year she would win the Fastnet with a corrected time of nineteen hours, proving to the skeptics that her prior victory was no fluke. The yawl and her crew would then return to New York for a ticker tape parade. The next summer, she would take first place in her class in the Bermuda Race and again dominate the 1933 Fastnet, and wins would follow regularly over the next decades. The 1936 edition of *The Rudder* would write after her Honolulu victory over twenty-one yachts, "This victory gives *Dorade* the unique distinction of having won every major ocean race in the yachting world today." She was an inflection point in the history of yacht design, her influence manifest in every yacht constructed over the next three decades. This is her complete story, from stem to stern, from her design by an unknown, nearsighted youngster who was to totally transform yacht racing and design in the ensuing decades, to her building at the Nevins' yard on Long Island, to her present life on the race course and on both coasts. Written by Doug Adkins, an active West Coast sailor and Concordia owner, and handsomely designed, the book, like its subject, has found a permanent and well-deserved place in the history of the world of sail.

Llewellyn Howland III: *No Ordinary Being:
W. Starling Burgess: Inventor, Naval Architect,
Poet, Aviation Pioneer, and Master of
American Design*
2015. 470 PP, 9½ × 8¾″ $65.00 HC

If there ever was an American polymath whose story was just waiting to be written, it was Starling Burgess. And if there was ever an author qualified, even eager, to take it on, it was Llewellyn Howland III. Both attended Milton Academy (where Burgess had invented and even patented a machine gun). His father, Ned Burgess, who died in 1890 when Starling was only twelve, had designed three America's Cup defenders in 1885, 1886, and 1887. All three won. Starling followed suit with three of his own in 1930, 1934, and 1937, including the immortal J-Boat *Ranger*. All of his won, too. In 1910, he built the first airplane to fly the skies of New England, was the only manufacturer to receive a patent to independently build aircrafts under the Wright Brothers' patents, and single-handedly designed and built the first seaplanes. His private life was in shambles—five successive wives and countless affairs. Children,

both legitimate and unacknowledged. But his genius as a designer was beyond dispute; he worked with Olin and Rod Stephens in designing the unbeatable *Ranger* for Harold Vanderbilt, with Buckminster Fuller in developing the Dymaxion, with the Navy Department in perfecting the conning tower and periscopes of submarines. The list of his associations and initiatives is endless: Michael Parker even claimed he had drawn the models for Times New Roman. Louis Howland made this biography his life's work. A descendant of the famous Howlands of Padanaram, a sailor from youth, an editor at Little, Brown, and later as an author and antiquarian bookseller, he knew all the players, in both their human and wooden incarnations, and also where most of the bodies (and there were more than a few, literally) were buried. Burgess comes across, even in print, as larger than life, a man of vast talents and equally vast flaws. This is the complete story, the entire history, related in lucid prose and accompanied by first-rate drawings and photographs. No costs were spared in the book's production, Monadnock paper, duotone printing, full-cloth binding, design by Sara Eisenman, and an absurdly low list price. We printed 2,500 copies and were sold out in three months, never to reprint.

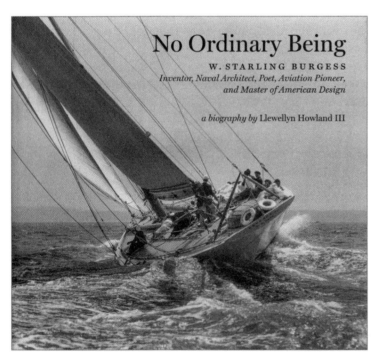

ABOVE: The jacket photo shows *Enterprise*, close hauled and driving to windward on a starboard tack, off Glen Cove in 1930. Sir Thomas Lipton had issued his fifth challenge for the America's Cup, the race to be held in 1930. Four syndicates were formed to answer the challenge; Burgess was Harold S. Vanderbilt's choice as a designer. The result was a J-class sloop with a revolutionary ultralight Duralumin mast and a heavy Park Avenue boom giving the mainsail a better shape. Manned (as were they all) by a professional crew, she beat out *Weetamie* in the trials and then thrashed Lipton's *Shamrock V* in straight races. Burgess would go on to design two more successful Cup defenders, the J boats *Rainbow* and, with Olin and Rod Stephens, perhaps the greatest of them all, *Ranger*. Louis would observe "His lasting fame as an American yacht designer was now assured. The duration of his fortune was a different matter."

ABOVE: Burgess's 112' yawl *Manxman* with her hollow 150' wooden mast from step to truck ghosts down Buzzards Bay in a 1948 photo by Norman Fortier

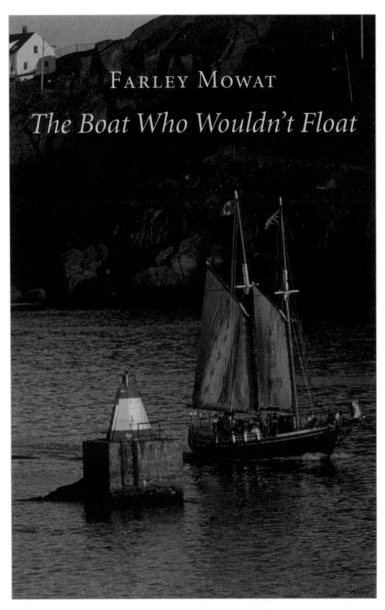

Farley Mowat: *The Boat Who Wouldn't Float*
2018. 296 PP, 5½ × 8½" $16.00 SC

The justly celebrated Canadian writer Mowat is at his finest in this classic tale of nautical misadventure. He admits early on, "Amongst the attitudes I had acquired from my father was a romantic and Conradian predilection for the sea and ships." Unable to overcome this fatal desire, he leaves Toronto in a rickety flatbed truck bound for Newfoundland where, he's been told, boats for sale are as common as cod. He finds more than he has bargained for when, late at night and half drunk, he manages to buy, sight unseen, a derelict coastal schooner—one that, as the story unfolds, requires every nautical repair known to man. And even afterward is still unseaworthy. Thus unwinds the story of the hopefully christened "*Happy Adventure*," the tale of a ship that, despite all efforts to save her, is clearly committed to doing her own thing, which often amounted to attempted suicide. Cajoling her, threatening her, even reading to her, sometimes works. But not always. Her cruise from the coast of Newfoundland, down the St. Lawrence, finally to receive a hero's welcome (against betting odds of her making it at 25 : 1) at the Montreal 1967 World's Fair Expo, slowly unfolds, the stuff of which legends are made. The ribs of the story are the journey, but the frame and planking are in the endless cast of characters Mowat encounters along the way, not least of whom is the intrepid Claire, soon to become his wife, along with a revolving crew that witnesses any number of appalling experiences. Part memoir, part tribute, and guaranteed laugh-out-loud funny, Mowat's series of close calls and near misses both dissolve and reaffirm the palpably ridiculous notion of buying, owning, maintaining, and sailing a wooden boat.

ABOVE: The extravagant (but extremely talented) dozen associates of the Godine Press standing before our equally extravagant offices at the Ames-Webster mansion in Boston's Back Bay. These were our first publishing offices, and we remained here eleven years.

was first engraved and later printed lithographically. But Edith Abbott (who, as a designer, has never received the credit she deserves, and was an excellent musician as well as calligrapher) undertook the transcriptions, following the authoritative and scholarly 1967 edition edited by Walter R. Davis. Martino Mardersteig set the text in Bembo, had line cuts made of her calligraphic pages, and undertook the printing, which included a stunning engraved title page, printed in red, by Leo Wyatt. He somehow managed to make the complex parts come together rather flawlessly. We issued the book in a boxed deluxe edition of 250 copies printed on Cartiera Magnani paper and bound with marbled sides and a cloth spine, a full-cloth trade edition and even in paperback. None sold well, but with the striking Leo Wyatt–engraved title page, it still stands out as a lovely example of our early letterpress efforts.

Peter Guralnick: *Lost Highway: Journeys & Arrivals of American Musicians*
1979. 374 PP, 6 × 9″ $9.00 SC, $19.00 HC

Peter and I had both attended the Roxbury Latin School together, and I was grateful when he approached me to publish his second book, a study of rockabilly, a genre that

Thomas Campion: *Selected Songs of Thomas Campion*
Selected & prefaced by W.H. Auden
Introduction by John Hollander
1973. 168 PP, 7¾ × 11⅛″ $7.50 SC, $15.00 HC, $40.00 *deluxe bound in quarter cloth with French marbled sides and contained in a slipcase*

A poet I especially wanted for our list was W.H. Auden. When presented with the temptation of our publishing anything he wanted, Auden came back with the idea of a selection of songs by the sixteenth-century Englishman Thomas Campion, the only example in English literature of someone equally gifted as a poet and a musician and a figure Auden admired extravagantly. Piece by piece the manuscript arrived over the next year, but his Introduction was (at least to me) so opaque and unintelligible that I wrote the poet John Hollander at Yale begging him to provide something a little more accessible and comprehensible. He obliged, and both were printed. The book was complex; we wanted to print transcripts of the songs themselves, but also facsimiles of the original music that had been written in such a way that three or four singers could sit around a table and read their respective parts from the same sheet. Before electronic typesetting, music

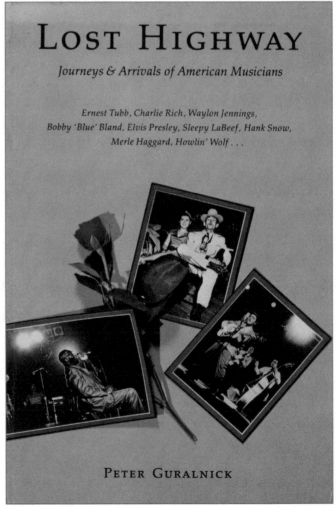

combined the best of country music and blues and those who mixed the two to create an explosive new sound defined by Elvis Presley and Sun Records in the fifties. These were the musical styles that defined American popular music and, in doing so, transformed American culture.

RLS was as conservative a prep school as existed on the East Coast, a place where five years of Latin were still mandatory, and hardly considered a likely breeding ground for rock historians. But Guralnick, who began his chapter on Presley with the sentence "Enough has been written about Elvis Presley to fuel an industry" would later go on to contradict his own edict by writing the definitive two-volume study of the American icon. His journey here starts with his examination of Charlie Rich, among rockabilly's early cult favorites who required twenty years to be noticed after repeated and self-inflicted failures; Waylon Jennings, who played bass for Buddy Holly, and was Johnny Cash's pill-popping roommate; Bobby "Blue" Bland, who began his career as valet to B.B. King; and Honky Tonk heroes like Ernest Tubb. The Venerable Ancients are all here as the music morphs into Hillbilly Boogie, and finally, a visual

and verbal examination of the enduring legacy of the blues as promulgated by Howlin' Wolf, Otis Spann, and Big Joe Turner. Between the lines is the story of how working musicians made a living, what it was like to be on the road day after day, playing one night stands before unfamiliar audiences… what it took to make it to the big time and the cost that success could, and often did, extract. An avatar of a brilliant career, the *Village Voice* pegged it as "The most emotionally and intellectually satisfying rock book yet to appear." The book, designed by Susan Marsh and set in Hermann Zapf's Palatino, was a triumph of integrating a long and detailed text with photographs of every stripe and quality, and adding a complex selected discography and an eclectic list of related monographs and articles. Peter really did his homework and knew his sources.

LEFT & ABOVE: Howlin' Wolf and Sleepy LaBeef, full-page portraits from Peter Guralnick's *Lost Highway*

Samuel Lipman: *The House of Music: Art in an Era of Institutions*

1984. 352 PP, 6 × 9″ $22.50 HC

When we published this, Sam was the Publisher of the newly minted *New Criterion* and a music critic for *Commentary*. He saw Western civilization disintegrating around him, and I suspect considered music a possible survivor, or at least a welcome cultural holdover from happier days. He was also an excellent pianist, almost concert grade, and married to another. In the twenty-four essays, he takes on Wagner, Shostakovich, Berlin's Philharmonic, the New York City Opera, and the obligatory Glenn Gould, whom he arguably defends as "without doubt the most interesting – in every meaning of that valuable word – pianist the public has heard." John Gross, a critic to be attended to, claimed "There are a few, a *very* few, music critics who would be well worth hearing even if you were tone-deaf, and Samuel Lipman is undoubtedly one of them. His great distinction is that he is good at taking music on its own term, and setting it firmly in a social and intellectual context; when he writes about it, he also addresses himself to broad cultural issues, and what he has to say is invariably penetrating and pungent." I might also add he was also invariably honest and often poignant. I once asked him why he had not pursued a career as a professional pianist. He answered, simply and somewhat wistfully, "My hands are too small."

M.B. Goffstein: *A Little Schubert*

Story and Pictures by M.B. Goffstein
Music arranged by Richard Woitach
1984. 42 PP, 7 × 7″ $11.00 HC

The minimalist Brooke Goffstein wrote this charming tribute to Schubert in 1972, and when published, it was selected as one of the ten *New York Times* Best Illustrated Children's Books of the year. Twelve years later at the suggestion of our newly acquired Publicity Manager, David Allender, we reissued it, using the original art and a handsome design by Jane Bierhorst. The story could not be simpler – a plump, shabbily dressed Franz Schubert is busily engaged writing music, music that no man had ever heard before, in his chilly garret. Occasionally he gets up to embrace his wife, but mostly he sits at his desk furiously composing. The drawings are lean and sure, miracles of minimalism, and Schubert's curly hair is a triumph of hirsute consistency, every lock remains exactly in place in image after image. When the temperature really sinks and he can't write anymore, he gets up, stamps his feet, claps his hands, and begins to dance. The book segues immediately into an arrangement of six dances, the so-called "Noble Waltzes," arranged for the piano by Richard Woitach and carefully calligraphed by Edith Abbot. The themes are thus memorialized just as Schubert wrote them down in that chilly room in Vienna around two hundred years ago.

John Langstaff: *The Christmas Revels Songbook*
Foreword by Susan Cooper
1985. 160 PP, 7½ × 9⅛″ $15.00 *flexible boards*

When I was growing up, Boston and Cambridge were still fairly small cities, and cultural eruptions of any size and quality did not go unremarked. I noticed most of my friends were trooping over to Sanders Theatre at Harvard to religiously take in Jack Langstaff's production of the Christmas Revels, an institution that has now gone national but at that time played to a faithful local audience. The presentations, emphasizing the musical Yuletide traditions of various countries, varied from year to year, but all of them contained a few predictable chestnuts for which audience participation could reliably be counted: "Dona Nobis Pacem," "The Gloucester Wassail," and, at intermission, "The Lord of the Dance," which took the entire audience into the chilly halls of Memorial Church in long, swaying lines with the orchestra playing from the balcony. Jack asked if we'd be interested in publishing a Revels Songbook, and we were very fortunate that Scott Kosofsky, both a musician and a very talented typographer, stepped in to commission the arrangements, set the music, and design the book. It remains, to my mind, the best single volume of Christmas music ever issued, combining the old standards with considerable fresh material and brilliant piano accompaniments. The lovely arrangement of that old Phillips Brooks favorite "O Little Town of Bethlehem," here set to the folk tune "The Ploughboy's Dream" by Ralph Vaughan Williams, is alone worth the price.

The Harvard Hillel Sabbath Songbook
1992. 288 PP, 7½ × 10¾″ $25.00 HC

This was another happy collaboration with Scott Kosofsky, who both designed the book and even provided "Hillel," a new Hebrew font designed especially for this volume. We were approached by the parents of Karen Avra Gordon, a student who died tragically while still a student at Radcliffe and to whose memory the book is dedicated. An active member of Harvard Hillel, she had faithfully observed the Sabbath, taking pleasure in singing the z'mirot, the hymns frequently accompanying the Sabbath meal that begins at sundown on Friday evening. The entire formalized ritual is explained and detailed in the text, beginning with the lighting of the candles and a hymn welcoming the angels of peace and tranquility and concluding with *Birkat Hamazon*, the Grace after the meal. Music books are always more difficult than they appear; the music has to be transcribed and set, and in this case English transliterations had to be properly placed under the notes. English reads from left to right; Hebrew from right to left. To fill in any white space Scott assembled a variety of fifteenth- and sixteenth-century Italian woodcuts of Biblical and Sabbath scenes. No songbook had ever been compiled of Shabbat tunes; this was a first–comprehensive, scholarly, handsome, and helpful. On a lark, we submitted the book to Martino Mardersteig's first competition of printing and design in Verona, where it was awarded the bronze medal.

LEFT: Georgia-born guitarist "Daddy Hot Cakes" is pictured on the jacket of *Blues Faces*.
BELOW: Clifton Chenier, the high priest of Zydeco

Sam & Ann Charters: *Blue Faces: A Portrait of the Blues*

Photographs by Ann and Samuel Charters
Introduction and Commentary by Samuel Charters
2000. 160 PP, 9½ × 8⅝″ $40.00 HC

For more than fifty years the blues, along with the singers who sang them and the musicians who played them, were nearly forgotten in this country. Not until Sam Charters published his seminal *The Country Blues* in 1959 did a new interest in this quintessentially American musical form gain traction. In the blues boom of the 60s and 70s, his articles, books, field recordings (dating back to the fifties), studio productions, and behind the scenes work with stage managers and record producers (not to mention the singers themselves) brought the blues to thousands of listeners. He would travel to Gambia and other states in West Africa to document and record their roots there; in the 1980s he would hang his hat as a record producer in Louisiana where he was among the first to record artists in the Cajun/Zydeco style and win a Grammy for his 1983 album with Clifton Chenier. He was to the blues what James Childs was to the English ballad. If the blues have a patron saint, Sam Charters is his name. His wife, Ann, was no slouch either. A PhD in English Literature from Columbia University, she wrote her thesis on Vladimir Mayakovsky and Lilya Brik, authored the first biography and edited the letters of Jack Kerouac and provided the photographs

for *Beats & Company: A Portrait of a Literary Generation.* This book is as much hers as his, for she provides almost all the photographs that complement his text. Together they were a formidable, and apparently irresistible, couple – they were invited into parlors, allowed to sit on porches, permitted to use their strobe lights and their tape recorders in homes throughout the South. They recorded some artists before they travelled north and made their mark on the South Side of Chicago – Muddy Waters, Otis Spann, Otis Rush, Johnny Shines, Wee Willie Dixon, Buddy Guy, Big Bill Broonzy, and more. But many never made it out of the South, or chose to stay there – Sleepy John Estes, Bukka White, Gus Cannon (who never gave up his banjo), Mississippi John Hurt, and finally the close relatives of the blues, western Louisiana's Zydeco, ruled over by Lafayette's Clifton Chenier and his close disciples Rockin' Dopsie and his Cajun Twisters. They, and many, many more, are recorded on these pages, comprising an irreplaceable archive created by this remarkable couple. Scott Kosofsky, our musical and typographic guru, deserves much of the credit for orchestrating and designing this book, a fitting tribute to a vital indigenous musical style.

MONK
10 1/2 x 13 INCHES

He played slowly when he played alone, weighing the silence between each note and chord. He sent dissonance into other dimensions and somehow found ways to shift silence. The patterns he played were portraits of his genius.

John Diebboll: *The Art of the Piano*
Introduction by Sandy Davis
2000. 96 PP, 5⅝ × 8″ $17.00 SC, $25.00 HC

On a visit to New York's Lincoln Center in 1999, I chanced upon their gallery in the basement and came across an exhibition displaying remarkable color renderings of designs for piano cases by the New York architect John Diebboll, a principal of Michael Graves & Associates. He made a living designing libraries, museums, hotels, churches, and private homes. Somehow he found time to turn his attention to the inviting, and generally visually vacant, landscape of the piano. I had not imagined that decorating piano cases and lids could be raised to the level of high art, but in these fanciful renditions of what Glenn Gould's Steinway or Bill Evans's Bösendorfer or Alfred Brendel's Viennese grand might have looked like, we encounter an entirely new dimension of musical and artistic imagination. Consider

what might result were an artist commissioned to design pianos that reflected the personality of a Cindy Sherman or Keith Jarrett, or even to reflect the spirit of a musical composition, say Philip Glass's *Metamorphosis* or an opera, perhaps *Aida* or *Carmen*? You have the two-dimensional flat plane of the lid to work with, but also the curves of the body, the complexity of the lid, and the fixed, static dimensions of the keyboard. With Diebboll, you see on display an informed imagination interpreting music, musicians, patterns, and even ideas through the idiom of art. And through some magic, both the music and the musicians come to life. This is the kind of book that would never pass muster at the marketing department of a commercial house (I can just hear the derisive hoots from an incredulous sales force), but I knew it would, over time, find its adherents. Every year I receive at least one letter politely asking what I was smoking, but it remains among my favorites – idiosyncratic, original, without any musical precedent.

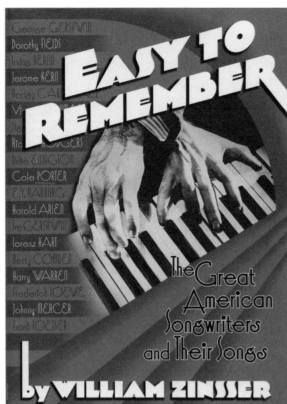

LEFT: Cover design by Katy Homans
BELOW: For endpapers, we chose sixteen different original playbills and posters announcing the openings of the various shows that Zinsser highlights in *Easy to Remember*. We printed eight at the beginning and eight at the end. They give a real sense of not only contemporary graphic esthetics but also the principal composers, lyricists, actors, directors, etc., involved in each of the musicals and movies.
OPPOSITE: The unusually clean, elegant and contemporary page designs by Michael Russem for our imposing folio celebrating the 200th anniversary of Boston's celebrated Handel and Haydn Society, America's oldest musical organization.

William Zinsser: *Easy to Remember: The Great American Songwriters and Their Songs*

2001. 280 PP, 7 × 10″ $35.00 HC

Bill is best known, and rightfully, for his bestselling book *On Writing Well*. But he was also an authority on the history and development of the American musical, and in this delightfully written and illustrated book, he details his lifelong love affair with American popular song – the thousands of wonderful tunes and lyrics written for Broadway musicals and Hollywood movies during a centennial golden age that began in 1928 with *Show Boat* and continues through today. These songs still form the standard repertoire for jazz singers and musicians, amateur theatrical and professional debuts. Who wrote them? For what stars and shows were they composed? Why are they so unforgettable? These are the questions Zinsser addresses and tries to answer, taking the reader on a tour not so much of the shows themselves, but of the personalities, the composers and lyricists, behind them. Through his lucid, enthusiastic prose, they come before his spotlight as flesh and blood – Jerome Kern, Cole Porter, Oscar Hammerstein, Richard Rodgers, Lorenz Hart, Harold Arlen, George and Ira Gershwin, Irving Berlin, Hoagy Carmichael, Stephen Sondheim – all of them are alive on these pages, enhanced by theatre bills and studio portraits, playbills and posters. While Bill *was* as interested in the people as the music, because he was also a more than able pianist and capable of approaching this history from three angles: the historical, the musical, and the personal. And it's this combination that makes the book so fascinating, along with his capacity to write evocative and lucid prose. For the endpapers, we assembled a grand galaxy of colorful sheet music, and the book was ably designed by Katy Homans and her associates.

Neff & Swafford: *The Handel and Haydn Society: Bringing Music to Life for 200 Years*
2014. 256 PP, 9 × 12″ $40.00 HC

In 2015, the Handel and Haydn Society, by far the oldest musical organization in America, celebrated its 200th anniversary. We were asked to produce a fully illustrated history, containing thirteen essays and countless illustrations and documents, to celebrate the event. It was worth the effort. From its New England roots in singing schools and musical societies through the formative years when its classical models were Handel (the contrapuntal godfather) and Haydn (then perceived as a musical innovator), the Society would go on to present premier performances of Handel's *Messiah*, Haydn's *Creation*, and Bach's *St. Mat-*

thew Passion. Their recent directors have included Christopher Hogwood and Harry Christophers. Above all, it has managed to survive, and in these essays one begins to understand not only the hard-earned success of a uniquely Boston institution but the struggles, defeats, and triumphs any musical organization that manages to prevail must endure. All this and more, set against the culture, history, and social background of a city that has always taken its musical culture seriously. How many other institutions, of any kind, have managed to survive for 200 years and maintain not only their original name but also their standards of excellence? We could have gone with an allusive design for this book, but instead turned to Michael Russem, whose clean, modern typographic grids and layout reflect the spirit of an institution that has always had the foresight to look as much to the future as to the past.

TERESA M. NEFF

THE SOCIETY AND ITS MEMBERS

JAMES SHARP joined H&H on October 15, 1816. He was a chorus member and soloist, served on the Board of Trustees three times, and served as vice president of the Society from 1828 to 1829. During a meeting to honor Benjamin B. Davis's 50th year as an H&H member, Sharp recalled how he became a member:

In 1816 I had passed twenty years of my early life in England,—that twenty years which usually determines and fixes a man's tastes and habits. Music, vocal music was my passion, and I had lived in a community that encouraged it.... and when, on Saturday, April 3, I went on board the ship *Minerva* for Boston, I gave to my friends my little musical library, supposing, of course, that I should never again, till I returned to England, hear an anthem, much less an oratorio.... I arrived in the town of Boston, and although a

STEVEN LEDBETTER

A NEW CENTURY: 1900–1967

IT IS RARE for a musical organization to be led by the same conductor for four decades or more. Such longstanding activity, especially in an organization made up mostly of amateur musicians, naturally generates warm feelings on the part of the members, feelings of gratitude for long years of devoted service, and also concerns that age may be diminishing the quality of the leader's work.

Carl Zerrahn had achieved a prodigious amount in building the musical quality of the Handel and Haydn Society chorus, at least during parts of his long tenure. Having begun his service at the age of twenty-six as a flutist, who had arrived in Boston with the Germania Orchestra in 1848, he turned his skill and energy to building the quality of the ensemble and enlarging its repertory. He also conducted choral organizations in Salem and Worcester for several decades. But after four decades with H&H, he was apparently losing steam, a fact that might have been hinted subtly to him. In any case, in 1894 he volunteered to retire, setting off several years of argument and crisis.

There was a strong movement to replace Zerrahn with B.J. Lang, who had been organist of the Society's concerts since 1859. Lang had many other strings to his bow. He was a composer, a busy teacher of organ and piano (his most significant pupil was the composer Arthur Foote), a creator of choruses—the all-male Apollo Club and the mixed Cecilia, which still exists. With his choruses, Lang was far more advanced in his choice of repertory than the Handel and Haydn Society had ever been (for some this may have been a mark against him), and he was an important exponent of Wagner, having been one of the leaders in American fundraising for the Bayreuth Festival. For two years Lang did take over the concerts, but then a long, hot summer of strife between partisans of Lang and of Zerrahn led to the return of Zerrahn for the 1897–1898 season.

OPPOSITE
Announcement for final H&H concert in Boston Music Hall, April 1900

147

HANDEL AND
HAYDN SOCIETY

MR. EMIL MOLLENHAUER, CONDUCTOR

MR. H. G. TUCKER, ORGANIST

LAST CONCERT OF HANDEL
AND HAYDN IN MUSIC HALL

ELIJAH

SUNDAY, APRIL 15, 1900, AT 7.30 P.M.

MME. GADSKI, SOPRANO
MISS MARIAN VAN DUYN, CONTRALTO
MR. CLARENCE B. SHIRLEY, TENOR
MR. GWILYM MILES, BASS

¶ TICKETS ON SALE AT MUSIC HALL DURING
THE WEEK BEGINNING APRIL 9. $2, $1.50, $1

WILLIAM F. BRADBURY, SECRETARY
NUMBER 369 HARVARD STREET, CAMBRIDGE

Nym Cooke: *American Harmony: Inspired Choral Miniatures from New England, Appalachia, the Mid-Atlantic, the South, and the Midwest*

2017. 280 PP *&* 192 PP, 12 × 9½" *two softcover volumes with flaps, in slipcase w/* CD $65.00
VOLUME ONE: New England Fuging Tunes, Plain Tunes, Anthems, Set Pieces, Elegies, and Patriotic Songs, 1770-1815
VOLUME TWO: Fuging Tunes, Plain Tunes, and Set Pieces from the Mid-Atlantic, Appalachian, Southern, Midwestern and Northeastern States, 1813-2008

I had known Nym for almost forty years when, finally, this formidable project, one that would occupy us for over three years, came into focus. While still a graduate student in Michigan, Nym had sent me a handwritten dummy of a book he was working on about the origins of American choral music – both religious and secular – a subject that had occupied him since his undergraduate years at Harvard. Over the decades, he became recognized as among the authorities on the subject and had even put together a performing group, also named "American Harmony," that gave recitals through the New England corridor. I rediscovered the dummy in my closet in Milton, tracked him down to where he was teaching in Western Massachusetts, and asked him if he would consider finishing what he had started three decades before. The result was a two-volume collection of early American choral tunes, complete with five indices, extensive biographies of the composers, and a CD. Publishing music is not easy; one has to first transform the tunes into musical notation, then set it, then ensure that the words from every verse of the tunes correspond to and are printed exactly under the proper notes or chords. Music reads vertically, lyrics horizontally. Susan Marsh had to experiment with three different typefaces before we found one that fit. She was probably the only designer in America who could have faced the challenges presented by this book and bring it off successfully.

This was a book that probably should have been initiated and funded by a major university press. Using Kickstarter for the first and last time, we managed to raise $37,000 toward the publication costs, but even with this as a subvention, the book, sewn, in a large format and in two volumes, should have been priced well over $100. The undertaking marked a major change of heart for me. Despite personal letters to every music and book editor I could think of, Nym's major effort, an enduring contribution to scholarship and music, was hardly noticed or reviewed. Even the hometown paper, *The Boston Globe*, gave it only a brief paragraph. This would never have occurred twenty or thirty years ago. A book of this importance and ambition would have received a half-dozen major reviews. It was heartbreaking, and it also made me realize my old dictum of "Act, then think" no longer applied. In this climate, one *had* to think – of costs and returns, of turnover, of hefty risks that we used to take instinctively but were no longer likely to pay off. The aftermath solidified my decision to sell the company and retire. If we couldn't make a book like *American Harmony* work in the marketplace and review climate of the twenty-first century, there was clearly no longer room for the kind of publishing I had championed for 45 years.

ABOVE: The title page of William Walker's 1854 edition of his "New Edition. Thoroughly Revised and Greatly Improved" of *The Southern Harmony, and Musical Companion*, published in Philadelphia and containing "Nearly one hundred new tunes, which have never before been published."

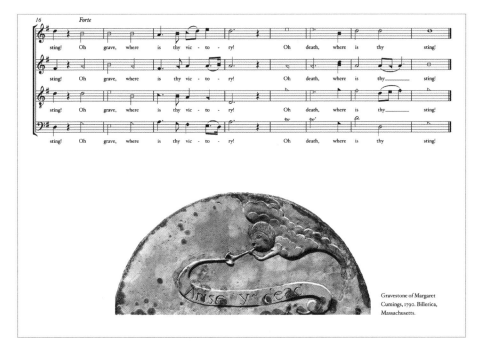

Gravestone of Margaret
Cumings, 1790. Billerica,
Massachusetts.

ABOVE: A sample page showing the gravestone of Margaret Cumings, 1790, of Billerica, MA and some staves from Walter Janes's hymn "Resurrection" with the words neatly fitted beneath the appropriate notes

ABOVE: The companion CD of Nym Cooke's choral group American Harmony singing 35 hymns and tunes, from 1770 to 1936, from the book

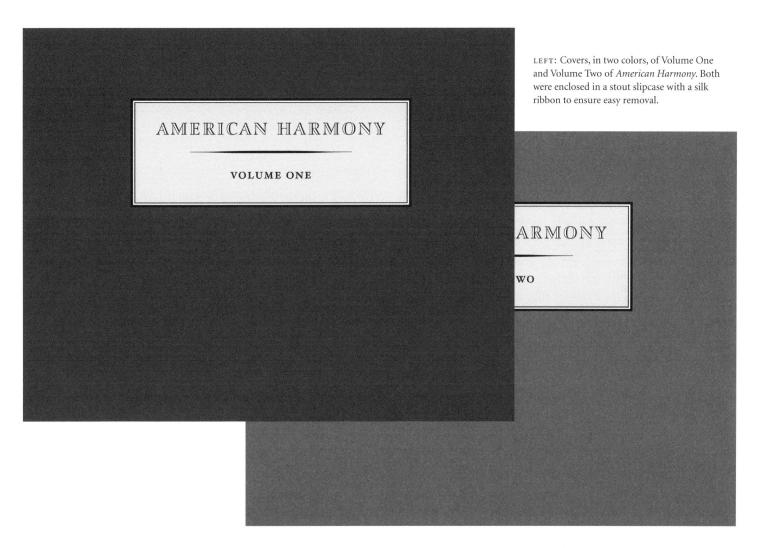

LEFT: Covers, in two colors, of Volume One and Volume Two of *American Harmony.* Both were enclosed in a stout slipcase with a silk ribbon to ensure easy removal.

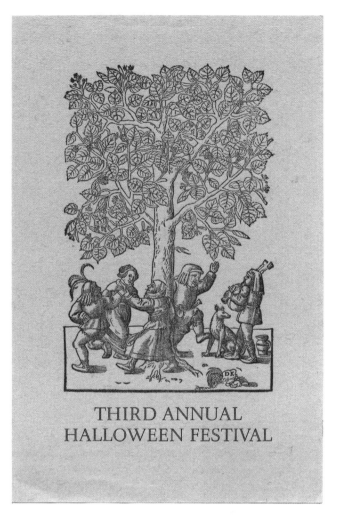

THIRD ANNUAL
HALLOWEEN FESTIVAL

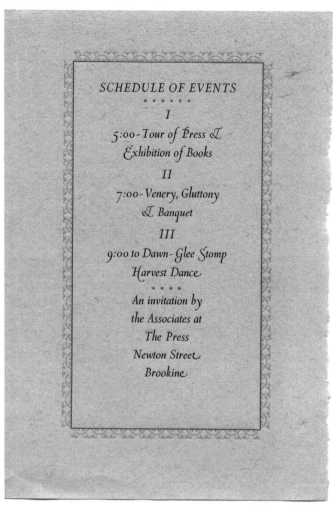

SCHEDULE OF EVENTS
* * * * * *
I
5:00 - Tour of Press &
Exhibition of Books
II
7:00 - Venery, Gluttony
& Banquet
III
9:00 to Dawn - Glee Stomp
Harvest Dance
* * * *
An invitation by
the Associates at
The Press
Newton Street
Brookine

DAVID R. GODINE
&
HIS LOYAL CREW
invite you to their
EIGHT ANNUAL
purely ceremonial but
totally unforgettable
HALLOWEEN FESTIVAL
to be held
Deo volente
at
The Fairy Palace
306 Dartmouth Street
from seven o'clock until
food & drink are exhausted.
Saturday, November 12
RES IPSA LOQUITUR

During our years in the Barn, and later at the Ames-Webster mansion, we made it a custom of hosting a Halloween party. These were congenial affairs, attended by customers, suppliers, friends and occasionally even celebrities like Bonnie Raitt. We provided a band and some food and drink, while the guests often conveyed and enjoyed all manner of hallucinatory drugs. The invitation invariably and deliberately contained at least one typo. Can you spot the one here?

OPPOSITE: This watercolor of a *Primula agleniana*, reproduced in Shulman's *A Rage for Rock Gardening*, was among the many new varieties the unappealing but intrepid Reginald Farrer introduced to England from his China expedition of 1920.

Gardening

Gertrude Jekyll on Gardening

Edited with a commentary by Penelope Hobhouse

1984. 336 PP, 5½ × 8¾″ $20.00 HC

It is hard to remember today just how seriously Gertrude Jekyll and the perennial border were taken by serious gardeners of late twentieth-century America. She was the high priestess of garden design, her place secure among the pantheon of garden greats. An artist by training, she turned to gardening late in life due to failing eyesight. Her first, and probably her most influential book, *Wood and Garden*, was published in 1899 and it incorporates many of the suggestions she would repeat in the books that followed: keep the choice of both plants and color schemes simple, understand the environmental needs of plants, and congregate varieties in groups with similar cultural requirements. She also encouraged her readers to be aware of and pay attention to context beyond the flowerbeds—

don't ignore the woodland, the wild flowers, and the flora of the surrounding countryside. Her genius for arranging colors and textures revolutionized the practice and philosophy of English landscape gardening. With the exception of her collaborations with Sir Edwin Lutyens, she planned gardens that made massive staffs obsolete, advocated hardy perennials over short-lived and labor-intensive annuals, advocated the use of first-rate species and cultivars. These she would deploy ingeniously in her herbaceous borders, emphasizing the importance of native species and advocating rugged shrubs and wildflowers over blowsy Victorian imports. She had a complete grasp of plant needs, an unmatched flair for composition and design, and, above all, an ability to write, to clearly and effectively express her ideas in words that were convincing and represented her long experience and practical knowledge. No better editor could be imagined than Penelope Hobhouse, author, nursery owner, and manager of the National Trust's Tintinhull. She cleverly arranges Jekyll's writings by month, provides her own commentary on modern usage, brings the plant nomenclature up to date, and recommends new and improved species and cultivars.

Edited by
PENELOPE HOBHOUSE

GERTRUDE
JEKYLL
ON
GARDENING

*Never before gathered in one volume, the
seminal writings and philosophy of the
First Lady of modern garden design.*

GERTRUDE
JEKYLL
ON
GARDENING

Edited with a commentary by
PENELOPE HOBHOUSE

DAVID R. GODINE · PUBLISHER · BOSTON

Graham Stuart Thomas: *The Art of Planting*

1984. 336 PP, 6½ × 9¼″ $25.00 HC

When we published this book in 1984 with our UK partners at J.M. Dent, the English gardening fad was probably at its peak in the US. Over those years, we had published some of the best from the other side of the pond – Rosemary Verey, Penelope Hobhouse, Ursula Buchan, Robin Lane Fox, and Gertrude Jekyll – but the acknowledged Dean of the English Garden was the modest and lucid Graham Stuart Thomas. Thomas approached gardening as a means to an end – the end being art, or, in his case, the ability to use living materials to provide shape, color, form, mass, light, and shadow. He achieved, and transmitted, this with an unparalleled understanding of what plants and shrubs can (and can't) do when properly chosen and cleverly combined. In the right hands, soil, and climate, they provide the desired aesthetic result. In chapters discussing the use of color, perspective, species, and style, he gives advice derived from years of practical experience. It is, in its way, as important a garden book as we ever published. But what we found out over time (and I found out myself through practical experience) is that unfortunately what works in the UK seldom translates well to the US. Our winters in the North are too cold, our summers in the Southeast too hot and damp and in the Southwest too dry, and rainfall does not come regularly or steadily to many parts of the country. In short, the aesthetics may be transferable, but the horticultural suggestions regarding species and cultivars often fail. People read these books, send away for some exotic cultivar or hybrid, keep them alive for maybe a season and, frustrated and disappointed, watch them disappear. It's not the fault of the English gardeners; it's the fault of US publishers (and to a degree, nurseries) who promote plants and shrubs that will never survive in the New World. I once had the pleasure of visiting Graham at his home. It was a modest row house in an unassuming neighborhood. Behind it, about the size of two squash courts, was the small nod to a "demonstration" garden. Everything under the sun seemed crammed in there, all of it growing happily. He had no room for special effects; this was an effort to see what *worked*. And most of that knowledge made its way into this book, still well worth reading, if only for the horticultural wisdom he has to share, rather than any specific practical applications.

 XXVIII A corner given to white and yellow at Cedar House, Norfolk, to blend with the grey-blue of the garage doors. On the barn wall are *Hydrangea petiolaris* and *Pyracantha rogersiana*; in the border are roses, *Senecio* 'Sunshine' and Golden Elder (*Sambucus nigra* 'Aurea'). It is a good example of not attempting too much in a small space.

XXIX The warm, full-tinted stone of Tyninghame, Berwickshire, demanded that colours should be complementary, thus yellows and white roses are the principal plants on this side of the house, while rich purple lavenders and sages are added to the whites and yellows on the east side.

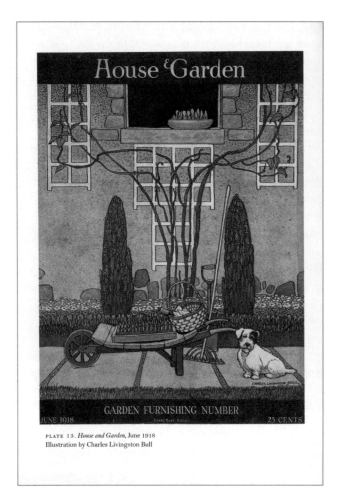

PLATE 13. *House and Garden*, June 1918
Illustration by Charles Livingston Bull

Virginia Tuttle Clayton: *The Once and Future Gardener*

1999. 352 PP, 7 × 10″ $40.00 HC

In the early decades of the twentieth century, gardening was serious business for a burgeoning and wealthy middle class, and nowhere was it explained and celebrated with more rigor and style than in the popular magazines of the period. For the average American, these were the medium of mass communication and there was one for every interest. They paid well and were read avidly. Every major gardener of the decades between the two wars wrote for them, instructing an eager middle class on what to do and how to do it properly. Many of the garden writers are names we still recognize as singularly fascinating voices – Louise Beebe Wilder, Fletcher Steele, Grace Talbot, and Mrs. Francis King, among others. But some of the best writing came from amateurs who wrote about their gardens with genuine intelligence and obvious enthusiasm. The best of these articles, over fifty written by some of the best horticultural experts of the day, were selected and reprinted in this fine compendium, illustrated by a seductive plate section displaying the magazine covers. These aren't stuffy historical reconstructions celebrating a lost America. They are still wonderfully fresh, pungent and pertinent, presented by people who had their hands in the dirt and grammar and rhetoric at their fingertips.

Sir George Sitwell: *On the Making of Gardens*
Introduction by Sir Osbert Sitwell
Foreword by John Dixon Hunt
2003. 168 PP, 5 × 7½″ $17.00 SC

A nervous breakdown drew Sir George Sitwell to Italy in the early years of the twentieth century and there he encountered the incomparable gardens of Tuscany, Rome, and its Lake District. In 1909 he would publish this small classic, a book reprinted many times since and one that saw and explained the continuum between the gardens of classical times, those of the Renaissance, and contemporary examples that had been renewed, revised, and sometimes even replanted in the nineteenth century. The book is part history (he had thoroughly read and studied the sources), part keen observation (he had been to visit every site personally and taken prodigious quantities of notes), part analysis (e.g. the difference between the Italian gardens of the sixteenth century and the French of the eighteenth are examined at length), and part literary experience. Its scented, rotund prose was a floral reflection of the excesses of the decade in which it was written, an era of Beardsley, Wilde, Morris, and the whole pre-Raphaelite sensibility. Sir George's sentences invoke music and magic in their descriptions of the mystical places where landscape, atmosphere, and manmade manipulations combine in artful conjunction. His style throughout is erudite, poetic, and fervent, completely out of tune with what you would find in a modern text. Above all, it is about garden *structure and design* (as opposed to plantings and horticulture). Sir George, an immaculate Edwardian gentleman, found his passion and was able, in this, his only book, to describe, illuminate, and publish it "wholly realized down to the last comma and the final full stop." Our edition contained an extended, equally scholarly foreword by John Dixon Hunt, illustrated with halftones of many of the gardens, fountains, villas, and vistas described in his book.

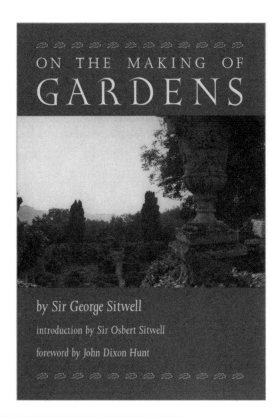

Nicola Shulman: *A Rage for Rock Gardening*
The Story of Reginald Farrer, Gardener, Writer, and Plant Collector

2004. 142 PP, 5 × 7½" $20.00 HC

George Gibson, my old friend, colleague, and bunkmate through a dozen Frankfurts, passed this book on to me with his strong endorsement. Sure enough, Nikki wrote like a dream, well enough to make even a misanthropic, ill-tempered man like Reginald Farrer come across as interesting, even appealing. No one wanted to issue it in the US, among other reasons because the central figure was unattractive, status seeking and distinctly unappealing. Nonetheless, in the words of the *London Evening Standard*, "She does the impossible; she tells the life of a dwarfish, rancorous, alcoholic, woman-hating plantsman – and contrives to make you love him." In this short book, a miracle of compression, Shulman manages not only to instill Farrer with a certain nobility, for collecting plants in nineteenth century was a dangerous adventure, but also explains how he became the foremost garden writer of his generation, essentially establishing a genre that not only democratized the activity but also put a garden book in every Englishman's library and a rockery in every backyard. There was a certain irony here; it's the unappealing Farrer whose writing and passion really brought gardening to the masses. And it is a real credit to the power of Shulman's prose that you almost grow to like him.

BELOW: The jacket and an interior plate show two watercolors by Farrer of plants he discovered in his 1920 expedition to China, the *Meconopsis prattii* and *Primula agleniana*.

Cypresses, Palazzo Giusti, Verona

ABOVE: The cover and a full-page illustration from Sitwell's *On the Making of Gardens* showing the formal allée of cypress trees at the Palazzo Giusti in Verona. Sitwell observes, "But it is possible to introduce a touch of imaginative beauty into almost any garden by finding the most perfect form for one of its features or by giving expression to the soul of some particular flower or tree as with... the cypress in the Giusti avenue at Verona."

Primula agleniana
(watercolor painted by Farrer in China, 1920)

LEFT: Jacket and an interior page from Jane Brown's *Tales of the Rose Tree* showing an illuminated autograph of King George VI in 1936 and Queen Elizabeth, the Queen Mother, photographed by Cecil Beaton strolling through the exploding rhododendron hedge at Windsor Castle in 1970
BELOW: A view of the Duke of Devonshire's extensive estate at Chatsworth, Derbyshire, in 1743 before Paxton's dramatic redesign in 1828

Jane Brown: *Tales of the Rose Tree: Ravishing Rhododendrons and Their Travels Around the World*

2004. 320 PP, 6 × 9″ $35.00 HC

I have always admired the lively and learned writing of Jane Brown. Her *Gardens of a Golden Afternoon* and *Vita's Other World* are classics of their kind. When we learned that the US rights to her latest book might be free, we jumped. Rhododendrons form a genus of almost endless variety, beauty, and habitat. Examples are found everywhere, from the jungles of Borneo to the swamps of the Carolinas. They inhabit almost every climate zone and comprise some 1,025 species. The curious history of Westerners' interaction with them is one of swashbuckling plant collecting and visionary gardeners, of colonial bullying and ecological destruction, of unexpected botanical successes and bitter business disappointments. It is all grist for Brown, and she grinds it exceedingly fine, taking the species from its origins fifty million years ago to the genetically enhanced hybrids of today. Her hope was to "construct a history of the genus Rhododendron that pays tribute to the mystery and majesty of these plants" and this she does with a scholar's thoroughness and the pacing and gusto of a born storyteller.

Charles Quest-Ritson: *The English Garden: A Social History*

2004. 284 PP, 7½ × 9¼″ $45.00 HC

Gardening is not only about plants and planting; it is also about lifestyle, money, and class. Among the rich, gardens are symbols of social and economic success; among the poor they are often a road to survival. Most books on gardening have concentrated on the development of garden design, styles, and fashions, but the whole story has to involve how they evolved in relation to the social and economic conditions of their times. Ritson attempts to put gardening into this context. He shows how major gardens have been altered through the generations in direct response to changes in English society while explaining the social and financial reasons why gardens evolved as they did. From 1500 to the present, he asks what owners wanted from their gardens. He poses and answers questions. "Why did people garden? What did they expect and get out of it? Who were regarded as the gardening experts and how much did it all cost? Were the gardens for food, recreation, ostentation, or just cut flowers? What was fashionable (and what was not) and how did taste and fashion change? He also answers questions most of us were too benighted to ask: How much did Humphry Repton charge for his

landscaping? From whom did Vita Sackville-West get the money to create Sissinghurst? What was the connection between Capability Brown and field sports? Which fruit was the ultimate status symbol of Restoration Society? Why were all the best Edwardian gardens created by the *nouveaux riche*? These questions are laid out and answered in this wide-ranging and highly readable account of English gardening through the ages. Accompanied throughout with full-color illustrations, it is an essential guide to how gardens matched the changing needs, moods, and aspirations of their owners, a book, in Anna Pavord's words, "written with verve, dash, wit, and style."

Kim Smith: *Oh Garden of Fresh Possibilities!: Notes from a Gloucester Garden*

2009. 224 PP, 7 × 10″ $35.00 HC

Kim Smith is the proprietor of a postage-sized backyard in coastal Gloucester where she grows a bewildering variety of annuals, perennials and small shrubs – everything from weeping willows to a full range of perennials. She is, as well, an artist, a decorator, and a devoted mother, and it was hard to say no to her carefully assembled collection of empirical advice aimed at the backyard gardener and designer. The illustrations, all of which she drew, are more than decorative; she was able, for example, to display the various and subtle hues of herbaceous peonies with exactitude. Her lists of preferred cultivars are born of real experience. Gardening books tend to be either too general, in which case they are of little use to anyone, or too geographically specific (the English gardening books, except when dealing with the broadest general principles, really do not travel well and have a shelf life of the average tulip). Kim's book is unusual for its broad perspectives, for she appreciates and expounds both the Western and the Eastern traditions, and with a specificity born of experience.

Elizabeth Barlow Rogers, Elizabeth S. Eustis, & John Bidwell: *Romantic Gardens: Nature, Art, and Landscape Design*
2010. 200 PP, 9 × 12″ $50.00 HC

Scenic vistas, winding paths, bucolic meadows, and rustic retreats conducive to solitary contemplation are just a few of the alluring features common to the Romantic garden. Landscape gardeners of the era learned to respect the inherent beauty of nature as it existed, nature they believed had been stifled and strangled by the rigid symmetry of the ancien régime. Free spirits in more ways than one, the Romantics looked on nature as a liberating force, a source of sensual pleasure, a font of moral instruction, religious insight, and artistic inspiration. They expected it to stir imaginations, clear minds, and relieve souls of burdens imposed by the social stresses and economic upheavals of the period. For this book, and the accompanying exhibition, the Morgan Library assembled an impressive array of text, books, prints, and manuscripts that displayed the core documents of the period. Taken together, they reveal the origins and the impact of these groundbreaking ideas, showing how they were implemented in private estates and public parks in England, Germany, and America.

Elizabeth Barlow Rogers: *Writing the Garden: A Literary Conversation Across Two Centuries*
2013. 302 PP, 5 × 7¾″ $28.00 HC

This collection of books, essays, and chapters, extracted from gardening books selected for the quality of the writing, not the efficacy of the horticultural advice, was put together by Mark Bartlett, our friend the former Head Librarian at the New York Society Library and Betsy Rogers, the woman from Texas who saw it her duty to save Central Park. Divided into twelve sections, beginning with "Women in the Garden" and ending with "Philosophers in the Garden," Rogers covers pretty much everything in between, providing cogent introductions to each section and highlighting the charms, idiosyncrasies, and appeal of each writer. Beautifully designed by Jerry Kelly, containing many color reproductions of jackets and bindings, interior spread and plates from the original books, shots of actual gardens in their glory, it is a bracing walk through the *literature* that is so essential to an understanding of garden history. With its delicious binding of green vines marching up the boards and its charming two-color title page, it is a small gem of a book – *sicut lilium inter spinas.*

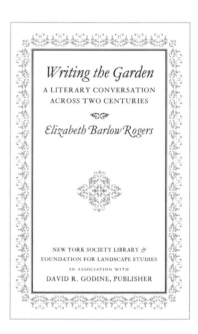

ABOVE: Jerry Kelly's striking two-color title page for Elizabeth Rogers's delightful selection of garden writing that also includes color images of iconic book jackets and interior scenes, this of Celia Thaxter among the poppies of her Appledore garden

FAR LEFT: Jacket of *Romantic Gardens* showing a detail of Humphry Repton's *View of the Welbeck Estate*, 1794, and Johann Heinrich Wilhelm Tischbein's 1787 portrait of *Goethe in the Roman Campagna*

Michael Valentine Bartlett & Rose Love Bartlett: *The Bartlett Book of Garden Elements*

2014. 272 PP, 9 × 11″ $40.00 SC *with flaps*

Once the horticultural bones of a garden have been established, and the plants and their whereabouts decided, the next question that generally arises is what man-made objects are required. Whether it's benches, bridges, or birdhouses, pavings stones, fountains or gazebos, this book is the "go-to" source for considering all the alternatives and finding the answers. In more 1,000 full-color photographs you'll find them all displayed and explained on these pages, not just the predictable "garden" varieties, but specimens from around the world: Jefferson's chinoiserie railings at Monticello, the curved Rose Pergola at Bodnant in Wales, Gaudí's fantastic paving wall mosaics in Barcelona, driveway gates made out of sheet metal in Christchurch, New Zealand. No, this is not a book of prefabricated, off-the-shelf commodities you can order from Amazon. Each is a handmade object, beautiful in itself, useful, original, one of a kind. Michael Bartlett came from a long line of gardeners. He began his garden design business in 1975, married Rose in 1980, and the two of them spent three decades travelling the world assembling the vast and encyclopedic archive of man-made garden objects that are the core of this book. The photos are selected from the more than one thousand gardens they visited in twenty-one countries. But the book is essentially a practical guide, providing gardeners with examples of the "best of kind" and allowing them to point to a photo and say, "Now, *that's* what I want." Whatever the challenge, the Bartletts had seen it and solved it. In twenty chapters, beginning with Allées and ending with Walls, they lay out the possibilities. Every chapter is preceded by a lengthy essay on the history and evolution of the structure in question. If it's man-made, useful, and elegant, you'll find an image of it in these pages, the standard reference for the best garden ornaments and elements. It was among the more challenging design projects we have encountered, and Sara Eisenman (who shares a love of gardening) was the perfect choice to put all the myriad pieces in their proper places.

BELOW: The Bartletts missed very little of any artistic importance in their international survey of garden elements: not benches, not birdhouses, not planters.

Barbara Paul Robinson: *Heroes of Horticulture*

2018. 272 PP, 7 × 12″ $40.00 HC

In a colorful and beautifully designed book Barbara Robinson introduces the reader to eighteen heroes of horticulture – community builders, plant explorers, and garden creators who collectively and individually have exerted a major impact on both our landscape and our institutions. Three of them worked to establish The Garden Conservancy, preserving exceptional gardens for public access. Others were instrumental in restoring (sometimes from scratch) public parks and abandoned spaces. Others took on the revitalization of major botanic gardens, spaces central to science, education, and public enjoyment. And some provide the book with incredible tales of plant exploration, traveling to the remote corner of the earth to return with plant species unknown to the West and working with hybridizers to preserve and improve new cultivars. The plants, ideas, and programs emanating from these heroes benefit garden lovers and gardeners across the country. But whether or not you're familiar with a spade and trowel, you can read these stories with a sense of wonder and admiration. These are the men and women who really did change our landscape, improve our public spaces and institutions, and engender real appreciation for gardening as an art as well as a pastime. The author, a lawyer by training, and a gardener through conversion, knew most of them personally. The affection she feels for them as people, as well as a sense of the challenges they endured and managed to overcome, shines through in her prose.

LEFT: The opening for Barbara Robinson's survey of the movers and shakers of the horticultural world, this spread displays just one section of the remarkable garden created by Frank Cabot at his stunning *Les Quatre Vents* in La Malbaie, Quebec, an undertaking of Olympian proportions that Robinson rightly considers "the Taj Mahal of gardens."

BELOW: A view of New York's Central Park, now a glory of the city but in large part saved from dissolution and disrepair through the singularly heroic efforts of Elizabeth Barlow Rogers

OPPOSITE: Interior spread from Bemelmans's *La Bonne Table*

Cooking & Cuisine

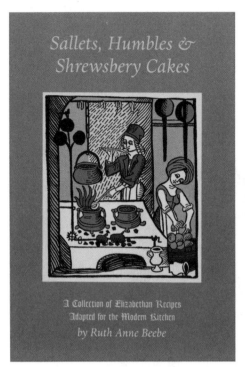

Ruth Anne Beebe: *Sallets, Humbles & Shrewsbery Cakes*

1976. 128 PP, 6½ × 9¾" $12.50 HC

This, the first of our sporadic and eclectic list of books on cooking and cuisine, was everything the modern cookbook is not. The text is scholarly, presenting a number of dishes that no modern cook would even consider, and the presentation is as much gastronomic and cultural history as an effort to cater to the latest dietary fad. The book was an attempt to recreate the past, to give the flavor of Elizabethan life, to provide historical insights into the circumstances that dictated Tudor eating habits and methods of food preparation. If you aren't seduced by the period, you had to love the design, typesetting, and printing by Mike and Winnifred Bixler. Seldom has a sober culinary exegesis received more loving care or beautiful printing. Elegantly illustrated with English woodcuts of the period, printed in red and set in Mike's favorite Dante typeface, it is a feast of letterpress. The recipes may appear somewhat dated, but they do provide a good cross-section of the skilled Elizabethan cook's repertoire and the kinds of food that were commonly served. By providing a compendium of genuine, historically accurate Elizabethan recipes, gathered, annotated, and (not unimportantly) tested, as well as instructions that make them accessible to the modern chef, Beebe makes a real contribution to the literature. In addition to the original recipes, she adapted and tested versions for the contemporary cook, including ingredients, measurements, and advice on what herbs were used to flavor and preserve. It's all here, from how ale was brewed to how to "fry an egg as round as a ball." This is real insight into the Medieval mind—its preconceptions, prejudices, and protocols, food for the plate and provisions for the mind.

Richard Olney: *The French Menu Cookbook: A Revised and Updated Edition of a Culinary Classic*

1985. 316 PP, 6⅝ × 10" $22.50 HC

Harry Ford, then a designer at Atheneum, was the man primarily responsible for Olney's introduction to American readers through the misleadingly titled *Simple French Food* published by Atheneum in 1974. I had the idea of commissioning him to update and revise it, urging him to write a more detailed description of the cuisine he loved and championed from a new fifteen-year perspective. Olney was a sybarite and a connoisseur in the best tradition—precise, demanding, and exacting. A brief taste of his language and approach to fine cuisine can be inferred from this paragraph on measurements: "The maniacal precisions of weights, measures, and oven temperatures imposed on modern cookbooks serve mainly to soothe feelings of insecurity in the timid cook; a blind respect for them will discourage self-confidence and the development of a tactile sense, which go hand in hand. Food should be an expression of a cook's personality. A recipe executed by two individuals will produce, thanks to individual sensibilities, two different dishes." This was no cookbook for "the timid cook"; Olney was a stern and exacting task master, easily the equal of Julia Child. The recipes may

have given a little leeway on measurements, but the directions for preparation, what wine and dessert would be appropriate, and the use of herbs, salt, and pepper were precise and explicit. Olney was promoting, in his words, "a convergence of all the senses, an awareness through touching, but also through smelling, hearing, seeing, and tasting that something is 'just right.'" We did our best to make the book "just right" and were blessed by the talents of the Boston designer Richard Bartlett, the fine illustrations by Judith Eldridge, and the choice of the just-released Galliard typeface of Matthew Carter. Printed in two colors with the Galliard italic doing its merry dance on the page, the ingredients somehow all came together. The result was our first real commercial success in the field and a book that still reads, and tastes, like the real thing.

Richard Olney: *Yquem*

1986. 168 PP, 9 × 10¾" $45.00 HC

When we published this title with Flammarion in 1986 at what was then a fairly ambitious price, I'd be the last to claim I knew anything at all about wine, and especially a really classy and expensive sauterne like Yquem. But we had published Richard Olney before, and I knew that any project that attracted that fastidious and scrupulous author (born, of all places, in Marathon, Iowa) was to be taken seriously. What I didn't realize is *how* seriously the Sauternes, a product of "the noble rot," produced at the vineyards of the Lur Saluces family on their ancestral vineyard bordering the Garonne River in the wine country that borders Bordeaux, were taken by wine aficionados. This was a wine with a history that went back 400 years; it was "wine of kings," a favorite at the Courts of the Czars, at the top of Thomas Jefferson's list of great white wines. The whole saga of family history, cultivating and harvesting the grapes, the composition of the soil and uniqueness

of the site, and the family's continued involvement in what can be a risky business, is thoroughly covered in Olney's text. The evocative color photographs by Michel Guillard document the family, the vineyards, and the personalities who tended and cultivated them. An unexpected bonus of publishing the book was a visit by the Duc to New York to celebrate the book's publication and where he hosted a series of formal dinners to which my wife Sara and I were invited. At each course we had the pleasure of tasting a new bottle, and a new year, of Château Yquem. Nights to remember with New York's culinary élite, and I can now distinguish a Sauternes from a Riesling.

Mary L. Hamady: *Lebanese Mountain Cookery*

1987. 288 PP, 6¾ × 10" $25.00 HC

When Mary and Walter Hamady were still a married couple and living in Mt. Horeb, Wisconsin, I drove from Iowa City to visit them with my sister. Mary, it turned out, was quite a cook, and she and Walter, whose grandparents were from the Lebanese Highlands, had put together a cookbook that they convinced me to publish by serving meal after meal celebrating its cuisine. With the two of them, their three children, and the two of us, every meal was a communal event, and this sense of familiar, informal family cooking, using recipes handed down from one generation to another, is what informs the book and its 200 recipes. Walter, one of the great printers and genuine originals of the past century, was still teaching, making paper, setting books, and publishing under his inimitable Perishable Press imprint. In short, he was doing everything – including, it seemed, bringing up three daughters and running a small farm. But he made time to design the book and cajoled his friend, Jana Fothergill, into providing the lovely and evocative halftone drawings that begin each chapter and manage to convey some sense of the lovely Lebanese high mountain scenery.

Samuel Chamberlain: *Clémentine in the Kitchen*

1988. 256 PP, 6½ × 9¼" $20.00 HC

Chamberlain was known to me primarily as an artist who, along with Stow Wengenroth, Thomas Nason, and John Taylor Arms, formed a New Englander foursome whose graphic work I most admired. I had no idea that *Clémentine*, written under the pseudonym Phineas Beck and really the first cookbook to seriously examine the mysteries of French cuisine, was the work of a man who had spent a dozen years in France and only left the little French cathedral town in Burgundy in 1939 when the threat of Nazi invasion became too real to ignore. With him came the family's longtime *cordon bleu* cook, Clémentine, repairing to the small Massachusetts harbor village of Marblehead. First published in 1943, our edition was completely reset and redesigned by Richard Bartlett to include a considerable number of Chamberlain etchings and dry-points, as well as original drawings. As Julia Child admitted, "French cooking was never the same after Clémentine came into our kitchens." I think the book succeeds on many levels, not least taking into account the grim events unfolding in Europe in the late thirties and putting them into a human framework, seen through the eyes of the determined Clémentine who has to struggle with – and triumph over – ingrained American customs, not to mention supermarkets, Francophobes, frozen and processed foods, and unfamiliar cookware. Chamberlain's daughter Narcisse, no mean cook and a superb editor in her own right, undertook rewriting the recipes and introducing new ones for the eighties.

Ludwig Bemelmans: *La Bonne Table*
Edited by Donald and Eleanor Fried

1989. 448 PP, 6 × 9" $14.00 SC ⲇ

The world mostly remembers the colorful Ludwig Bemelmans for his timeless *Madeline* series, but here we have the best of what he wrote (and illustrated) on the subject he knew, and loved, best – food and drink, cooking and eating. Assembled by his friends Donald and Eleanor Fried from letters, journals, articles, published writings, unpublished drawings, and scribbles on the backs of napkins, it is as close to an autobiography of this remarkably versatile and talented man as we are likely to see. The reader is transported behind the scenes of the great hotels of Europe and America – including the immortal *Hôtel Splendide*, *La Tour D'Argent* in Paris and *Le Pavillon* in New York. It recalls memorable dishes (including recipes) eccentric kitchen geniuses who created them, astonishing patrons who ordered them, legendary wines, and the occasions they toasted – all presented in a rich, piquant prose sauce. He remembers, with mixed emotions, his lives as a busboy and a waiter, as well as the qualities that make a perfect maître d'. He muses over great menus and great eaters. In all of this, and especially in the drawings seamlessly integrated into the text, his extraordinary charm shines through. He once wrote the Frieds, when asked for a self-evaluation, a note that says it all, "Just say then: a curious, complicated being who is driven by an excess of energy which he tries to discipline but since it is like wild horses it runs away with him. He works with a fury, and lives as though it were the last day on earth. He is overly kind, overly generous – and hides it under a cloak of arrogance. He paints or writes the night through, is never where he says he will be, changes his mind constantly, drinks, smokes, and eats to excess, but fortunately has the constitution of an ox." You get the picture.

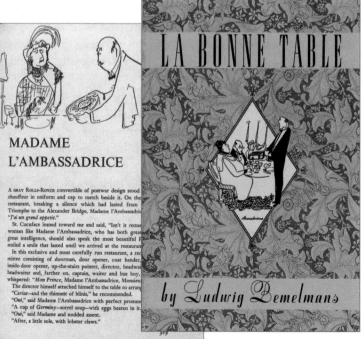

Nicolas Freeling: *The Kitchen Book & The Cook Book*

1991. 368 PP, 5½ × 8¼" $16.00 SC

Freeling, best known for producing some of the best modern crime novels, began his life as an apprentice chef in a large French hotel and continued working in the field professionally for many years. Here, combined into a single volume, are two memoirs of those years; the first his life in the kitchen, the second his life as a chef, each a bracing blend of both the literary and the culinary with recipes such as cinnamon lamb stew and the perfect bouillabaisse embedded in a consistently entertaining text. Our initial printings combined the two books, reproducing the original editions published in 1970 and 1972 respectively. Although similar, they were a mismatched set in both their typography and pagination. In 2014, we hired Michael Russem to reset and repaginate them sequentially so they now look like identical twins rather than distant cousins. No less than M.F.K. Fisher called them "two of the best books about cooking in the English language." Like the Bemelmans, the memoir is illustrated with line drawings, in this case by the talented and witty John Lawrence.

Raymond Sokolov: *Fading Feast: A Compendium of Disappearing American Regional Foods*

1999. 352 PP, 6 × 9" $17.00 SC

In the early 1980s, on assignment from the American Museum of Natural History, Raymond Sokolov was sent on an interesting culinary mission. He crisscrossed the continent not in search of buried dinosaur bones but traditional regional cuisines. Travelling from Maine to California, he returned with an archive of recipes that few at the time seemed eager to preserve or even claim had any importance – recipes such as boudin blanc, persimmon fudge, an old-fashioned New England clambake, and, for the truly adventuresome, roast bear paws. The resulting essays, here collected and arranged in book form, were intended to describe, celebrate, and ultimately codify these quintessentially regional recipes. Since its publication, *Fading Feast* has proven to be not a farewell but a forerunner of renewed interest in these regional treasures. Cookbooks have sprung up like weeds celebrating local cuisines, local chefs, and local (sometimes *really* local) foods. But this culinary incunable, written with passion and panache, and including eleven essays not included in the original hardcover version, was a harbinger of a movement to discover and record our "regional foods" (not *cuisine*, thank you).

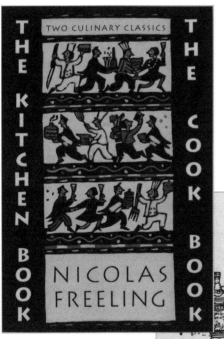

LEFT: This whimsical and inviting cover was designed by Lucinda Hitchcock.

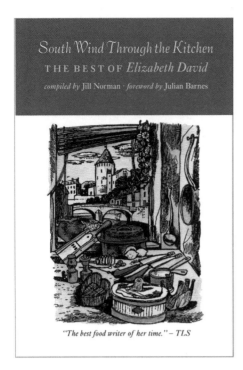

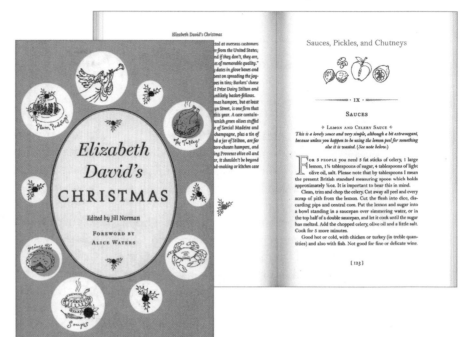

Elizabeth David: *South Wind
Through the Kitchen*
Compiled by Jill Norman
Foreword by Julian Barnes
2006. 414 PP, 6 × 9″ $19.00 SC

Elizabeth David's Christmas
Edited by Jill Norman
Foreword by Alice Waters
2008. 224 PP, 5½ × 8¼″ $26.00 HC

The *New Yorker* observed, "If we were to bushwack our way back to the true source of American food culture, we would find that it was not Julia Child, but Elizabeth David. [Her] recipes are all charm."

Both these books were, for this reader, not only "all charm," but great reading, even for someone who didn't fancy himself in any way a cook. She was, first and foremost, a *writer,* and by bringing charm and anecdotes and history and opinions, all expressed in lucid and bracing prose, she made cooking as much of a joy to read about as to engage in. Our first title *South Wind through the Kitchen* reprinted some of her best writing – essays on Provence and Paris, instructions on the challenges of rolling puff pastry and the ease of making pizza. We tend to forget what a gastronomic wasteland both the United States and England were after WWII. The legend, as Julian Barnes spells it out, went something like this: "The poor benighted Brits, mired in Spam and over-cooked vegetables, believing olive oil was something you bought at the pharmacy to clear wax from your ears, were hauled into culinary awareness by E.D." (as she was affectionately known). Mostly true: austerity rationing was in effect in the UK until 1954, and it was indeed David, with her *Book of Mediterranean Food*, who opened the windows to those balmy Mediterranean breezes and French herbs

and flavorings. Canned ham gave way to sea salt, sprigs of rosemary, whole basil leaves, seasonal produce, and fresh pasta. All of it drenched in olive oil. But it wasn't the recipes alone – it was her *writing*. She was stimulating, opinionated, informative, and funny. An equally diverting companion in both the kitchen and the library. She brought the continental cuisine to England's shores and then to America's. It's no wonder that James Beard called her "probably the greatest food writer we have." For Alice Waters, "she was the champion of simplicity and beauty in the kitchen, the defender of the authentic and the seasonal, and the ultimate arbiter of taste and proportion." As *South Wind* gathered the best from her previous books, *Christmas* was the result of Jill Norman's efforts to gather her notes and jottings surrounding that most challenging and stressful of family meals, the Christmas dinner. Much of the work had been done before her death. The fixings were all there; they only required a good cook (and editor) to prepare them. The classics are present and accounted for: the turkey (but also goose) and stuffing, the sauces, the pies, the Christmas pudding. But the main thrust of the book is to relax and enjoy yourself. Her hope was that the host or hostess "be spared the annual orgy of spending, the jammed streets, the frantic shoppers in the stores …" the whole circus of what she described as "The Great Too Much" that quickly morphed into "The Great Too Long." This book allows you to enjoy the holidays reading rather than slaving over a stove. But if you want a clear-headed account of how to prepare a proper Christmas dinner, it's all there. When Queen Elizabeth presented E.D. the C.B.E. in 1986, she asked her what she did. She answered, "Write cookery books, Ma'am." To which the Queen replied, "How useful." In two short words, she spoke for all of us – useful then, and useful now.

✒ *Typography*

✒ TYPE REVIVALS

What are they?
Where did they come from?
Where are they going?

by JERRY KELLY

Jan van Krimpen: *The Mechanical Cutting of Punches*

Introduction and Commentary by John Dreyfus
1972. 104 PP, 6⅝ × 9¾" $15.00 HC

When we began printing in the barn, among the very first hot metal faces we acquired from the venerable Dutch firm of type casters and printers, Joh. Enschedé en Zonen, were Jan van Krimpen's *Cancelleresca Bastarda* (in all three sizes) and a full range of Romulus. While still active at the heart of the business and a strong believer in new letter forms, Van Krimpen had been commissioned by Phil Hofer of Harvard's Houghton Library in July 1953 to deliver a calligraphic manuscript on a subject near and dear to his heart. He complied, but with qualifications. He would respond,"The only interesting thing, in my opinion, is I think the problem I mentioned to you; a problem which I doubt I shall ever be able to solve for myself. How can a living design, made by human hand, eye (& heart) be adequately rendered by the mechanical means now in use of producing type?" In Van Krimpen's day, that "mechani-cal means" still involved cutting type from metal using machinery operated by trained artisans, but even then this ancient skill was being replaced by two-dimensional photographic masters. Today it involves the manipulation of points on a computer screen. But the question still hangs in the air: to what degree does a mechanical reproduction, by whatever means, capture or distort what was originally a drawn letter of the human hand? Two years and twelve letters later, he would write to Hofer in November 1955, "… the manuscript is finished; Laus Deo." Van Krimpen's letter was as beautiful in its calligraphy as it was meaningful to its author. The commentary and transcription were provided by John Dreyfus, a leading expert on his work, who takes issue with many of Van Krimpen's arguments and conclusions (especially his disapproval of Stanley Morison's efforts at Monotype to reissue classic faces) while providing substantive evidence to support his case. Printed in a specially tinted paper to match the original, designed by Bram de Does and Sem Hartz, both working at Enschedé, it was co-published with the Department of Printing and Graphic Arts at Harvard's Houghton Library.

BELOW: Facsimiles of Jan van Krimpen's distinctive cursory hand-writing, printed on a specially tinted paper to imitate the original, in which he presents his case for and against the use of mechanical methods to reproduce human handiwork

machine are two different tools from which fundamentally different achievements should be asked. I am coming back to this.
But you and anybody else who might care to read this letter I refer to the pages in Updike's book I have mentioned.
Updike's merit lies, I think, more in his having seen so early — in a time when the Bentons and Pierponts, inventors or inventors and improvers, still were the indisputed masters and directors of the engraving machine — that there was something, nay very much, wrong than in what he points out as, in his opinion, favourable developments or in prescriptions for further improvement. That, for instance, his observation that "each size is a law unto itself" has become obsolete — since nowadays all users of engraving machines know and conform
13

modified some oddities of his handiwork — and so needs not being dealt with separately. Will Updike, who has known the type and must have seen the patterns, have been satisfied with the flexibility of Wiebking's machine? In his criticism, quoted by Rogers, there is a restriction that leaves room for doubt: The late D. B. Updike, in his monumental work Printing Types, wrote: "It appears to me one of the best Roman founts yet designed in America, and, of its kind, the best anywhere." What Updike has wanted to imply with the insertion "of its kind" we are unlikely ever to know.
I have read, and re-read several times, Morison's A Tally of Types and I have been unable to find that the subject of this letter should be even the slightest point to him. This is made possible by the fact that
19

ART OF THE PRINTED BOOK
1455–1955

MASTERPIECES OF TYPOGRAPHY

THROUGH FIVE CENTURIES

FROM THE COLLECTIONS OF THE

PIERPONT MORGAN LIBRARY

NEW YORK

ABOVE: The recto title page of Joe Blumenthal's accessible exploration of five centuries of fine printing. The book was set in Baskerville with shoulder notes in Bulmer, but the title and date are composed in the carefully letterspaced full caps of Eric Gill's Perpetua. Note the touch of a master: the carefully mitred dash between the two dates. The subtitle was set in Bulmer caps. It may look simple, but there were hours of work involved in getting those letters to fit so perfectly. The right page shows a reproduction of a page from Melchior Pfinzing's 1517 edition of the *Theuerdank*, a series of adventures the Emperor Maximilian encountered in search of a bride. The extravagant swash letters and tightly set fraktur blend seamlessly with the woodcut illustration.

Joseph Blumenthal: *Art of the Printed Book, 1455–1955*
1973. 208 PP, 9 × 12⅛″ $30.00 HC

We had no idea, when we first began publishing exhibition catalogues from The Pierpont Morgan Library for distribution to the "trade," that luck would present us with Joe Blumenthal's memorable overview of fine printing through five centuries. This was an exhibition, it could be argued, that the Library was destined to support and a book Joe was born to write. No one, not even Stanley Morison, had taken the whole scope of fine printing, from the Gutenberg Bible through its final days of hot metal, and presented such a coherent and fluid narrative of its development and influence. Joe was, in this sense, a great synthesizer and storyteller, and this is what made the book so successful—this and the fact that he and Charles Ryskamp, the Library's director, had the good sense not to insist on a typical exhibition catalogue but rather a standalone narrative, told with the insight of a practitioner and typographically arranged with the eye of a first-rate designer. The plate section following the text, printed duotone by the Meriden Gravure Company, superbly captured the detail and majesty of the original pages. It was set in Blumenthal's favorite combination, Baskerville for the text and Bulmer for the display. The text for the first few editions were printed letterpress at The Stinehour Press of Lunenburg, VT. The page from the Gutenberg Bible was a foldout. The exhibition, as well as the book, was widely and favorably reviewed in the New York press, and what we thought would have limited and local appeal turned into an early "bestseller." Over time, it went through six printings and sold over 20,000 copies in hardcover. Joe was as immensely pleased as we were surprised.

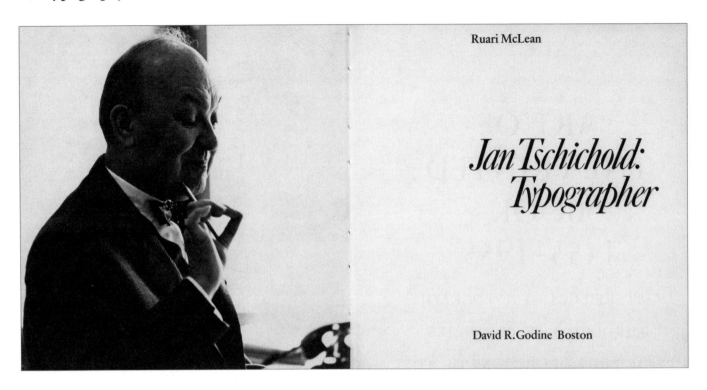

Ruari McLean: *Jan Tschichold: Typographer*
1975. 160 PP, 9½ × 9½" $25.00 HC

When we published this title in 1975, the author was probably better known in America than his subject, Jan Tschichold, a typographer and designer few had heard of and whose name fewer still were capable of spelling. But McLean, always a few decades ahead of his time, recognized what a major part he had played in typographic history. He had basically redesigned the entire output of the Penguin list at the invitation of Sir Allen Lane and his list of dos and don'ts should be required reading. He had died just a year before, among the first generation of "modern" European typographers, and certainly among the most lucid, original, intelligent and influential. Since his native language was German, few of his books had been translated into English and until this publication, there had never been a full appraisal in English of his personal history, achievements, or influence. McLean had published a translation of his *Typographische Gestaltung* or *Asymmetric Typography* in 1967, but little was known of Tschichold's early career in Germany, his imprisonment by the Nazis, his escape to Switzerland in 1933, his career in the UK revamping the Penguin list, or his later work after his return to the Ticino in Switzerland where he remained until his death. Profusely illustrated, it provides a full overview of his work, presenting many of his early designs never seen before in an English language publication and including the first and only translations of his most important essays. A full chapter is devoted to his years at Penguin and, at the end, is a selected list of books by and about him. The index

ABOVE: Ruari McLean's early investigation of the influential Swiss perfectionist Jan Tschichold

reads like a "Who's Who" of twentieth-century typography. McLean ends with a sentence that more or less says it all: "He has shown, more clearly than anyone else, that the true task of the typographer is not so much in the broad sweep and the dashing effect, which draws the applause, as in the less obvious, infinitely more difficult and painstaking task of getting *all* the details right–with elegance."

Eric Gill: *The Letter Forms and Type Designs of Eric Gill*
Notes by Robert Harling
1977. 64 pp, 7¼ × 7¼″ $12.50 HC

An Essay on Typography
New introduction by Christopher Skelton
1998. 150 pp, 4¼ × 6⅝″ $20.00 HC

Gill was the most protean of the twentieth-century lettering artists, at home cutting letters on stone and wood, equally adept at designing entire fonts, and perfectly comfortable writing manifestos on the side on everything from clothing to art theory. But I think his real love was in design. In his manifesto, *An Essay on Typography*, really the first of English-language modernist polemics, he lays down the law for the correct composition and layout of book pages. The original was published and printed in 1931 on a lovely, grey English handmade paper and is a wonder, but the later letterpress edition, reissued and revised, in 1936 containing additional material, revisions and a new chapter at the end, is the one on which ours is based. The typesetting of the unjustified lines (which he championed) is a perfect rag right; the *mise en page* and the title page are perfect. If Gill had one flaw as a designer, it was in his chronic inability to create decent figures, i.e. numbers, a failing he shared with van Krimpen. But his Perpetua and Joanna are bright, original and inscriptional, and we have used both to great effect, especially the Perpetua Titling, which is perhaps the finest font of full caps cut in the twentieth century. His greatest fault as a human being was perhaps that he took his conversion to Catholicism, and especially the absolution conferred by confession, a little too literally and often used it as an excuse for bias, deviance and abuse. But he was hardly alone in leaving the Church of England; Morison, Bridges, Chesterton, T.S. Eliot, and many more, looking for a higher and tighter religious structure, would join the Church of Rome before the century was finished. His *Essay* was the first major book he published, and it remains to this day an indispensable reference for anyone interested in the art of letter forms and the presentation of graphic information.

ABOVE: Pages from Robert Harling's examination of Eric Gill as a type and letter designer with sample pages from Gill's wseminal *An Essay on Typography*

Joseph Blumenthal: *The Printed Book in America*

1977. 268 PP, 7½ × 10¾″ $30.00 HC

Following his exhibition at the Morgan, Joe was asked by Edward C. Lathem, then Librarian of Dartmouth College, if he would write a parallel book concentrating on the printed book in America. Joe attacked the proposition with his usual thoroughness and enthusiasm and from the unique perspective of a printer, not an historian. As Joe probably knew, truth be told, there wasn't much "fine printing" in America until De Vinne at the end of the nineteenth century, and Joe had to stretch a little to find any examples in the seventeenth and eighteenth centu-ries. Benjamin Franklin's *Cato Major* may have been a peg above the average printing then found in the colonies, but, compared to what was happening on the continent, it was small beer. Still, it was the first overview to appear from this perspective and as always, his design and the production were exemplary. The book was somewhat smaller in format than the Morgan volume, but still set in Baskerville with Bulmer and Perpetua as the display faces. And, as always, the giveaway swelled rule. I find his adulation of Bruce Rogers a bit excessive, and think that he should perhaps have given more space to his own Spiral Press and to the twentieth century, when America really *could* hold its own with Europe in terms of fine book design and manufacture. Still, the book, again printed letterpress at Stinehour with the plates struck in at the end by Meriden Gravure, is handsome, balanced, and often referenced.

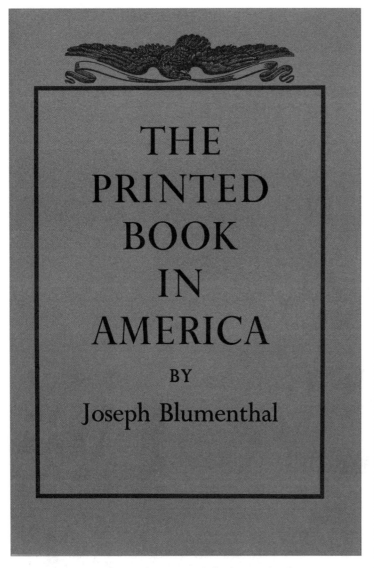

NEWARK
A SERIES OF ENGRAVINGS ON WOOD BY
RUDOLPH RUZICKA
WITH AN APPRECIATION OF
THE PICTORIAL ASPECTS OF THE TOWN
BY WALTER PRICHARD EATON

THE CARTERET BOOK CLUB
NEWARK · NEW JERSEY
1917

33 Rudolph Ruzicka. The Carteret Book Club, Newark, New Jersey. *Newark.* (Engravings on wood by Ruzicka; text by Walter Prichard Eaton.) 1917. 9¼ x 12.

RIGHT: This sample page from Blumenthal's *The Printed Book in America* shows an example of D.B. Updike's Merrymount Press printing of *Newark.* Ruzicka fulfilled the hopes of The Carteret Book Club that he "would find beauty and some grandeur where most people see only industrial blight" in the city. Printed as a generous quarto, it included five full-page color illustrations printed by hand by Ruzicka in an edition of 200 copies.

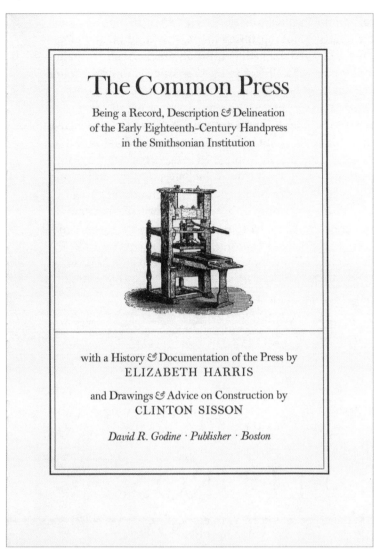

ABOVE: A detailed drawing of the original wooden Benjamin Franklin press in the Smithsonian Institution. Little changed over 300 years; Gutenberg could have walked in, looked it over, and immediately started printing.

Elizabeth Harris: *The Common Press*

Drawings and Construction Advice by Clinton Sisson 1978. 124 PP, 8½ × 11″ $15.00 HC *with a separate suite of plans, eight separate folio mechanical drawings folded to fit into a separate sleeve, two volumes enclosed in a slipcase*

It is a mystery to me how or why we decided to take this on. But like many specialized books (and we've done very few more specialized than this), it sold to a grateful, if astonished, audience. In it, Harris and Clinton give the history and clear schematic drawings for building the enduring wooden press, one very similar to the ones Isaiah Thomas or Benjamin Franklin would have been using in the late eighteenth century before the iron press supplanted them. The folding plans, issued in a separate folder and close to life-size, are detailed, the building instructions clear and methodical. Not made for riveting reading, but as a "how to" book, we've never done better.

Elizabeth Harris was the Curator of Graphic Arts at the Smithsonian Institution when this book was written.

It housed many battered veterans, including the original used by Benjamin Franklin, closely related to thousands that had served printers' needs for centuries. Gutenberg could have walked into the museum, instantly understood its construction and mechanism, and begun printing immediately. This was, in essence, the same press he used to print the Bible in 1455, and its descendants would spread wit and wisdom, sense and sedition, for four hundred years. Its history, antecedents, and construction had never been fully documented, and Harris's account, accompanied by a suite of eight detailed line drawings by Clinton Sisson, allow any ambitious amateur the tools needed to build an exact replica from scratch. This was a small miracle of a book, designed by Stephen Harvard, set in Monotype Bell, printed and bound entirely at Stinehour Press with the text and the line drawings in two folders enclosed in a matching slipcase, all for the absurd price of $15.00.

Fleuron Anthology

Chosen and with a Retrospectus by Sir Francis
Meynell and Herbert Simon

1979. 376 PP, 8½ × 10⅞″ $22.50 SC

Published between 1923 and 1930, the seven volumes of
"The Fleuron: A Journal of Typography" were the justly
acclaimed New Testaments in their field. The first four
volumes were edited by Oliver Simon, who then passed
editorial control to Stanley Morison, who commented, in
his postscript to the seventh and final volume, "Nobody
ever made a penny profit from it." The set has become
increasingly rare and correspondingly expensive. I wish
we could take some little credit for initiating this anthology, but the credit goes to Sir Francis Meynell and Herbert
Simon for choosing the 22 articles and to The Curwen
Press, whose exemplary printing and typesetting can been
seen in the original four volumes, and again in this reissue,
for resetting and reprinting them. This "Journal of Typography" covered the field graphically, intellectually, visually,
and typographically for years, presenting countless seminal
articles from the leading authorities of the day. It justly
came to be considered the primary record of the printing
renaissance that both the US and the UK were experiencing
in the early years of the twentieth century. Along with the
articles came a newly minted "Retrospectus" on "English
Printing before The Fleuron" by Oliver Simon and Francis
Meynell. Sheets from the UK had been imported by The
University of Toronto, from whom we bought sets, commissioned Mike Bixler to print and design a Fleuronesque
cover and title page, and sold the book in softcover for
$22.50. It was, and remains, the best one-volume overview,
an ample snapshot of the key players and products of one
of typography's most exciting decades.

BELOW: A page from Paul Beaujon's (AKA Beatrice
Warde's) essay "On Decorative Printing in America."
The page shows the modernist William Addison
Dwiggins's bravura use of his handcut stencils to
form an ingenious design as well as the perfection
of his handwriting, almost indistinguishable from
the titling capitals

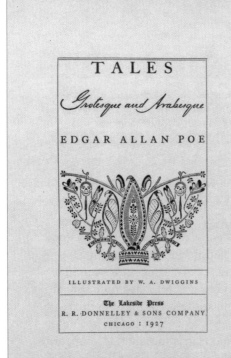

Fig. 6. *Title-page from Mr W. A. Dwiggins' edition of Poe's* Tales
(Chicago, Donnelley, 1927)

259

ABOVE: A new cover designed, set, and printed letterpress by Michael Bixler
for Meynell & Simon's *Fleuron Anthology*

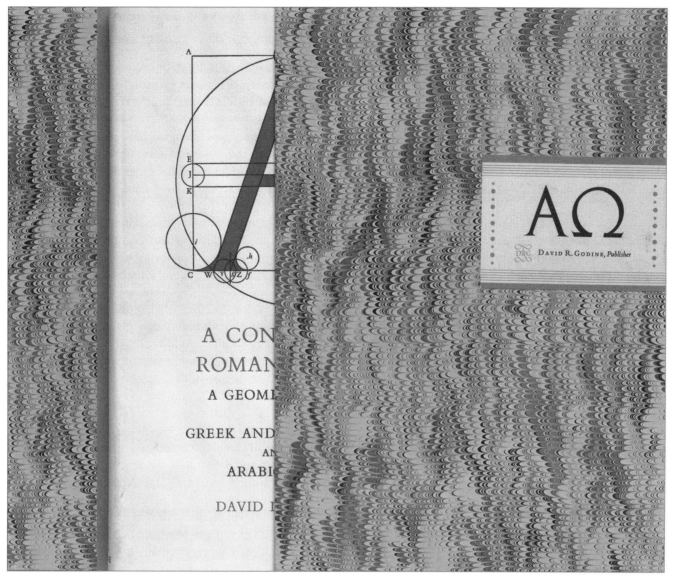

David Lance Goines: *A Constructed Roman Alphabet*

1982. 192 PP, 8 × 12″ $50.00 HC, $150.00 *limited edition in a slipcase with extra suite of letters inserted*

The idea of using mathematical and geometric principles to construct a "perfect" alphabet goes back to the fifteenth century and is probably first and best manifested in the manuscripts of Felice Feliciano, all created in the 1460s. But Moille, Durer, Pacioli, Fanti, Verini and Tory, among others, each tried to bring some rational (i.e. geometric and mathematical) formulae to what had been (and probably should remain) the visual and manual construction of the roman capitals, letters that found their fullest antique expression in the Trajan column of Rome. Here David Lance Goines, a prolific and talented printer, poster designer, and artist from Berkeley, tried his hand and

generated what are, to my mind, quite astonishing results, recreating both the Roman and Greek capitals as well as a complete set of figures and the ampersand. The book was printed letterpress in two colors on Mohawk Superfine paper from linecuts of the drawings at The Stinehour Press, which under the direction of Rocky Stinehour and Freeman Keith, did a magnificent job of printing the Monotype Bembo while not underinking the solids. To be sure, these books appeal to few beyond the lunatic fringe, but both the conception and the execution of what is a totally artificial set of rules is here so perfectly printed that one forgets the forced mechanics and just stands back to admire the astonishing results. Goines engaged in an exercise that no one had seriously attempted in 300 years, and the outcome was a series of Roman and Greek capitals that could hold their own with any of their predecessors. Everyone involved in this project was proud of the results.

Walter Tracy: *Letters of Credit*

1986. 224 PP, 6⅞ × 9¾″ $27.50 HC

Some four years before Lawson's *Anatomy*, Walter Tracy, the thirty-year head of typographic development at British Linotype, foresaw that the development of photo-typesetting and type design via the computer was not only encroaching on traditional technology but was, in fact, inevitable. He saw his customers "bewildered by the number and variety of typefaces now available" and concluded that merely accumulating facts about them "squirrel-fashion" was no longer sufficient. For him what was needed was some practical system of evaluation; what was necessary was "to acquire a sense of values and to develop the ability to make judgements about the quality of the typefaces I was using." And reading this book with its pungent prose and prescient predictions, one is left with no doubt that Tracy indeed *had* opinions, firm opinions, about legibility, kerning, the proportion and form of the roman letter as well as italics, bold face, figures and san serifs. He ends the books with discussion of four type designers: Van Krimpen, Goudy, Koch, and Dwiggins, as well as a final chapter on Stanley Morison's only venture in the field of type design: Times Roman. This title, as with many others, came to us through the good offices of Gordon Fraser in the UK and its talented typographer Peter Guy, who, along with John Ryder at the Bodley Head, served in many ways as our publishing partners in the UK.

Alexander Lawson: *Anatomy of a Typeface*

1990. 432 PP, 6 × 9″ $25.00 SC, $40.00 HC

Alexander Lawson was, for decades, a beloved instructor of typography at the Rochester Institute of Technology, where he kept alive a certain respect for the traditions of the past and taught generations of students the rudiments of type and typographic design. This book, long in print and much admired, is a summation of his familiarity with, indeed his passion for, type, and especially hot metal. In it he divides all type into basic families, in his words "just thirty from the many thousands that have appeared since the fifteenth century." He describes the lineage and branches of the families he discusses in some detail, offering complete synopses of many of the faces as well as affectionate appraisals of the types themselves, not to mention their designers and engravers. I created the cover montage by setting type for the cover label, proofing and tying it up, and then placing it on a brass galley placed above the upper-case half of a California job case. My Milton workshop still houses sixteen different hot metal faces, most in multiple sizes. Were he alive today, Lawson would doubtless be astonished, and probably gratified to witness the number of fonts available, the list of alternate sorts and characters they contain, and the ease by which they can be accessed and used on an ordinary computer. His aim was never to exalt one face and denigrate another, or to argue that too many fonts already existed. On the contrary, the book is "addressed to the person who believes the opposite—that the subtleties of refinement as applied to roman letters have yet to be fully investigated and that the production of the perfect printing type remains a goal to be desired as much by contemporary as by future typographers."

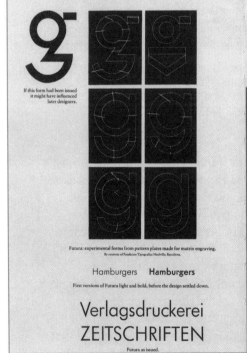

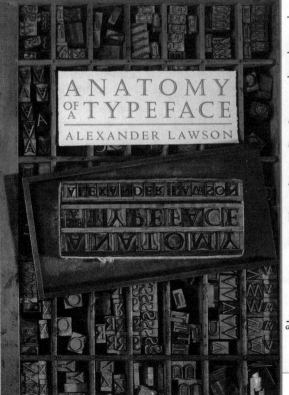

ABOVE: An interior page from Tracy's *Letters of Credit* RIGHT & FAR RIGHT: Front jacket of Lawson's survey of type families showing the title set and tied up on a galley tray over the upper-case half of a California job case and a page from the book displaying Matthew Carter's lively Galliard italic, based loosely on the italics of the sixteenth-century punchcutter Robert Granjon, released by Linotype in 1978, and proof that extraordinary new faces are still being created.

John Dreyfus: *Into Print: Selected Writings on Printing History, Typography and Book Production*

1994. 410 PP, 6 × 9″ $65.00 HC

This fine potpourri of a volume was the result of the combined efforts of myself and David Way, the publisher of the British Library, to persuade John Dreyfus to finally put between covers a selection of the important, often seminal, articles, essays, and lectures he had published as bibliographer, typographer, and internationally renowned historian of printing. The result is a compendium of his best, a singular contribution to the literature of typographic scholarship and research. They reveal interests covering a wide range of subjects from both sides of the Atlantic. There are discussions of particular typographers, such as Giovanni Mardersteig, Stanley Morison, Eric Gill, P. J. Conkwright, Bruce Rogers, and Jan van Krimpen; private presses; the Doves, the Cranach, the Stanbrook Abbey; typefaces, such as Baskerville and Sabon; issues of manufacture and design, e.g. "Matrix Making and Type Design at the Monotype Works 1900–1913"; and the

types created by Giovanni Mardersteig. As the Assistant University Printer and Adviser to Cambridge University Press, a close collaborator to the Monotype Corporation, president of the Association Typographique Internationale and the Wynkyn de Worde Society, and member and frequent speaker at the Double Crown Club, Dreyfus was command central for all matters typographic in the UK, the US, and Europe. His bibliography of The Nonesuch Press, his examination of the collaboration between Eric Gill and Robert Gibbings in creating *The Four Gospels*, and his essay on the aborted 1940 exhibition at Cambridge's Fitzwilliam Museum that ultimately evolved into "Printing and the Mind of Man" are models of clarity and primary source investigations. Containing over ninety illustrations, designed by John Trevitt and printed at the Stamperia Valdonega in their VAL Dante, it's a book that does justice to the man who inherited the mantle of Stanley Morison and wore it proudly for five decades.

BELOW: John Dreyfus is seen here with a bemused smile standing before the statue of Laurens Coster in the town square of Haarlem, where some Dutch still believe that he, not Gutenberg, was the inventor of movable type and printing.

RIGHT: The initial exhibition for the groundbreaking "Printing and the Mind of Man" was held at Cambridge's Fitzwilliam Museum in 1940 but shortly aborted because of fear of German bomb attacks. This page from his essay connects that modest initiative to the far larger "Printing and the Mind of Man" exhibition suggested by John Carter and held at Earls Court and the British Museum in 1963. The engravings by Reynolds Stone show, below, the critical mechanism of Gutenberg's invention, the two-piece mould surrounded by strikes and matrices and, above, the title of both the exhibition and catalogue, a phrase that may well have been inspired by the Jefferson Memorial in Washington, D.C. : "I have sworn upon the altar of God eternal hostility against every form of tyranny over the mind of man."

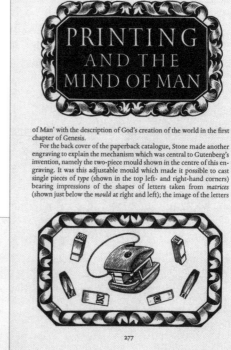

John Dreyfus below the Monument to Laurens Coster in Haarlem, 1992.

INTO PRINT

Selected Writings on Printing History, Typography and Book Production

JOHN DREYFUS

DAVID R. GODINE
Publisher
BOSTON

John S. Fass and The Hammer Creek Press
Edited by Eugene M. Ettenberg and Jackson Burke
1998. 64 PP, 5½ × 8″ $35.00 HC

Fass and his tiny "Hammer Creek Press" are known today mostly by typophiles and a small band of collectors, his minuscule editions and rare ephemera, printed on a diminutive Albion handpress, collected by only a handful of the faithful. His great supporters were Herman and Aveve Cohen of New York's famed and beloved Chiswick Book Shop, and they assiduously promoted his work while providing him moral and financial support over his lifetime. When given the chance to publish a checklist of the press, a brief history of the man and some pages of samples of his work, I leapt at the opportunity, knowing full well that this, like most of our eclectic typography books, would be embraced by true believers who probably never numbered more than a few hundred. The resulting small volume, printed letterpress from polymer plates and with a number of fine color reproductions of the title pages and the ephemera is the result. As a designer, Fass was every bit the equal of Rogers, most especially in his delicate and sensitive use of ornaments. As a printer, working on the tiny Albion handpress and the typecases that he stored beneath his bed at the YMCA, he was unsurpassed.

Stanley Morison: *A Tally of Types*
Edited by Brooke Crutchley, with an Introduction by Mike Parker
1999. 152 PP, 6⅛ × 9¼″ $16.00 SC

This was the final incarnation of a typographic classic, first issued as a limited edition by the Cambridge University Press in 1953 and sent by its director, Brooke Crutchley, as a Christmas keepsake to his favorite customers. Later, it was reissued by CUP, with Morison's notes on the typefaces unchanged but containing an appendix and endnotes. We provided a facsimile of this trade edition with a new Introduction by Mike Parker, a man supremely equipped to write it. He had followed Harry Carter to the Plantin-Moretus Museum in 1957 to continue inventorying their formidable collection of sixteenth-century types and punches. In 1960 he went to the Mergenthaler Linotype Company, to supervise the expansion of their hot metal library and was among the principal founders of Bitstream, among the first American foundries to supply digital type. At the core of the book are Morison's discussions of the various type revivals made available by English Monotype and, in what make the book especially attractive, with each of his long essays set in the typeface under discussion. Thus it becomes a useful specimen book; you are not only reading about Bembo; you are actually seeing what it looks like on the printed page. Parker says it well in his new Introduction: "It tells of the creation of a group of typefaces that lie at the heart of the library of book faces we all use today in our new world of digital communication." It also presents Morison (who like D. B. Updike never had the "benefit" of a college education) at his best – opinionated, eclectic, offering his characteristic blend of erudition and insight. It also presents, for the first time, a real look at the key players, the constant friction between Morison of Fetter Lane in London and Frank Hinman Pierpont, autocrat of the Works at Salfords, to the management genius of Harold Duncan and William Burch and the cooperation and enthusiasm of Walter Lewis and then Brooke Crutchley. Anyone who has witnessed a Monotype machine in action, with all 20,000 moving parts, will understand the prodigious effort involved in making, and then bringing these contraptions and typefaces, near perfect in their way, real triumphs of design, engineering and production.

LEFT: Samples of the ephemera printed by John Fass on his tiny Albion handpress. None of these pieces, many printed in more than one color, is much larger than a playing card.

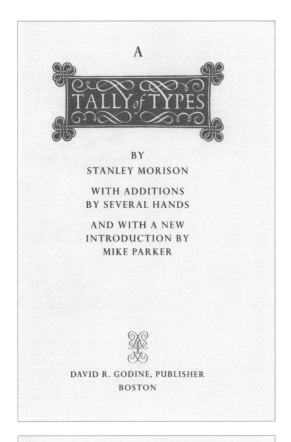

ABOVE: Opening page from one of the essays on monotype faces contained in Morison's *A Tally of Types*

ABOVE RIGHT: The fine calligraphy of Jerry Kelly is displayed on this cover for the revised edition of the Grolier Club exhibition catalogue. This new edition included all of the original descriptive data that further illuminated the full-page illustrations from each book from each year of the twentieth century.

Jerry Kelly & Martin Hutner: *A Century for the Century: Fine Printed Books 1900–1999* 2003. 144 PP, 9 × 12″ $45.00 HC

This book attempts, and largely succeeds, in selecting and discussing one hundred books for the twentieth century distinguished for their typography, illustration, or both. The authors were scrupulously careful to provide a real overview of what was happening in western typography, for the books included come from the US, the UK, Spain, Italy and Germany. The first edition was printed to accompany an exhibition of the hundred books at The Grolier Club in New York, but their edition didn't include the excellent notes on the books that Jerry and Martin had prepared. We shipped the files to China, set the notes (which amounted to about a paragraph for each title) and reprinted it. Jerry provided the calligraphy for the jacket. Reading this from cover to cover gives a fine and fairly comprehensive overview of who was doing what in the realm of fine printing and design throughout the last century. The choice of illustrations is excellent – each title is illustrated with most pages and spreads reproduced in full color.

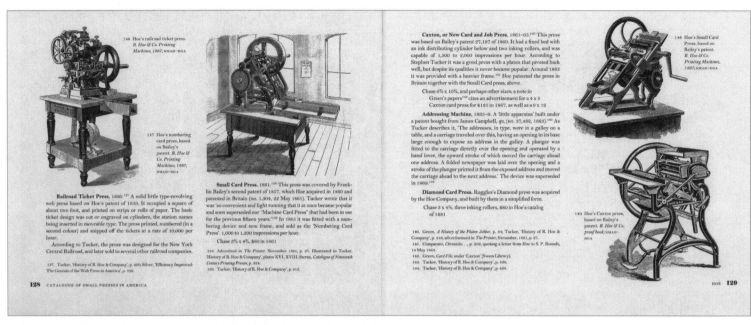

ABOVE: A spread from Elizabeth Harris's comprehensive survey of small, nineteenth-century American presses showing a quartet of the bewildering varieties available to small boys and small shops engaged in what was America's most competitive and widespread industry

Elizabeth Harris: *Personal Impressions: The Small Printing Press in Nineteenth-Century America*

2004. 200 PP, 11 × 8⅜″ $40.00 HC

This was another title undertaken with the formidable Susan Shaw, but by this time Elizabeth Harris had left US soil to raise sheep (or perhaps goats) in the UK. But the subject matter of the book is totally American: how an entire generation of entrepreneurial youth was introduced to, and frequently supported by, small and inexpensive hand presses which, with a brief instruction book and a few fonts of type available through the mail, could print everything from business cards to letterheads. Printing was the most competitive and widespread industry of nineteenth-century America. Every city not only boasted its larger presses for printing catalogues, books and newspapers, but a host of small shops, putting out everything from stationery to playbills to tickets. Many of the publishing giants of the twentieth century, F. N. Doubleday, George Mifflin, Henry Houghton, Donald Brace and even the legendary Alfred A. Knopf began their careers in the printing plant or manufacturing office. This definitive and richly illustrated survey of the small presses produced in this country in the nineteenth century is the first history devoted to these lovely, useful and prodigiously varied machines. Elizabeth Harris meticulously examined the minefields of the American patent office to track down the registration dates of the presses and then carefully ferreted out the tortuous business records of the small companies that manufactured them. Tony Kitzinger, a fine designer whose work I had known and admired for decades, patiently undertook the design and somehow composed spreads that made sense of an almost endless array of wood engravings, photographs, and line cuts.

Roberto de Vicq de Cumptich: *Men of Letters & People of Substance*

Preface by Francine Prose

2008. 96 PP, 5⅝ × 8″ $15.00 SC

Graphic artists (who follow each other closely) do recognize genius when they see it, and it would be difficult to not acknowledge that Roberto de Vicq's website and book *Bembo's Zoo* were milestones in creative graphic design. This book does for letters what his *Zoo* did for animals; for in this new effort de Vicq takes the typefaces and ornaments (known affectionately in the trade as "dingbats") and combines them to form the faces of his literary heroes. Thus the ten letters of Saul Bellow's name gives us, in the typeface of Gill's Golden Cockerel, his face (unmistakable) and the twelve letters of Carter's Miller provides us with the very anxious visage of George Orwell. There's more. In the second part he combines type ornaments and icons to suggest a face with singular attributes – pride, fear, fanaticism, surprise. Mother Nature here appears made up of flower cuts and Father Time from wall clocks. These are not drawings; they are images arranged from the creative combinations of discrete graphic forms. They are created on a computer screen, not in a composing stick. They are the face, or rather the faces, of the future.

Printed throughout in two colors, giving both the birth and death dates of the various subjects, as well as the number of times the various sorts are used in the construction of the image, this typographic offering is quirky, personal, and valuable – wholly original, totally inventive. In these typographic assemblies, here transformed into recognizable and ingenious portraits, de Vicq has managed, in the words of Francine Prose, "to make the alphabet sing."

Jerry Kelly: *The First Flowering: Bruce Rogers at the Riverside Press, 1896–1912*
2009. 96 PP, 5¾ × 8⅞" $25.00 HC

BR's years at Riverside were probably the happiest of his life, which, considering how miserable he usually sounded, probably isn't saying very much. In a decade when "limited edition" books, and especially the repercussions of Morris and his Kelmscott *Chaucer* were resonating in "arts and crafts" Boston, he was given practically a free hand by Houghton Mifflin to issue books in small quantities that would do the company proud – and perhaps make a little money on the side. He would run what was virtually a separate division at the Riverside Press on the bank of the Charles River in Cambridge and was empowered to choose everything from the texts to the paper, to oversee every detail of the book's production. This sweet little book by Jerry Kelly not only provides a complete bibliography of the special editions produced there under his reign, reproducing 36 of his charming title pages and some interior spreads, but also establishes that he was asked to leave, almost certainly "with tears in his eyes," by George Mifflin, his longtime supporter, probably the combined result of Henry Houghton's death in 1906, Rogers's imperious personality, and his salary ($110,000 in today's dollars). I always found it somewhat bizarre that Rogers and his work have commanded so much ink while other printers of the century, Fred Anthoensen, John Anderson, Bert Clarke, Carroll Coleman, John Fass, and Frederic Warde have been almost entirely ignored. Like T. E. Lawrence, whose *Odyssey* he would later design, BR had a perfect genius for (deliberately) backing into the limelight, and as a personality, only Warde was more difficult or perpetually dissatisfied.

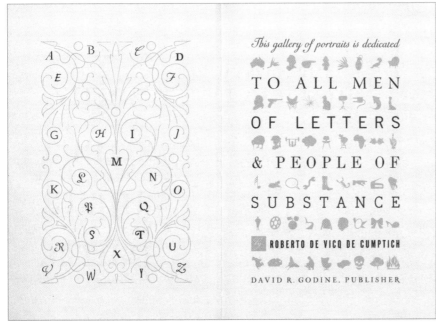

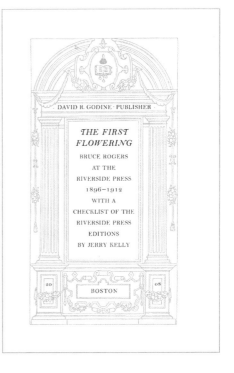

Simon Loxley: *Printer's Devil: The Life and Work of Frederic Warde*

2013. 208 PP, 5¾ × 9″ $45.00 HC

Until this book, Warde had been virtually ignored by biographers, and with good reason. He was feckless, sometimes deliberately duplicitous, and often knavish. He is probably best known as the husband of Beatrice Becker, whom he married, brought with him to England in 1923 and then virtually abandoned to the tender ministrations of Stanley Morison in the ensuing years. But Warde deserves his page in history – he was a prodigious letter writer and kept in constant contact with men like Kittredge at Donnelley and Kent at the Metropolitan Museum; he remained a long-time friend and frequent collaborator with Bruce Rogers; and he worked closely with Mardersteig, printing one of the Officina Bodoni's most beautiful books, *Crito*, in his Vicenza typeface. He worked closely with Morison in the UK (until Morison's simmering affair with his wife became too obvious and embarrassing to ignore) and later with George Macy at the Limited Editions Club, for whom he engineered, designed, and acted as editor for the first volume of *The Dolphin*. But his slippery personality, his inability to really stick with any one job or employer, and perhaps above all, his early death, prevented him from achieving the recognition he deserved. Loxley, in this definitive biography, examines his life and work with qualified admiration and exemplary objectivity, restoring Warde to his rightful place along the key figures of the typographic renaissance of the twenties and thirties.

Valerie Lester: *Giambattista Bodoni: His Life and His World*

2016. 256 PP, 7 × 10″ $40.00 HC

Lester's is the first biography in English of the great eighteenth-century typographer, printer, and punchcutter, Giambattista Bodoni. Leaving his small mountain village of Saluzzo, he traveled to Rome in 1758 to apprentice under Cardinal Spinelli at the Catholic Propaganda Fide press. There he learned all aspects of the printing craft, but his real genius lay in type design and punchcutting, a craft he would pursue his entire life. In 1768, at age 28, his life changed abruptly when the Duke of Parma invited him to abandon Rome and direct the ducal press. He would remain there his entire life overseeing a vast variety of printing, from the mundane to the glorious. This is one book where the writing and "the world" the hero inhabits are considerably more interesting than the subject. Bodoni in and of himself was not particularly fascinating; his time was completely occupied with cutting punches and directing the activities of the press. But the times themselves were exceedingly interesting, as was the culture, and even the food (a key component of the narrative) that surrounded him. These were turbulent and fragile political times for Italy, and Parma was a key player in the drama. A constant cast of fascinating characters enlivened the ducal court while visiting Bodoni in his shop. Parma was politically Italian but very much French in its taste and culture. The illustrations of the city, the press, the pages of the books he designed, even of the nearly 45,000 matrices he engraved, are compelling. And Lester is an author who manages to bring all of it to life. She fills it with intrigue and scholarship, slyly inserting culinary asides and details that go beyond his workshop but show a real appreciation for the work itself. It will be considered the biography of record of the great printer for years to come.

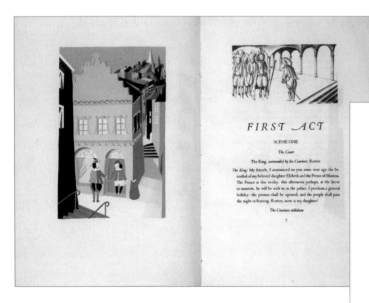

ABOVE: A specimen spread designed by Frederic Warde from Loxley's *Printer's Devil*
RIGHT: The title page and a sample illustration from Lester's biography of Bodoni showing a page from his first *Manuale typografico* of 1788 saluting Saluzzo, his beloved hometown, and set in Papale, the largest typeface in the specimen book

Robert Bringhurst: *Palatino: The Natural History of a Typeface*

2016. 296 PP, 5½ × 9″ $65.00 HC

On 4 June 2015, the world lost one of its greatest practitioners of the graphic arts. Born in 1918, Hermann Zapf made his mark as book designer, type designer, binding designer, teacher, and advocate. But as a calligrapher, the world has seldom seen his equal. And this book, researched and written by poet, translator, polymath, and type traveller Robert Bringhurst does both the man and his typeface, probably the most calligraphic and widely used of all Zapf's book faces, full justice. Taking Palatino as his main theme, he reaches back through its long and fascinating history, tracing developments, with all their many (and often minute) permutations and iterations, from its genesis as a hot metal face in 1949, through its brief interlude in film setting to its present incarnation in the digital world. And while Palatino is the theme, many variations can be found in its extended family, the variants between foundry and linotype, Michelangelo, Sistina, Aldus, Heraklit, Phidias, Zapf Renaissance, PostScript Palatino, Aldus Nova, and more. *Much* more. More than you would ever believe existed. But beyond the painstaking and extensive research into the type and its offspring, the book is a convincing argument that artists who create letters can, and should, be judged by the same standards and held in the same esteem as composers who write music, artists who paint on canvas, and poets who put words in the proper order. They are all cut from the same cloth. Bringhurst poses the question, "Can a penstroke or a letterform be so beautiful it will stop you in your tracks?" In this groundbreaking, seminal and original book, a towering figure in the field affirms: "It can." Anyone willing to read this fascinating book, issued in 1,000 copies with The Book Club of California, will have to agree with him.

Jerry Kelly: *Type Revivals*

2019. 200 PP, 8 × 11″ $40.00 HC

Whether they realize it or not, type revivals form an essential part of every typographer's tool kit. The older classics, Baskerville, Bembo, Garamond, and Bodoni are ubiquitous, often embedded fonts in standard operating systems' collections. They serve, and will continue to serve, their users well, trusted go-to tools of the best professional designers. Yet all these and many more – Bembo, Caslon, Fournier, and Centaur among many others – are revivals, recreations of obscure and often lost originals. Or in the rare cases where the originals can actually be located, are translations into digital fonts that can be used on modern computers. And this is just the "roman" side of the story; the italics are often an entirely separate saga. In almost every case, there is, and has to be, deliberate selection, revising and reformatting to make these letters we take so much for granted suitable for modern use. In this fine and original survey, Jerry Kelly guides the traveller through the thickets of these modifications, adjustments, and occasionally perversions. By interpreting modern versions of earlier iterations, he is able to present a clear and concise discussion of their origin, permutations, and digital availability. He also provides broad hints as to which versions should be embraced and which avoided. Anyone poised to select a typeface for a book or project should read this book.

LEFT: A page from Zapf's second *Manuale Typographicum* showing an excerpt of Plato's *Phædrus* set in his Greek "Heraklit" with the German translation in "Aldus"

ABOVE RIGHT: A seventeenth-century display of the Granjon italic that provided a close model for Galliard, the italic of Matthew Carter's lively modern revival. Note the lovely lower-case "g" and the distinctive "r."

Mark Argetsinger: *A Grammar of Typography*

2020. 536 PP, 8½ × 12″ $65.00 HC

In 1856, Owen Jones published his magisterial folio, *A Grammar of Ornament,* in which he attempted to display, in full color and all their ornamental and decorative variety, forms from around the world. Argetsinger takes for himself the same task in the realm of typography, looking to the past for models that demonstrate taste and display a thorough familiarity with materials, balance, and the demands of readability. Books attempting to instruct both the novice and expert on the intricacies and challenges of book design have been issued for centuries, but none have appeared in recent decades with the reach, depth, detail, or attention to modern applications as this sweeping study. A distinguished designer whose roots (and probably heart) are with hot metal, Argetsinger has been witness to more changes in the past three decades than the world has seen in four hundred years – from small pieces of lead, tin, and antimony, to film, to binary codes. How, he asks, in this fluid and evolving environment, do we absorb the lessons of the past, lessons that suggested the right choice of typefaces, paper, margins, leading, letter and word spacing, and binding and bring them (almost literally) from the age of Gutenberg into the era of the computer screen and the internet? How does a typographer who holds dear the traditions and lessons that have governed a craft for over five centuries deal with complexities of the digital age?

These questions are answered, sequentially, and comprehensively, in a series of chapters that deal with every aspect of modern book design and production – from the choice of typeface, spacing, leading, and margins to the choice of paper and specifications for binding (right down to the headbands). The author delves deeply into the minutiae (often unseen and unappreciated) of letter spacing and kerning, hyphenation and justification. He discusses "house style" and how this may vary from publisher to printer. The result, fully illustrated with examples and captions, is an unparalleled resource for anyone looking to the past for guidance and to the present for advice on how to utilize modern design programs – especially Adobe InDesign – as a means to carry on the finest traditions of typography and bookmaking. For anyone sitting before a screen, wondering where and how to begin designing a book that is elegant, legible and visually appealing, this over-500-page guide is the bible. And it was a fine and fitting terminal note on which to end five decades of publishing books exemplifying and examining this endlessly fascinating subject.

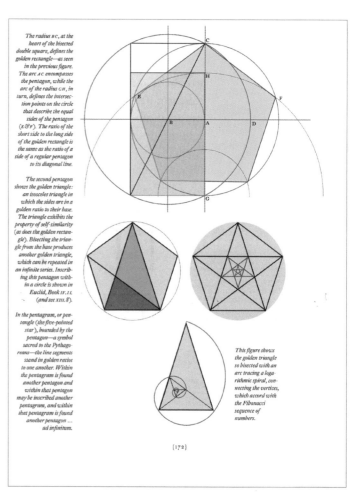

OPPOSITE: A fold-out spread from Morison's *Early Italian Writing Books* showing Marc Antonio's 1598 effort to generate a uniform geometric solution to the creation of roman capitals

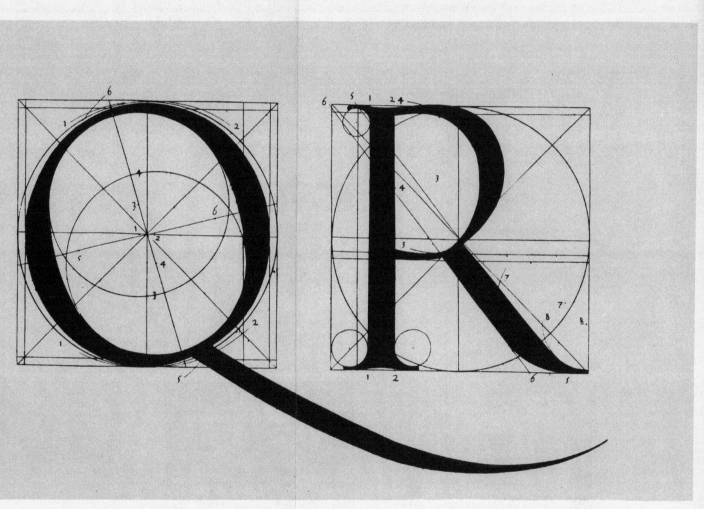

13. Marc'Antonio Rossi, *Giardino de scrittori*, 1598, [plate 9].

Alfred Fairbank: *Augustino da Siena*

1975. 104 PP, 7 × 9⅝″ $30.00 HC

This is a facsimile of the superb writing manual of Augustino da Siena, a title of great rarity and the last of the great sixteenth-century writings manuals to be cut in wood. To celebrate the 75th birthday of the great calligrapher and scholar Alfred Fairbank, we conspired with Susan Shaw's Merrion Press to issue this facsimile of the 1568 edition, with an erudite and perceptive Introduction by Fairbank and a complete facsimile of the book, printed from linecuts by Vivian Ridler at the Oxford University Press. Like all of Susan's productions, the design and printing were perfection, and this title, in its appearance and binding, makes no apologies to the excellent twentieth-century predecessors produced by Warde, Mardersteig, and Morison.

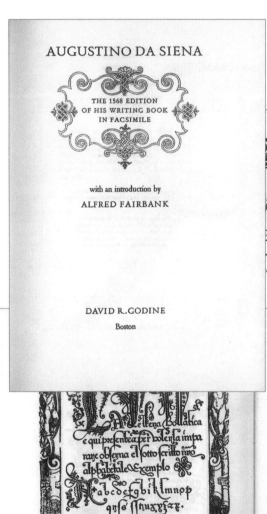

ABOVE TOP & LEFT: The cover, title page and two sample spreads from Augustino da Siena's 1568 writing manual show the extraordinary facsimile woodcut pages Vivian Ridler printed letterpress from linecuts.

THE LITTLE ABC BOOK OF
RUDOLF KOCH

A Facsimile of Das ABC Büchlein
With a Memoir by Fritz Kredel and a

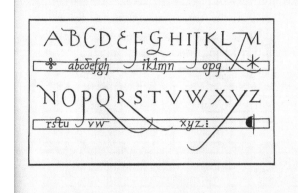

LEFT: Title and interior page from Rudolf Koch's *The Little ABC Book* displaying a page of the master's calligraphy

BELOW & RIGHT: A woodcut page from writing master Vespasiano Amphiareo's 1548 Venetian writing book, *Un novo modo d'insegnar,* with the jacket design by Berthold Wolpe

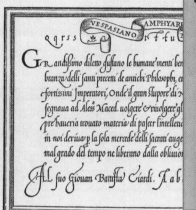

SCRIBES AND SOURCES

Handbook of the Chancery Hand
in the Sixteenth Century

*Texts from the Writing-Masters
selected, introduced and translated by*

A.S. OSLEY

with an account of John de Beauchesne by

BERTHOLD WOLPE

7. From Vespasiano Amphiareo, *Un novo modo d'insegnar a scrivere,* Venice, 1548.

Rudolf Koch: *The Little ABC Book*
Memoir by Fritz Kredel
Preface by Warren Chappell
1976. 80 PP, 8¾ × 5½″ $12.00 HC

To celebrate the hundredth anniversary of Koch's birth, our friend Warren Chappell suggested we reissue *Das ABC Büchlein,* originally calligraphed by Koch and Berthold Wolpe, cut in both wood and metal by Fritz Kredel and Gustav Eichenauer and first published by Insel Verlag in 1934, the year of Koch's death. We issued simultaneous co-editions with The Merrion Press in England, the Typophiles of New York, and The Klingspor Museum in Germany. Warren Chappell, himself a distinguished artist, historian, and calligrapher, provided the Preface. With the help of Dr. Hans Halby, we shot the alphabets from a copy of the limited hand press edition from Koch's personal library. Finn Typographic set the two essays by Chappell's and Koch's friend and associate, Fritz Kredel, in Trajanus and Meriden Gravure printed the book on Mohawk Superfine. It was then, and remains, the best, and certainly the most affordable, synopsis of Koch's remarkable calligraphic alphabets in print, and when the hardcover sold out, we reissued it in paper a few years later.

A.S. Osley: *Scribes and Sources*
Texts from the Writing-Masters selected, introduced and translated by A.S. Osley
1980. 272 PP, 6⅞ × 9¾″ $25.00 HC

In an age where the keyboard and computer have taken over our lives, it's hard to remember that people often used to write their letters and addressed their envelopes *by hand.* There was, in the sixties and seventies, a wide-spread interest in how to create beautiful letters, the root of the word "calligraphy," a movement that began in the Northwest, inspired by teachers like Lloyd Reynolds at Reed College (at whose work Steve Jobs once looked on in amazement) and in the East by Paul Standard, the Pentalic Corporation and its publications, and even by public schools where the italic hand was routinely taught. The roots of the italic hand can be traced to the Renaissance with scribes like Arrighi, Tagliente, and Palatino, who gave us both the term "writing master" and also produced the models for what we now take for granted: the italic letter. Their writing manuals, often cut in wood, printed in the thousands, published in Italian, French, German, Spanish, and Latin, provided an eager public with both instructions and models. In those days before audio transmission, a person's position was detected and reflected by their written hand. It is no surprise that Elizabeth I wrote beautifully. In this classic survey of the best manuals produced in the 200 years following Arrighi's first efforts in Rome, designer and scholar A.S. Osley presents his pick of the finest, illustrates them, translates them, and gives additional excerpts from the books of Fanti, Cresci, Augustino da Siena, Yciar, and more. Each translation is fully illustrated with both examples of the lettering and full-page specimens of the letter forms. This is not an instruction manual, and doesn't try to be. It doesn't tell you how to form the letters but rather provides primary source material – what the actual masters wrote about their approach to calligraphy – and gives necessary, but sparing, examples of their work. For full synopses of their various letter forms, refer to Kay Atkins's *Masters of the Italic Letter.*

Christopher de Hamel: *A History of Illuminated Manuscripts*

1986. 256 PP, 8½ × 11″ $45.00 HC

The Medieval manuscript, written by hand, sometimes requiring years of work, often gloriously illustrated with illuminations, elaborate decoration, and historiated initials, is among the gilded glories of Western art. After monasteries collapsed, empires crumbled, and princes and potentates perished, these books, thousands of them, survived, their gold and silver illumination and splendid calligraphy still brilliant and fascinating. They provide our best surviving link with the mind and culture of Medieval and Renaissance Europe, containing both visual and verbal information invaluable to cultural historians.

This tour, starting with the earliest monastic Gospel books and proceeding through the sophisticated Books of Hours of the Renaissance, is conducted by Christopher de Hamel, former head of Western Manuscripts at the British Library and subsequently of the Western Manuscripts Department at Sotheby's. He analyzes and describes different manuscript types, placing them in their cultural and historical settings. He considers the history of scripts, the iconography of the symbols, the techniques and use of materials, and the formal organization of the scriptoria. He asks, and convincingly answers, the questions "Who made books?" "To what use were they put and how were they fashioned and decorated?" "Who read them and how were they marketed and commissioned?" and answers

them in chapters as inclusive as "Books for Emperors," "Books for Students," and "Books for Everybody." The narrative is written by a scholar but directed at a general audience, and the book delivers what the title demands: full-page, detailed spreads of all kinds of manuscripts with color plates reproducing the extraordinary illumination, calligraphy, and manuscript pages from all eras and places. By understanding the creation and dissemination of these small wonders, the reader sees how learning, both visual and textual, spread throughout Europe leading, finally, to the invention of printing by Gutenberg in 1455, catapulting the written word into the realm of the printed word and starting an entirely new revolution.

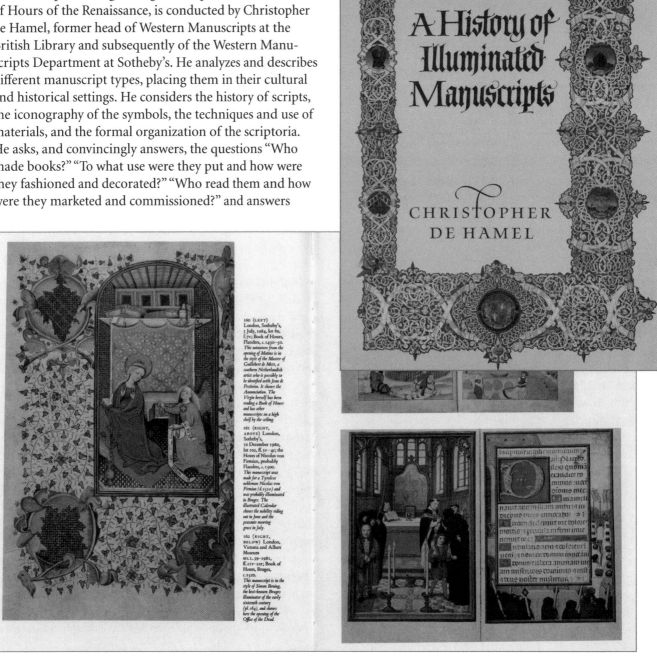

Nicolete Gray: *A History of Lettering: Creative Experiment and Letter Identity*
1986. 256 pp, 6⅞ × 9⅝″ $30.00 hc

This book, unlike any other I know of, has a concentrated focus. It is *not* a book about how letters are drawn. It is *not* a book that concerns itself primarily with the closely allied subjects of calligraphy, typography, type design, and handwriting. It concentrates on lettering in its cultural context. How the letters of the alphabet change in relation to ambience and culture. By providing illustrations that start with ancient Rome and proceed through modern times, it covers a lot of ground. Gray, personally acquainted with actual techniques as well as history, is interested in the alphabet's changing form, and most especially of the Roman capitals. She explores how they have evolved to meet – and reflect – social, artistic, and technical demands. In other words, she directs a laser at the letters themselves,

tracing how they evolved through centuries, examining periods of experimentation and retrenchment and paying special attention to the forces that necessitated changes in form. The text gives a general survey of early inscriptions, providing analyses of hitherto unclassifiable letters and giving credit to outliers, avoiding the mainstream whose forms appear regularly through the centuries. Scholarly but never pedantic, speculative but providing the necessary evidence, it is the result of a lifetime of thinking about the alphabet and its central role in the intellectual evolution of mankind. With more than 300 illustrations, from Roman inscriptions to neon lighting, from engraved writing books to constructivist posters, it's a guided tour through a forest of variants, permutations, and wildly individual interpretations, written, inscribed, stonecut, sandblasted, and engraved on every imaginable surface. It is a book that opens your eyes to the infinite possibilities presented by the 26 soldiers that changed the world.

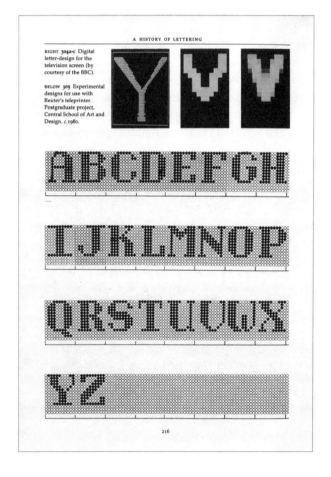

ABOVE & RIGHT: You can infer from the collage on the cover to Nicolete Gray's examination of lettering that this is going to be an eclectic ride. Here displayed are cropped examples of everything from street and shop signs to Medieval manuscripts and Roman capitals. In its breadth of unconventional sources and startling connections, the book does not disappoint.
OPPOSITE TOP LEFT & LEFT: Jacket and an interior spread from De Hamel's *A History of Illuminated Manuscripts*

Kathryn A. Atkins: *Masters of the Italic Letter*
Foreword by James W. Wells
1988. 186 PP, 11¾ × 9″ $45.00 HC

Kay Atkins was a part of the Newport, Rhode Island calligraphy mafia that converged around the John Stevens stone cutting shop at 29 Thames Street captained by John "Fud" Benson and which included such luminaries as Alexander Nesbitt, Howard Glasser, Raphael Boguslav, John Hegnauer and Brooke Roberts. She had been working for years, primarily at Chicago's Newberry Library, assembling data and photographs for this useful and original book in which she compares, letter by letter, both upper and lower case, the designs of the twenty-two greatest early writing masters, from Fanti in 1514 to Beauchesnes in 1610. The predictable greats are all here – Arrighi, Tagliente, Palatino, Cresci, to name just a few. Lesser-known masters are equally represented: Yciar, Wyss, Moro Brun, and Hondius. In an invaluable chapter, she isolates more than 2,500 individual letters of the 22 scribes, to provide actual comparisons of their subtle differences of form and composition. Atkins provides facsimiles of the title pages and sample spreads from various masters. Why it took us so long to sell through this book, I will never know. It was as good as anything of its kind, and for practicing calligraphers it provides an incomparable opportunity to contrast and compare what solutions were contrived for every letter.

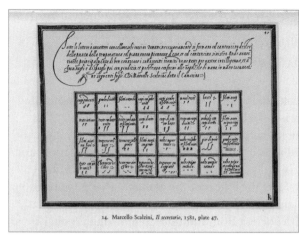

LEFT: An early example of an engraved calligraphy manual, Marcello Scalzini's *Il secretario* of 1581, from Morison's *Early Italian Writing-Books*

14. Marcello Scalzini, *Il secretario*, 1581, plate 47.

Stanley Morison: *Early Italian Writing-Books: Renaissance to Baroque*
Edited by Nicolas Barker
1990. 224 PP, 5½ × 8½″ $65.00 HC

Before his death in 1967, the renowned English typographic historian Stanley Morison had drafted a major work examining the history and development of Italian writing books. The text, which was the result of years of investigation and visits to libraries in the UK, US, and the Continent, was always a subject close to his heart. Close to completion, it was sent to Jim Wells, the Curator of the Wing Collection of the famous Newberry Library in Chicago, for final editing and revision. Wells returned the manuscript with massive notes, which Morison undertook to incorporate, and then passed over to Nicolas Barker for final editing. Dedicated to Carla Marzoli, who first commissioned it, it is finally published in this elegant format, printed by Martino Mardersteig and containing twenty-

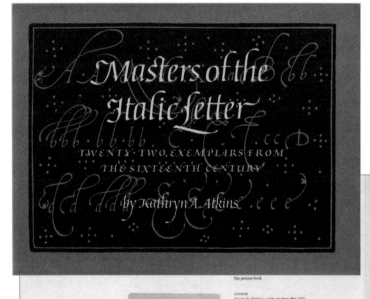

LEFT: The cover and an interior spread, featuring the early 1524 writing book of Giovannantonio Tagliente with the title to the left and the recto page displaying the italic capitals, along with their variants, cut in wood by Eustachio Celebrino

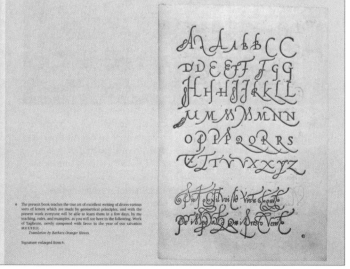

one duotones. In it Morison examines the calligraphy of the primarily woodcut manuals of the sixteenth century – Arrighi, Ugo da Carpi, Tagliente, Celebrino, Amphiareo, and Cresci – and ends with a brief discussion of the engraved books that succeeded them in the seventeenth century, offering commentary on the work of Rossi, Leoni, Segaro, Perricioli, Ruinetti, and Antonozzi. It was not only the last of Morison's texts to be printed but also indispensable for the serious scholar of letters and their development, a book covering and displaying the most important (and most beautiful) examples of the calligrapher's art.

William Hildebrandt: *Calligraphic Flourishing: A New Approach to an Ancient Art*
1995. 128 PP, 7½ × 9⅛″ $16.00 SC

Probably no one would think that a title as narrow as this would go into three printings, but Bill's book, concentrating on the narrow but challenging corner of the calligraphic tradition of creating a flourish, was a success from the outset. Perhaps one reason is that it was set in a typeface he designed himself – in fact, he designed and set the entire book; all we had to do was shoot the pages and print. Calligraphy had, I think, its golden years in the US under the influence of Lloyd Reynolds at Reed on the West Coast and Paul Standard on the East Coast with the Newberry Library, James Wells and the Wing Collection in between. During the sixties, everyone was buying calligraphic pens, reading Edward Johnston, Alfred Fairbank, and Berthold Wolpe and trying to write like Arrighi. It was a fad and a good one. I wish it had lasted longer.

ABOVE & BELOW: The cover and a spread from Bill Hildebrandt's *Calligraphic Flourishing*, entirely written, designed, illustrated and typeset in Bill's own typeface and including the extensive and inventive designs he had created to add flourishes to his italics

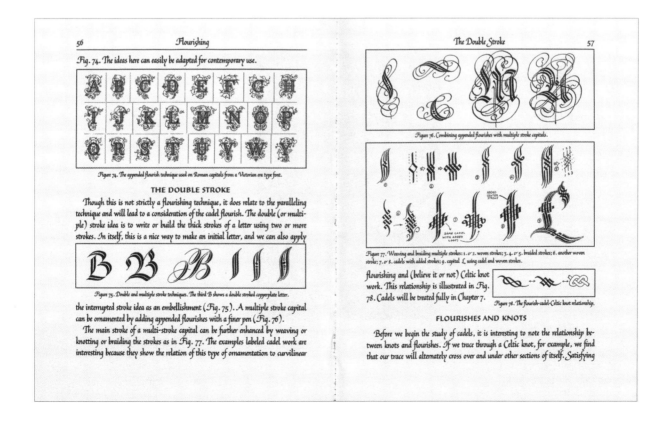

Artist & Alphabet: Twentieth Century Calligraphy and Letter Art in America
Curated by Jerry Kelly and Alice Koeth
Introduction by Donald Jackson
2000. 136 PP, 8 × 11″ $50.00 HC

From the 1950s, as Lloyd Reynolds began teaching at Reed College, Father Catich's books on Roman lettering began to appear, and Paul Standard was championing italic in New York, calligraphy began to take hold as a legitimate art form in America. In those happy days before the internet, when microchips and the keyboard took the place of ink and paper, handwriting still stood as a personal attribute. A younger generation recognized this, pushed along by companies like the Pentalic Corporation offering both broad nib pens and books of instruction on the correct formation of classic italic letter forms. In 2000, we joined forces with the Society of Scribes and the American Institute of Graphic Arts to publish a volume celebrating and illustrating the best work of the century. A committee was formed and immediately selected twenty-eight historic figures central to the revival. The plates include at least one work from each, in full color and gloriously printed by The Stinehour Press. The list and the examples are eclectic: W.A. Dwiggins's impeccably hand-lettered page for the first issue of *The Fabulist*, Hermann Zapf's "Declaration of Independence," Sheila Waters's *Roundel of the Seasons*, Rudolf Koch's handwritten page from *Das ABC Büchlein*, examples from all three members of the Benson family, letterheads by George Salter and logos by Phil Grushkin – an entire galaxy of calligraphic luminaries that still stands today as the best compendium of calligraphy this country produced. The reader is provided not only with the widest display of lettering talent in America, but also extremely helpful capsule biographies of the practitioners.

Alice: A Survey of Her Calligraphy
Compiled with an Introduction by Jerry Kelly
Foreword by Donald Jackson
2017. 144 PP, 8 × 11½″ $50.00 HC

New Yorkers who walked down Madison Avenue in the 60s, 70s, and 80s would recognize her masterful posters for the Morgan Library. Scribes in the US and around the world know her from her celebrated workshops. Her work has adorned innumerable book jackets (including some of ours), certificates, announcements, and testimonials. She is Alice Koeth, known professionally simply as Alice, and although among the most respected contemporary calligraphers, her work had never been gathered and presented, a vast majority of it remaining unknown and unseen. This book presents the best of a career that spanned over sixty years, displaying an artistry that exemplifies taste, wit, total command of material and technique, and, in Donald Jackson's words, a "spirit" – her attitude – "that sings through every one of her illustrations in this book." The range is impressive; brushes, italic nibs, Coit and Automatic pens, even the smallest speedball points. The results comprise everything from the large posters with which the Morgan would advertise its major shows to tiny alphabets, doodles, and delightful drawings. Printed on a fine heavyweight paper, this book does justice to a woman of modest demeanor and major achievements.

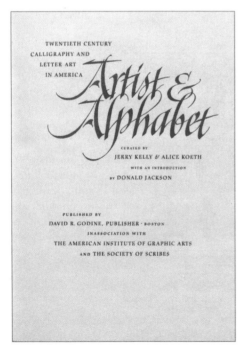

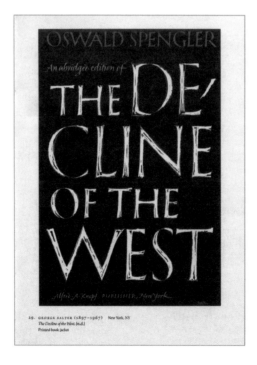

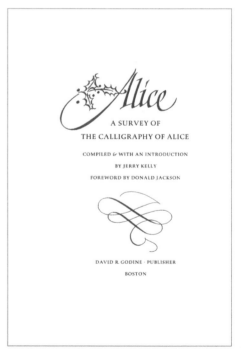

ABOVE & RIGHT: The title page with the calligraphy of Alice Koeth and a sample interior page showing the virtuosity of George Salter

ABOVE: The title page gives some idea of the wit and calligraphic talents of Alice Koeth.
OPPOSITE: A page of pomegranates from the *Herbal* of Mattiolo, published in Prague in 1563

Natural History

POMEGRANATE

GEORGE STUBBS

Anatomical Works

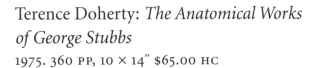

ABOVE & OPPOSITE: These three finished drawings of Stubbs show a tiger, human figure and fowl. As the dissection proceeded, he would make–from these and subsequent detailed drawings–printing plates using the stipple engraving technique he had perfected to capture the nuances of his pencil studies. This was his last major initiative, a testimony, in Doherty's words, to his "concern with the scrupulous observation of natural facts… considered as an individual entity, and all were composed with the most rigorous thought and exacting taste into coherent and stable designs."

Terence Doherty: *The Anatomical Works of George Stubbs*

1975. 360 PP, 10 × 14″ $65.00 HC

With good reason, Stubbs is perhaps best known for his animal portraits, and he was arguably the greatest horse painter who ever lived. His monumental *Anatomy of a Horse,* published in 1766, was instantly recognized as an artistic and scientific triumph. But the original drawings for his last great work, the comparative drawings of a human, a fowl, and a tiger, had disappeared until they were discovered by Sir Basil Taylor at the Worcester Free Public Library, where they had languished unknown for over two centuries. This was, therefore, not only the first book to publish these remarkable drawings in full, along with the exceedingly rare suite of engravings he made after them, but also to include complete facsimiles of both *The Anatomy of the Horse* and *A Complete New System of Midwifery* along with all the then-extant drawings. These included the Worcester drawings as well as twenty-four studies made for the *Anatomy* recently discovered at the Royal Academy. Doherty, himself an anatomist, provided

an introduction charting Stubbs's growth, and placing in perspective the appalling difficulties under which an eighteenth-century anatomist was forced to practice. Stubbs, a man of protean strength and determination, was, in my view, a better artist than anatomist (just look at the somewhat androgynous drawings of his "groom")–but as a self-taught engraver obsessed with thoroughly understanding the workings of the human and animal anatomy, he was the equal of Leonardo. Tom Rosenthal of Secker and Warburg talked me into taking an unconscionable number of copies at a ridiculous cost and had it not been for a fairly substantial order from the ever-generous Paul Mellon, a staunch advocate of Stubbs, I think we would still be paying off the debt. Ruari McLean designed this doorstop of a book, setting the text in Baskerville, and Meriden Gravure shot the originals from Worcester. The Westerham Press in Kent, with whom we were to work repeatedly in years to come, did an admirable job of reproducing the delicate, highly nuanced drawings.

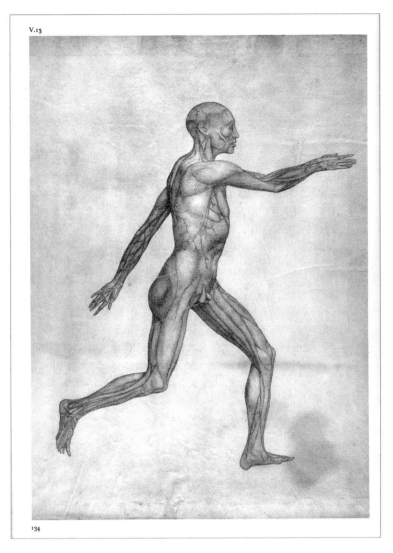

Marcus Goldman: *In Praise of Little Fishes*
Illustrated by Craig Ronto
1977. 152 PP, 5¾ × 8¾″ $10.00 HC

Marcus Goldman was a remarkable man, a retired professor of English whose specialty was the Renaissance and who spent his early life fishing the small streams and ponds of the Middle West and developing a particular fondness not for trout, salmon, or steelhead, but the "little fishes" – a modest school whose attractions he captures with Waltonian eloquence and simplicity in these brief forays. We encountered him at age 83, living in Norwell, and proof positive that, as the proverb provides, "Allah does not subtract from a man's life the days spent fishing." He must have been a good father as well as an infectiously enthusiastic angler, for his son, who wrote the affectionate Introduction, turned out to be a distinguished ichthyologist. We gave Darrell Hyder full control of the book and commissioned Craig Ronto to provide line drawings of the sixteen species discussed. Darrell did a magnificent job; in its small compass, this is among the most satisfactory books, in the writing, design, and production, to appear under my imprint. I look at it today and would not change one iota, the perfect "multum in parvo" package.

S. Dillon Ripley: *Rails of the World*
Illustrated by J. Fenwick Lansdowne
1977. 432 PP, 10 × 14″ $75.00 HC, $400.00 *deluxe in slipcase, bound in quarter leather with a signed and numbered original black-and-white lithograph by Lansdowne*

This has always been among my favorite titles. For two years, I had begged Dillon Ripley, then the Secretary of the Smithsonian Institution and, among his many other accomplishments, a distinguished ornithologist, to try us for a book. So when he called and announced that he wished to produce a book on "rails," I was thrilled – anticipating a book on steel rails and steam locomotives. "No," he explained patiently, "a widely diffused family of birds with bright beaks and long legs." Ripley, it turned out, was the world authority on the elusive and flightless family of birds, the *Rallidae*, and this represented his life's work. He was determined to create an ornithological classic, and, as both a bookman and collector, he knew the precedents and the competition. He hired Crimilda Pontes,

LEFT: The binding, title and sample pages from Marcus Goldman's *In Praise of Little Fishes*
RIGHT: The dust jacket displaying the artistry of J. Fenwick Lansdowne for the imposing study of the family *Rallidae* by S. Dillon Ripley

the Smithsonian's first official graphic designer, to design it; the Canadian artist Fenwick Lansdowne to illustrate it; and Martino Mardersteig to print it. While visiting the Stamperia Valdonega in Verona, I saw the progressive proofs – up to eight separate color passes for each of Lansdowne's paintings. My fondest memory was visiting Crimilda at the National Zoo in Washington, where she was trying to coax a resident rail to walk through a box of finely sifted sand. Photographed at a raking angle, those tracks provided the endpapers. This was a large book, in format the largest we had issued, but it was impeccably designed and printed. It remains, as Dillon had hoped, a classic in the field.

Marie Angel: *Bird, Beast & Flower*
Watercolors by Marie Angel
Poetry selected by Ian Parsons
1980. 64 PP, 7½ × 10½" $11.00 HC

An Animated Alphabet
Introduction by Anne Anninger
Foreword by Philip Hofer
1996. 64 PP, 5⅝ × 8" $13.00 SC *with flaps* ℙ

Printed at the Westerham Press in the UK, the book shown below could be put almost anywhere – poetry, children's books, calligraphy, fine printing. But because Angel's real and obvious passion was for animals – all kinds from hummingbirds to elephants – I'll place it here. She was for decades probably the finest "illuminator" to come out of Europe. Her original manuscripts, always on vellum, are small works of genius, combining her elegant calligraphy with brilliant delineations of wildlife. The poetry selection by Ian Parsons depicts that "social union" of nature seen by poets past and present – from Blake's "The Tyger" to Frost's "The Tuft of Flowers," 48 poems from 35 poets, each of them with an (often historiated) initial letter by Ms. Angel. We printed this on a fine offwhite sheet, close to vellum shade, and commissioned Alice Koeth to provide the spirited calligraphy for the jacket and title page.

LEFT ABOVE, ABOVE, LOWER LEFT, RIGHT: The exuberant calligraphy of Alice Koeth for both the title page and jacket of *Bird, Beast & Flower* provides a fine balance to Marie Angel's detailed drawings and the chaste typography of the poetry.

Later, in 1996, we issued a full-color edition of her *Animated Alphabet.* Commissioned by Philip Hofer for the Houghton Library, it had been published by the Library in black and white in 1970, but it hardly did justice to the delicacy and vibrancy of these remarkable miniatures. Marie would say as much (in her own polite fashion) in a letter to Philip Hofer, "I was rather disappointed when I heard that the *Animated Alphabet* was to be in monochrome, but I can understand so well how expensive it must be to produce the drawings in colour." With the help of the gracious Anne Anninger, we were able to rephotograph all 28 drawings and print them at C & C Offset in China on a paper as close to the original vellum as we could find. It was, as Anne commented, "a new edition that does justice both to the subtlety and delicacy of Marie Angel's designs and to the exquisite color of her original drawings .... It would have given great pleasure to the late Philip Hofer to see the wish of his long-time friend and collaborator finally realized."

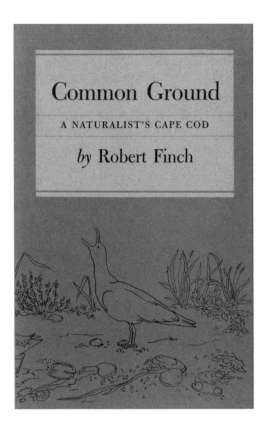

LEFT & BELOW: The cover and two interior vellum miniatures of the vellum drawings Philip Hofer commissioned from Marie Angel for her *An Animated Alphabet*
ABOVE RIGHT: Richard Bartlett's jacket and Amanda Cannell's drawing for Robert Finch's *Common Ground*

Robert Finch: *Common Ground: A Naturalist's Cape Cod*
Drawings by Amanda Cannell
1981. 160 PP, 5¾ × 9¼″ $13.00 HC

This was the first book of Robert Finch, a respected Cape Cod naturalist, whose essays were first written as "Soundings" and appeared as weekly nature columns in four Cape Cod newspapers. They became something of a legend. His locus was entirely the Cape, that sandy, scrub-oaked, tough, mutable spit of land that juts out from Massachusetts like a beckoning arm. In these expressive essays, Finch bears witness to the power of nature, the fierce nor'easters that batter the coast, the inexorable erosion of wind and tide, but also of its wonders, the migration of the herring, the call of a loon. The writing is all first-person; the book begins with his one-night stand, cold, hungry, and thirsty, in a dunes shack outside Provincetown. For Finch, it was "one man's response to the changing face of this curved peninsula." And it is beautiful, a mixture of Thoreau, Beston, and the Bible. Its publication was in every way a South Shore production: the author a full-time Cape Codder since 1963 and resident of Brewster, the designer Richard Bartlett of Cotuit, and the typeface Caledonia, designed by the great American book and type designer W.A. Dwiggins. The drawings by Amanda Cannell, the laid paper from Monadnock Mills, and the full-cloth binding stamped in two colors provided additional appeal. Along with Goldman's *Little Fishes* and Beston's *Herbs and the Earth,* another small jewel in this category.

Henry Beston: *Herbs and the Earth*

Woodcuts by John Howard Benson
Introduction by Roger Swain
1990. 168 PP, 5½ × 8″ $18.00 HC

I knew this book from an Anchor Books edition, and when Kate Barnes informed me that the rights were free, I jumped at the chance. Written at Chimney Farm, his retreat and later his home on the shores of Lake Damariscotta in Nobleboro, Maine, the text is learned, graceful, and far ranging, drawing on references to herbs and herbal lore from sources as broad as Shakespeare and the Bible. We were extremely lucky to locate the original woodcuts, engraved by the great American calligrapher and artist, John Howard Benson. Our friend, Roger Swain, then a rising television star and a regular columnist for *Horticulture* magazine, wrote an eloquent survey of Beston's life and work, commenting that although he would always be best known for *The Outermost House* and would go on to write other books, "*Herbs and the Earth* had an intensity about it that evokes the herbs themselves, as if, pressed between its pages, their aroma had seeped into the paper. Beston felt that the last paragraphs – his 'Epilogue in Spring' – were 'the best he ever wrote.'"

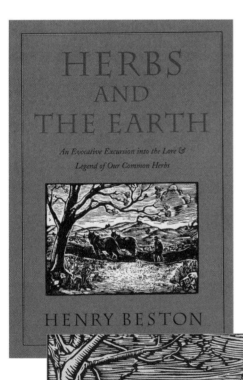

LEFT & LEFT BELOW: The fine letterpress printing of the first edition in Linotype Caslon at Maine's Shagbark Press gave real authority to Benson's woodcuts and Beston's text.

Joseph Wood Krutch: *Herbal*

1995. 256 PP, 9 × 12″ $27.50 HC

In this lovely book, Joseph Wood Krutch, among the most accomplished writers and naturalists this country produced in the last century, examines the discoveries of herbalists from ancient times to the present. The Bible tells us, and herbalists believed, that God began his work on earth by creating a garden in which everything had its purpose. Each plant was there for a reason, to cure a specific ill, and wisdom lay in the ability to identify that purpose and apply it. And if readers want to see how specific these properties were, they have only to consult a text that examines in detail six creatures and a hundred plants. As an example, daffodils could exterminate rats, provoke urination, and when reduced to ashes, provide relief to a toothache on the right side of the month. (What would relieve one on the left side is not mentioned.) The woodcuts chosen to illustrate the text are from the folio of Mattiolo, published in Prague in 1563, among the first to be clearly based on firsthand observation of original material. But the real delight is Krutch's prose. Just read this sample from the closing paragraph of his Introduction: "Closely regarded, every one of the individual plants will be found useful, beautiful, or wonderful – and not infrequently all three. Perhaps the charm of the Herbalists (and certainly the one this book would especially like to suggest) is just that they are more likely than the modern scientist to impart a sense of beauty and wonder – both of which the scientist may feel, but considers it no part of his function to communicate."

Eleanor Mathews: *Ambassador to the Penguins: A Naturalist's Year Aboard a Yankee Whaleship*

2004. 368 PP, 6 × 9" $30.00 HC

In 1912, a young naturalist named Robert Cushman Murphy was offered the opportunity of a lifetime – to spend two years aboard the last Yankee whaleship to sail out of New Bedford in search of whales off the coast of Antarctica. Only recently married, Murphy had understandable regrets about leaving his wife Grace after only a few months together, but he saw this as his chance, perhaps his only chance, to voyage to the ends of the world, to record life aboard a wooden brig still serving a dying industry, one that had once made New Bedford among the richest towns in America. He had the opportunity to bring back specimens of birds and wildlife then unknown to science. What he didn't know was that this was to be the beginning of a brilliant career at the institution sponsoring him, New York's Museum of Natural History. During the voyage Murphy kept a diary packed with his observations, both as a naturalist and as a means to record a way of life soon to

disappear. When not taking photographs, he was catching birds, watching his shipmates chase penguins, harpoon whales, and boil down their stripped carcasses for the oil. His journal reveals a man who relished the work around him, and his record of the trip, *Logbook for Grace,* became a bestseller. His granddaughter, Ellie Mathews, took that diary, updated it, and supplemented it with never-before-published information and his own photographs, miraculously still intact at the Museum in his archive. Presenting his voyage in a third-person voice, she updates it for the modern reader as a story of seafaring life at the turn of the century, a portrait of an industry still under sail, and soon to be transformed by the harpoon gun. His account of this natural history expedition set the standards for all that followed. It is a classic, rightly described as "a book to set on the shelf beside *Moby-Dick* and *Two Years Before the Mast.*"

Robert Leonard Reid: *Arctic Circle: Birth and Rebirth in the Land of the Caribou*

2010. 240 PP, 6 × 9" $28.00 HC

Published in 2010 after a long gestation, this is part autobiography, part adventure, part natural history, and part ecology. An adventurer and serious climber, Reid had never set foot north of the 55th parallel, but he was determined to see for himself the Arctic, a land that Elisha Kent Kane had described as "Horrible, horrible – a dwelling place of darkness and death." Reid was somewhat more

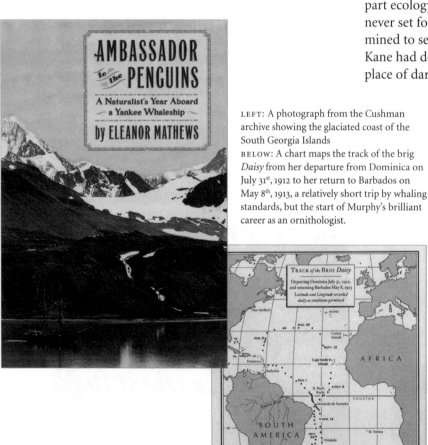

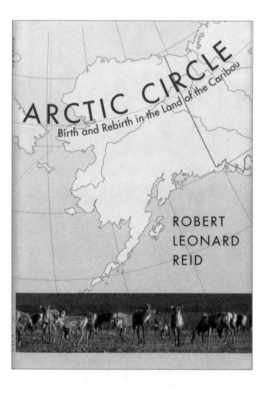

LEFT: A photograph from the Cushman archive showing the glaciated coast of the South Georgia Islands

BELOW: A chart maps the track of the brig *Daisy* from her departure from Dominica on July 31st, 1912 to her return to Barbados on May 8th, 1913, a relatively short trip by whaling standards, but the start of Murphy's brilliant career as an ornithologist.

sanguine and especially fascinated by the migration of the Porcupine Caribou Herd, which, braving swollen rivers with icebergs the size of trucks, wolves, and treacherous terrain, makes the longest land migration of any animal on earth. On the eve of his sixtieth birthday, Reid sets out to fulfill a vow made to a friend, an environmental activist who had begged him to visit the newly established Arctic Wildlife Refuge before it was despoiled by oil exploration. "Come and see the Great Land. Then write about what you find." The result is a poignant, eloquent, almost mystical journey into the far reaches of the Arctic where he indeed encounters the Porcupine Herd while taking in, firsthand, the last great unspoiled North American wilderness.

Gavin Maxwell: *Ring of Bright Water*

2011. 340 PP, 6 × 9″ $19.00 SC

This volume brings together under one cover the Scottish otter stories of Gavin Maxwell: *Ring of Bright Water* (1960), *The Rocks Remain* (1963), and *Raven, Seek Thy Brother* (1968). The first was a huge international bestseller, the result of a trip he took to the marshes of Iraq in 1956, returning with Mijbil, an abandoned otter (which turned out to be a new subspecies) he brought home with him in a crate to his home at Sandaig, a remote and isolated town on Scotland's western coast. There he led an idyllic, if isolated, life. The book, its title after a poem by Kathleen

Raine, his former (if ultimately platonic) partner, provided fame and a swarm of uninvited visitors. But through it he became the outspoken defender of the species, saving it from senseless hunting and attempting to ensure its survival. Maxwell was a complex, eccentric, and tortured man, haunted by the ghosts of his past and upbringing, the results of which we watch in the two subsequent books. His life slowly unwinds as fame, fate, and fire conspire against him. He has problems with the otters and their keepers. He loses his friends and endures heartbreak and disappointment at every corner. But he writes with rare eloquence and honesty about his birth, his upbringing, his devotion to his beloved Scottish Highlands and its wildlife, and especially his passion for a species that became almost synonymous with his name. What Dian Fossey was to gorillas and Jane Goodall was to chimpanzees, Maxwell was to otters. And you're drawn to him for this passion as well as his refusal to abide by the social norms of his generation and class. We reset all three books to be consistent and included many of his line drawings and sketches, a fitting tribute to a man who was forthright about his shortcomings and failures, refused to ignore the darker aspects of his nature, and whose life, in both its greatness and tragedy, still comes across as somehow enduringly noble.

BELOW: Jacket and a color spread showing Toru Sonohara carrying our aging author across the Kongakut River, a string of arctic char, and, well above the Arctic Circle, the nesting sites of Arctic terns

ABOVE LEFT: *The author's arrival at the campsite on the Kongakut River, assisted by Toru Sonohara.* (PHOTOGRAPH BY SHAUN T. GRIFFIN)
ABOVE RIGHT: *Shaun T. Griffin and Arctic char.* (PHOTOGRAPH BY TORU SONOHARA)
BELOW: *Kongakut River camp.*

ABOVE: *Arctic terns.*
BELOW: *"Toru's Garden."*

Robert McCracken Peck: *The Natural History of Edward Lear*

Foreword by David Attenborough

2016. 224 PP, 7 × 10″ $40.00 HC

Lear, if he is remembered at all today, is generally associated with his nonsense verse and his limericks. But he began his career as an artist and a naturalist, and his book on parrots set the mold for what would follow, decades of impressive deluxe folios containing ornithological renderings of species printed in full color on full-page plates that technology had finally made possible. Lear would exploit this medium, using it to illustrate everything from the simple line drawings accompanying his limericks to detailed topographical plates of the many countries he would visit that were every bit the equal of his ornithological efforts. Like so many Englishmen of his generation, he was shockingly precocious; his illustrations for the parrot family were published when he was only eighteen. It is something of a miracle that Lear lived to a ripe old age and was able to excel in at least three disciplines—as a natural history artist, as a landscape painter, and as a writer. He was plagued by ill health his entire life, including epilepsy. He had to leave England for a healthier climate, but still managed to travel extensively throughout Europe and the Middle East. And his topographical drawings of the countrysides he visited are every bit the equal of his ornithological renderings. He was beloved by his patrons, but especially by their children for whom he would compose jingles, nonsense verse, and limericks, often accompanied by his self-deprecating self-portraits. Robert Peck was a publisher's dream, thoroughly organized, in full command of his subject, and cognizant that we were determined to do right by him and his book. The edition of 4,000 copies sold out almost immediately and has since been reprinted, slightly revised, by the Princeton University Press.

ABOVE & RIGHT: A spread from Robert Peck's *The Natural History of Edward Lear* showing the artist's talents as a watercolorist

OPPOSITE: A characteristically detailed and revealing pen drawing by Mark Livingston serving to illuminate the humor, if not absurdity, of *The Adventures of Jonathan Corncob*

BOTTLED FURY

M. Livingston Del.

The Adventures of Jonathan Corncob,
Loyal American Refugee
Foreword by Noel Perrin
Drawings by Mark Livingston
1976. 152 PP, 5¼ × 8¾″ $9.00 HC

Many books are forgotten for good reasons, but a few are resurrected because they deserve it. This, the story of a picaresque, putatively American hero, cowardly, vain, amorous, and totally without partisan scruples (an early model for MacDonald's *Flashman*), is among them. Probably written by a British naval officer and first published in London in 1787, it is an unknown American masterpiece of irreverence, sustained humor, and outright scatology (reading the first chapter gives a good idea of why it was never published in America before this edition) – and, in Ned Perrin's opinion, the best novel to emerge from the American Revolution. Jonathan Corncob, who, as the title suggests, is more prone to lust than national loyalties, leaves rural Massachusetts, after impregnating the equally wanton Miss Desire Slawbunk in a bundling encounter gone awry, to serve on an American privateer. After a brief interlude of looting and skirmishes, he finds himself posted on a British man-o'-war, and presently winds up in New York City. There he spends his time making cattle raids into New Jersey with a cohort of Loyalists and personal raids on a New York society girl named Dinah Donewell, a creature of breeding and impeccable family who promptly transmits at least six varieties of venereal disease. After recovering, Jonathan hurries off to more adventures: with slaves and slave owners in the Barbados; with a Royal Navy officer, who is among the few characters in the book actually more cowardly than Jonathan; and finally, in more trouble than usual, back to New York for a reunion with Desire. The book takes no prisoners on either side; both the rustic Americans and the haughty British are equally culpable and ridiculous. It is, to the Revolution, much what Heller's *Catch-22* was to WWII, rich in black humor and the absurd. The illustrations, by Mark Livingston, a young Virginian who had recently graduated from Williams College and had done equally fine work for Knopf and Grossman, are nothing short of brilliant – detailed line drawings that capture all the raunchy humor, political inanities, and outrageous action of the text. They are among the finest artwork we ever commissioned.

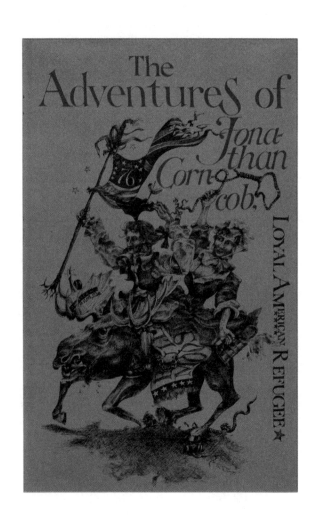

Will Cuppy: *The Decline and Fall of Practically Everybody*
Drawings by William Steig
1984. 256 PP, 5½ × 8¼″ $11.00 SC

That the American humorist, Will Cuppy, never lived to see the success of this book seems affectingly appropriate. He was plagued his entire life by rotten luck, and although his research was impeccable and his writing style inviting, it was not until Edward R. Murrow read *Decline and Fall* on three successive evenings on his evening CBS TV broadcast in 1950 that the book took off and remained on the bestseller list for months. It was, in effect, the first bestseller created by media exposure. Here you'll encounter Nero and Cleopatra, Alexander the Great and Attila the Hun, Miles Standish and Lady Godiva. You think there's no more to be written about Lucrezia Borgia or Christopher Columbus? You're wrong. Cuppy did his homework and as improbable as some his exposures may appear, they are all entirely accurate. On display is Cuppy footloose in the footnotes of history. We have remained obdurately loyal to Cuppy and brought out all four of his remaining titles over the years, many of them illustrated by the young and talented William Steig.

L. Rust Hills: *How to Do Things Right: The Revelations of a Fussy Man*
1993. 320 PP, 6 × 9″ $23.00 HC

Rust Hills, for years the fiction editor at *Esquire,* was among my college heroes. He had an editor's ear for just the right word and phrase and these three books, all originally issued by Doubleday, were my companions at college and used again with my family on whom I would fatuously inflict "How to Organize a Picnic" or "How to Eat an Ice Cream Cone," trying hard to not dissolve into helpless laughter. The subtitle "Memoirs of a Fussy Man" doesn't begin to describe how shatteringly funny compulsive fussiness can be, especially when it is usually employed as camouflage for a personality that is obviously and helplessly inclined towards entropy and chaos. The three books "age" along with the author. In the first, it's all about organizing life's messy challenges, albeit on a minor level. The second considers what life might be like without a job and the third looks mortality squarely between the eyes. Hills never abandons his sense of humor, but the reader begins to realize that, as time passes, the writer is reluctantly figuring out that life isn't entirely about fun and games.

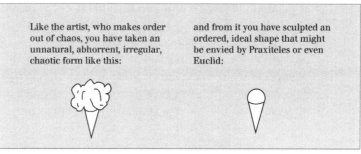

Like the artist, who makes order out of chaos, you have taken an unnatural, abhorrent, irregular, chaotic form like this:

and from it you have sculpted an ordered, ideal shape that might be envied by Praxiteles or even Euclid:

LOUIS XIV

Louis XIV was born rather suddenly in 1638. His parents, Louis XIII and Anne of Austria, were married for twenty-two years without having a baby.[1] Because of the long delay, the infant was called Louis Dieu-Donné, or Louis the God-Given. He was afterwards known as Louis le Roi Soleil, or Louis the Show-Off. Extremely dull as a child, he gradually developed this characteristic

[1] *Louis XIII stayed away from his wife for fifteen years at one stretch. He didn't seem to be interested.*

113

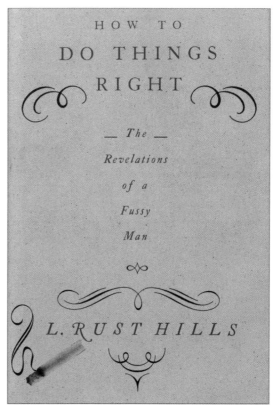

Richard Watson: *The Philosopher's Diet*

1998. 128 PP, 5½ × 8¼" $15.00 SC

"Red" Watson was a professor of Philosophy at Washington University for decades, and I suspect that our affiliation with authors from that fine institution–Gass, Nemerov, and Elkin–may have led him to us with the suggestion that we reissue his *Philosopher's Diet*. In terms of actual results, all you really need to know (substantively) about this book is articulated in the first sentence, expressed with the usual Watson clarity and pungency: "Fat. I presume you want to get rid of it. No normal, healthy person on the good green earth ever got thinner without cutting down on caloric intake, do a few exercises, don't eat so much, and you will lose weight." The rest of the book is just a riff on that simple instruction. But losing weight isn't the real point. It's the how and why that fascinates Watson–the philosophy behind the avoirdupois. As he is quick to point out, it is not easy. It requires will power, discipline, and a sense of purpose. He puts it on the line. Losing twenty pounds and keeping it off is probably the most difficult initiative you will undertake, and you need to do it not only for your health, but because it will prove to yourself that you are capable of taking control of your own life. Interspersed with exhortation, instructions, and examples from adventures in spelunking (Watson was a world-class cave crawler) are the philosophical positions of Hume, Pascal, Kierkegaard, and especially his favorite, Descartes. There are few books that take on the combined challenges of discovering the meaning of the universe and eliminating fat in the same breath, and Red approached both issues with the zeal of a Southern Baptist preacher and philosophy scholar. For our money, the most erudite, fascinating, and eccentric book ever written on the perennially fascinating subject of weight control–a combination of common sense, Cartesian philosophy, and the presumption that attempts to understand both the mysteries of weight loss and the universe are somehow compatible, even sympathetic, ambitions.

Allan Miller: *Mad Amadeus Sued a Madam*

Illustrated by Lee Lorenz

Introduction by Roger Angel

1999. 64 PP, 5⅝ × 8" $10.01 *(get it?)* SC ¶

The palindrome, for anyone unfamiliar with it, is a series of letters, words, or phrases that have the odd property of reading the same backward as they do forward. As in the title of the book. We realized when we took this on that the world attracted to it was somewhat circumscribed, consisting of the fanatics who are outrageously adept at solving crossword puzzles or using all seven of their Scrabble chips. Confirmed addicts seem to find as much satisfaction in a gem like "Sununu's tonsil is not Sununu's" (a big hit in New Hampshire) or that sex shop favorite "Strap on No Parts" as the discovery of a new planet. But in this book for both aficionados and beginners is a delightful compendium of "a furtive collection of letters which, weirdly and all on its own, resembles itself perfectly when looked at from the other end." Expanding on the possibilities inherent in Miller's dotty two-way examples are the madcap drawings of the *New Yorker* cartoonist Lee Lorenz.

The Sporting Life

Stanley Murphy: *Martha's Vineyard Decoys*
1978. 172 PP, 10⅛ × 9¼″ $17.50 HC

It was the spring of 1978, and I was sitting at my desk in the basement of 306 Dartmouth Street when I took a call from one Stan Murphy from Martha's Vineyard. He had, he explained, finished his book on the duck decoys of the island and was looking for a publisher. I put on my high hat and explained that we were not in the business of publishing local history, but world-class fiction, distinguished poetry, and other work of immortal import, etc, etc. Stan listened politely and told me he'd call back the following week. Which he did. With the same response. The next week (I remember this well; it was early February, not a favorable month for a boat ride), he called to say he was on the Vineyard ferry, had hired a rental car, and was coming to my office to show me the book. He reassured me that it was all laid out, everything was in place (he'd done this himself), and it was ready to go to press. How could I refuse? Stan, as it turned out, was a delightful human being, a portrait artist of some note, and he had, indeed, laid out an entire book on this somewhat esoteric subject. He offered to pay for the book; he guaranteed he would not allow us to lose any money. He was gracious, modest, and determined, desperate to see it published. I couldn't say no. It was, after all, the definitive history on the subject, and although the photography was mediocre and the typography appalling, a book not likely to be repeated, I agreed and we put it on the fall list.

Here's what I remember next. I was giving a talk in St. Louis and, naturally, was selling the local bookstores. These were my first sales calls of the season. I came to a prosperous suburb, and the buyer began going through the list and (understandably) I tried skipping over this one.

"No," she said, suddenly perking up, "I have two customers for that one. Send me three." This happened again and again. Evidently there was a fanatic market out there for these small blocks of wood cleverly carved to lure unsuspecting water birds to their doom. And people were willing to pay high prices for them, *really* high prices. As in $25,000 and more. What was $17.50 for a book? Taking a hint, I immediately called back to the office and told them to increase the print run from 1,200 to 1,500. We had listed the book with a pre-pub price of $17.50 until December 31st and $25.00 thereafter. By the end of the year we had sold every copy. So much for fine printing, non-lining figures, elegant typography, and breathtaking halftones. Get the facts out (in this case about the decoys as well as their makers), make it readable and affordable, and pick a subject in which your book is the best book (and in this case, the *only* book) available, and you will sell out your stock.

Peter Berg: *The Art of Ogden M. Pleissner*
Introduction by Thomas S. Buechner
1984. 132 PP, 11¾ × 10⅞″ $45.00 HC

When Peter Berg approached me with the idea of a book on Ogden Pleissner, I had never heard of the man. But a visit to the Shelburne Museum on the shores of Lake Champlain, which holds his major collection, convinced me that this was indeed a virtuoso, probably the finest sporting artist to work in watercolor since Winslow Homer. His reputation was immense, and this was the first title to examine both his life and work. His supporters thought nothing of buying out both the deluxe and special editions, containing extra suites of prints and a large, unpublished watercolor reproduced full size, mailed in a tube.

RIGHT: Although Pleissner is best known and celebrated as a sporting artist, his talents as a water colorist encompassed a variety of places and subjects. Below is his finely detailed portrait of a Paris street scene at dawn executed in 1961.

Joseph D. Bates, Jr.: *The Art of the Atlantic Salmon Fly*

Line drawings and color frontispiece by Henry McDaniel

1987. 256 PP, 8½ × 11″ $50.00 HC

A special edition of 250 copies in slipcase with extra suite of the plates, and a deluxe edition of 85 copies, with extra suite of plates, bound in quarter leather by Claudia Cohen with a hand-tied Colonel Bates pattern salmon fly.

Joseph Bates, or "Colonel" as he styled himself, was humorless, driven, passionate about salmon, and even more passionate and knowledgeable about the marvelous concoction of fur, feathers, and tinsel that occasionally attracts them. He had the foremost private collection of salmon flies and was an authority on their construction, history, evolution, and idiosyncrasies. Why Atlantic salmon, which cease to feed as soon as they begin their trek to their spawning beds, are interested in flies, at least as food, remains a mystery, but over the decades, thousands of patterns have been developed, some very specifically attached to certain locales and rivers. The best are presented in this fine book, designed by Freeman Keith and printed by The Stinehour Press. Half the battle, of course, was simply selecting, and then arranging and photographing, the flies, and this was not as easy as it sounds for, under lights, the flies cast an unmistakable shadow. Here, Joe cleverly arranged for them to be shot on a sheet of clear Plexiglas. We issued the book in three editions: the trade, a special, and a deluxe with a hand-tied fly mounted within a debossed French matte. All sold out almost instantly. And, as promised, we never reprinted.

Faith Andrews Bedford: *The Sporting Art of Frank W. Benson*

2000. 272 PP, 11 × 9″ $65.00 HC

Benson has always been among my favorite artists. Born in Salem, he was shortly thereafter given a shotgun by his father and spent a good part of his youth shooting shore birds along the North Shore. He was a student and later an instructor at Boston's newly founded Museum School, where he formed a lifelong friendship with Edmund Tarbell. He spent a few summers in Dublin, NH coming under the influence of Abbott Thayer and Joseph Lindon Smith and later, continuing his studies in Europe, was exposed to the Impressionists, most especially to the brushstrokes and color palette of Manet. On his return to the US, he would marry and buy a summer home on North Haven overlooking the Thoroughfare and spent the rest of his summers there rusticating with his lovely daughters and printing small editions on his etching press. The author traces his love affair with hunting, fishing, sailing, and the outdoors that provided the inspiration for an elegant string of paintings, watercolors and etchings from life spent in the *plein air* he clearly held dear.

RIGHT: A guide poles a wooden canoe down a Canadian river as the sport in the bow plays a salmon in this typical watercolor by Frank Benson. Lorraine Ferguson expertly combined the extended text with the numerous images.

Charles B. Wood III: *Bibliotheca Salmo Salar*
A Selection of Rare Books, Manuscripts, Journals, Photographic Albums & Ephemera on the Subject of Atlantic Salmon Fishing
2017. 248 PP, 8½ × 11″ $75.00 HC

Every activity generates its own literature, but few have generated as much enthusiasm – some of it incredibly esoteric, most of it interesting and much of it downright irresistible – as salmon fishing. As a species, they demand clean, fast-moving fresh water, and in the past decades they have seen their southern runs on America's eastern coast entirely eliminated. What remains are a few closely guarded rivers in Iceland, Canada, Great Britain, and Scandinavia. All of them relatively inaccessible, all of them beautiful, and all of them pristine. As a distinguished antiquarian bookseller and avid fisherman, Wood has pursued these fish (at no mean expense) for decades, and has what is probably the most extensive collection of books about them in private hands. For this selective bibliography, he selected 230 of the most interesting titles (some of them so rare they might be encountered once in a lifetime) and arranged them by country and date. All are illustrated in full color. What makes the book a pleasure is the knowledge he brings to bear on the subject – not only as a bookman, but also as a reader and fisherman. He knows the rivers, and often the people who fished them and authored the books. He knows what qualifies as "quality material" – either an elusive, fugitive mimeographed memoir or a treasured limited edition. For collectors, the book is considered the last word. For the rest of us, it makes the expense and travel almost unnecessary. We issued this in both a trade edition of 800 copies and a signed and numbered deluxe edition of 85, bound in quarter leather by Gray Parrot with three additional handsomely produced and rare pamphlets. Certainly among the more specialized titles this company ever issued, but also among the most delightful.

LEFT: The jacket of Charles Wood's bibliography of salmon literature with the John Benson cypher Godine pressmark and the elegant calligraphy of Jerry Kelly, the book's designer
BELOW: A sample spread showing three books issued with hand-tied flies, including one of our own *The Art of the Atlantic Salmon Fly*, with the flashy hand-tied "Colonel Bates" pattern inset in a debossed roundel

OPPOSITE: This is one of Robert Lawson's more unforgettable illustrations for Munro Leaf's immortal *Ferdinand the Bull*. The original artwork, we discovered to our surprise, still existed at New York's Morgan Library, so we had it entirely reshot from the originals for our Latin-language edition by Elizabeth Hadas, and the results were a considerable improvement over the English-language version.

Outliers & Other Works of
Unclassifiable but Undeniable Genius

Giorgio De Santillana & Hertha von Dechend: *Hamlet's Mill*

1970. 540 PP, 6 × 9″ $7.00 SC

Among the very first Nonpareils we reprinted, and originally published by Gambit Publications with whom we shared offices on Dartmouth Street, this book presents a theory of preliterate science that is, as *The Washington Post* claimed, "wonderful to read and startling to contemplate. If this theory is correct, both the history of science and the reinterpretation of myths have been enriched enormously." Drawing on scientific data as well as historical and literary sources, the authors argue that our myths are the result of a preliterate astronomy, a science whose accuracy and power was suppressed and then forgotten by the Greco-Roman world. What was "science" before the Greeks? And what if one could prove that all myths have a single and common origin in celestial mythology? What if, in other words, what we now think of as mythology was really a series of stories and ciphers invented for the purpose of perpetuating complex arithmetic and astronomical data? If this sounds far-fetched, read this genuinely original and seminal thesis, one that throws into doubt many of our assumptions about the development of early science and the transmission of knowledge.

F. Washington Jarvis: *With Love and Prayers*

Foreword by Peter J. Gomes

2000. 368 PP, 6 × 9″ $17.00 SC

For thirty years, from 1974 to 2004, "Tony" Jarvis was the headmaster of The Roxbury Latin School (or, as he referred to it, "The One, True School"). Founded in 1645 and in 2020 celebrating its 375th anniversary, it is the oldest school in continuous operation in North America and also my alma mater. It is fair to say that Tony not only saved this "little nursery" as Cotton Mather describes it, but transformed it into the vibrant and caring community it is today. Every day of the week, the boys of the six classes would march into "Hall," there to sing a hymn, get their marching orders for the day, and often listen to a short homily, most often delivered from the pulpit by the headmaster. This is a collection of Tony's best advice, delivered from the heart and through experience, to a room of adolescent boys about the challenges they would face as young men destined, in the words of the school's charter, to "serve Church and state." He believed strongly, and articulated clearly that "To those to whom much has been given, much is to be expected." These weren't sermons about duty to God; they were summons to action in the real world, to moral behavior, to what he tersely termed "Values to Live By." We mistakenly thought we were simply doing the school a favor by putting his words between covers. A total miscalculation. Four printings later, we are convinced of the effect his advice has exerted on an entire generation of anxious parents and students who were told, in words of tough love, that the world wasn't fair and would be full of disappointments and that they might be just as well off, emotionally, financially, and educationally, graduating from a state university as Harvard.

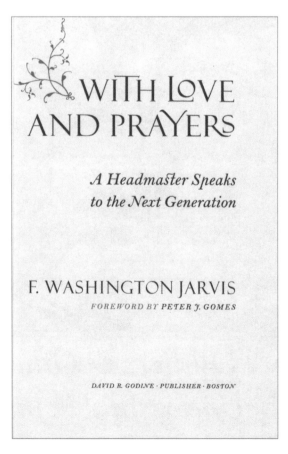

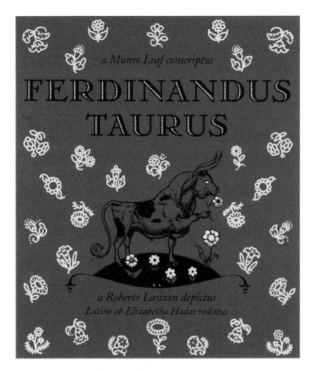

Munro Leaf: *Ferdinandus Taurus*
Illustrated by Robert Lawson
Translated into the Latin by Elizabeth Hadas
2000. 84 PP, 7 × 8⅛" $18.00 SC

Elizabeth Hadas was deceased when we published her fine translation of Munro Leaf's classic. Everyone knows the story of the peace-loving, tranquil bull who was briefly but dramatically catapulted into action by sitting on a bee. But probably only a select few knew it had been translated, along with a full glossary, into Latin for the benefit of students of the Spence School in NYC. And fewer still will recall its remarkable history or the enormous impact the book had when it was first published in 1936, two months following the outbreak of the Spanish Civil War. Some saw it as a commentary *on* the Spanish Civil War. Some interpreted it as pro-fascist, others as anti-Franco. Many saw it as a manifesto endorsing pacifism. The book was burned in Germany and banned in Spain. When Berlin fell in 1945, the USIA had 30,000 copies printed and distributed to German school children in an effort to promote peace and reconciliation. Before its publication, the president of Viking put his money on Pène du Bois's *Giant Otto*, saying "*Ferdinand* is a nice little book, but *Giant Otto* will live forever." Who remembers *Giant Otto* today? By 1938, *Ferdinand* was selling 3,000 copies a week. It knocked *Gone with the Wind* from the top of the bestseller list. It has been translated into 60 languages. Every year, the Swedes rerun the Disney version on Christmas Eve. Leaf was incredulous; he just wanted to write something original for his friend Robert Lawson that did not, for once, feature a dog or a cat. He settled on a bull. We were fortunate to find the original art at The Pierpont Morgan Library, and were able to reproduce it more carefully than the original English-language edition. Of course, the color and design of the cover is so iconic that many folks ordering our edition assumed it was indeed the original, but were probably too embarrassed to admit their mistake and return it.

Peter Korn: *Why We Make Things and Why It Matters*
2013. 184 PP, 6 × 9" $25.00 HC

This is as much autobiography as polemic, following Peter's career as a carpenter on Nantucket, his move to Philadelphia as a nascent furniture maker, to Aspen, Colorado, as a resident craftsman, and finally to Rockport, Maine, where as the founder and prime mover of the Center for Furniture Craftsmanship, he turns out every year another cycle of craftsmen in wood. Above all, it is an eloquent argument for the pleasure, indeed the necessity, of making things with one's hands, with the joy of both conceiving and then converting an idea to a physical object—something of worth, beauty, permanence, and practicality. The title says it all: this is an attempt to explain our innate impulse to use our minds and hands, as well as an argument for why this matters in a world where these impulses are blocked, blunted, or buried. In an age where the term "handmade" has echoes of the quaint and fussy, this title sets forth a bracing and convincing argument for the "aristocracy of the hand."

BELOW: The simple, striking and wholly appropriate jacket design of Korn's book was the inspired work of Michael Russem, who managed to bring, despite his background as a letterpress master printer, a clean and modern sensibility to our jackets and interiors. I strongly suspect the simple originality of this jacket was in large part responsible for the book's success.

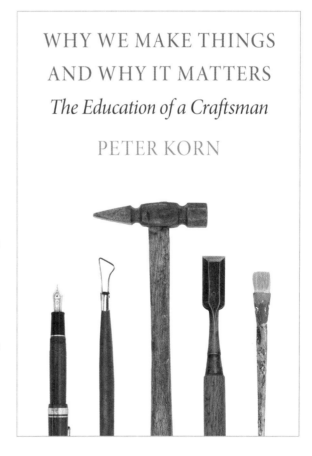

Charlton & Roth: *Speaking of Dogs: The Best Collection of Canine Quotables Ever Compiled*

Doggedly assembled by James Charlton
Fetchingly illustrated by Arnold Roth
2017. 152 PP, 5¼ × 7½" $18.00 SC *with flaps*

Who doesn't love dogs? Well, truth be told, my parents didn't, and it wasn't until I was married that we began assembling our noble string. But if you hold your canine pets (we have two) in any regard, this is a book that contains the best that was ever said about them, and in just about every language–who can resist, as an example, Kafka: "All knowledge, the totality of all questions and all answers, is contained in the dog." Containing quotes from pundits and poets, artists and authors, politicians, musicians, and petty thieves, there's something new and memorable in here for everyone. Charlton arranges the quotes into neat categories, simplifying your task of finding precisely the right quotation to fit your mood, your dog's mood, or conversational demands. Hungry? Look under Dog Food. ("My pit bull was choking on his dinner. I squeezed his stomach and our neighbor's cat shot right out.") Lonely? Try Love and Loyalty. ("Thorns may hurt you, friends desert you, sunlight turn to fog, but you're never friendless, ever, if you have a dog.") Aging: you'll be soothed by Old Dogs. ("There are three faithful friends; an old wife, an old dog, and ready money.") Greatly enhanced by the charming line drawings of Arnold Roth, cartoonist and illustrator, of dogmatic profundity and unleashed wisdom, this litter has the best that was ever written about man's best friend. And if in doubt, remember what Mark Twain said: "Heaven goes by favor; if it went by merit, you would stay out and your dog would go in."

William H. Armstrong: *Study Is Hard Work*

2000. 84 PP, 5½ × 8⅛" $18.00 SC 🐦

Written long before computers, cell phones, or the internet, written when homework assignments were written out with a pencil longhand on ruled paper and students had to consult a physical dictionary to confirm a spelling, published when there were actually discrete disciplines and books were *the* medium of teaching, when authors didn't mind prefacing their books with a Latin quotation, *Study Is Hard Work* is the prehistoric fossil of our list. And it still sells like hotcakes. For in it, for teachers and educators, parents and students, the beloved author of *Sounder* has offered the most lucid and accessible text ever written on acquiring and maintaining study skills. Yes, studying *is* an art, just like playing the piano. Divided into its component parts–mathematics, history, composition, languages, using the library, creating a précis–it observes that different skills engage different parts of our brain. Armstrong, a teacher for forty years, attacks these individually, provides clear and pragmatic instruction on how they can be approached and subdued. More importantly, he addresses the issue of time management: how best to use the study time you're allotted. But the title gives a hint at the tone, and the opening quotation from Ovid says it all: "Before the high gates of excellence, the Gods have placed sweat." We receive more mail about this book than any we've published, mostly from grateful parents who claim the book saved their child's life–and sometimes their sanity.

Dogs are better than human beings, because they know and do not tell.
EMILY DICKINSON

The more I see of the representatives of the people, the more I admire my dogs.
ALPHONSE DE LAMARTINE

The more I see of men, the more I like dogs.
MADAME DE STAEL

The average dog is a nicer person than the average person.
ANDY ROONEY

~ 114 ~

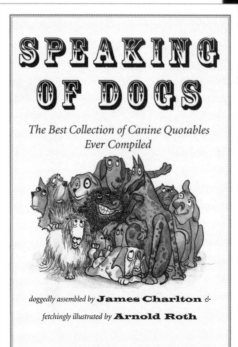

LEFT: The sample spread and cover art displays the consistently wacky drawings by Arnold Roth and a selection of sample canine comestibles from Emily Dickinson to Sigmund Freud.

The house of Godine contains many rooms, and the following may provide its visitors some hints for navigation.

The information below the authors and titles provides

A) The date of the original publication. If the book was issued simultaneously in hard and softcover, both are noted. If not, assume that this is the date at which the first edition, in either soft or hardcover, originally appeared.

B) Number of pages, including blanks but not including the endpapers.

C) The dimensions in inches of the trimmed book block (i.e. not the binding), width preceding height, and rounded off to the nearest $\frac{1}{16}''$.

D) The list price. All of these have been rounded up to nearest nickel (e.g. a title selling for $14.95 is listed as $15.00). These little marketing schemes trying to fool people buying a $15 book into thinking they are only spending $14 have always appeared foolish to me.

E) The format in which the book was originally issued. HC = hardcover SC = paperback

The following symbols refer to the various imprints, really separate lists, we have created over the years.

🐦 NONPAREIL These are titles that are reprints we have either licensed from other publishers or reset and reissued from previous editions. In many cases they include new Introductions, Forewords or Afterwords; these have been noted. The sizes and designs vary, but all are noted as "A Nonpareil Book." The name comes from a size of type, but it also refers to a species of bird (duly appropriated) and a kind of candy. The literal translation is, of course, "without equal," but that seems a little too self-serving.

● VERBA MUNDI Literally "words of the world," these are books that have all been translated from a foreign language (although not every translated book on the list is so categorized). These books do have a uniform design and size, both in paperback and hardcover, although the designs have evolved over the decades.

🌐 IMAGO MUNDI This series exclusively contains illustrated books and they are all printed in a uniform format of $8\frac{5}{8} \times 9\frac{3}{4}''$. One may wonder why; when we first initiated this list, most fine printers were using sheet-fed machines that could take a 23 × 35″ sheet. If one prints in twelves (six pages to a side), the maximum page size you could extract, given gripper allowances and trim, was as above. The horizontal format was chosen because most of the original artwork and photography we were illustrating was horizontal.

℘ POCKET PARAGON This was an effort to take mostly illustrated books with texts and publish them in a small and affordable format. They were meant to be "reading" books, or at least easily portable. And also to take advantage of the benefits allowed by offset printing: the easy combination of text and image.

A few other thoughts worth mentioning

A) This is not intended to be a complete, or even nearly complete, bibliography of DRG titles published over the past five decades. That is for a braver soul to undertake. These are simply my favorites, hopefully interesting, occasionally significant titles that have been chosen purely on the basis of personal affection. Tastes *are* personal. My apology for any of *your* favorites that have been omitted.

B) The length of copy bears no relationship to the book's importance, reception or its sales. The books have been selected purely on the basis of subjective prejudice. My own. And there are cases where I have been clearly carried away.

C) Many of these titles appeared over the years in a variety of different costumes. For example, Andre Dubus's *Separate Flights* has had at least six different jackets and covers. Consistency has never been a strong suit of this company. The ones selected for illustration in this checklist attempt to show a variety but by no means every edition.

D) It has been impossible to list all the people who have been affiliated with this little ship of fools over fifty years, many of them in very significant ways. Not just authors, illustrators, designers and manufacturers, but also the endless parade of employees, interns and fellow travelers without whose aid and support the ongoing survival of the company would have been impossible. For these omissions, my sincere apologies; it is not for lack of affection, but merely lack of space.

We have frequently printed the word Democracy. Yet I cannot too often repeat that it is a word the real gist of which still sleeps, quite unawaken'd, notwithstanding the resonance and the many angry tempests out of which its syllables have come, from pen or tongue. It is a great word, whose history, I suppose, remains unwritten, because that history has yet to be enacted. It is, in some sort, younger brother of another great and often-used word, Nature, whose history also waits unwritten.　　　　　　WALT WHITMAN

THE WHOLE PRESENT SYSTEM of the officering and personnel of the army and navy of these States, and the spirit and letter of their trebly-aristocratic rules and regulations, is a monstrous exotic, a nuisance and revolt, and belong here just as much as orders of nobility, or the Pope's council of cardinals. I say if the present theory of our army and navy is sensible and true, then the rest of America is an unmitigated fraud.

Walt Whitman

David R. Godine, Publisher
The First Ten Years · 1970 – 1980

GODINE FOR CHILDREN

The top two posters, printed at Enschedé in gravure, were issued to celebrate our 1971 edition of Whitman's *Specimen Days*. The upper left poster shows a photograph by Thomas Eakins shortly before Whitman's death with the text set in Zapf's Optima, while the right displays the calligraphy of Bram de Does. The lower two silk-screen posters were designed and illustrated by Lance Hidy with lettering by Stephen Harvard to celebrate our first decade and the introduction of our children's list.

Clockwise from upper left: A poster announcing the publication of Stephen Williams's book on Maine's Sabbathday Lake Shakers; Louise Fili's design celebrating Koch's tribute to craft with the DRG press mark designed by Stephen Harvard; DRG contemplating a stick of type with the bank, cases of type and hanging pica rulers in the background in a silkscreen celebrating our 40ᵀᴴ anniversary by Glenna Lang; Leslie Cabarga's sly retro tribute to at least one discerning customer eyeing a Godine book.

The Godine Press, specializing in fine letterpress printing, is now offering a limited selection of distinctive stationery. The design and printing reflect the Press's unique letterpress capabilities, where a balance of inking, type, and impression are crucial in obtaining the finest results. The type faces used are: Centaur, a traditional Renaissance face designed by Bruce Rogers; Lutetia, a modern face designed by van Krimpen; and Cancelleresca Bastarda, also by van Krimpen, with elegant swash letters. The typographical designs, adapted from commissioned orders, combine with fine papers to offer beautiful and reasonably priced personalized stationery.

DAVID R. GODINE
cordially invites you to
a Tea
to be held at
THE GROLIER CLUB
on April twenty-eighth
from four-thirty to six o'clock
at the Clubhouse
47 East 60th Street
New York, New York

⁊

RSVP *regrets only*

JOSEPH MOXON
DEFINES THE DUTIES
OF A TYPOGRAPHER
IN HIS TREATISE
'MECHANICK
EXERCISES'

BY A TYPOGRAPHER,
I do not mean a printer, as he is Vulgarly accounted, any more than Dr. Dee means a Carpenter or Mason to be an Architect: But by a Typographer, I mean such a one who, by his own Judgement, from solid reasoning with himself, can either perform, or direct others to perform, from the beginning to the end, all the Handy-works and Physical Operations relating to TYPOGRAPHIE.

This broadside, printed letterpress in an edition of one copy, honors & describes the extraordinary work of beloved John Kristensen on the occasion of his 60th birthday. David R. Godine on 11:3:10.

BEA: '99

HERMANN HESSE
The Magic of Books

Among the many worlds that man did not receive as a gift from nature but created out of his own mind, the world of books is the greatest. Every child, when he first draws on his slate and makes his first attempt to read, thereby takes the initial steps into an artificial and highly complicated realm whose laws and rules of play are too much to learn and fully employ in any one lifetime. Without the word, without the writing of books, there is no history, there is no concept of humanity. And if anyone wants to try to enclose in a small space in a single house or single room the history of the human spirit and to make it his own, he can only do this in the form of a
COLLECTION OF BOOKS.

Designed, composed & printed letterpress by David R. Godine in an edition of 100 copies on the occasion of the BEA exhibition held in Los Angeles. Reprinted from Reading in Bed, edited by Steven Gilbar, Godine, 1995. Scratchboard illustration provided by Wesley Bates.

LEFT: A selection of letterpress ephemera, all printed on our Vandercook proofing press, displaying just a small sample of the variety of announcements, pronouncements and propaganda issued over the years

The Friends & Associates of
Yale University Library
& David R. Godine
are invited to an exhibition of
Books & Ephemera
printed and published by
The Godine Press

On view October–December
The Sterling Memorial Library
Art of the Book Room
Yale University, New Haven

WALT WHITMAN
Assurances

I need no assurances—I am a man who is preoccupied, of his own Soul;
I do not doubt that whatever I know at a given time, there waits for me more, which I do not know;
I do not doubt that from under the feet, and beside the hands and face I am cognizant of, are now looking faces I am not cognizant of — calm and actual faces;
I do not doubt but the majesty & beauty of the world are latent in any iota of the world;

I do not doubt there are realizations I have no idea of, waiting for me through time, and through the universes—also upon this earth;
I do not doubt I am limitless, and that the universes are limitless — in vain I try to think how limitless;
I do not doubt that the orbs, and the systems of orbs, play their swift sports through the air on purpose — and that I shall one day be eligible to do as much as they, and more than they;
I do not doubt there is far more in trivialities, insects, vulgar persons, slaves, dwarfs, weeds, rejected refuse, than I have supposed;
I do not doubt there is more in myself than I have supposed — and more in all men & women—and more in my poems than I have supposed;
I do not doubt that temporary affairs keep on and on, millions of years;
I do not doubt interiors have their interiors, and exteriors have their exteriors — and that the eye-sight has another eye-sight, & the hearing another hearing, and the voice another voice;

I do not doubt that the passionately-wept deaths of young men are provided for — and that the deaths of young women, & the deaths of little children are provided for;
(Did you think Life was so well provided for — and Death, the purport of all Life, is not well provided for?)
I do not doubt that wrecks at sea, no matter what the horrors of them—no matter whose wife, child, husband, father, lover, has gone down — are provided for, to the minutest point;
I do not doubt that shallowness, meanness, malignance, are provided for;
I do not doubt that cities, you, America, the remainder of the earth, politics, freedom, degradations, are carefully provided for;
I do not doubt that whatever can possibly happen, any where, at any time, is provided for, in the inherences of things;
I do not think Life provides for all, and for Time and Space—but I believe Heavenly Death provides for all.
GODINE·BOSTON·1970·HIDY FEC.

FOR A CENTURY, between roughly 1820 and 1920, before dust jackets hid them from view, a "trade" or "publisher's" binding was what a potential buyer encountered when considering a book. Careful attention and considerable craftsmanship was lavished on these wonders of the decorative arts, especially in England in the fifty years between 1840 and 1890. A fine example is shown here, designed by W. R. Tymms and published in 1865. When I began in 1970, the binding, the unseen poor stepchild of the manufacturing process, was already in decline. The better publishers, Knopf and Farrar, Straus & Giroux leading the pack, still often used full cloth, headbands, even top-edge stain to cover their books.

Many of them were even sewn in signatures. Today you can pick almost any trade book off the shelves and hardly find a hint of cloth. Almost all are "perfect bound," among the great misnomers of the industry. Even head and foot bands, which cost pennies, have all but disappeared. The binding is the last opportunity a publisher has to save a few cents and, after paying too much for the book, a king's ransom in royalties, a few too many three-martini lunches, and a stern note from the accounting department demanding costs be cut, this is where the nickels and dimes are saved. We're far from perfect, but we do pay attention to bindings and occasionally come up with some worthy of the tradition. A selection of a few of my favorites is shown below.

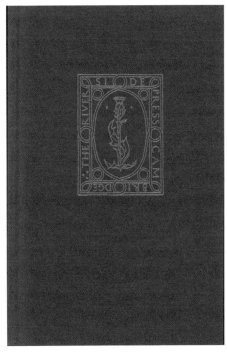

At the end of most Godine titles readers will encounter a "colophon," a brief paragraph identifying the typeface in which the book has been set and often its designer, edition size, and other details of manufacture. As I claimed earlier, authors don't create books; they create texts. It is up to the publisher to convert words into physical objects and this effort requires and involves a conflation of talents – editors, proofreaders, designers, paper manufacturers, printers and binders – who remain invisible, out of sight and often unacknowledged. Very few readers buy books because of their manufacturing merits or quality of design, but these talents, from around the world, are as much responsible for what we take for granted as the authors supplying the texts. They also provide an endless source of entertainment, for every book requires a constellation of decisions from the typeface used, its size, its leading, its measure, to the color of the foot and head bands. And no two books are alike, each title presenting a unique set of challenges demanding a long list of individual and discrete decisions. These decisions often involve people: their compatibility, their specialties, their levels of competence, and yes, their prices for the work to be done. Below is an abbreviated list of some of the associations this company has enjoyed over the years. With these names come my personal and heartfelt gratitude – both for the work they produced and the attention they paid our titles over the decades.

A selective list of typefaces used in Godine books over the past fifty years including, where known, the designers, sources and manufacturers

Bembo (English Monotype)
Baskerville (English Monotype/Mergenthaler Linotype)
Bell (English Monotype)
Bodoni (International Typeface Corp./Bauer)
Caledonia (W.A. Dwiggins; Mergenthaler Linotype)
Cancelleresca Bastarda (Jan van Krimpen;
    Joh. Enschedé en Zonen)
Caslon Old Face (Stephenson Blake/Mergenthaler Linotype)
Caslon (Carol Twombly; Adobe Systems)
Centaur & Arrighi (Bruce Rogers & Frederic Warde;
    English Monotype)
Dante (Giovanni Mardersteig; English Monotype)
Dante VAL (a PostScript version developed at the
    Stamperia Valdonega)
Ehrhardt (English Monotype)
Electra (W.A. Dwiggins; Mergenthaler Linotype)
Fournier (English Monotype)
Galliard (Matthew Carter; Mergenthaler Linotype)
Garamond (English Monotype/Mergenthaler Linotype)
Garamond (Robert Slimbach; Adobe Systems)
Golden (Scott-Martin Kosofsky after William Morris)
Golden Cockerel (Eric Gill; International Typeface Corp.)
Hillel (Scott-Martin Kosofsky)
Janson (Nicolas Kis; D. Stempel/Mergenthaler Linotype)
Joanna (Eric Gill; English Monotype)
Lutetia (Jan van Krimpen; English Monotype)

Mentor (Michael Harvey)
Miller (Matthew Carter; Carter & Cone)
Minion (Robert Slimbach; Adobe Systems)
Montaigne Sabon (Scott-Martin Kosofsky after Tschichold)
Nofret (Gudrun Zapf-von Hesse)
Optima (Hermann Zapf; D. Stempel/Linotype AG)
Palatino (Hermann Zapf; D. Stempel/Linotype AG)
Plantin (English Monotype)
Perpetua (Eric Gill; English Monotype)
Poliphilus & Blado (English Monotype)
Primer (Rudolph Ruzicka; Mergenthaler Linotype)
Rilke (Jerry Kelly)
Sabon (Jan Tschichold; D. Stempel/Linotype AG)
Sabon Next (Jan Tschichold & Jean François Porchez)
Spectrum (Jan van Krimpen; English Monotype)
Trump Mediäval (Georg Trump; C.E. Weber/Linotype AG)
Van Dijck (Christoffel van Dijck & Jan van Krimpen;
    English Monotype)
Walbaum (English Monotype)

Jacket & Book Designers

Michael Babcock	Martino Mardersteig
Richard Bartlett	Susan Marsh
Jane Bierhorst	Ruari McLean
Michael Bixler	Barry Moser
Joseph Blumenthal	Wynne Patterson
Dean Bornstein	Mark Polizzotti
Robert Bringhurst	William Reuter
Anne Chalmers	Michael Russem
Lisa Clark	Carl W. Scarbrough
Barbara DeWilde	Herbert Spencer
Robert Dothard	Roderick Stinehour
Sara Eisenman	John Trevitt
Virginia Evans	Carl Zahn
Lorraine Ferguson	
Louise Fili	
Daphne Geismar	
Carol Goldenberg	## *Calligraphers*
Howard Gralla	
Philip Grushkin	Marie Angel
Peter Guy	John E. Benson
Walter Hamady	Tim Girvin
Stephen Harvard	Howard Glasser
Richard Hendel	Philip Grushkin
Lance Hidy	Stephen Harvard
Lucinda Hitchcock	Michael Harvey
Katy Homans	Jerry Kelly
Darrell Hyder	Alice Koeth
Jerry Kelly	G.G. Laurens
Freeman Keith	George Laws
Barbara Knowles	Richard Lipton
Scott-Martin Kosofsky	Mark Livingston
Marshall Lee	Barry Moser
Lorraine Louie	Jim Sadler
	John Stevens
	Julian Waters

Index

ABOVE: DRG printing with his daughter Maddy, and amused by his son Addison who is clearly delighted with something he has just eaten.

ABOVE: On the night of July 23, 1986, Andre Dubus stopped to assist two motorists on the highway just north of Boston. A car collided with their vehicle, crushing both his legs. His right leg was amputated above the knee and for three years he endured pain and extensive physical therapy. As Andre had no medical insurance to help pay the bills, we decided to organize four literary benefits to help raise money. The readings at the Charles River Hotel in Cambridge included Ann Beattie, E.L. Doctorow, John Irving, Gail Godwin, Stephen King, Tim O'Brien, John Updike, Kurt Vonnegut, and Richard Yates. With their help we managed to raise just over $100,000 to help defray his medical costs. Andre described the accident and its aftermath in poignant detail in his collection of essays, *Broken Vessels*, a finalist for the Pulitzer Prize. Seen here are Andre Dubus, Stephen King and John Irving on the night of their reading. Andre died in 1999 at the age of 62. Photograph © Roger Farrington.

A Abbott, Edith, 186
ABC Et Cetera: The Life & Times of the Roman Alphabet (Humez), 70
Absolutely Wild (Webster), 165
Ackerman, Peter, 169
Acme Printing, 114
Adair, Gilbert, 38
Adams, Richard, 168
Adkins, Douglas, 182
Adventures of Jonathan Corncob, The, Loyal American Refugee, 248, 250
Adventures of Uncle Lubin, The (Robinson), 160
African, The (Le Clézio), 40, 41
Agee, James, VIII, 2
Age of Wonders, The (Appelfeld), 37
Ahab's Wife (Naslund), 24
Aiken, Joan, 162
Alice: A Survey of Her Calligraphy, 238
Allender, David, IX, 155, 188
All My Mirrors Lie (Rubin), 44
All of It, The (Haien), 22
All Sail Set: A Romance of the Flying Cloud (Sperry), 176
Alone at Sea: Gloucester in the Age of the Dorymen, 1623–1939 (Morris), 174–175
Alpern, Andrew, 140
Alpha to Omega: The Life & Times of the Greek Alphabet (Humez), 70
Alvord, Douglas, 23
Always a Body to Trade (Constantine), 19
Ambassador to the Penguins: A Naturalist's Year Aboard a Yankee Whaleship (Mathews), 246
American Bookman (typeface), 47
American Boy's Handy Book, The (Beard), 153–154
American Girl's Handybook, The (Beard), 153, 154
American Harmony: Inspired Choral Miniatures from New England, Appalachia, the Mid-Atlantic, the South, and the Midwest (Cooke), 194
American Masterpieces: Singular Expressions of National Genius (Wilmerding), 134
Anatomical Works of George Stubbs, The (Doherty), 240
Anatomy of a Typeface (Lawson), 222
Ancestors (Maxwell), 22
Andalusian Poems (Middleton and Garza-Falcon), 50
Anderson, John, 94
And The Whale is Ours: Creative Writing of American Whalemen (Miller), 174
Angel, Marie, 243, 244, 266
Angel, Roger, 252
Angle of Geese and Other Poems (Momaday), 44
Anglin, Clint, 110
Angus, Ian, 64, 65
Animal Fables from Aesop (McClintock), 159–160
Animated Alphabet, An (Angel), 243–244
Anne of Green Gables (Montgomery), 159
Anninger, Anne, 243, 244
Antigone Greek, 70
Apollinaire, Guillaume, 46–47
Appel, Odette M., 110
Appelfeld, Aharon, 37
Arctic Circle: Birth and Rebirth in the Land of the Caribou (Reid), 246–247
Ardizzone, Edward, 148, 166
Argetsinger, Mark, 230
Armstrong, William, 260
Arrighi (typeface), 2, 12, 97, 266
Artist & Alphabet: Twentieth Century Calligraphy and Letter Art in America, 238
Artist in Venice, An (Van Doren), 129
Art Museums of New England, The (Faison), 126–127
Art of Ogden M. Pleissner, The (Berg), 254
Art of Planting, The (Thomas), 199–200
Art of the Atlantic Salmon Fly, The (Bates), 255
Art of the Piano, The (Diebboll), 191
Art of the Printed Book (Blumenthal), 93, 215
Ascensius Press, 51
As I Walked Out One Midsummer Morning (Lee), 84
As We Were: American Photographic Postcards (Vaule), 117–118
Atkins, Kathryn A., 233, 237
Attenborough, David, 248
At the Edge of the Light: Thoughts on Photography & Photographers, Talent & Genius (Travis), 65
Aubrey, John, 78–79
Aubrey's Brief Lives (Aubrey), 78–79
Auden, W. H., 186
Augustino da Siena (Fairbank), 232
Autobiography of Michel de Montaigne (Lowenthal), 78
Azarian, Mary, 15, 50, 51, 152, 154

B Babcock, Michael, 171, 266
Badenheim 1939 (Appelfeld), 37

Bakke, Kit, 25
Banville, John, 21
Barba, Susan, IX, 55, 84
Barker, Nicolas, 236
Barlow, Joel, 2
Barnes, Julian, 212
Barnes, Kate, 51
Baron, Mary, 44
Bartlett, Mark, 204
Bartlett, Michael Valentine, 205
Bartlett, Richard, 138, 209, 210, 244, 266
Bartlett, Rose Love, 205
Bartlett Book of Garden Elements, The (Bartlett), 205
Bascove, Anne, 128
Baskerville (typeface), 44, 93, 215, 218, 240, 266
Baskin, Leonard, VIII, 2
Bates, Joseph D. Jr., 255
Bates, Wesley, 25
Bator, Thomas E., 99
Battle for Gaul, The (Julius Caesar), 96
Baudelaire, Charles, 48
Bayley, Nicola, 168
Bear (Engel), 25
Beard, Adelia, 153
Beard, Daniel C., 153
Beard, Lina, 153
Beasts in My Belfry (Durrell), 86
Beaton, Cecil, 202
Beattie, Ann, 31
Beaujon, Paul (Beatrice Warde), 220
Bedford, Faith Andrews, 255
Beebe, Ruth, 208
Behan, Brendan, 75
Bell (typeface), 2, 3, 219, 266
Bellos, David, 38, 42, 77
Bembo, 30, 97, 186, 221, 266
Bemelmans, Ludwig, 210
Beneath the Streets of Boston (McKendry), 163
Benson, Frank, 255
Benson, John E., 6, 30, 266
Benson, John Howard, 245
Benson, Richard, 114, 117
Berg, Peter, 254
Bernard, Liza, 171
Bestiary or The Parade of Orpheus (Apollinaire), 46–47
Beston, Henry, 51, 167, 245
Bethlehem in Broad Daylight (Doty), 55
Bibliotheca Salmo Salar (Wood), 256
Bidwell, John, 204
Bierhorst, Jane, 188, 266
Big Six, The (Ransome), 160
Bilu, Dalya, 37
Bird, Beast & Flower (Angel), 243
Birds and Beasts (Smith), 13
Bixler, Michael, IX, 9, 46, 59, 110, 208, 220, 266
Bixler, Winnifred, 9, 208
Blagden, Allen, 132
Blake, Quentin, 164
Blake, Stephenson, 266
Blinn, Carol, 9
Blue Faces: A Portrait of the Blues (Charters), 190
Blumenthal, Joseph, 93, 215, 218, 266
Boat Who Wouldn't Float, The (Mowat), 184
Bodoni, Giambattista, 228
Bodoni (typeface), 52, 266
Bodwell, Josh, 28, 31, 266
Bonne Table, La (Bemelmans), 210
Book of Cape Cod Houses, A (Doane), 142
Boreman, Thomas, 5
Borges, Jorge Luis, 35
Bornstein, Dean, 15, 118, 266
Borstal Boy (Behan), 75
Boston (Whitehill), 94
Boston Raphael, The (Rathbone), 99
Boston Trustee, The (Bator and Seely), 99
Bowler, Peter, 71
Boylan, Anne M., 153
Braham, Jeanne, 67
Bravo, Álvarez M., 111
Brett, Simon, 54
Bringhurst, Robert, 229, 266

Broken Blockhouse Wall, The (Peck), 44
Broken Vessels: Essays (Dubus), 62
Brown, Andreas, 118
Brown, Jane, 202
Brown, J. Carter, 176
Brown, Richard, 79, 104, 122
Brown, Susan, 123
Browne, Thomas, 7
Browning, Robert, 2
Brumfield, William, 137
Bryant, Audrey, 159
Bryer, Elizabeth, 42
Buchan, John, 24–25
Buechner, Thomas S., 254
Bulmer (typeface), 215, 218
Burke, Jackson, 224
Burlen, Robert, 7
Burnett, Frances Hodgson, 157
Busch, Frederick, 20
Busiest Man in England, The: A Life of Joseph Paxton, Gardener, Architect & Victorian Visionary (Colquhoun), 84
Buzzati, Dino, 41

C Cabarga, Leslie, 263
Caesar, Julius, 96
Caledonia (typeface), 244
Calligraphic Flourishing: A New Approach to an Ancient Art (Hildebrandt), 237
Cambridge University Press, 8
Cameron, Julia Margaret, 106
Campion, Thomas, 186
Cancelleresca Bastarda (typeface), 2, 4, 214, 266
Cannell, Amanda, 244
Canzano, Fran, 110, 114
Caponigro, Paul, 117
Carduff, Chris, 22
Carl Zahn, 266
Carter, Matthew, 209, 266
Carter, Sebastian, 7
Carter, Will, 7
Case-Hoyt, 125
Caslon (typeface), 245, 266
Caslon Old Face (typeface), 5, 266
Catherine Certitude (Modiano), 39
Causley, Charles, 45
Centaur (typeface), 6, 11, 12, 150, 266
Century for the Century, A (Kelly and Hutner), 225
Chakraharti, Vishan, 140
Chalmers, Anne, 266
Chamberlain, Narcisse, 210
Chamberlain, Samuel, 210
Chambers, Roland, 87
Chappell, Warren, 233
Charleston & Other Stories (Donoso), 37
Charlton, James, 260
Charters, Ann, 190
Charters, Samuel, 190
Chateau (Maxwell), 22
Chelmaxioms (Mandelbaum), 46
Chiarenza, Carl, 114
Child's Christmas in Wales, A (Thomas), 148
Childers, Erskine, 27
Christmas Oratorio, The (Tunstrom), 39
Christmas Revels Songbook, The (Langstaff), 189
Chronicles of Pantouflia, The (Lang), 151
Cider with Rosie (Lee), 84
Civil Disobedience (Thoreau), VIII, 2
Clarendon Press, 7
Clayton, Virginia Tuttle, 200
Clémentine in the Kitchen (Chamberlain), 210
Coast of California, The (Killion), 12
Coburn, Alvin Landgon, 32–33
Cochin (typeface), 13
Cocteau (Steegmuller), 76
Cogito Ergo Sum: The Life of René Descartes (Watson), 80
Cohen, Claudia, 255
Cohen, Stu, 120
Collected Essays, Journalism, and Letters of George Orwell, The (Orwell), 64–65
Collected Stories. 1948–1986 (Morris), 34
Colquhoun, Kate, 84
Common Ground: A Naturalist's Cape Cod (Finch), 244
Common Press, The (Harris), 219

Complete Plain Words, The (Gowers), 70
Conkwright, P. J., 94
Constantine, K. C., 19
Constructed Roman Alphabet, A (Goines), 220, 221
Conzett and Huber, 125
Cooke, Nym, 194
Coolidge, A. Knight, 176
Cooper, Susan, 189
Coot Club (Ransome), 160
Corner in the Marais, A: Memoir of a Paris Neighborhood (Karmel), 140–141
Correspondence: An Adventure in Letters (Hall), 26
Corrigan, Dennis, 71
Corsiglia, Betsy, 141
Cottage Garden Alphabet, A (Wisnewski), 170
Country of the Pointed Firs (Jewett), 23
Craveri, Benedetta, 77
Criminal Convictions: Errant Essays on Perpetrators of Literary License (Freeling), 63
Cross Country Runner, The (Dubus), 29–30
Crossette, George, 92
Crutchley, Brooke, 8, 224
Cunliffe, Barry, 96
Cunningham, Kim Webster, 165
Cuppy, Will, 251
Curbstone Press, 40
Curwen Press, The, 220
Cygnet Press, 8

D Dalton, Max, 169
Dalven, Rae, 45
Dance Me Outside: More Tales from the Ermineskin Reserve (Kinsella), 34
Dance of Death, The (Holbein), 8, 9
Dante (typeface), 9, 35, 59, 110, 208, 223, 266
Davenport, Guy, 63, 81
David, Elizabeth, 212
Davis, Sandy, 191
Davis, Walter R., 186
Day, Fred Holland, 111
Deagon, Ann, 44
Deaths Duell (Donne), 8
Dechend, Hertha von, 258
Decline and Fall of Practically Everybody, The (Cuppy), 251
De Hamel, Christopher, 234, 235
Democratic Art, The: Pictures for a 19th-Century America (Marzio), 126
DePol, John, 15
De Santillana, Giorgio, 258
Desert (Le Clézio), 40
Desperate Characters (Fox), 18
Desperate Measures (Starbuck), 44
Devlin, Harry, 138
DeWilde, Barbara, 266
DeWolf, Gordon, 11
Dezmazières, Erik, 35
Dialogues of Alfred North Whitehead, The (Price), 82–83
Diana & Nikon: Essays on the Aesthetics of Photography (Malcolm), 61
Dick, Oliver Lawson, 78–79
Dickey, James, 6
Dickson, C., 40
Diebboll, John, 191
Disappearances (Mosher), 21
Disobedience of Water, The (Naslund), 24
Distant Trumpet, A (Horgan), 22–23
Doane, Doris, 142
Dodds, Gordon, 122
Does, Bram de, 6, 8, 91, 214, 262
Doherty, Robert, 110
Doherty, Terence, 240
Donne, John, 8
Donnelly, Richard, 181
Donoso, José, 37
Doolittle, Hilda, 74
Door in the Wall, The (Wells), 32
Dorade (Adkins), 182
Doren, Adam Van, 129
Dorfman, Elsa, 59, 108
Dothard, Robert, 95, 266
Doty, Mark, 55
Down to the Sea: The Fishing Schooners of Gloucester (Garland), 174–175
Dresser of Sycamore Trees, A (Keizer), 79
Dreyfus, John, 8, 214, 223
Droeshout, Martin, 8
Dubus, Andre, 28–31, 62

Dufy, Raoul, 46–47
Duhamel, Peggy, IX, 1
Duncan, Robert, 80
Dunlop, Geoffrey, 41
Dunwell, Steve, 95
Durrell, Gerald, 86
Durst, Seymour, 140
Dwiggins, William Addison, IX, 220, 266

E Eakins, Thomas, 91, 262
Eakins Press, 47
Early Children's Books and Their Illustrations (Gottlieb), 93
Early Italian Writing-Books: Renaissance to Baroque (Morison), 236
Early Italian Writing Books (Morison), 230
Easy to Remember: The Great American Songwriters and Their Songs (Zinsser), 192
Ehrhardt (typeface), 174, 266
Eichenauer, Gustav, 233
Eisenman, Sara, 28, 60, 119, 133, 181, 183, 205, 266
Eldridge, Judith, 208, 209
Electra (typeface), 95, 266
Elizabeth David's Christmas (Norman), 212
Elkin, Stanley, 31
Elliott, T. J., 11
Elsa's Housebook (Dorfman), 108
Emerson, Ralph Waldo, 66
Emily Dickinson in Southern California (Kennedy), 44
Engel, Marian, 25
Engell, James, 56–57
English Country Traditions (Niall), 13
English Garden: A Social History, The (Quest-Ritson), 202–203
Engravings, The (Gill), 14
Entries (Oliver), 44
Epstein, Joseph, 70
Erhardt (typeface), 8
Ervin, Booker Telleterro, 80
Essay on Typography, An (Gill), 14, 216, 217
Ettenberg, Eugene M., 224
Eustis, Elizabeth S., 204
Evans, Virginia, 266

F Faber & Faber, 84
Fadiman, Anne, 171
Fadiman, Clifton, 171
Fading Feast: A Compendium of Disappearing American Regional Foods (Sokolov), 211
Fairbank, Alfred, 232
Fair Sun (Barba), 55
Faison, S. Lane, Jr., 126
Falconer, John, 175
Famine (O'Flaherty), 19
Farmer's Alphabet, A (Azarian), 152
Farnsworth, Ward, 72
Farnsworth's Classical English Metaphor (Farnsworth), 72
Farnsworth's Classical English Rhetoric (Farnsworth), 72
Farnsworth's Classical English Style (Farnsworth), 72
Farrer, Reginald, 196, 201
Fass, John S., 224
Fauna and Family (Durrell), 86
Fell, Bishop, 7
Fell (typeface), 7
Ferdinand the Bull (Leaf), 256
Ferdinandus Taurus (Leaf), 259
Ferguson, Lorraine, 266
Fern, Alan, 91
Fiction and the Figures of Life (Gass), 60
Fiedler, Leslie, 62
Fiedler of the Roof: Essays on Literature and Jewish Identity (Fiedler), 62
Field & Forest Handybook, The (Beard), 153, 154
Fields, Kenneth, 44, 74
Fields of Peace (Tice), 112
Figures of Thought (Nemerov), 59
Fili, Louise, 263, 266
Fillets of Plaice (Durrell), 86
Finch, Robert, 244
Finn Typographic, 233
First Flowering, The: Bruce Rogers at the Riverside Press, 1896 1912 (Kelly), 227
First Person Rural (Perrin), 60
Five Decades of the Burin: The Wood Engravings of John DePol (Godine), 15
Five Women (Musil), 38
Flanagan, Thomas, 19, 32
Fleuron Anthology, 220
Flora Exotica (Hnizdovsky and DeWolf), 11

Fo'c'sle, The (Rossiter), 167
Fortier, Norman, 183
Forty Days of Musa Dagh, The (Werfel), 41
Fothergill, Jana, 208
Four Adventures of Richard Hannay, The: The Thirty-Nine Steps, Greenmantle, Mr. Standfast, and The Three Hostages (Buchan), 24–25
Four Colour Print Group, 123
Four Gospels, The (Gill), 15
Fournier (typeface), 266
Four Seasons, The (Azarian), 15
Fourth Dimension, The (Ritsos), 45
Fox, Paula, 18
Franchiser, The (Elkin), 31
Frank, Stuart, 181
Frank Sutcliffe: Photographer of Whitby (Hiley), 108
Fraser, Gordon, 108
Fraser, James, 108
Freeling, Nicolas, 63, 211
Freiberg, Malcolm, 93
French Menu Cookbook, The: A Revised and Updated Edition of a Culinary Classic (Olney), 208–209
Fried, Donald, 210
Fried, Eleanor, 210
Fry, Roger, 106

G Gallant, Aprile, 117
Galliard (typeface), 138, 209, 222, 229, 266
Gallimard, Antoine, 40
Gambit Publications, 258
Garamond (typeface), 13, 78, 127, 229, 266
Garden, The (Marvell), 4, 5
Garland, Joseph, 174
Garvey, Eleanor, VII, 8
Gary, Romain, 42
Garza-Falcon, Leticia, 50
Gass, William, 31, 33, 59
Gassendi, Pierre, 2
Gehenna Press, VIII, 2, 3, 5
Geismar, Daphne, 100–101
Generous Days, The (Spender), 3
Genius of Common Sense: Jane Jacobs and the Story of The Death and Life of Great American Cities (Lang and Wunsch), 85
Geography of the Imagination (Davenport), 63
George Eastman House, 110
Georges Perec: A Life in Words (Bellos), 77
Germain, Sylvie, 40
Gertrude Jekyll on Gardening (Jekyll), 198
Giambattista Bodoni: His Life and His World (Lester), 228
Gibson, Eric, 134
Gibson, George, IX, 71, 201
Gilbar, Steven, 67
Gilbert, Thomas W., 104
Gill, Eric, 14, 15, 216, 217, 266
Girvin, Tim, 34, 59, 266
Giving Up the Gun: Japan's Reversion to the Sword, 1543–1879 (Perrin), 96
Godine, David R., IX, 15, 160
Goffstein, M. Brooke, 188
Goines, David Lance, 220, 221
Golden (typeface), 160, 266
Goldenberg, Carol, 33, 125, 266
Golden Cockerel, 14, 15, 226, 266
Gold in Azure (Brumfield), 137
Goldman, Jane, 38
Goldman, Marcus, 242
Gomes, Peter J., 258
Good Babies, Bad Babies (Lawrence), 156
Goodman, Bill, IX, 18, 19, 21, 30, 32, 37, 75, 127, 153
Gordon, Mary, 128
Gordon Fraser, 222
Gorey, Edward, 28
Gottlieb, Gerald, 93
Gottlieb, Robert, 59
Goudy, Bertha, 32
Goudy, Fred, 32
Gowers, Ernest, 70
Gralla, Howard, 47, 56, 174, 266
Grammar of Typography, A (Argetsinger), 230
Granby, Alan, 178
Grand Resort Hotels of the White Mountains, The: A Vanishing Architectural Legacy (Tolles), 139
Grasso, Rita, 20

Gray, Nicolete, 235
Gray Parrot, 3, 256
Great Camps of the Adirondacks (Kaiser), 144–145
Great Houses of Britain (Nicolson), 136
Great Northern (Ransome), 160
Greenbaum, Sidney, 70
Greenberg, Alvin, 44
Gregorian, Vartan, 41
Grossman, Richard, 66
Grushkin, Philip, 74, 266
Guarnaccia, Steven, 34
Gunn, Thom, 44
Guralnick, Peter, 186, 187
Gurwitz, Gary, 113
Guy, Peter, 108–109, 222, 266
Gypsies & Other Narrative Poems, The (Pushkin), 54

H Hadas, Elizabeth, 256, 259
Hadas, Rachel, 44
Hadsel, Christine, 130
Hadzi, Dimitri, 9
Haien, Jeannette, 22
Halby, Hans, 233
Half-Life (Purcell), 121
Hall, Donald, 44, 50, 68, 74
Hall, N. John, 26
Hall, Roger, 122
Halliday Lithograph, 95
Hamady, Mary, 209
Hamady, Walter, 209, 266
Hamlet's Mill (De Santillana and Dechend), 258
Handel and Haydn Society, The: Bringing Music to Life for 200 Years (Neff and Swafford), 193
Hand of the Small-Town Builder, The: Vernacular Summer Architecture in New England, 1870–1935 (Pfeffer), 143
Hannavy, John, 108–109
Harling, Robert, 216, 217
Harper & Row, IX, 20, 34
Harris, Elizabeth, 219, 226
Hartman, Charles O., 44
Hartz, Sem, 214
Harvard, Stephen, 60, 219, 262, 263, 266
Harvard Hillel Sabbath Songbook, The, 189
Harvey, Michael, 175, 266
Hasty Pudding, The (Barlow), 2
Hawkes, Kevin, 162
Hayden, Sterling, 174
Head of the Bed, The (Hollander), 44
Heaney, Seamus, 21
Heartaches of a French Cat, The (McClintock), 159
Hecht, Anthony, 9
Hendel, Richard, 126, 137, 266
Hennessey, Robert, 117
Herbal (Krutch), 238, 245
Herbs and the Earth (Beston), 245
Heroes of Horticulture (Robinson), 206
Hidy, Lance, VIII, IX, 2, 3, 4, 5, 79, 91, 106, 108, 125, 262, 266
Hildebrandt, William, 237
Hiley, Michael, 108
Hill, Susan, 156
Hillel (typeface), 189, 266
Hillers, John Karl, 92
Hills, L. Rust, 251
History of Illuminated Manuscripts, A (De Hamel), 234, 235
History of Lettering: Creative Experiment and Letter Identity, A (Gray), 235
Hitchcock, Lucinda (Lucy), 59, 160, 211, 266
Hnizdovsky, Jacques, 11, 13
Hoban, Russell, 164
Hobhouse, Penelope, 198
Hofer, Evelyn, 98
Hofer, Philip, VII, 8, 9, 243, 244
Hogarth Press, 106
Holbein, Hans, 8, 9
Holbein: The Paintings of Hans Holbein the Younger (Rowlands), 127–128
Holdouts! The Buildings That Got in the Way (Alpern and Durst), 140
Hollander, John, 44, 186
Homans, Katy, IX, 8, 61, 110, 192, 266
Honeymoon (Modiano), 39
Hood, Stuart C., 41
Hoover, Paul, 39
Hopkins, Gerard Manley, 6

Horgan, Paul, 22–23
Horowitz, Alan, 113
House of Music: Art in an Era of Institutions, The (Lipman), 188
House Tells the Story, The: Homes of the American Presidents (Van Doren), 144
Howard, Richard, 48
How Baseball Happened: Outrageous Lies Exposed! The True Story Revealed (Gilbert), 104
Howe, Ilana Wiener, 33
Howe, Irving, 18, 33
Howland, Llewellyn,, III, 180, 182, 183
How to Do Things Right: The Revelations of a Fussy Man (Hills), 251
How Tom Beat Captain Najork and His Hired Sportsmen (Hoban), 164
Hugo, Harold, VII, 91, 94
Humez, Alexander, 70
Humez, Nicholas, 70
Hunger of Memory (Rodriguez), 75
Hunt, John Dixon, 200
Hurst, Heather, 52
Hutchinson, Bradley, 50
Hutner, Martin, 225
Hyder, Darrell, 242, 266
Hyland, Janice, 178

I *Images and Shadows: Part of a Life* (Origo), 79
In/Direction (Greenberg), 44
Ingenious Contrivances, Curiously Carved (Frank), 181
Inner Sky, The (Rilke), 54
In Praise of Little Fishes (Goldman), 242
Instant Lives (Moss and Gorey), 28
In the Blood A Memoir of My Childhood (Motion), 84
In the Heart of the Heart of the Country and Other Stories (Gass), 33
Into Print: Selected Writings on Printing History, Typography and Book Production (Dreyfus), 223
Invisible Years: A Family's Collected Account of Separation and Survival during the Holocaust in the Netherlands (Geismar), 100–101
Iris Origo (Moorehead), 82

J Jackson, Donald, 238
Jacobs, Jane, 85
Jan Tschichold: Typographer (McLean), 216
Jarvis, F. Washington, 103, 258
Jewett, Sarah Orne, 23
Joanna (typeface), 217, 266
Joh. Enschedé en Zonen, 6, 214, 266
John S. Fass and The Hammer Creek Press, 224
Johnson, Pamela, 156, 162
Johnson, Samuel, 4, 64
Johnson Sampler, A (Curwen), 64
Joseph Banks: A Life (O'Brian), 76
Journal of Madam Knight, The (Knight), 93
Judge and His Hangman & The Quarry, The (Constantine), 19
Jussim, Estelle, 111, 114

K Kaiser, Ernst, 38
Kaiser, Harvey, 144
Karmel, Alex, 140
Karmel, Pepe, 46
Karsh, Yousuf, 119
Katz, Leslie, 47
Kazin, Alfred, 91
Keith, Freeman, VII, 221, 255, 266
Keizer, Garret, 79
Kelly, Jerry, 15, 102, 204, 225, 227, 229, 238, 256, 266
Kelly, Robert, 81
Keneally, Thomas, 150
Kennedy, X. J., 44
Kennerley, Mitchell, 32
Kepler (Banville), 21
Kermode, Frank, 38
Keynes, Geoffrey, 7, 8
Kiely, Benedict, 21, 32, 75
Killion, Tom, 12
King of the Birds, The (Ward), 171
Kinsella, W. P., 44
Kirstein, Lincoln, 47
Kitchen and the Cook Book, The (Freeling), 211
Kitzinger, Tony, 226
Klimt, Gustav, 38
Klingspor Museum, The, 233
Kneeling Orion (Barnes), 51
Knight, Sarah Kemble, 93

Knowles, Barbara, 156, 266
Knowlton, Tim, 99
Koch, Rudolf, 233
Koeth, Alice, 238, 243, 266
Kogawa, Joy, 20
Korn, Peter, 259
Kosofsky, Scott-Martin, 78, 160, 189, 190, 266
Kotzwinkle, William, 27, 155
Koura, Patricia, 119
Kramer, Hilton, 22
Kredel, Fritz, 233
Krimpen, Jan van, 2, 4, 6, 12, 70, 214, 266
Krutch, Joseph Wood, 245
Kumler, Kipton, 109

L Land, Edwin, 114
Landscapes of the Mind (Chiarenza), 114
Lang, Andrew, 151
Lang, Glenna, 85, 172, 263
Langstaff, John, 189
Lankes, Julius John, 14
Lansdowne, J. Fenwick, 242–243
Lapides, Michael, 180
Lark Rise to Candleford (Thompson), 26
Last, Yong Hee, 125
Last Englishman: The Double Life of Arthur Ransome, The (Chambers), 87
Last Giants, The (Place), 163
Last Letter to Father Flye (Agee), 2
Last of the Hill Farms, The: Echoes of Vermont's Past (Brown), 122–123
Lattimore, Richmond, 52
Laughlin, James,, IV, 81
Laurens, G. G., 48, 266
Lawrence, James, VIII, 4
Lawrence, John, 156, 211
Laws, George, 148, 149, 154, 266
Lawson, Alexander, 222
Lawson, Robert, 256, 259
Lawton, Nancy, 37
Leaf, Munro, 256, 259
Lebanese Mountain Cookery (Hamady), 209
Le Clézio, J. M. G., 40–41
Lee, Laurie, 84–85
Leithauser, Brad, 53
Leithauser, Mark, 53
Les Fleurs du Mal (Baudelaire), 48
Lester, Valerie, 228
Lettered Creatures (Leithauser), 53
Letter Forms and Type Designs of Eric Gill, The (Gill), 217
Letters for the New England Dead (Baron), 44
Letters of Credit (Tracy), 222
Letter to a Friend, Upon the Occasion of the Death of His Intimate Friend, A (Browne), 7
Libanus Press, 97
Library of Babel, The (Borges), 35
Life A User's Manual (Perec), 38
Light Within the Light, The (Braham), 67
Likes of Us, The: America in the Eyes of the Farm Security Administration (Cohen), 120
Lindbergh, Anne, 162
Lindsay, John V., 140
Lines II: A Half-Century of Yacht Designs by Sparkman & Stephens, 1930–1980 (Stephens), 176–177
Lipman, Samuel, 188
Little ABC Book, The (Koch), 233
Little Princess, A (Burnett), 157
Little Red Riding Hood (Wisnewski), 164, 170
Little Schubert, A (Goffstein), 188
Livingston, Jane, 111
Livingston, Mark, 248, 250, 266
Llewellyn, Howland,, 180
Logan, William, 44
Loker, Chris, 102
London Perceived (Pritchett), 98
Lonely Typewriter, The (Ackerman), 169
Longfellow, Henry Wadsworth, 52–53
Looking at Death (Norfleet), 116
Lorenz, Lee, 252
Lost Highway: Journeys & Arrivals of American Musicians (Guralnick), 186–187
Lotte Jacobi (Moriarty), 122
Louie, Lorraine, 37, 266
Lowenthal, Marvin, 78
Loxley, Simon, 228

Lun, Aleksandra, 42
Lutetia (typeface), 6, 12, 266
Lützelburger, Hans, 8, 9

M McClintock, Barbara, 159
McCoy, Roy, 137
McCullough, David, 144
McCurdy, Michael, 45, 93
McDaniel, Henry, 255
McElroy, John Harmon, 98
McFee, William, 176
McGrath, Harold, VIII, x
McKendry, Joe, 163
MacKenzie and Harris, 6, 150
McLaren, Keith, 179
McLean, John, 99
McLean, Ruari, 216, 240, 266
McNair, Wesley, 51
Mad Amadeus Sued a Madam (Miller), 252
Madame du Deffand (Craveri), 77
Mades, Leonard, 37
Malcolm, Janet, 61
M. Álvarez Bravo (Livingston), 111
Mandelbaum, Allen, 46
Mann, Sally, 113
Man Who Liked Slow Tomatoes, The (Constantine), 19
Man Who Liked to Look at Himself & A Fix Like This, The (Constantine), 19
Man Who Lived Alone, The (Hall), 50
Marcus, George, 125
Marcus, Norman, 140
Mardersteig, Giovanni, 35, 266
Mardersteig, Martino, 12, 186, 236, 242, 266
Maritime Maverick: The Collection of William I. Koch (Granby and Hyland), 178
Marking the Moment (Blagden), 132
Marks, Carol, 40
Marsh, James, 21
Marsh, Susan, 187, 194, 266
Martha's Vineyard Decoys (Murphy), 254
Martin, Hardie St., 37
Marvell, Andrew, VIII, 2, 4
Marx, Leo, 91
Marzio, Peter C., 126
Massingham, H. J., 26
Masters of the Italic Letter (Atkins), 233, 236
Mathews, Eleanor, 246
Matter of Time, A (Purcell), 121
Mattiolo, 238, 245
Maxwell, Brooke, 22
Maxwell, Gavin, 247
Maxwell, William, 22
Mazur, Gail, 44
Mazur, Michael, 48
Mechanical Cutting of Punches, The (Krimpen), 214
Medieval Bestiary, A (Elliott and Tyler), 11
Medieval Latin Lyrics (Stock and Kredel), 12
Mefisto (Banville), 21
Memoirs of Hecate County (Wilson), 18
Men of Letters & People of Substance (Vicq de Cumptich), 226–227
Men of Roxbury (Jarvis), 103
Mercantile Printing, 113
Merchant of Prato (Origo), 97
Meriden Gravure Company, VII, 215, 218, 233, 240
Merrion Press, The, 232, 233
Merrymount Press, 218
Metcalf, Pauline, 138
Meynell, Francis, 220
Middleton, Christopher, 50
Millard, Charles, 114
Miller, Allan, 252
Miller, Henry, 81
Miller, Pamela A., 174
Miller (typeface), 226, 266
Mills, Lauren, 159
Miner, Mary-Jean, 141
Minion, 266
Miss Alcott's Email: Yours for Reforms of All Kinds (Bakke), 25
Missee Lee (Ransome), 160
Missing Person (Modiano), 39
Moccasin Telegraph and Other Tales, The (Kinsella), 34
Modiano, Patrick, 39, 40
Momaday, N. Scott, 44

Moment of War: A Memoir of the Spanish Civil War, A (Lee), 84
Monadnock Summer: The Architectural Legacy of Dublin, New Hampshire (Morgan), 142
Montague, Amy T., 8
Montaigne Sabon (typeface), 78, 266
Montgomery, L. M., 159
Moorehead, Caroline, 82
Moral Reflections on The Short Life of the Ephemeron (Boreman), 5
Morgan, William, 142
Moriarty, Peter, 122
Morison, Stanley, 97, 220, 224, 236
Morris, John N., 174
Morris, Wright, 34
Moser, Barry, 16, 46, 66, 67, 266
Mosher, Howard Frank, 21, 79
Moss, Howard, 28
Motion, Andrew, 84
Mowat, Farley, 184
Murphy, Robert Cushman, 246
Murphy, Stanley, 254
Murray, Timothy D., 15
Musil, Robert, 38
Mussey, Robert D., Jr., 133
Mutual Friend, The (Busch), 20

N   Naslund, Sena Jeter, 24
Natural History of Edward Lear, The (Peck), 248
Near Thing for Captain Najork, A (Hoban), 164–165
Ned Kelly and the City of the Bees (Keneally), 150
Neff, Teresa M., 193
Neild, Julie, 26
Nemerov, Howard, 30, 59
New Directions, 47
New England Days (Caponigro), 117
Newhall, Beaumont, 106
Newman, Arnold, 106
Niall, Ian, 13
Nicolson, Nigel, 136
Nightfire (Mazur), 44
Nixon, Bebe, 115
Nixon, Nicholas, 115
No Art without Craft: The Life of Theodore Low De Vinne (Tichenor), 83
No Ordinary Being: W. Starling Burgess: Inventor, Naval Architect, Poet, Aviation Pioneer, and Master of American Design (Howland), 183
Norfleet, Barbara, 116
Norman, Jill, 212
Northern Calendar, A (Sadoff), 44
Not Forgotten (Gilbar and Stewart), 67

O   *Obasan* (Kogawa), 20
O'Brian, Patrick, 76
Obscene Bird of Night, The (Donoso), 37
O'Flaherty, Liam, 19
Ogden Codman and the Decoration of Houses (Metcalf), 138
Oh Garden of Fresh Possibilities (Smith), 203
Old Man at the Railroad Crossing (Maxwell), 22
Old Man Mad about Drawing (Place), 163
Oliver, Raymond, 44
Olney, Richard, 208, 209
On Being Blue (Gass), 59
Once and Future Gardener, The (Clayton), 200
On Eagle Pond (Hall), 68
One Hundred Portraits (Moser), 16
One Mind's Eye: The Portraits and Other Photographs of Arnold Newman (Newman), 106
On the Making of Gardens (Sitwell), 200
On the Wind: The Marine Photographs of Norman Fortier, 180
Optima (typeface), 107, 262, 266
Origo, Iris, 79, 97
Orion on the Dunes: A Biography of Henry Beston (Payne), 89
Orwell, George, 59, 64–65
Orwell, Sonia, 64, 65
Osley, A. S., 233
Outermost House, The (Beston), 51, 167
Over by the River (Maxwell), 22
Oxford University Press, 232

P   Palatino (typeface), 7, 61, 187, 266
Palatino: The Natural History of a Typeface (Bringhurst), 229
Palimpsests, The (Lun), 42
Palpable Elysium, A (Williams), 81

Paragon Park (Doty), 55
Parker, E. F., 27
Parker, Mike, 224
Parker, Olivia, 18, 110
Parsons, Ian, 243
Partch, Harry, 81
Patchen, Kenneth, 80
Patterson, Wynne, 145, 266
Payne, Daniel G., 89
Pearce, Clark, 133
Pearson, Norman Holmes, 74
Peck, John, 44
Peck, Robert McCracken, 248
Peiresc & His Books (Gassendi), 2
Penelopeia: A Novel in Verse, The (Rawlings), 52
People with AIDS (Nixon), 115
Perec, Georges, 38
Perpetua (typeface), 22, 215, 217, 218, 266
Perrin, Ned, 154
Perrin, Noel, 60, 96, 153, 250
Personal Impressions: The Small Printing Press in Nineteenth-Century America (Harris), 226
Peter and the Wolf (Prokofiev), 149
Peter Duck (Ransome), 160
Pfeffer, W. Tad, 143
P.H. Emerson: Photographer of Norfolk (Turner and Wood), 108
Philosopher's Diet, The (Watson), 252
Photographs (Kumler), 109
Pickering Press, 94
Picts and the Martyrs, The (Ransome), 160
Pied Piper of Hamelin, The (Browning), 2
Pigeon Post (Ransome), 160
Pigfoot Rebellion, The (Hartman), 44
Place, François, 163
Plantin (typeface), 266
Plea for Captain John Brown, A (Thoreau), 2
Plume, Ilse, 150
Poliphilus & Blado, 266
Polizzotti, Mark, IX, 24, 141, 266
Pontes, Crimilda, 242, 243
Portraits and Elegies (Schnackenberg), 44
Portraits of American Architecture: Monuments to a Romantic Mood, 1830-1900 (Devlin), 138–139
Powell, Tristram, 106
Practicing Stoic, The (Farnsworth), 72
Prairie Fires and Paper Moons (Brown), 118
Prelude, The (Wordsworth), 56–57
Prettiest Love Letters in the World, The: Letters between Lucrezia Borgia and Pietro Bembo 1503–1509 (Shankland), 97
Price, Lucien, 82–83
Primer (typeface), 266
Printed Book in America (Blumenthal), 218
Printer's Devil: The Life and Work of Frederic Warde (Loxley), 228
Pritchett, V. S., 98
Prokofiev, Sergei, 149
Prose, Francine, 226
Prospector, The (Le Clézio), 40–41
Purcell, Rosamond, 121
Pushkin, Alexander, 54

Q   *Quentin Corn* (Stolz), 156
Quest-Ritson, Charles, 202

R   Rabb, Theodore K., 129
Race for Real Sailors, A (McLaren), 179
Rae, Susan, 3
Rage for Rock Gardening, A (Shulman), 201
Rails of the World (Ripley), 242–243
Rampant Lions Press, 7
Ransome, Arthur, 87, 160
Rapoport Printing, 109
Rathbone, Belinda, 99
Rather Elegant than Showy: The Classical Furniture of Isaac Vose (Mussey and Pearce), 133
Rawlings, Jane, 52
Raymond, Michael, 56–57
Regarding Heroes (Karsh), 119
Reid, Robert Leonard, 246–247
Reidel, James, 41
Remington, Frederic, 52–53
Rescuing Mouse, The (Warde), 2

Rexroth, Kenneth, 81
Rhymes of a PFC (Kirstein), 47
Rich, Howard, 142
Richardson, Robert D., IX, 46, 88–89
Riddle of the Sands, The (Childers), 27
Ridler, Vivian, 232
Riley, James Whitcomb, 172
Rilke, Rainer Maria, 38, 54
Rilke (typeface), 266
Ring of Bright Water (Maxwell), 247
Ripley, S. Dillon, 242
Ritsos, Yannis, 45
Robinson, Barbara Paul, 88, 206
Robinson, W. Heath, 160
Rocksburg Railroad Murder & The Blank Page, The (Constantine), 19
Rockwell, Martha, VIII, 3
Rodarmor, William, 39
Rodriguez, Richard, 75
Roger Fenton of Crimble Hall (Hannavy), 108–109
Rogers, Bruce, 12, 227, 266
Rogers, Elizabeth Barlow, 204
Roman (typeface), 97
Romantic Gardens: Nature, Art, and Landscape Design (Rogers, Eustis, and Bidwell), 204
Ronto, Craig, 242
Roots of Heaven, The (Gary), 42
Rosemary Verey: The Life & Lessons of a Legendary Gardener (Robinson), 88
Rosenthal, Tom, 106
Ross, David, 82
Rossell, Deac, 109
Rossiter, Nan Parson, 167
Roth, Arnold, 171, 260
Rotten Island (Steig), 146, 155
Rowlands, John, 127
Roylance, Dale, 5
Rubin, Larry, 44
Run of the Mill, The: A Pictorial Narrative of the Expansion, Dominion, Decline and Enduring Impact of the New England Textile Industry (Dunwell), 95
Russem, Michael, 192, 193, 211, 259, 266
Russo, Richard, 31
Rust, Graham, 156, 157
Ruzicka, Ivan, 6
Ruzicka, Rudolph, 94, 218
Ryan, Stephen, 150
Ryder, John, 108, 222
Ryskamp, Charles, 93

S Sabon, 78, 266
Sacrificial Years, The (Whitman), 98
Sad-Faced Men (Logan), 44
Sadler, Jim, 266
Sadoff, Ira, 44
Sail and Steam: A Century of Maritime Enterprise, 1840–1935 (Falconer), 175
St. Onge, Sarah, 48
Saki (H. H. Munro), 153
Sakwa, Jacqueline, 33, 176
Sallets, Humbles & Shrewsbury Cakes (Beebe), 208
Salter, George, 238
Samuelson, François, 38
Sarah and Simon and No Red Paint (Ardizzone), 166
Say What You Mean!: A Troubleshooter's Guide to English Style and Usage (Trask), 71
Scarbrough, Carl W., 35, 72, 120, 142, 163, 177, 180, 266
Schelkun, Greg, 5
Schnackenberg, Gertrude, 44
Schreiber, Jan, 44
Scribes and Sources (Osley), 233
Sculpture of Auguste Rodin, The (Tancock), 125
Seacoast Maine (Tice), 112
Searches and Seizures (Elkin), 31
Searls, Damion, 54
Second Sight (Mann), 113
Secret Garden, The (Burnett), 157
Secret Water (Ransome), 160
Sedgwick, Ellery, 94
Seed Leaves (Wilbur), 7
Seely, Heidi A., 99
Selected Photographs (Tice), 112
Selected Poems: 1951–1975 (Causley), 45
Selected Prose of John Wesley Powell (Crossette), 92
Selected Songs of Thomas Campion (Campion), 186
Sempé, 39

Separate Flights (Dubus), 30–31
Servello, Joe, 155
Shadows and Moonshine (Aiken), 162
Shagbark Press, 245
Shankland, Hugh, 97
Sherlock in Love (Naslund), 24
Shimmer of Joy: One Hundred Children's Picture Books, A (Loker), 102
Short Shorts: An Anthology of the Shortest Stories (Howe), 33
Shulman, Nicola, 201
Siegal, Calvin, 180
Signs of Life (Parker), 110
Simmonds, Harvey, 47
Simon, Herbert, 220
Simon, Oliver, 220
Siskind, Paul M., VIII, 88
Sisson, Clinton, 219
Sitwell, George, 200
Sitwell, Osbert, 200
Skelton, Christopher, 14, 217
Slave to Beauty: The Eccentric Life and Controversial Career of F. Holland Day, Photographer, Publisher, Aesthete (Jussim), 111
Slimbach, Robert, 266
Small Victories: One couple's surprising adventures building an unrivaled collection of American prints (Williams), 129
Smallwood, Norah, 106
Smith, Kim, 203
Smith, Richard Shirley, 97
Smith, William Jay, 13
Snow, C. P., 22
Sobieszek, Robert A., 106, 110
Sokolov, Raymond, 211
So Long, See You Tomorrow (Maxwell), 22
Song of Hiawatha, The (Longfellow), 52–53
South Wind through the Kitchen (David), 212
Spacks, Barry, 44
Speaking of Dogs: The Best Collection of Canine Quotables Ever Compiled (Charlton and Roth), 260
Specimen Days (Whitman), 91, 262
Spectrum, 266
Spender, Stephen, 3
Sperry, Armstrong, 176
Spirit of Fact, The: The Daguerreotypes of Southworth and Hawes, 1843–1862 (Sobieszek and Appel), 110
Spitzer, Philip, 30
Splendor of the Heart (Richardson), 88–89
Sporting Art of Frank W. Benson, The (Bedford), 255
Stamperia Valdonega (typeface), 12, 223, 243, 266
Starbuck, George, 44
Starting from Troy (Hadas), 44
State of Ireland, The (Kiely), 32
Steegmuller, Francis, 76
Steig, William, 155, 251
Stephens, Olin J., II, 176
Stevens, John, 70, 159, 266
Stewart, Dean, 67
Stinehour, Roderick (Rocky), VII, 44, 221, 266
Stinehour Press, The, VII, 30, 35, 44, 91, 93, 215, 218, 219, 221, 238, 255
Stolz, Mary, 156
Stone and Steel: Paintings & Writings Celebrating the Bridges of New York City (Bascove), 128
Stories, Fables & Other Diversions (Nemerov), 30
Story of Befana: An Italian Christmas Tale (Plume), 150
Story-Teller, The (Saki), 153
String Too Short to be Saved (Hall), 50, 74
Stryker, Roy, 120
Stuart, Gilbert, 99
Stubbs, George, 240
Studley Press, The, 117
Study Is Hard Work (Armstrong), 260
Sullivan, Nancy, 44
Sunbelly (Fields), 44
Superior Person's Book of Words, The (Bowler), 71
Superpower: The Making of the Berkshire Locomotive (Weitzman), 158
Suspended Worlds: Historic Theater Scenery in Northern New England (Hadsel), 130–131
Swafford, Jan, 193
Swain, Roger, 245
Swallowdale (Ransome), 160
Swallows and Amazons (Ransome), 87, 160–161
Swimmer in the Secret Sea (Kotzwinkle), 27

T *Tale of John Barleycorn (or From Barley to Beer), The* (Azarian), 154
Tales of the Rose Tree: Ravishing Rhododendrons and Their Travels Around the World (Brown), 202
Tally of Types, A (Morison), 224
Tancock, John, 125
Tartar Steppe, The (Buzzati), 41
Taylor, Tom, 50
Taylor, Welford Dunaway, 14
Teaching the Penguins to Fly (Spacks), 44
Telling It (Sullivan), 44
Tennyson, Alfred Lord, 106
Theatrical World of Angus McBean, The (Wilson), 118
There is No Balm in Birmingham (Deagon), 44
They Came Like Swallows (Maxwell), 22
Thomas, Dylan, 148
Thomas, Graham Stuart, 199
Thomas Todd Company, 110
Thompson, Flora, 26
Thoreau, Henry David, VIII, 2
Thorn, John, 104
Thrashin' Time (Weitzman), 158
Tice, George, 112
Tichenor, Irene, 83
Time Will Darken It (Maxwell), 22
Titcomb, Caldwell, 82
Titherington, Jeanne, 20, 151, 153
Toad to a Nightingale (Leithauser), 53
To His Coy Mistress (Marvell), VIII, 2
Tolles, Bryant F., Jr., 139
To the Air (Gunn), 44
Town of Hill, The (Hall), 44
Town of No & My Brother Running (McNair), 51
Tracy, Walter, 222
Trask, R. L., 71
Travis, David, 65, 119
Trevitt, John, 223, 266
Tribute to Freud (H. D.), 74
Triggs, Stanley, 122
Trio: The Tale of a Three-legged Cat (Wisnewski), 170
Trouble in Bugland (Kotzwinkle), 155
Trump Medieval (typeface), 33, 137, 266
Tschichold, Jan, 216, 266
Tuchman, Barbara, 97
Tunstrom, Goran, 39
Turner, Peter, 108
Turtle, Swan (Doty), 55
200 Years of American Sculpture (Tancock), 125
Tyger Voyage, The (Adams), 168
Tyler, Gillian, 11
Type Revivals (Kelly), 229
Typophiles, 233
Tyranny of the Normal: Essays on Bioethics, Theology and Myth (Fiedler), 62

U *Unbroken Circles: The Campground of Martha's Vineyard* (Miner), 141
Unpublished Letter of Junipero Serra, An (Browning), 2
Updike, Daniel Berkeley, 218
Updike, John, 18
Upon Some Midnights Clear (Constantine), 19
Urban Romantic: The Photographs of George Tice (Tice), 112

V Van Dijck, Christoffel, 79, 266
Van Dijck (typeface), 4, 13, 46, 79, 266
Van Doren, Adam, 129, 144
Vaule, Rosamond, 117
Venetian Vespers, The (Hecht), 9
Verey, Rosemary, 88
Verlag, S. Fischer, 41
Vicq de Cumptich, Roberto de, 226
Victorian Photographs of Famous Men & Fair Women (Cameron), 106
Views from the Island (Wadsworth), 6
Vile, Scott, 51
Void, A (Perec), 38
Voigt, Erna, 149
Vulture, The (Johnson), 4

W Wadsworth, Charles, 6, 7
Walbaum, 266

Wally the Wordworm (Fadiman), 171
Ward, Helen, 171
Warde, Beatrice, 2, 12
Warde, Frederic, 220, 228, 266
Warner, Sylvia Townsend, 22
Waters, Alice, 212
Waters, Julian, 21, 161, 266
Watson, Richard, 80, 252
Waugh, Teresa, 77
Way, David, 223
Webster, Dennis, 165
We Didn't Mean to Go to Sea (Ransome), 160
We Don't Live Here Anymore (Dubus), 28–29
Weingarten, Roger, 24
Weiss, Murray, 125
Weissbort, Daniel, 39
Weitzman, David, 158
Wells, H. G., 32
Wells, James W., 236
Wells, Jim, 236
Werfel, Franz, 41
Werner, Arno, 3, 4
Westerham Press, 240, 243
When the Frost is on the Punkin (Riley), 172
Where the Deer Were (Barnes), 51
Whitcut, Janet, 70
Whitehill, Walter Muir, VII, 94
Whitman, Walt, 91, 98
Why We Make Things and Why It Matters (Korn), 259
Wilbur, Richard, 7
Wilkins, Eithne, 38
Williams, Dave H., 129
Williams, Jonathan, 81
Williams, Stephen, 263
Wilmerding, John, 132, 134
Wilson, Edmund, 18, 78
Wilson, Frederic Woodbridge, 118
Winchester, Simon, 129
Winks, Robin, 19, 24–25
Winter Father, The (Dubus), 28–29
Winter Holiday (Ransome), 160
Wiseman, Anne, 96
Wiseman, Peter, 96
Wisnewski, Andrea, 164, 170
With Love and Prayers (Jarvis), 258
Woitach, Richard, 188
Wolf, Eelco, 114
Wolff, Tobias, 31, 62
Wolpe, Berthold, 233
Woman in Black, The (Hill), 156
Wood, Antony, 54
Wood, Charles B., III, 256
Wood, Richard, 108
Woodcut Art of J.J. Lankes, The (Taylor), 14
Wood Engraving (Moser), 16
Woolf, Virginia, 106
Wordsworth, William, 56–57
World of William Notman, The (Dodds, Hall and Triggs), 122
World Within the Word, The (Gass), 60
Wormell, Christopher, 13
Worry Week, The (Lindbergh), 162
Wreck of the Deutschland, The (Hopkins), 6
Wright, Barbara, 39
Writing the Garden: A Literary Conversation Across Two Centuries (Rogers), 204
W. Thomas Taylor, 13
Wunsch, Marjory, 85
Wyatt, Leo, 186
Wylie, Andrew, 22

Y *Year with Emerson, A* (Emerson), 66
Yquem (Olney), 209

Z Zahn, Carl, 114
Zapf, Hermann, 7, 61, 187, 229, 262, 266
Zinsser, William, 192

As always, this title was made possible by a confluence of talents. First, I'd like to thank
longtime colleague, ally and friend George Gibson for reading the entire text
and providing pages of helpful suggestions. The lovely Ally Findley,
who started her career at Godine as a fall intern and quickly rose
in the ranks, proofread and edited the manuscript, discovering all
manner of embarrassing omissions and errors. I thank her for her
gracious, patient and expert help. Carl Scarbrough, Jerry Kelly and
Michael Russem carefully and closely read the manuscript,
providing invaluable suggestions and corrections.
Sara Eisenman, wife, helpmate, and expert designer, worked in
a room alongside my third-floor study, laying out the book
page by page and image by image, urging me to cut
or clarify where necessary and generally putting
up with totally unnecessary outbursts of temper and
irascibility. Special thanks to Julia Featheringill,
for her excellent photography.
Michael Babcock oversaw the production
and the transfer of files to Czechoslovakia. Finally,
my thanks to David Allender, the company's
present publisher, and its new owner, Will Thorndike,
for steadfastly encouraging and supporting
this publication in a difficult and challenging
year for everyone involved with publishing. The
real thanks, of course, go to the legions of
contributors – authors, editors, designers, production
managers, paper manufacturers, printers and
binders – who remained loyal
to this company,
provided it with
their best work
through a half-century,
and gave life to these books.

This book has been set in Minion,
a product of the team assembled at Adobe Systems
under the leadership of Fred Brady whose crew single-handedly
changed what was possible for type and typesetting in the digital era.
The type, designed by Robert Slimbach as a member of their Adobe Originals
family and released in 1990, is based on a synthesis of Renaissance designs, most
notably the roman designed by Griffo for Aldus in 1495 and the Garamond family
that appeared in the mid-sixteenth century. The italic is modelled strongly after the
chancery handwriting of the Papal scribes and the italic used by Aldus in his wildly
popular *libelli portatiles* series of portable octavos published in the early 1500s. Both
types were somewhat narrowed and modified for modern use but retain all the
earmarks of their Renaissance heritage. As Mr. Slimbach would write, "The design
grew out of my formal calligraphy, written in the Aldine style. By adapting my
hand lettering to the practical concerns of computer aided text typeface design,
I hoped to design a fresh interpretation of a classical alphabet." The name
Minion is derived both from the name given to a particular small size
of type and also from its current meaning, a "faithful servant." Godine
was among the very first trade publishers to employ the type for a
trade book, and we have gratefully used it, and its entire family
of ornaments, old style figures, small and swash capitals and
ampersands, in all their various weights and sizes ever since.

The book was typeset and designed by Sara Eisenman

Printed and bound in the Czech Republic
by PBtisk in an edition of
1,500 copies

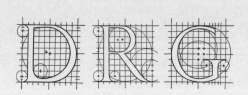